Living Forms of the Imagination

Living Forms of the Imagination

Douglas Hedley

t & t clark

Published by T&T Clark International
A Continuum imprint
The Tower Building, 11 York Road, London SE1 7NX
80 Maiden Lane, Suite 704, New York, NY 10038

www.continuumbooks.com

British Library Cataloguing-in-Publication Data
A catalogue record for this book is available from the British Library.

Typeset by Data Standards Limited, Frome, Somerset, UK.
Printed on acid-free paper in Great Britain by Athenaeum Press, Gateshead,
Tyne & Wear

ISBN-10: 0567032949 (hardback)
0567032957 (paperback)
ISBN-13: 9780567032942 (hardback)
9780567032959 (paperback)

For Clemens and Justin

Contents

Acknowledgements

I am very grateful to the Arts and Humanities Research Board for sabbatical leave during Easter term 2004. I am also very grateful to the Theology Faculty of Durham University for electing me to the Alan Richardson Lectureship in Lent term 2004 – special thanks to David Brown and Ann Loades. Gratitude is also due to St John's College and Stephen Sykes for accommodating me and providing such a stimulating theological environment.

Part of Chapter three first appeared as 'La perception de cdieu et la vision de L'invisible chez William Alston' in *Revue de théologie et de philosophie*, 134 (2002), pp.175–185. A version of Chapter 4 appeared in Ingolf U. Dalferth and Hans-Peter Grosshans, *Kritik der Religion Zur Aktualität einer unerlidigten philosophischen und theologischen Aufgabe* (Tübingen, Mohr Siebeck, 2006), pp.187–217 and a version of Chapter 5 appeared in Hermann Deuser, *Metaphysik und Religion* (München: Gütersloher Verlagshaus, 2007), pp. 60–88. I am grateful to the editors of these works for permission to re-use these materials.

This book has its basis in lectures given at the École Pratique des hautes Études in Paris during March 2002. Thanks to my host Philippe Hoffman, and to Denis O'Brien, Alain Segonds and Wayne Hankey. In Munich I have continued to profit from Werner Beierwaltes and Jan Rohls and in Athens from Sylvana Chrysakopolou. The members of Natural Theology Group in London have cheerfully listened to parts of the book and the Trialogue group in Bristol has provided great stimulus. I am grateful to colleagues in the British Society for the History of Philosophy, especially Sarah Hutton; the British Society for the Philosophy of Religion and the European Society for the Philosophy of Religion. I have particularly benefited from the insights and learning of Anthony O' Hear, John Rist, Mark Wynn, John Cottingham, John Dillon, Barry Fleet, Gordon Graham, Stephen Clark, Jane Heal, Raymond Geuss, Charles Moseley Émile Perreau-Saussine, Michael Allen, Rémi Brague, Ingolf Dalferth, Wilhelm Dupré, Roger Trigg, Chris Insole and Ilona Roth. Charles Taliaferro, Philip Clayton, David Leech, Russell Re Manning, Chloë Starr and James Vigus read parts or the whole text. David Grummet, Geoff Dumbreck, Chloë Cyrus-Kent, Russell Hillier and Chris Ryan were an invaluable support in the final stages of the preparation of the manuscript. Thanks to Thomas Kraft and his impressive team at T&T Clark, especially Tim Bartel. None of the above is responsible for any remaining errors, infelicities or asperities.

Thanks to the Master, Fellows and Staff of Clare College, The Divinity

Faculty and library and many colleagues throughout the university, not least the staff of the Cambridge University Library. I have discussed the central topics in this book regularly with Brian Hebblethwaite and George Watson. Geoffrey Rowell, Robert Murray SJ and Basil Mitchell sowed very early seeds in my mind, while my debt to Margaret Barker is unfathomable.

The book is dedicated to Clemens and Justin, who will soon know why their father was *so* interested in *The Lord of the Rings* and *The Chronicles of Narnia*.

Cambridge
January 2008

Prologue

Yet I am the necessary angel of earth
Since, in my sight, you see the world again[1]

This book is consciously written in a tradition of Christian Platonism, but it emphasizes the eschatological-mythical dimension of Platonism and the apocalyptic-*Christus Victor* gospel of Christian faith. It is a fusion of narrative *and* natural theology. My thesis is that a reductive concept of reason inspired the unprecedented exaltation of the concept of imagination in Romanticism and that we are still confronted by many of the great issues of the Romantic era. Much analytic philosophy operates with this reductive sense of reason, while much post-Heideggerian phenomenology fails to address the legitimate challenge of the Enlightenment and reverts to a quasi-positivism of the 'gift'.

Rather than appeal to the great tradition of inferential proofs of divine existence, or even the claim of distinguished philosophers and theologians that the Divine can be experienced directly, the present work reflects upon those indirect apprehensions of transcendent reality: the forms of imagination. This means the irreducible creativity of human beings that distinguishes them in kind from the rest of the animal kingdom. Through the 'inner eye' of imagination, finite beings can apprehend eternal and immutable Forms.

It is pre-eminently through the poets that we can best appreciate the real drama of human ethical existence as an apocalyptic struggle between good and evil and a journey of the soul to God. In the *Phaedrus*, the soul is described in mythical terms as a charioteer employing winged horses in a journey of the soul beyond the physical cosmos to join the celestial cavalcade of the gods and contemplating the supercelestial ideas, and Plato's image was taken up and transformed by the syncretism of early Christian apologists up to Dante and Milton. In pursuing the insights of the poets I include such theologically unlikely figures as Marcel Proust, Thomas Mann and Patrick White as well as Christian Romantics like Coleridge, Wordsworth and Hölderlin. I do not propose, however, a vague religious universalism but argue for a robust concept of the uniqueness of the Christian revelation. I argue that a major obstacle to reflective faith is a failure of imagination.

---

1 W. Stevens, *Collected Poetry and Prose* (New York: Library of America, 1997), p. 423.

1

The retrieval of the Romantic legacy

Since Xenophanes, theology has had to confront the challenge that religious belief is merely a sham. In the wake of the European Enlightenment Spinoza, Marx, Nietzsche and Freud have reinforced this challenge by suggesting further motives for the phantastical illusion. Much contemporary criticism of religion consists of some kind of illusion theory. Yet clearly many of the most significant aspects of the contemporary world are shaped by religious traditions, aspirations and conflicts.

Those who regard chimerical fancies to be the foundation of religious beliefs and action are compelled to view the world as an Augean stable of ignorance and delusion. Ironically, today, Western philosophy, which has such deep monotheistic traditions, plays a significant role in disseminating this pessimistic view of human culture and society. Indeed, belief in God is often assumed to be quite incompatible with the enquiring spirit of the genuine philosopher.

The challenge of the Enlightenment inspires three responses. One is the broad acceptance of the illusion theory, e.g. Hume; another is the rejection of the validity of the Enlightenment challenge *tout court*, e.g. Karl Barth; and the third is the Romantic attempt to answer the Enlightenment critique, while accepting the seriousness of its challenge. My proposal is in the Romantic vein. It is an account of religious belief which tries to grasp and explicate the genuine force and vitality of religious belief, without wilfully ignoring the Enlightenment, but acutely aware of its limits. It attempts to give a robust account of traditional Christian claims about the reality of God and revelation, rejecting any identification of religion with ethics or aesthetics. However, I share the traditional liberal desire to try to meet the cultured despisers of religion on common territory, and to try to reflect on the persisting force of the Enlightenment critique of Christianity. It may be objected that Shelley, Keats and Byron espoused atheism and Blake was a religious maverick, but I am using the term 'Romantic' in a rather specific and narrowly English sense to mean the Coleridgean–Wordsworthian legacy. I hope the meaning of the tag will become clear for the purpose of my argument, even if Romanticists feel uneasy about such liberties of expression.

The book is neither a historical survey of the concept of the religious imagination, nor an analysis of the concept of imagination. Rather, I employ the idea of imagination to explore various traditional problems in philosophical theology: critiques of religion; knowledge of God; evil and freedom; inspiration and revelation; and religion and society. This discussion combines both a systematic and a historical component. There are no presuppositionless strategies in the humanities, no timeless arguments. Much valuable reflection is the exercise of becoming aware of, and making explicit, the assumptions of our intellectual-imaginative frameworks. I present a hermeneutically nuanced exploration of some perennial themes and problems in Christian philosophical theology.

The topic of imagination has nothing like the significance it possessed in the eighteenth and early nineteenth centuries. The concept of imagination has humble beginnings in antiquity and medieval thought, rises to eminence after the Renaissance and Enlightenment in the Romantic period, and then suffers a steep decline in the twentieth century. The relevance of its conceptual trajectory for theology seems to me quite clear. I wish to argue that our nineteenth-century ancestors had insights which we have since lost. Though certain philosophers, such as Sartre and Bachelard, have been intrigued, indeed obsessed, by the philosophical significance of the imagination, twentieth-century philosophers more typically sought to deflate its Romantic aura and its metaphysical pretensions. Ryle, for example, argued with great eloquence and vigour that imagination is not a *sui generis* mental faculty. Being imaginative, in his view, is just a characteristic of diverse sorts of verifiable-observable behaviour. The influence of Wittgenstein (whether correctly interpreting him or not) generated much hostility towards the role and even the idea of the very existence of inner images, a hostility which in turn has exerted considerable influence upon theology. Since mental images clearly play a role in the work of creative artists, the relation between philosophy of mind and aesthetics is of deep significance for any theological construal of imagination.

The history of the concept has its own interest and fascination. However, it should not be overstressed. Ancient Greek has no concept for art or religion and yet it would be an egregious error to conclude that they possessed neither. In particular, I am convinced that historiographies of the imagination tend to make too much of a supposed gulf between the mimetic imagination of antiquity and the Middle Ages, and the imagination as a constructive and productive power in the modern age. This overlooks the manifold meanings of 'mimesis' and underrates the fascination in the ancient and medieval world with artistic creativity and indeed with creativity in general.

Dante assures us that God has no hands or feet, though Scripture legitimately uses such language to speak of the reality of God, and he believes that his *Commedia* can and should lead his readers to spiritual truths through its imaginative power and *ingegno*. In the Scriptures, faith tends to be opposed to sight, not to knowledge. Hence imagination, for all its pitfalls and limitations, can be the vehicle of 'awakening' to an invisible world: 'Faith is the substance of things hoped for, the evidence of things not seen' (Hebrews 11.1).

Between Harnack and Barth?

In theology the reason for the eclipse of imagination as a concept lies in the dominance of an *Offenbarungspositivismus* of the Barthian stamp. According to this account, appeals to imagination are tainted with human frailty and hubris. In philosophy the reason why the imagination has fallen from the central role it played for Hume or Kant is more complex. The simple answer is the role of the 'linguistic turn'. A quasi-nominalist obsession with language in both the analytic and the phenomenological traditions meant that language came to replace imagination as the key to the relation of mind to world.

I wish to explore the ramifications for theology of the theory of imagination in Samuel Taylor Coleridge. After considering the reasons for the eclipse of the concept of imagination, I shall argue for the persisting relevance of Coleridge in so far as he produces a body of thought which engages with problems of contemporary interest. I follow Charles Taylor's *Sources of the Self* in arguing that Romanticism was not obliterated by modernism (or even post-modernism) but its impact and influence is ubiquitous in contemporary thought. My sympathy for the Romantic legacy places the project much closer to Charles Taylor than to Alasdair MacIntyre. Whereas MacIntyre sees no possible compromise between the Christian inheritance and the Enlightenment legacy and is deeply pessimistic about the resources of contemporary reflection, Taylor is more sanguine about the sources and prospects of contemporary subjectivity.

Imaginative irreducibility

My debt to Taylor can also be seen in my argument for the irreducibility of human self-understanding to models derived from experimental science.

I wish to argue that critics of religion, particularly reductionistic atheists who wish to 'explain' religion in evolutionary terms, suffer themselves from a radical failure of imagination (akin to those ubiquitous flat-footed productions of Wagner whose staging deliberately tries to defuse any sense of the sublime, as if trying to judge the quality of a painting with their noses and fingers). A Titian or Raphael canvas will have a certain smell and texture, but a critic who judged the work on this basis would be making an elementary error. A contemporary Gallic scourge of priestcraft, Pascal Boyer, can point (with the wickedly withering *esprit* of a Voltaire or Diderot) to a contemporary tribal group, the Fang people, who find absurd the Christian story of the Fall of Adam and Eve.[2] He might have asked the same question about the Prometheus myth of the ancient Greeks, and the stern and profound vision of Aeschylus in *Prometheus Bound*. There is a schoolboy pleasure in demoting the pillars of civilization to primitive illusions, and as Paley said of Gibbon, 'who can refute a sneer?'

Metaphysical reductionism inspired by the success of the physical sciences, especially recent molecular biology, creates an unprecedented challenge for reflective religious belief: ontology is confined to scientific description. Christian theology in particular has a long tradition of 'faith seeking understanding'. This project is rendered implausible, if not totally incoherent, if the reductionist project prevails. In Anglophone discussions of religion there have been many forms of anti-reductionism

---

2 P. Boyer, *Religion Explained: The Evolutionary Origins of Religious Thought* (New York: Basic Books, 2001), p. 297.

in philosophical theology. This book argues that the concept of imagination must play a core role in any successful anti-reductionist account.

The role of imagination in psychology, ethics and aesthetics provides a good analogy for thinking about the imagination in religious belief. In dealing with the inner lives of other human beings, or with moral values or aesthetic qualities, we need to employ the imagination: to suppose; form hypotheses; empathize or engage imaginatively with alien people or worlds. The imaginative skills required remain very different from any quantifiable account of items and events in time and space, and yet remain necessary for the acquisition of genuine knowledge. Just as we use the imagination to relate to other minds, appreciate beauty and understand goodness, we need imagination to engage with God's action in the world.

There is an important distinction between the incomprehensibility and the utter and radical unknowability of God. If God were wholly unknowable, the latter religion would be impossible. We can know the Divine through imaginative analogy and belief in the scale of Being. This knowledge is symbolic, though not merely figurative. God is veiled – and the world is at an epistemic distance from God.

I link the Taylorian principle of the irreducibility of human self-understanding with the Platonic conviction that the lower is derived from, and participates in, the higher; and that the sensible is the 'spissitude' or thickening of the intelligible (Henry More). This Platonic tenet is the basis of my attempted retrieval of the Romantic (and non-figurative) idea of the symbol. With this I articulate an account of evil and atonement, and using Austin Farrer's work I develop a theory of historical revelation.

Experiential Platonism

Throughout this book there is much discussion of the Platonic legacy in the Christian inheritance. In Emmanuel College in Cambridge we can see Origen and John Scotus Eriugena in two stained-glass windows, as well as later Emmanuel worthies like the Cambridge Platonists Peter Sterry and John Smith. Notwithstanding my conscious apology for, and defence of, this tradition, I wish to forestall a cetain misunderstanding of my project. I reject what one might designate as the 'Socratic error', the view expressed classically in the *Theaetetus* that knowledge requires the capacity to give an adequate account or justification of true beliefs. Against this rationalist strand in Plato, I press for recognition of the more poetic and imaginative apprehension of the Forms, which eludes articulation. Plato's own use of myths, particularly in the *Phaedrus*, can be seen as the source of this poetic-imaginative Platonism throughout the centuries, especially in Shakespeare, Milton and Wordsworth.

The relevance of this construal of 'Platonism' for philosophical theology is momentous. Traditionally, the Platonic leaven in much Christian theology has produced a repeated oscillation between radical apophaticism and ultra-rationalism, between Pseudo-Denys and Anselm, Bonaventure and Leibniz, de Maistre and Hegel. All are committed to the Christian Platonic *itinerarium mentis in Deum* expressed so vividly in the image of the soul's chariot. But thinkers in the Platonic tradition all lurch from extreme rationalism to excessive agnosticism. More recently, Heidegger's celebrated critique of the rationalist legacy in Platonism has inspired a retrieval of the apophatic bequest. Yet neither extreme, I believe, is properly compatible with Christian theology. The Phaedran-imaginative-poetic Platonism I am advocating avoids this uncomfortable pair of alternatives. With its basis in the experiential apprehension of the divine presence in the world, it envisages the world as a sacrament of the transcendent Godhead, and history as the mysterious theatre of divine action.

In the first chapter I explore the broader significance of imagination for theology and consider the view, advanced in many histories of thought, that 'imagination' remains mimetic until the Romantic period and then becomes creative and productive through Kant and the Romantics. In contrast I suggest that it is important to distinguish between the word and the object. In modern thought imagination is crucially employed by Spinoza as a tool to criticize the claims of theism. Plato's theory of the Forms and his use of myths is evidently the employment of imagination to compensate for the limitations of discursive thought: imagination can 'body forth' the unseen Forms. In Romanticism this Platonic legacy is expressed with unparalleled vigour.

In the second chapter I consider the human imagination from a variety of perspectives: psychological-psychoanalytic, metaphysical, epistemo-logical and aesthetic. I concentrate on the contributions of Coleridge and Collingwood. I aver that creativity is an inalienable and irreducible part of the human mind, and is a necessary component of the ancient conviction in the infinite value of the human soul as made in the image of God.

Since the creative power of the mind points to a transcendent source, in Chapter 3 I consider two models of mystical theology in philosophical theology and observe in both a failure to pay heed to the proper role of the imagination as 'Reason in its most exalted mood', and explore why Wordsworth is preferable.

The Wordsworthian account of the soul's sense of divine presence leads us in Chapter 4 to consider whether this is fantasy or legitimate. In this chapter I explore the view that religion is essentially symbolic, and that the Romantic view of symbol in Coleridge or Schelling has much to commend it.

In Chapter 5 I turn from religion to the apocalyptic dimension of ethics, in which the 'ought' of obligation expresses the supernatural within us, so that the moral life is quite rightly seen by the great Christian poets Dante or Shakespeare as both exile and pilgrimage towards an absolute Good.

The view of ethics as apocalyptic leads on in Chapter 6 to the importance of stories and the question of narrative from a Parmenidean perspective. Drawing upon C. S. Lewis and J. R. R. Tolkien, I argue that the power of the story resides in its religious and metaphysical implications and the intimation of that perfection whose centre is everywhere and circumference nowhere.

In Chapter 7 I turn to the specifically Christian story and pursue Austin Farrer's attempt to employ poetic imagination as a key to understanding scriptural inspiration, in which images are the primary content of revelation.

Finally, in Chapter 8, I consider the 'social imaginary', in which the fabric of our common life is suffused by the symbols and icons, the ideas and memory, of a historical culture. This 'imaginary' has a deep, though often neglected, Christian structure.

Common to all these chapters is the highly suggestive image of the chariot. In Chapter 1, I present the patristic fusion of the theophany of Ezekiel and Plato's vision of the 'plane of truth' approached with the chariot of the soul. Chapter 2 uses the idea of the wheels within the wheels of Ezekiel's vehicle as an image of divine indwelling and double agency, while Chapter 3 reflects on the opposite dimension of the vision, namely the inscrutable, numinous quality of the theophany, and the transcendental mood conveyed by both Plato and Ezekiel. Chapter 4 explores how a core symbol, like the chariot, represents an instance of the tautegorical sublime, which resists any reductive translation or allegory. Indeed, Chapter 5 presents the ethical life in apocalyptic terms as a battle of the soul, and the chariot as an image of the human agent's ineluctable interior journey. It is because we need to see our lives within a certain narrative that story or myth exerts such a binding force upon the human imagination. As *merkabah*, the ascending or descending chariot expresses the widespread longing for coherence and unity, which is answered by the Christian Logos. If the chariot is an image of the rational control of the charioteer, it is also an image of the pre-theoretical, subconscious energies guided by the soul. Chapter 6 explores how story or myth can address the soul at this pre-theoretical level. Chapter 7 deploys the image of the chariot as a paradigm of providence and power, Christologically construed. The final chapter draws on the vision of the city through the eyes of St John the Divine in Patmos, as he transforms Ezekiel's vision into a contemplation of the City of God and the consummation of all things, bringing the chariot's journey to an end.

Religious belief is indeed a feat of imagination; a product of human faculties. Yet Farrer liked to speak of double agency – certain acts which are at once authentically human and yet the channels of divine influence. I wish to speak of the anagogic imagination to designate such a reciprocal relation: the human construction of symbols of God which at the same time constitute divine epiphany. Like Farrer, I wish to produce an account of the imagination which culminates in a theory of inspired images which is based on the doctrine that man is made in the image of God. In this manner I wish to avoid the Scylla of a crude theological anthropomorphism and the Charybdis of a desiccated projectivism. My aim is to produce a 'conjectural' theology in the mode of Nicholas of Cusa's *De coniecturis* (1442). It is significant that the Latin word *conjectura* and the Greek word σύμβολον share the same root meaning of throw together (conjicere, συμβάλλειν: to throw together). Neither the inspired symbols of revelation nor the great conjectures about God are mere fantasies, since the imagination of the human soul mirrors, however darkly, the fecundity of the divine mind.

1

Religion, Romanticism and Imagining Modernity

It is not surprising, therefore, that, while theology alone is not philosophy, the question of the *possibility* of theology has been, and to some extent still is, the principal philosophical question.[1]

Ovid's great work, *Metamorphoses*, appeared at a time when Graeco-Roman mythology was already dying and during the metamorphosis of a ritually executed Galilean Jew into the Redeemer of the world. The religion of the 'pale Galilean' (Christianity) was the force which ultimately supplanted the old pagan narratives, as John Milton in 'On the Morning of Christ's Nativity' presents Christ driving away the pagan deities. Indeed, Milton's *Paradise Lost* is the last great Christian epic in Europe. Milton is contemporary and conversant with major developments in cosmology. He does not, like Donne, rue the 'new Philosophy'. He met Galileo (the 'Tuscan artist' in book I of *Paradise Lost*), and Raphael in book VIII of *Paradise Lost* seems to mock the Ptolemaic cosmos. Nature constitutes a 'book of God' but the rest

> From man or angel the great architect
> Did wisely to conceal[2]

But was not Milton the last great imaginative articulation of Christianity? Was not his epic, like Ovid's, wrought during the death knell of its mythic basis? Has not modern science and technology, to paraphrase Keats somewhat, clipped the angel wings of the Platonic imagination and unwoven the rainbow? Is modern science not the harbinger of the traumatic experience of disenchantment inaugurated by the new science expressed in Pascal's memorable words, 'Le silence de ces espaces infinis m'effraie'? Modern despisers of religion are aware that it still haunts the contemporary imagination. Popular Western culture, from *Star Wars* to *The Lord of the Rings* and the Chronicles of Narnia, is clearly still fascinated by the Christian vision. The demise of anti-religious secular ideologies such as Communism, National Socialism and Italian fascism in the twentieth century and the growth of militant Islam and fundamentalist Christianity in the later twentieth century (reinforced by the impact of 9/11) means that many modern inheritors of the legacy of the radical Enlightenment are searching for explanations of the persistence of

---

1 R. Scruton, *A Short History of Modern Philosophy* (London: Routledge, 1995), p. 5.
2 J. Milton, *Paradise Lost*, VIII, 72–3.

religious belief in terms of physiological and neurological causes: all can be explained by the survival of the genome.

The Bible presents a vast cosmic drama of Fall and redemption, sin and salvation. How can it survive the realization since Copernicus that the world is not the centre of the universe? How can religion survive the loss of the soul implicit in Darwinian biology, as the highest values of human beings, love, duty, honesty, sympathy, are grounded in the evolutionary process rather than the soul made in the image of God? Has not the Christian imagination been superseded by the imaginary generated by science?

Is not modern culture the result of a progressive disenchantment of the world? A century ago the great German sociologist Max Weber gave an oration to young scholars, 'Wissenschaft als Beruf', in the magnificent Grosse Aula in the Ludwig Maximilians Universitität in Munich.[3] Weber observed that the modern world is one of re-emergent polytheism. The beautiful, the true – to say nothing of the good – have no overarching unity in contemporary culture. The legacy of this is a science stripped of values, art devoid of beauty, ethics divorced from truth – a milieu in which the very idea of science itself, and the process of rationalization which it ushered in, cannot be justified with scientific or rational tools. The loss of the inherited monotheistic vision through the progress of science has generated an unavoidable relativism. Hence the death of God has generated a battle of reawoken idols. For all the notes of elegiac loss in Weber, he holds fast to the sense of an inexorable process of secularization in the occidental imagination. Karl Löwith famously challenged the legitimacy of the modern idea of progress in his *Meaning in History* by exposing it as a 'secularisation' of the 'eschatological pattern' of Christian progress.[4] Thus Löwith questioned the vaunted superiority of the 'modern' over medieval and antique cultures. Hans Blumenberg responded to Löwith's challenge by conceding that modernity has to be understood within the boundaries of certain historical, intellectual and cultural traditions. However, Löwith pleads for the *legitimacy* of modernity as the emancipation and affirmation of human autonomy and rationality against the theological absolutism of late medieval nominalism. Modernity's genetic roots in the historical struggle against the Gnostic implications of a nominalism grounded in a *potentia absoluta* do not invalidate the positive assertions of modern humanity.

Notwithstanding the subtlety and interest of Blumenberg's vigorous assertion of the legitimacy of modernity, Löwith is quite correct to reveal the extent to which the Christian imagination has shaped occidental culture. The pattern of Paradise–Fall–Redemption is still very deeply entrenched, so that ostensibly anti-religious movements like Marxism or some forms of psychology depend on it. A crucial figure is that of Rousseau and his visceral critique of the alienated state of human beings

---

3 M. Weber, 'Wissenschaft als Beruf', in *Max Weber: Gesamtausgabe*, ed. W. J. Mommsen and W. Schluchter with B. Morgenbrod (Munich: Mohr Siebeck, 1992), pp. 99–101.
4 K. Löwith, *Meaning in History: The Theological Implications of the Philosophy of History* (Chicago: Chicago University Press, 1970), p. 2.

in modern institutions. Beethoven's Ninth Symphony paradigmatic is another index of the pattern of salvation emerging in secular form. The nineteenth- and twentieth-century novel is structured on the pilgrim's progress. Rousseau's eponymous *Émile* is a copy of the profoundly Christian *Robinson Crusoe*.

Although Christian theology was subject to unprecedented critique and erosion of its power and prestige in Europe through biblical criticism, the attack on miracles, and the exposure of its institutional privileges, it managed to sustain a remarkable grip upon the European imagination. It is perhaps telling that Blumenberg's work *Höhlenausgänge* saw the philosophical challenge in the wake of the failure of metaphysics as one of relinquishing the unrealizable demand for ultimate meaning and significance implicit in the absolute metaphor of the cave and its implicit or explicit corollary – the demand for emancipation.[5] This melancholy note of resignation in the later Blumenberg is nevertheless a reminder of the residual power of the Christian-Platonic legacy. Blumenberg is deeply akin to Nietzsche. For Nietzsche, the Madman proclaiming that 'God is dead' is unnoticed by the crowd. The crowd still exists within an imaginary framework of values largely dictated by (obsolete) Christian belief. On this view, the death of God is an event of which our culture has not become sufficiently aware. Those surrounding the Madman have not properly internalized the consequences of the 'death of God'. Both Nietzsche and Blumenberg view contemporary culture as still in the thrall of the Christian imaginary. The metaphysical apparatus that has supported our values has disappeared.

Images and idolatry

It is easily forgotten that the concept of God is traditionally as much an integral part of the philosophical curriculum as the soul or freedom, and most of the greatest philosophers from Aquinas to Descartes, Locke or Kant were theists. But philosophy traditionally covered most of those intellectual problems between grammar and Divine revelation! In the last few centuries its scope and ambition have been severely restricted. Contemporary philosophers are often puzzled why God might be thought as a philosophical topic at all, transcending – in the worst possible sense of the world – both reason and imagination, and providing a basis for superstition and delusion.

Modern theology has inherited a largely negative conception of the imagination. This is linked to the critique of metaphysics as idolatrous, which has its roots in Heidegger and Bergson and the deconstruction of the *visual* paradigm of truth as totalitarian gaze.[6] Bergson's philosophy of

---

5 H. Blumenberg, *Höhlenausgänge* (Frankfurt am Main: Suhrkamp, 1989).
6 C. Pickstock, *After Writing: On the Liturgical Consummation of Philosophy* (Oxford: Blackwell, 1998), pp. xiii, 90–1, 103–4.

duration and his critique of the tyranny of the visual in the Platonic *eidos* stands as the root of the 'cinematological instinct' of theological thought.[7] Cognate to this is Heidegger's celebrated critique of metaphysics as the vision of Being, i.e. the idealization of static presence over and against the ephemeral flux of becoming from Plato's cave. In the shadow of Friedrich Nietzsche, Martin Heidegger regarded modern philosophy as a baneful aberration derived from Plato's momentous misconstrual of truth as *veritas logica*, and as the divine light in Augustinianism down to Descartes. This philosophical legacy has led to the spatialization of reality, technology, etc. Heidegger's strictures on metaphysics as idolatry become fused with Levinas's Hebraic iconoclasm in which Hellenic ontology is idolatry,[8] and in Derrida there is subsequently an interesting fusion of elements of radical Protestantism and Hebraic iconoclasm. Heidegger was fascinated by radical Protestantism: Schleiermacher, Kierkegaard and Luther determined his early reading of Augustine and Paul. Rosenzweig, Buber and Lévinas have all shaped phenomenology in the French tradition. Hence imagination receives a gloomy estimate at the hands of the Gallic avant-garde.[9] In their eyes, it is too closely tied to the appalling humanistic project, from which Heidegger disassociated himself in favour of thoughts about Being. And of course, Spinoza, Marx, Freud and Nietzsche all play a highly significant role in this tradition as searching critics of the bogus fantasies of the Christian bourgeoisie. Foucault concludes his *Les Mots et Les Choses* with his hyberbolic anti-humanism:

> L'homme est une invention dont l'archéologie de notre pensée montre aisément la date récente. Et peut-être la fin prochaine ... on peut parier que l'homme s'effacerait, comme à la limite de la mer un visage de sable.[10]

Spinoza and the challenge of the imagination

It is a singular irony that Spinoza, who was such a formative force in the development of Romanticism, should have developed a stringent rationalistic critique of religion as generated by the inadequate and confused ideas of imagination.[11] In the appendix to part I of the *Ethics*,

---

7 H. Bergson, *Creative Evolution* (London: Macmillan, 1954), p. 333.

8 Although there is a strong Hellenic component in Levinas, see J.-M. Narbonne, *Lévinas et l'héritage grec* (Paris: Vrin, 2004).

9 M. Jay, *Downcast Eyes: The Denigration of Vision in Twentieth Century French Thought* (Berkeley, Calif.: University of California Press, 1993). For a theological exception, see D. Grumett, *Teilhard de Chardin: Theology, Humanity and Cosmos* (Leuven: Peeters, 2005), pp. 139–68.

10 M. Foucault, *Les Mots et Les Choses* (Paris: Gallimard, 1966), p. 398.

11 Benedictus de Spinoza, *Ethics*, I, app., ed. G. H. R. Parkinson (Oxford: Oxford University Press, 2000), pp. 111–12.

Spinoza is adamant that the confusion of imagination with understanding is at the root of theism.[12]

Spinoza is drawing upon ancient debates concerning the religious 'imagination'. This becomes apparent when one considers the challenge of Xenophanes to any rational or 'natural' theology: that the Ethiopians and Thracians formed gods in their own likeness. Those philosophers like Plato and Aristotle who wished to avoid the materialism of the Ionian scientists or the relativism of the Sophists and to develop a theory of a supreme principle had to consider scrupulously the projectionist critique. The development of 'natural theology' in Athens postulated a movement from within to outside the 'cave' of immediate and untutored experience and up the divided line to the supreme transcendent Good. Plato produced an argument in the *Republic* that poets should be censored,[13] but resorted to 'likely tales' about a cosmic demiurge, winged chariots and heavenly judgement of the soul. Aristotle was critical of the value of such 'myths' but the austerely intellectual God of book XII of the *Metaphysics* nevertheless draws the world with the beauty of the beloved. The vision of God in Athenian metaphysics was developed with enormous imaginative as well as argumentative force.

Spinoza takes up the old challenge of Xenophanes and places it at the centre of his critique of theism. Imagination contains 'all those ideas which are inadequate and confused',[14] and is inferior to discursive reason and the highest cognitive level, rational intuition. Rational intuition grasps the necessity of all events in the universe as proceeding from the divine substance. But 'those who do not understood the nature of things, but only imagine them, affirm nothing of things and take imagination for understanding, they therefore firmly believe that there is an order in things, ignorant as they are of things and their own nature'.[15]

Deluded by their imaginations, men are given to employ concepts like 'good', 'bad', 'freedom', 'contingency' and 'God' as a personal agent. In his *Theologico-Political Treatise* Spinoza exploits this theory of imagination to undermine three foundations of theology: miracles, prophecy and Scripture. Since all modes necessarily express the one unique and infinite substance, miracles are impossible a priori. Though men's imaginations are stimulated by the idea that God can be shown to exist when nature 'breaks her accustomed order',[16] reason can correct this folly, since 'if anyone asserted that God acts in contravention to the laws of nature, he, *ipso facto*, would be compelled to assert that God acted against His own nature – an evident absurdity'.[17] Prophets have unusually 'vivid imaginations, and not . . . unusually perfect minds'.[18] The prophets are full of

12 See L. Strauss, *Spinoza's Critique of Religion* (Chicago: The University of Chicago Press, 1965), pp. 215–23, and also H. Laux, *Imagination et religion chez Spinoza: La potentia dans l'histoire* (Paris: Vrin, 1993).
13 Plato, *Republic* 377–89.
14 Spinoza, *Ethics*, II, prop. 41; p. 149.
15 Ibid., I, app.; p. 110.
16 Benedictus de Spinoza, *Theologico-Political Treatise*, VI (New York: Dover, 1951), p. 81.
17 Ibid., VI; p. 83.
18 Ibid., II; p. 27.

vulgar and crude anthropomorphisms, and contradict one another. Prophecy thus needs to be subjected to rational critique. Similar strictures apply to Scripture as a whole, since it 'does not aim at explaining things by their natural causes, but only at narrating what appeals to the popular imagination, and doing so in the manner best calculated to excite wonder, and consequently to impress the minds of the masses with devotion'.[19]

The basic Platonic intuition and the mediating imagination

Richard Rorty writes:

There was, we moderns may say with the ingratitude of hindsight, no particular reason why this ocular metaphor seized the imagination of the founders of Western thought . . . The notion of 'contemplation,' of knowledge of universal concepts or truths as Θεωρία, makes the Eye of the Mind the inescapable model for the better sort of knowledge.[20]

Plato's basic intuition is that habitual human life is akin to being in a dark cave with intimations of a transcendent domain of Forms culminating in the Form of the Good. The good life consists in striving to ascend to this transcendent source. The language he uses for these Forms is tantalizing. The most dynamic descriptions of the ideas come in the quasi-mythical passages of the charioteer, the demiurge, or Diotima's speech. Plato's philosophy is presented in dramatic form. He expressly subordinates 'imagination' to 'reason' and yet is a supremely imaginative philosopher who consciously employs 'likely tales' in order to pursue his metaphysical concerns.[21] The idea of Socrates as a midwife is also highly imaginative.

Plato was the poet who initiated a great quarrel between philosophy and poetry. In his hierarchy of souls that enjoy the vision of the intelligible, the poet is placed in a very inferior position.[22] There is, admittedly, a tension in Plato himself between the demand for knowledge conceived as articulate rational comprehension which at least in principle can be taught (book VII of the *Republic*) and those aspects in the dialogues, especially the myths (or rather mythic poems), the *Seventh Letter* and the *Phaedrus*, which suggest a view of knowledge as also eluding exhaustive definition. He is inclined to prefer the latter conception to the former. The *locus classicus* is the 'heaven-sent madness' of the *Phaedrus*:

19 Ibid., VI; p. 90.
20 R. Rorty, *Philosophy and the Mirror of Nature* (Oxford: Blackwell, 1980), pp. 38–9.
21 J. A. Stewart, *The Myths of Plato* (London: Centaur, 1960); L. Brisson, *Plato the Myth Maker* (Chicago: University of Chicago Press, 1998).
22 Plato, *Phaedrus* 248e.

If a man comes to the door of poetry untouched by the madness of the Muses, believing that technique alone will make him a good poet, he and his sane compositions never reach perfection, but are utterly eclipsed by the performance of the inspired madman.[23]

One of the major tenets of Platonism is the conviction that there is a surplus of ultimate meaning that transcends any attempt to express it: the Good is 'beyond being'. There is an *experiential* if not definitional knowledge. This is a genuinely Platonic component. Notwithstanding Plato's insistence upon the importance of close reasoning and argument, all reasoning presupposes those truths which the soul intuits immediately. The classic expression is the image of the yearning of the winged soul in the *Phaedrus*[24] or the vision of love expounded by Diotima as recounted by Socrates in Plato's *Symposium*.

Plato bequeathed an interest in a rationality which transcends the discursive or inductive and yet is not a projection of anthropomorphisms. That is to say, there is an interest in certain images and 'stories' and a keen sense of their limitations. Yet, as Hegel insisted against Kant, to set limits is to transcend them. Here is the Plato of the *myths* as well as the Plato of the *dialectic*: the residual poet in the philosopher; the Plato who is not just a logician but 'of all philosophers . . . the most poetical',[25] and who is drawing upon the kind of experiences or feelings which are characteristic of religious and aesthetic encounters. It was this side of Plato's mind, the transcendent mood, for which Aristotle had little sympathy, even if he shared the intellectualism of his teacher and mentor. Aristotle's criticisms of the Platonic Ideas can be traced to a tendency to be overly literal in his interpretation of Plato's language. Sir Philip Sidney, like Shelley later, saw Plato as 'essentially a poet' and the myths and the dialogues, indeed the dramatic structure of his works, are for Sidney an instance of 'which who knoweth not to be flowers of poetry did never walk into Apollo's garden'.[26] This estimate is most apt in relation to the *Phaedrus*. Hackforth follows the great Wilamowitz in his view that in this dialogue the poet in Plato 'definitely gets the upper hand'. It is clear that in this dialogue Plato is quite exceptionally conscious of the value of the imaginative, as against the rational, power of the human soul; and that consciousness finds expression both in the

23 Ibid., 245a. Cf. Henry More on Plato, Plotinus and *enthusiasein*: ('those diviner sort of Philosophers, such as *Plato* and *Plotinus* . . . upon the more then ordinary sensible visits of the divine Love and Beauty descending into their enravished Souls, profess themselves no less moved then what the sense of such expressions as these will beare, *anakineisthai, exbakhiousthai, enthousian, enthouiasein*. To such Enthusiasm as this, which is but the triumph of the Soul of man inebriated, as it were, with the delicious sense of the divine life, that blessed Root and Originall of all holy wisdom and virtue, I must declare myself as much a friend, as I am to the vulgar fanatical Enthusiasm a professed enemy'. *Enthusiasmus Triumphatus* (1662; repr. Los Angeles: The Augustan Reprint Society, 1966, p. 45).

24 Plato, *Phaedrus* 248–9.

25 Sir Philip Sidney, *A Defence of Poetry*, V. Plato Banished the Poets; 'Refutation, Four charges: ed. J. A. van Dorsten (London, Oxford University Press, 1966), p. 58.

26 Ibid., 'What Poetry Is'; p. 20.

'inspired' Socrates himself and in his exaltation of inspired divination and poetry.[27]

The emphatic espousal of the imagination as a cognition coincided with a revival of Platonism. Keats's assertion, 'I am certain of nothing but of the holiness of the Heart's affection and the truth of the Imagination',[28] or Wordsworth's affirmation in *The Prelude* that imagination is but 'reason in her most exalted mood',[29] represent a clear debt to Platonic sources, even though the identification of reason and imagination seems explicitly denied by just that tradition. Perhaps the reinforcement of the achievements of Newtonian physics throughout the eighteenth century encouraged a dimension of Platonism which has been one of its most potent legacies to contemporary consciousness, a doctrine latent in Plato and Neoplatonism, but only explicitly articulated in Renaissance and Romantic developments: the tenet of the special dignity of the creative imagination drew upon a tradition of thought stretching beyond seventeenth-century Cambridge to fifteenth-century Florence. The poet sees the realm of Being in the flux of Becoming: true poetry is the mimesis of reality and not of appearance.

Creative imagination or mimesis

> Oh Plato! Plato! you have paved the way,
> With your confounded phantasies, to more
> Immoral conduct by the fancied sway
> Your system feigns o'er this controlless core
> Of human hearts, than all the long array
> Of Poets and romancers . . .[30]

Popular histories of the imagination tend to present a shift from conceiving the imagination as essentially representing or mimetic to the productive or creative model of the imagination in the modern period. The concept of imagination does indeed play a humble role in the antique and medieval philosophical tradition.[31] However, we should be wary of assuming an unproblematic relationship between ancient and modern concepts. There is often no exact equivalent between the different concepts; or, conversely, what we mean by the concept of 'imagination' may be implicit in the work of a philosopher even if different terminology is employed. 'Imagination' is not the only word which might be used to explore the phenomenon. The Greeks had no word for religion, but we still discuss their versions of it.

27 R. Hackforth, *Plato's Phaedrus* (Cambridge: Cambridge University Press, 1955, p. 61.)

28 *The Letters of Keats, 1814–1821*, ed. H. E. Rollins (Cambridge, Mass.: Harvard University Press, 1958), vol. 1, p. 184.

29 William Wordsworth, *The Prelude: The 1805 Text*, XIV, 19.6 (Oxford: Oxford University Press, 1984), p. 233.

30 Lord Byron, *Don Juan*, cant 1, st. 116, ll. 1–6.

31 G. Watson, 'Imagination and Religion in Classical Thought', in J. P. Mackey (ed.), *Religious Imagination* (Edinburgh: Edinburgh University Press, 1986), pp. 29–54.

We should remember that aesthetics as a philosophical discipline is a very recent development in the history of thought. The term 'aesthetics' is a coinage of the eighteenth-century German philosopher Alexander Baumgarten. The very term seems to usher in an age of subjectivism and expressivism, in contrast to the classical and medieval tradition of art as essentially representative: *mimesis*.

Stephen Halliwell, however, has eloquently attacked such a schematic view of the history of thinking about art and argues for 'a significant degree of both historical and conceptual continuity'.[32] He also warns against any straightforward translation of *mimesis* as imitation, and insists that *mimesis* in some of the key ancient thinkers often includes rather than excludes expression.

Plato uses the language of *mimesis* in a large variety of philosophical contexts, not least in his allegories of the Sun, the Divided Line and the Cave and in the creation myth of the *Timaeus*, where 'the world itself is a mimetic creation, wrought by a divine artist who, at one point in the *Timaeus* (55c6), is expressly visualized as a painter . . .' Hence philosophers might be deemed for Plato "interpreters of a cosmic work of art" '.[33]

And, as noted above, Plato famously banished the artists. Clearly Plato's position on art is ambivalent – we have both his critique of Homer and Hesiod and his evident fondness for Pindar and the language of mysteries. Plato's attack on the arts is based on an epistemological argument concerning imitation – they take us further away from the Ideas and towards the unruly nature of passions. Artists are like Sophists in that they do inadequate justice to the concerns of truth, taking us two stages away from reality and arousing dangerous and disturbing passions. Aristotle challenges this account: imitation (*mimesis*), he counters, is quite normal and this is just how children learn. Over the question of the problematic passions aroused by the arts, Aristotle considers the process of catharsis in tragedy to be an instance of how an art form purifies the emotions and passions. Plotinus pursues Aristotle's defence of art against Plato. Yet his approach is inspired by a thoroughly Platonic metaphysics. Rather than a distraction, art becomes an organ of philosophical knowledge. The artist creates on the basis of a vision of the Forms, *natura naturans* rather than *natura naturata*, and his work represents this ideal noetic realm rather than the empirical domain. The vision of the great poet, say, is the view of the world from the perspective of the inner eye. Plotinus argues that since artists possess beauty, they make up what is defective in things. For Phidias too did not make his Zeus from any model perceived by the senses, but understood what Zeus would look like if he wanted to make himself visible. Plotinus thinks that 'the material did not have this form, but it was in the man who had it in his mind even before it came into the stone; but it was in the craftsman, not in so far as he had hands and eyes, but because he had

32 S. Halliwell, *The Aesthetics of Mimesis: Ancient Texts and Modern Problems* (Princeton, NJ: Princeton University Press, 2002), p. 8.
33 Ibid., p. 71.

some share of art'.[34] Plotinus is claiming that Phidias employs his 'active' imagination in shaping his statues. Here is the probable source of Michelangelo's famous remark that he thought of his statue as buried in the marble.

Yet we should be wary of thinking that these later Platonists were utterly at odds with their own tradition. Plato employs the language of myth, symbol and metaphor in order to convey both the absolute and binding *normative* force of the transcendent Forms as *realities*: they are absolute patterns (παράδειγματα); or even forces (δυνάμεις) in which the sensible world participates (μέθεξις). And yet Plato suggests that no adequate description or definition of these Forms is possible. The mind quite properly experiences truth, goodness or beauty to command assent as a reality of experience, without which science, society and creativity would collapse.

This normative quality of the realm of values is particularly difficult to express in factual terms. The properties which demand assent look rather odd compared to the properties of physical objects. The values of being true, beautiful or good are often said to possess a 'magnetic' quality. We are drawn towards such qualities, and yet their relation to the tangible physical properties of objects is puzzling. One cannot readily read off an 'ought' from the observable 'is', even with a fine microscope. They are particularly perplexing for the mere 'lover of sights and sounds.'[35]

Truth, beauty and goodness are all examples of the normative in this strong Platonic sense. Plato was impressed by mathematical truths for this reason. Once one recognizes a belief to be true, one sees that it *should* be believed. There is a gap between the usefulness of a belief and its truth.[36] In fact it is puzzling, as both Alvin Plantinga and C. S. Lewis have observed, how the epistemological optimism of modern science can be justified on a purely evolutionary basis. Only the most resolute pragmatist will deny that many truths are not *useful*, and conversely many useful beliefs are not *true*. Furthermore, if our minds are best understood as products of the struggle for survival on the savannah, the capacity of the human mind to probe into quantum or astrophysical domains is most surprising.

Similarly with beauty. 'De gustibus non est disputandum', says the relativist, but qualities of the *Oresteia* of Aeschylus have produced admiration and continuity of esteem through the ages. Marxism explains responses to art in terms of class and status. More recently sociobiology likes to speculate about genetic dispositions to prefer certain shapes and colours, even landscapes like Poussin's which remind us of the savannah. Yet as many philosophers, from Plato to Kant, have observed, aesthetic appreciation is characteristically disinterested. The enjoyment of beauty, phenomenologically at least, is quite distinct from the

---

34 Plotinus, *Enneads*, V.8.1 20–2, in *Plotinus*, tr. A. H. Armstrong. Loeb Classical Library (Cambridge, Mass.: Harvard University Press, 1984), vol. 5, p. 237.
35 Plato, *Republic* 476bff.
36 See A. O'Hear, *Beyond Evolution: Human Nature and the Limits of Evolutionary Explanation* (Oxford: Clarendon Press, 1997).

satisfaction of desire or the longing for possession. If the Marxists or sociobiologists are correct, we are quite deluded in imagining that we admire beauty for its own sake. Murdoch makes an eloquent case for the Platonic view:

> Good art, thought of as a symbolic force rather than statement, provides a stirring image of a pure, transcendent value, a steadily visible enduring higher good, and perhaps provides for many people, in an unreligious age without prayer or sacraments, their clearest *experience* of something grasped as separate and precious and beneficial and held quietly, and unpossessively in the attention.[37]

Most important for Plato is the *ethical* dimension of the normative. As moral beings we feel the clash between inclination and duty. Not just the sense of the inherent preciousness of life but our most visceral instincts clash with the sacrifices demanded in wartime. Horace's *dulce et decorum est pro patria mori* has been abused and justly criticized but is a striking testimony to a widely accepted code of duty to society which can have appalling consequences for individuals. It would be cynical and implausible to think that the ravages of the two world wars of the twentieth century can be *explained* in biological terms.

Socrates is an image of goodness, and one which reverses the biological and cultural approbation of the admirable. Just as the outwardly beautiful and aristocratic Alcibiades, with his baleful vices, is overwhelmed and outshone by the inner beauty of Socrates, so the injustice of the Athenian court is condemned by his calm but resolute courage.

The basis for epistemological, ethical and aesthetic judgement, Plato avers, must reside in a transcendent principle, perceived by what he refers to as the 'eye of understanding'.[38] The idea ($\delta\acute{o}\xi\alpha$) has the primary sense of visible forms and appearances (cf. $\epsilon\tilde{i}\delta o\varsigma$), and is linked to the verb $\epsilon\tilde{i}\delta o\nu$ (I saw). Both are cognate with both the Latin *videre* and the German *Wissen*. Many other central epistemological terms in Plato possess this strong visual component, e.g. $\delta\acute{o}\xi\alpha$ and $\theta\epsilon\omega\rho\acute{i}\alpha$. Thus Plato uses the symbol of the eye to convey the power and immediacy of the soul's apprehension of immaterial realities.

I say the *symbol* of the eye because here we are not speaking of mere metaphor or of useful fictions, but the facts of the spiritual life, without which morality collapses into prudence or convention, truth into utility, and beauty into the pleasurable. Truth, beauty and goodness are facts, yet they elude description in objective terms, and seem to vanish upon analysis. Goodness or evil are not locatable in space and time, but are as palpable to the reflective mind as mathematical objects or conscious thoughts. That murder is wrong is an eternal and immutable truth, or as firm and secure as many empirical claims, whatever the details about debates concerning embryos or euthanasia. All parties agree, in discus-

---

37 I. Murdoch, 'Against Dryness', Encounter, 16 (January 1961), 16–20.
38 ($\acute{\eta}$ $\tau\tilde{\eta}\varsigma$ $\delta\iota\alpha\nu o\acute{i}\alpha\varsigma$ $\acute{o}\psi\iota\varsigma$, *Symposium* 219a.).

sions of the ethics of abortion or euthanasia, stem cell research or cloning, that murder is wrong; they differ only over its definition.

Imagination all compact

At this point the imagination is necessary. The ideal world can be grasped, however obliquely, by the imagination. Hence Coleridge defines imagination in the *Lay Sermons* as 'that reconciling and mediatory power' which incorporates the 'Reason in Images of the Sense'.[39] It is able to substitute for the failings of pure rationality by 'bodying forth' unseen Forms. Shakespeare is almost paraphrasing the *Phaedrus* in his famous lines from *A Midsummer Night's Dream*:

> The lunatic, the lover, and the poet
> Are of imagination all compact.
> One sees more devils than vast hell can hold;
> That is the madman. The lover, all as frantic,
> Sees Helen's beauty in a brow of Egypt.
> The poet's eye, in a fine frenzy rolling,
> Doth glance from heaven to earth, from earth to heaven.
> And as imagination bodies forth
> The forms of things unknown, the poet's pen
> Turns them to shapes, and gives to airy nothing
> A local habitation and a name.[40]

In the *Phaedrus*, Socrates defends the divinely inspired madness of poetical frenzy, which he compares with the divine gift of erotic madness. This fourth frenzy – the inspirational power of beauty to transform the soul into the object of its aspiration – is the real *skopos* of the dialogue. The poet, like the lover, is responding to genuine spiritual beauty: to the experience and presence of the Divine in the world. Plato notes that the 'learned' will sneer, but the wise will appreciate the truth of supersensible beauty.[41] Hackforth identifies the 'learned' as those who hold materialistic and mechanistic philosophical positions.[42] Such thinkers, like the later Hobbes, refuse to acknowledge the difference between arousal and inspiration. Plato is reflecting upon the power of physical beauty to unleash great energy: for example, the Trojan war, fought over Helen. The dialogue is concerned with sustained submission of the heart and the discipline of the imagination required to follow real beauty and not false and delusive delights. It is concerned with inspiration in its highest form.

---

39 S. T. Coleridge, *Lay Sermons*, ed. R. J. White (Princeton, NJ: Princeton University Press, 1972), p. 29.
40 William Shakespeare, *A Midsummer Night's Dream*, V.i.7–17.
41 Plato, *Phaedrus*, 243ff.
42 Plato, *Phaedrus*, tr. R. Hackforth (Cambridge: Cambridge University Press, 1952), p. 62.

Brann describes Plato's *Phaedrus* as 'the first text in which the relationship between desirous passion, eros, and the imagination is explicitly articulated'.[43] It is a complex dialogue which covers such topics as beauty, knowledge, love and rhetoric. Modern commentators tend to regard the main subject of the dialogue to be rhetoric, which has inspired Derrida's celebrated critique of Plato.[44] Coleridge is clearly well aware of the *Phaedrus* when he observes of numerous ancient passages that 'book knowledge was held in contempt for its emptiness and even reprobated for its tendency to inflate the mind and thus unfit it for communion with immediate truths'.[45] It was a dialogue which was especially important for the Platonic school, especially for the so-called Neoplatonists, who saw the dialogue as theological and concerned with beauty. The primary point of the dialogue is not the superiority of speech over writing but the immediate beholding of the Divine (the Good) and communion with the Divine over and against other purported forms of knowledge.[46]

I wish to argue throughout this work for Plato's *ontology* while relaxing his *epistemological* requirements. Aesthetic experience provides compelling instances of intuition and immediacy and Neoplatonism views art as providing images of intelligible reality. Armed with this Neoplatonic modification, Ficino, Sir Philip Sidney, Spenser and the Metaphysical Poets, and Wordsworth could produce a thoroughly Platonic theory of

the Poets, . . .
. . . Men endowed with highest gifts,
The vision and the faculty divine,[47]

Coleridge's view of the aesthetic imagination is very close to Shakespeare's depiction of the poet 'in a fine frenzy', as is evident from his remarkable poem 'Kubla Khan'. Shakespeare's poet, in turn, is rooted in Plato's *Phaedrus*. In that dialogue the great central myth of the soul's chariot vision of intelligible truth comes in the second speech, where Socrates rejects his own critique of love in favour of rationality. Here Socrates presents love as a divinely inspired madness. Coleridge in 'Kubla Khan' picks up on this motif of the inspired poet:

For he on honey-dew hath fed,
And drunk the milk of paradise.[48]

There is an ancient pedigree for this thought – even for the imagery of honey – in Plato's *Ion*:

43 E. Brann, *The World of the Imagination: Sum and Substance* (Lanham, Md: Rowman and Littlefield, 1991), p. 762.
44 See Y. Rinon, 'The Rhetoric of Jacques Derrida II: *Phaedrus*', *Review of Metaphysics*, 46 (1993), pp. 537–58.
45 S. T. Coleridge, *Logic*, ed. J. R. de J. Jackson (Princeton, NJ: Princeton University Press, 1981), p. 32.
46 M. J. B. Allen, *Marsilio Ficino and the Phaedran Charioteer* (Berkeley, Calif.: University of California Press, 1981).
47 William Wordsworth, *The Excursion*, I, 77.
48 S. T. Coleridge, ' Kubla Khan', ll. 53–4.

The poets tell us that they gather songs at honey-flowing springs, from glades and gardens of the Muses, and that they bear songs to us as bees carry honey, flying like bees. And what they say is true. For a poet is an airy thing, winged and holy, and he is not able to make poetry until he becomes inspired and goes out of his mind and his intellect is no longer with him.[49]

Platonism generates a *via media* between the rationalistic reductionist, who avers that that which cannot be verified is not, and the subjectivist, who is content with 'imaginative patterns' and who denies any need for external or absolute principle. The imagination, for the Platonist, labours upon materials already furnished by the experience of those absolute standards proper to ethics and religion.

The central tenet of Neoplatonism is the ascent of the soul to God, the ascent from love of the visible and temporal to that of the invisible and eternal: the noetic world supports and sustains the visible world through continual creation. The imagination, in Wordsworth's sense as 'Reason in her most exalted mood', is the capacity to see the world as disclosing that which transcends the spatio-temporal. This experience is described in the *Phaedrus* and the *Symposium* – and in Philo, Eriugena, Dante, Ficino, Michelangelo, Spenser and Henry More, and by William Wordsworth in *The Prelude*. The *Phaedrus* presents the doctrine of intellectual love, in which the knowledge of the intelligible is kindled by the sense of visual beauty, and Plato did portray the intelligible world imaginatively as 'outside' and 'above'. Forms are incorporeal and can only be seen by the intellect.

Behind this idea of imagination lies that of the *image*.[50] The transcendent archetype as the source of the image is immanent in the image. In the Platonic tradition there is the tenet that the material world is shaped by the intermediary of the 'plastic' spirit of nature, the immanent aspect of divine intelligence. The material realm, for the Neoplatonist, is – though subject to decay – not alien to the soul because it is produced by the non-deliberative intelligence of the World-soul. The apparently inanimate exhibits intelligence. Our planet, and indeed the entire physical universe, is a dynamic and harmonious unity that mirrors the unity of the noetic cosmos. The realm of nature is not simply the sum of its parts – whether in the Stoic sense of a living continuum or in the Epicurean sense of being ultimately a mere collection of disparate atoms. Nature is a harmonious unity because it is an image or expression of the divine mind. It is weaker and less valuable than the Intellect, but nevertheless possesses its own derivative goodness – which Plotinus defends vigorously against the Gnostics. Here we have the ideas of both nature as a veil and the book of nature. The Western imagination (*sit venia verbo*) is not necessarily Promethean but, in Pierre Hadot's sense, Orphic. The roots of the Romantic concept of imagination in Coleridge lie in Neoplatonism and

49 Plato, *Ion* 534a–b.
50 Aloys de Marignac, *Imagination et Dialectique: Essai sur l'expression du spirituel par l'image dans les dialogues de Platon* (Paris: Les Belles-Lettres, 1951).

the Romantic reception of the late antique metaphysics of nature and mythology. The concept of imagination or φαντασία is especially notable in Porphyry as the mode of the embodied soul in using images, because it cannot attain to purely noetic or discursive thought.⁵¹ On the other hand, nature itself is the product of the World-soul's lower part, a bridge between the intelligible and the visible. Nature is mythic for the Neoplatonists because it simultaneously manifests figures and shapes and signs whose real significance remains hidden – unless, of course, the observer employs φαντασία, the fount of both myth and nature. Coleridge writes:

> The material universe, saith a Greek philosopher, is but one vast complex MYTHOS (i.e. symbolical representation): and mythology the apex and complement of all genuine physiology.⁵²

This Neoplatonic theory had a great impact via Paracelsus and Boehme up to the Romantics. 'Phantasie' or 'fancy' was reserved for the much inferior faculty contrasted by Coleridge with 'imagination'. ⁵³

But the main issue is not epistemology but metaphysics. Plotinus says that 'every particular entity is linked to that Divine Being in whose likeness it is made'.⁵⁴ Macrobius writes:

> Since, from the Supreme God mind arises, and from Mind, Soul, and since this in turn creates all subsequent things and fills them all with life, and since this single radiance illumines all and is reflected in each, as a single face might be reflected in many mirrors placed in a series . . . the attentive observer will discover a connection of parts, from the Supreme God down to the last dregs of things, mutually linked together and without a break. And this is Homer's golden chain, which God, he says, bade hang down from heaven to earth.⁵⁵

Hence despite the fallen state of humanity (whether *more Platonico* as the τόλμα/foolhardy estrangement from the Source, or in Christian terms),⁵⁶ within human intelligence there is a special kinship with the Divine which enables the knower to perceive nature as reflecting its divine source. We need symbols because we belong to two worlds. The love of the visible and the invisible are closely linked. Without love of the finite, the longing for the infinite would be extinguished. Stewart says:

---

51 P. Hadot, *Porphyre et Victorinus* (Paris: Études Augustiniennes, 1968), vol. 1, pp. 182–9.
52 S. T. Coleridge, *The Friend* (Princeton, NJ: Princeton University Press, 1969), vol. 1, p. 524; cf. Sallustius, *De deis et mundo* III, 3.
53 K. Goldammer, *Paracelsus in der deutschen Romantik* (Vienna: Gesellschaften Österreichs, 1980); J. Engell, *The Creative Imagination: Enlightenment to Romanticism* (London: Harvard University Press, 1981).
54 Plotinus, *Enneads* IV.3.10; cf. S. Leclercq, *Plotin et l'expression de l'image: les paradoxes du réel* (Mons: Sils Maria, 2005). See also P. Dronke, *Imagination in the Late Pagan and Early Christian World: The First Nine Centuries AD* (Florence: Sismel, 2003).
55 Quoted in A. Lovejoy, *The Chain of Being: A Study of the History of an Idea* (Cambridge, Mass.: Harvard University Press, 1961), p. 63.
56 Plotinus, *Enneads*, V.1.1 1ff. On the concept of τόλμα, see A. H. Armstrong, *The Cambridge History of Later Greek and Early Medieval Philosophy* (Cambridge: Cambridge University Press 1967), pp. 242–5.

'Platonism is love of the unseen and eternal cherished by one who rejoices in the seen and temporal.'[57] He observes that the philosopher or theologian is likely to deal with truth, beauty and goodness either as abstractions or through asceticism. The poet, in contrast, sees the objects of the visible world with the 'eye of steady imagination' as 'altered into their own eternal meaning' . . . sees them become 'vehicles of the unseen and eternal world which is substantially present in them behind the veil of their sensible attributes'.[58]

In *The Prelude* XIV, Wordsworth speaks of 'amplitude of mind'. This is

1. The experience of a transcendent beauty and the mood of love.
2. The capacity to recall the mood as the function of the imagination, which does not change the items as such yet rather sees them as they are 'illumined'.
3. Reason as 'the intuitive comprehension of the intelligible system of the universe' in which temporal items and events body forth the eternal.[59]

Imagination sees events as symbols:

> This spiritual love acts not, nor can exist
> Without Imagination, which in truth,
> Is but another name for absolute power
> And clearest insight, amplitude of mind,
> And reason, in her most exalted mood.[60]

But this is not a credulous longing for nature as an elaborate code which can be – as it were – allegorized. The mind perceives a resemblance which is grounded in the interpenetration of different levels of reality; this is the fruit of an insight which is the product of imagination not fantasy. Beauty, Truth and Goodness are present in objects of the world of sense but not as *abstractions*.[61] The Ideas are not unattainable abstractions but the ultimate facts of the universe perceived in their intrinsic value. The noetic cosmos (the mind of God) includes all the sensible cosmos, and Plotinus employs the language of touch to describe it. The intelligible cosmos that is the Mind of God is independent of particular manifestations. Here the separation is not spatial, because Forms are not in space. Wordsworth is speaking of the presence and translucence of the Divine – the spiritual or intelligible world in the domain of sense perception.

Coleridge speaks of imagination as bringing the whole soul of man into activity. He is explicit about the role of the imagination in a total response to God. The poet, the lover and the theologian are united by

---

57 J. A. Stewart, 'Platonism in English Poetry', in G. G. Stewart (ed.) *English Literature and the Classics*, (Oxford: Clarendon Press, 1912), p. 30.
58 Ibid., p. 31.
59 Ibid., p. 36.
60 William Wordsworth, *The Prelude*, XIV, 188–92.
61 Ibid., p. 42.

their use of imagination. However, 'the lover and the poet at least look at something and see it.'[62] The theologian should also endeavour to do so. Austin Farrer insists that the 'chief impediment to religion in this age'[63] is the loss of the capacity to contemplate:

> no one ever looks at anything at all: not so as to contemplate it, to apprehend what it is to be that thing, and plumb, if he can, the deep fact of its individual existence. The mind rises from the knowledge of creatures to the knowledge of their creator, but this does not happen through the sort of knowledge which can analyse things into factors or manipulate them with technical skill or classify them into groups. It comes from the appreciation of things which we have when we love them and fill our minds and senses with them and feel something of the silent force and great mystery of their existence. For it is in this that the creative power is displayed of an existence higher and richer and more intense than all.[64]

Here is 'joy' in the Wordsworth/Coleridgian sense.[65] The contemplative mood of 'joy' in Coleridge's poem 'Dejection' is explicitly linked to his 'shaping spirit of Imagination'.[66] Ruskin exclaims: 'to see clearly is poetry, prophecy, and religion, – all in one.'[67] It is such imaginative moods which 'lift', as Shelley puts it in his *Defence of Poetry*, 'the veil from the hidden beauty of the world'. The joy described by some of our greatest poets can be seen as the pinnacle of an imaginative component in cognition which is evident in mundane experience and extends to very elevated experiences of the world as a coherent and purposive theatre of divine agency. One might think here of Coleridge's view of how Wordsworth can modify 'objects observed' – that for which 'custom had bedimmed all the lustre', endowing them with the 'depth and height of the ideal world'.[68] In such a way, Coleridge muses that Wordsworth in 'imaginative power' is closest to Shakespeare and Milton. Using Wordsworth's lines from 'Elegiac Stanzas, Suggested by a Picture of Peele Castle', Coleridge reflects upon Wordsworth in the following way:

> To employ his own words, which are at once an instance and an illustration, he does indeed to all thoughts and to all objects add the gleam,

62 A. Farrer, *Reflective Faith: Essays in Philosophical Theology* (London: SPCK, 1972), p. 37.
63 Ibid.
64 Ibid., pp. 37–8.
65 One might compare Farrer with Coleridge: 'Hast thou ever raised thy mind to the consideration of EXISTENCE, in and by itself, as the mere act of existing? Hast thou ever said to thyself thoughtfully, IT IS! heedless in that moment, whether it were a man before thee, or a flower, or a grain of sand?': *The Friend* (London: Routledge, 1969), vol. 1, p. 514.
66 S. T. Coleridge, *Poems*, ed. J. Beer (London: Dent, 1986), p. 282.
67 J. Ruskin, *Modern Painters*, (London: George Allen, 1898), III.iv.xvi.278.
68 S. T. Coleridge, *Biographia Literaria*, vol. 1, ed. J. Engell and W. J. Bate (Princeton, NJ: Princeton University Press, 1983), p. 80.

The light that never was on sea or land,
The consecration and the poet's dream[69]

Such a paean to 'joy' can be misleading for us, especially since purely secular writers like Virginia Woolf or Proust with his 'moments bienheureux' have accustomed us to imaginative epiphanies with no residual religious content. And many will associate Romantic epiphanies with pantheism. Yet I suspect that the concept of 'joy' is best understood as a name for the exalted mood of the contemplative liaison of the empirical eye and mind's eye by which the poet perceives items of sense experience as conveying beyond themselves the divine source.

To speak of the contemplative imagination is to reflect upon the relation of the empirical eye and on what our great metaphysical bard William Shakespeare calls 'the mind's eye'.[70] Wordsworth's power lay primarily in this creative liaison of empirical eye and mind's eye. And he was convinced that the poet's imaginative capacity is dependent upon the capacity to penetrate truths obscured by the narrower constraints of physical science and to envisage the hidden shape of reality. Here we are not so much talking of imagination in the sense of possession of mental images, the Kantian 'transcendental' power of the imagination, or make-believe, but the imagination which enables the theist to see the world as real facts – discrete, apparently discordant and often grievously painful – and respect them as such and at the same time to see these parts as belonging to a whole which one can affirm as grounded in a wholly good and transcendent God. This contemplative imagination is not the much-discussed capacity for 'seeing as', which is important. Whatever we see is seen *with the mind*. Significant is the capacity to see *both x and y*. It is a capacity of the religious mind to see symbols, as Coleridge observes: 'living *educts* of the Imagination, . . . consubstantial with the truths, of which they are the *conductors*' as opposed to the 'unenlivened general-ising Understanding'.[71] It is not that the religious mind fails to see the same objects in the world as the purely secular observer, since to see them in *exclusively* religious terms would be what the eighteenth century called rampant 'enthusiasm' or what we might designate madness. It is rather the sober capacity to see the same objects as *both* themselves *and* conductors or symbols of another dimension of reality. Theists like Descartes, Boyle and Gassendi were quite happy to yoke together the God of Christianity and the new mechanical science, but many Platonists were much more averse to implications of the scientific revolution, and sceptical of any easy rapprochement. The claim of the Lakeland poet was to 'see into the life of things' by

an eye made quiet by the power
Of harmony, and the deep power of joy[72]

---

69 Ibid., vol. 2, p. 151.
70 *Hamlet*, I.i.12.
71 Coleridge, *Lay Sermons*, pp. 28–9.
72 William Wordsworth, 'Lines Written a Few Miles above Tintern Abbey', ll. 47–8.

Atheism for Coleridge or Wordsworth can be construed as a failure of imagination. Through imagination, the reality of certain *facts* can be experienced and hence the mind emancipated from what Coleridge calls 'the despotism of the eye'[73] and open to the impact of certain objects upon the soul. A Caspar David Friedrich landscape is a good instance of an appeal to both the empirical and the inner eye. His depictions have a certain realism and yet are aimed at an effect upon the soul rather than any purely visual experience. Milton is even more extreme. He writes:

Mine eyes he closed, but open left the cell
Of fancy, my internal sight.[74]

The blindness of the poet, whether Milton or Homer, is itself an image of the work of imagination. We are not mirrors of nature in any crude representational sense, and the Christian faith is a fidelity to the invisible causal joint between God and the soul, through the dark glass of our reason and imagination.

The chariot of the soul:
Phaedrus and Ezekiel fused

Wallace Stevens says of Plato's great chariot of the soul in the *Phaedrus*:

We recognize at once in this figure Plato's pure poetry and at the same time we recognize what Coleridge called Plato's dear, gorgeous nonsense. The truth is that we have scarcely read the passage before we have identified ourselves with the charioteer, have, in fact, taken his place, driving his winged horses, are traversing the whole heaven.[75]

On the contrary, we shall see that Coleridge was far from thinking that Plato's chariot was nonsense, and how much he derived from Christian tradition in this respect.

The chariot is a primordial image, from the Lord Krishna, the charioteer of the *Upanishads*, to Apollo the Sun God. It is often employed as a model or image for the nature of the self, whether in the *Bhagavadgita* or Plato's *Phaedrus*. Buddhism perhaps reflects both the Greek and the Indic traditions when it employs the image of the chariot in order to argue for a composite theory of the self. In a famous passage from the *Questions of King Menander*, the monk Nagasena draws an analogy between a chariot and the self in order to defend the Buddhist view of the self to the Hellenistic King Menander (or Milinda), ruling in north-west India in the middle part of the second century BC. The king challenges the Buddhist denial of a permanent self. The monk replies that a chariot is composed of a pole, axle, wheels, frame, reins, yoke, spokes and goad and yet not one of these elements *is* the chariot. The

---

73 S. T. Coleridge, *Biographia Literaria*, vol. II (London: Routledge: 1983), p. 107.
74 John Milton, *Paradise Lost*, VIII, 460–1.
75 Stevens, *Collected Poetry and Prose*, p. 643.

monk is able to persuade the king to agree that the term 'chariot' is a 'practical designation' which refers to a composite item. So, the analogy claims, should we think of personal identity. The Buddhist tradition has an eclectic representative in Western thought in Schopenhauer, as Charles Taylor observes:

> The greatest, the most influential misanthrope of the nineteenth century – the great 'pessimist' – was Schopenhauer. In a sense what Schopenhauer offered was an expressivism with the value signs reversed. For he took the idea of nature as a source, a power which comes to expression in things. This power 'objectified' itself in the different realities we see around us, and these 'objectifications' constituted a hierarchy, all the way from the lowest, most inanimate level to conscious beings at the summit.
>
> This all-pervading power is the Schopenhauerian will. But it is not a spiritual source of good . . . Schopenhauer's reversal of sign relative to Romantic expressivism is strangely reminiscent of the hyper-Augustinian reactions to Christian humanism. Indeed, the notion of a spiritual force uniting nature plainly descends from Renaissance neo-Platonism and its doctrine of love. Ficino is one of the ancestors of expressivism, as we have seen. Continuing this parallel, we can say that what the Jansenists were to St. François de Sales or Camus, Schopenhauer was to Schelling and Hegel. Within their expressivist metaphysic, he introduces radical vitiation. The source from which all reality flows as expression is poisoned. It is not the source of good, but of insatiable desire, of an imprisonment in evil, which makes us miserable, exhausts us, and degrades us.[76]

Schopenhauer's impact upon Nietzsche and Freud was seminal, ushering in a widespread vitalistic pessimism in its wake. In the twentieth century the influence of this vitalism was powerful in figures like Bergson, Heidegger and Wittgenstein. Wittgenstein's debt to Tolstoy and Schopenhauer informs his hostility to metaphysics and emphasis upon ethics and compassion. The emphasis upon the body and its passions, instinct or form of life rather than reason has obvious roots in rejections of Cartesianism or Neo-Scholasticism, or the Hellenic-Christian legacy more generally. Yet just as the 'lady doth protest too much', so the insistence upon the somatic, passionate nature of humanity itself is an index of the felt tension between flesh and spirit, inclination and conscience, instinct and intellect in reflective human life. Neither extreme asceticism nor naturalism/vitalism seems satisfactory. The divisions of human experience, expressed so memorably by St Paul, abide. And these, for a Christian, are symptoms, not the cause, of deeper malaise. The imagination is linked to the soul's longing for God. Austin Farrer shares with his great North African namesake, St Augustine, a concentration upon the unique nature of the soul:

76 C. Taylor, *Sources of the Self: The Making of the Modern Identity*, (Cambridge: Cambridge University Press, 1989), p. 442.

The soul is unique when compared with that which is not a soul; for if we are classifying created things, we must put the soul all by itself on one side of the main division, and on the other the whole host of things which the soul knows, loves, hates, feels, manages, copes with and exploits. But though the soul is unique by comparison with all that is not soul, it is in this respect not unique, that there are many souls, yours and mine and the next man's, and these have a common nature, and I can know something about several such. But God is uniquely unique.[77]

In Christian tradition, Platonism and Indic thought the uniqueness of the soul is given dramatic expression in the image of the chariot. The rider represents the rational part of the soul, the horses the sensitive dimension of the psyche and its drives, while the chariot often for the physical body. The chariot is also a striking image of what Farrer terms double agency – it can be both a fiery divine chariot and human vehicle. God is a reality immanent and active in his creature through his continual creative power, and yet the soul possesses the capacity for both humiliation or ascent.

All statements about God are enigmatic, like those of the soul. Farrer then faces an objection: is he not just reducing theology to poetry? Farrer's reply is that the metaphors of the poet illuminate the real analogy between the items compared. The poet, however, is not worried about the accuracy of the analogy. In theology 'we must get behind the poetry to the real analogies'.[78] Farrer states at this point that personal analogies are best: God can be compared with human will and intellect but not with human passions. Farrer takes the example of the phrase 'the eternal spirit' as an example of this work by analogy. It expresses the paradoxical coincidence of living personality and the immutability of mathematical verity.

The great constructs of the religious imagination are not beguiling fantasies but living educts of spiritual truths. Whereas much theology of the last century emphasized the gap between humankind and God, the imagination is evidence of a high estimate of human potential. Coleridge claimed:

> In the imagination of man exists the seeds of all moral and scientific improvement . . . The imagination is the distinguishing characteristic of man as a progressive being; and I repeat that it ought to be carefully guided and strengthened as the indispensable means and instrument of continued amelioration and refinement.[79]

The Platonic dimension is evident in those key images of the cave, the chariot, and the doctrine of *anamnesis* with its theological correlates of the

---

77 Farrer, *Reflective Faith*, pp. 34–5.
78 Ibid., p. 36.
79 S. T. Coleridge, *Lectures, 1818–1819 on the History of Philosophy*, ed. J. R. de J. Jackson (Princeton, NJ: Princeton University Press, 2000), vol. 2, p. 193.

divine spark and the doctrine of illumination. The central idea-image is
that of the *ascent*.

Austin Farrer develops an explicit metaphysical principle of the 'union
of will with the primal Will'.[80] The only God who can mean anything to
the human mind is the God about whom the human will has something
to do.[81] Furthermore, the analogy between finite and infinite creativity is
central for Farrer. He states: 'We know that the action of a man can be the
action of God in him'.[82] This is the paradigmatic instance of double
agency. Brian Hebblethwaite insists that Farrer does not speak of the
paradox of double agency as contradiction. It appears paradoxical only
because of our inadequacies – 'we lack access to the "causal joint" of
supernatural and the natural'.[83] As Farrer says, double agency is a
paradox which 'arises simply as a by-product of the analogical
imagination'.[84] Farrer uses the literary analogy of the author who 'has
the wit to get a satisfying story out of the natural behaviour of the
characters he conceives'.[85] But though the source of divine action remains
hidden, the effects are obvious.

Coleridge speaks of the

> living *educts* of the Imagination; of that reconciling and mediatory
> power, which incorporating the Reason in Images of the Sense, and
> organizing (as it were) the flux of the Senses by the permanence and
> self-circling energies of the Reason, gives birth to a system of
> symbols, harmonious in themselves, and consubstantial with the
> truths, of which they are the *conductors*. These are the Wheels which
> Ezekiel beheld when the hand of the Lord was upon him, and he
> saw visions of God as he sate among the captives by the river of
> Chebar. *Whither soever the Spirit was to go, the wheels went, and thither
> was their spirit to go: for the spirit of the living creature was in the wheels
> also.* The truths and the symbols that represent them move in
> conjunction, and form the living chariot that bears up (for *us*) the
> throne of the Divine Humanity.[86]

One might note that 'living chariot that bears up (for *us*) the throne of the
Divine Humanity'. One is reminded of Dante's divine chariot of the
Church, which draws upon both Ezekiel and the Revelation of St John
and Milton's 'Chariot of Paternal Deitie'.[87] Those words of Coleridge
have a close parallel in Henry More's various reflections upon this

---

80 A. Farrer, *Faith and Speculation: An Essay in Philosophical Theology* (Edinburgh: T&T Clark,
    1988), p. 10.
81 Ibid., p. 70.
82 Ibid., p. 66.
83 B. Hebblethwaite, *Philosophical Theology and Christian Doctrine* (Oxford: Blackwell, 2005),
    p. 140.
84 Farrer, *Faith and Speculation*, p. 66.
85 A. Farrer, *A Science of God?* (London: Geoffrey Bles, 1996), p. 76.
86 Coleridge, *Lay Sermons*, p. 29.
87 Dante, *Purgatorio*, XXX, 1ff.; Milton, *Paradise Lost*, VI, 750ff.

passage in Ezekiel, as More also takes the passage Christologically: the rider in the chariot is 'The Heavenly Humanity of the Son of God'.[88] But like More, Coleridge employs the chariot as a model of the ascent of the human mind to God, an *itinerarium mentis in Deum*.

Let me consider the image of the chariot in the first chapter of the book of Ezekiel. The book begins with the words:

> as I was among the exiles by the river Chebar, the heavens were opened, and I saw visions of God.[89]

In Ezekiel's vision we have a very obscure object surrounded by four 'living creatures' like an eagle, an ox, a lion and a man. Ezekiel's vision has similarities to the mandala symbolism of Eastern religions – symbols of wholeness. The analogy with mandala symbolism is in the image of the cherubim and the wheels. There are four creatures, each one possessing four faces and four wings, and each facing in four directions. Four is a common symbol of perfection. The fiery chariot with its wheels expresses the creative energy of the psyche – the divine-human form in fire seems to express the realization of the Divine in man and its transformative energy. Its flight represents transcendence. The vision is an image of the sublime creative energy and power of the Divine; but it is also an image of the soul's longing for God – to become a rider in the chariot.

The blazing eyes of the strange vehicle or object described by the prophet Ezekiel constitute a fine symbol of the vision of God, and the Ezekiel vision was the starting point for the mystical tradition of the Merkabah mystics of medieval Iberia, which formed the foundation of the Hasidic movement. Moreover, there is a tradition of Christian commentary whereby the enthroned man above the chariot is a prophecy of Christ. And yet with the Platonic resonance of Coleridge's passage – 'self-circling energies of the Reason' – is there not a barely conscious reference to the celestial chariots contemplating the Ideas? The chariot is 'living' and the educts of the imagination are 'living'. Here we find, apart from the biblical reference, the (Neo)Platonic associations of the ebullient creative plenitude of the intelligible realm where 'every idea is living, productive, partaketh of infinity and . . . containeth an endless power of semination'.[90] Coleridge writes:

> In the state of perfection, perhaps, all other faculties may be swallowed up in love, or superseded by immediate vision; but it is on the wings of the CHERUBIM, i.e. (according to the interpretation of the ancient Hebrew doctors,) the *intellectual* powers and energies, that we must first be borne up to the 'pure empyrean'.[91]

88 Henry More, *The Immortality of the Soul* (London, 1713), p. 440.
89 Ezekiel 1.1b.
90 Coleridge, *Lay Sermons*, p. 23–4.
91 S. T. Coleridge, *Aids to Reflection*, ed. J. Beer (London: Routledge, 1993), p. 20f.

The *Phaedrus* was a dialogue which was especially important for the Platonic school, especially for the so-called Neoplatonists, who saw it as theological and concerned with beauty. At the centre of this tradition was the vision of the soul as a winged charioteer using winged horses, one light and the other dark, encircling the celestial sphere and straining to contemplate the Ideas. The domain above the heavens is the realm of true being, which can only be grasped by reason. This vision sustains the gods, but cannot properly be attained by mortals who, having both a good and a bad horse, cannot sustain their place in the heavenly cavalcade and fall to earth. The soul, however, longs to regrow her wings and return to her celestial origin. Upon seeing beauty, the soul is reminded of true spiritual beauty, the recollection of which leads to the regrowth of wings. Thus what men call *eros* is named by the gods *pteros*, or 'winged'. Beauty can awaken the soul to its true destiny with an experiential power. Plato uses the language of awe:

> Few are left who retain a sufficient memory. These, however, when they see some likeness of the world above, are beside themselves and lose all control, but do not realize what is happening to them because of the dimness of their perceptions.[92]

Of all the Ideas, beauty has the most luminous gripping immediacy, and has a more pervasive attractive power than Ideas such as justice. Coleridge stands within this Neoplatonic tradition in so far as he seems to interpret Plato as referring to those truths which transcend strict verbal articulation. The primary point of the dialogue is not the superiority of speech over writing but the immediate beholding of the Divine (the Good) and communion with the Divine over against other purported forms of knowledge. Plato is using an image of the mystical chariot as a symbol of the journey of the soul to God, and characteristically as an image of self-control and reason.

And in Plato's *Phaedrus* the myth of the charioteer functions as a symbol of the philosophical ascent of the mind and a vision or theophany. The image of the chariot was then associated by Alexandrian Platonists with the vision of God in the first chapter of the prophecy of Ezekiel. This link between Greek and Hebrew images and ideas has a clear precedent in Philo of Alexandria (30 BC–45 AD), who integrated the Phaedran myth of the heavenly chariots into his theology. The divine Logos is pictured by Philo as a charioteer. It is a link, prima facie quite bizarre, in the early patristic fusion of the 'chariots' or 'vehicles' of *Phaedrus* 250ff. and Ezekiel 1.[93]

Origen (184/5–245) lived and worked in Alexandria, and as the first really significant Christian Platonist developed the scattered thoughts of the first Christian humanists, Justin Martyr and Clement of Alexandria, into a rigorous system. He writes:

92 Plato, *Phaedrus* 250, tr. W. Hamilton (Harmondsworth: Penguin, 1973), p. 56.
93 A. G. R. Christman, *Ezekiel's Vision of the Chariot in Early Christian Exegesis* (Ann Arbor: UMI, 1995).

I do not doubt that Plato learnt the words of the *Phaedrus* from some Hebrews and that . . . it was after studying the sayings of the prophets that he wrote the passage where he says *'No earthly poet either has sung or will sing of the region above the heavens as it deserves'*, and the following passage in which this also occurs: 'Ultimate being, colourless, formless, and impalpable, visible only to the mind that is guide of the soul, round which is the species of true knowledge, lives in this place.'[94]

Origen produces a version of the Attic Moses which was to be reformulated by Ficino in the fifteenth century and would influence Cambridge Platonists like Cudworth and Coleridge. In his 27th Homily on Numbers, Origen produced two interpretations of the story of the Exodus: first, as the conversion from paganism to Divine Law, but second, as the journey of the soul back to God on the model of Plato's *Phaedrus*. In *Contra Celsum* the Platonic journey of the soul is compared to Jacob's ladder,[95] which of course is further evidence of Plato plundering Moses.

The soul as a winged chariot, the fusion of Ezekiel with the *Phaedrus*, although first mentioned in Pseudo-Justin (Marcellus of Ancyra?), was the work of Origen, especially through his highly allegorical Alexandrian exegesis. In her work *What Did Ezekiel See?*, Angela Christman has produced a thorough and illuminating account of how Origen produced a Christological reading of Ezekiel that was immensely influential upon later writers, and has defended the sublimity of Ezekiel's vision of the divine incomprehensibility as surpassing even Plato's own magnificent apocalypse in the *Phaedrus*.[96] Yet Ambrose, Augustine's great teacher in Milan also viewed both Ezekiel and the *Phaedrus* as presenting a model for the ascent of the soul and a model of the Christian life.[97] In Pseudo-Macarius the vision of the ascent becomes a cipher for the paradoxical ascent of the soul and the indwelling of the Divine: the soul searching for Christ finds Christ bearing it up.[98] This wealth of patristic speculation on the chariot carried on into the Middle Ages and beyond.[99]

Marsilio Ficino (1433–1499), the primary source of early modern and Romantic Platonism, was absorbed by this image of the chariot.[100] Coleridge, while an undergraduate at Cambridge, wrote a prize poem on astronomy. The Greek original is lost but it is preserved in translation by Robert Southey. In this poem Coleridge uses the explicit imagery of

---

94 Origen, *Contra Celsum* VI, 19; tr. H. Chadwick (Cambridge: Cambridge University Press, 1953), p. 332.
95 Genesis 28.12–13.
96 A. Christman, *What Did Ezekiel See? Christian Exegesis of Ezekiel's Vision of the Chariot from Irenaeus to Gregory the Great* (Leiden: Brill, 2005).
97 Ibid., pp. 105ff.
98 Ibid., pp. 130ff.
99 See M. Lieb, *The Visionary Mode: Biblical Prophecy, Hermeneutic and Cultural Change* (Ithaca, NY: Cornell University Press, 1991).
100 M. J. B. Allen, *The Platonism of Marsilio Ficino: A Study of his 'Phaedrus' Commentary, its Sources and Genesis* (Berkeley, Calif.: University of California Press, 1984).

the *Phaedrus* when he speaks of the 'Chariots of happy Gods' and his own desire

> To roam the starry path of Heaven,
> To charioteer with wings on high,[101]

We also find explicit references to the soul sprouting wings or the horses of the celestial chariots drinking ambrosial nectar:

> For Hope with loveliest visions soothes my mind,
> That even in Man, Life's winged power,
> When comes again the natal hour,
> Shall on heaven-wandering feet
> In undecaying youth,
> Spring to the blessed seat;
> Where round the fields of Truth
> The fiery Essences for ever feed;
> And o'er the ambrosial mead,
> The breezes of serenity
> Silent and soothing glide for ever by . . .
>
> I may not call thee mortal then, my soul!
> Immortal longings lift thee to the skies:
> Love of thy native home inflames thee now,
> With pious madness wise.
> Know then thyself! expand thy wings divine![102]

The command to 'Know then thyself!' is of particular interest. Charles Griswold Jr argues that the topic of self-knowledge is the key to the *Phaedrus*.[103] The reference to the Delphic oracle and the Christian Platonic interpretation of it is as old as Augustine and Macrobius. In the fifth century AD Macrobius writes:

> Hence in a diatribe both witty and pungent a famous quotation was used seriously: 'From the sky has come to us the saying, "Know thyself" '. Indeed, this is said to have been the advice of the Delphic oracle. To one desiring to know by what path blessedness is reached the reply is, 'Know thyself'. The maxim was inscribed on the front of the temple at Delphi. A man has but one way of knowing himself, as we have just remarked: if he will look back to his first beginning and origin and 'not search for himself elsewhere.' In this manner the soul, in the very cognizance of its high estate, assumes those virtues by which it is raised aloft after leaving the body and returns to the place of its origin; in fact a soul that is permeated with the pure and subtle stuff of the virtues does not become defiled or burdened with

---

101 Quoted in J. Beer, *Coleridge the Visionary* (London: Chatto and Windus, 1970), p. 298.
102 Quoted ibid., pp. 299–300.
103 C. L. Griswold, *Self-knowledge in Plato's 'Phaedrus'* (New Haven Conn.: Yale University Press, 1986).

the impurities of the body, nor does it seem to have ever left the sky which it has always kept in sight and thought.[104]

Plato's attack on the arts is closely linked to his rejection of the pessimistic anthropology of the tragedians. Hence, while for the tragedians 'Know thyself!' means 'Know thy limits and don't upset the gods!', Plato takes the Delphic oracle/imperative to mean 'Know the rational divine within!'

Yet the image of the chariot, so often associated with regal deities and power – one might think of the celestial chariot of Zeus or Apollo, or even the thunderous rolling of Thor's chariot in pagan northern mythology – can also be used to refer to a spiritual power derived from self-knowledge and knowledge of nature which has little relevance to regal deities in dead mythologies. Patrick White in his seminal *Riders in the Chariot*[105] describes four dislocated lives in which each shares a common vision, as well as experience of the Divine and spiritual transformation through suffering. The central image of the novel is the vision of the chariot in Ezekiel, a passage much loved by Blake and which is read by one of the characters, an exile from Nazi Germany called Himmelfarb (the word 'Himmel' having connotations of both sky and heaven). Miss Hare, Himmelfarb, the benevolent Ruth Godbold (again *nomen est omen*), and the barely educated and sexually abused aboriginal painter Alf Dubbo, are all 'Riders in the Chariot', and all find spiritual power and energy in the midst of worldly failure or ignomy. As Hölderlin writes:

Wo aber Gefahr ist, wächst
Das Rettende auch.[106]

The elderly maid, Miss Hare, dwells in a (decaying) house called Xanadu. The name 'Hare' has connotations of timidity and flight, but is a common image in Christian iconography of human frailty and dependence upon God. Yet the chariot stands for a core element of what Jerome McGann has called the Romantic Ideology. McGann writes:

One important feature of Romantic Ideology . . . is the belief that poetical works can transcend historical divisions by virtue of their links with Imagination, through which we see into the permanent life of things.[107]

104 Macrobius, *Commentary on the Dream of Scipio*, tr. W. H. Stahl (New York: Columbia University Press, 1952), pp. 124–5. See also J. Flamant, *Macrobe et le néo-platonisme latin, à la fin du IVe siècle* (Leiden: Brill, 1977), and A. Hüttig, *Macrobius im Mittelalter: Ein Beitrag zur Rezeptionsgeschichte der Commentarii in Somnium Scipionis* (Frankfurt am Main: Peter Lang, 1990).
105 P. White, *Riders in the Chariot* (London: Eyre & Spottiswoode, 1956).
106 F. Hölderlin, 'Patmos' in *Gedichte* (Stuttgart: Philipp Reclam, 2003), p. 88.
107 J. J. McGann, *The Romantic Ideology: A Critical Investigation* (Chicago: University of Chicago Press, 1983), p. 114.

McGann quotes Wordsworth:

Imagination – here the Power so called
Through sad incompetence of human speech,
That awful Power rose from the Mind's abyss
Like an unfathered vapour that enwraps,
At once some lonely Traveller. I was lost;
Halted without an effort to break through;
But to my conscious soul I now can say –
'I recognise thy glory', in such strength
Of usurpation, when the light of sense
Goes out, but with a flash that has revealed
The invisible world, doth Greatness make abode[108]

McGann dismisses the central Romantic view of the imagination as an escapist illusion, regarding the enhanced awareness of an 'inner, spiritual self' as the evasion of pressing political and economic concerns.

In his acknowledgement of Blake's love of the chariot in Ezekiel, Patrick White is quite conscious of the Romantic appropriation of this ancient mystical Christian and Jewish image of the vehicle of the soul and employs it as a key symbol for his novel about life in twentieth-century Australia. This shows, to my mind, the extent to which what McGann and others disparage as the 'Romantic ideology' has persisted in exerting a creative force in contemporary literature.

'Extremes Meet' was one of Coleridge's favourite adages, and the reluctance of late-twentieth-century Marxists to do justice to the Romantic imagination mirrors the equally stout incredulity of the nineteenth-century Benthamites. The persistence of Romantic themes in a great twentieth-century novelist like Patrick White suggests that this Romantic legacy is still potent. Miss Hare expresses very early in the novel the dislocation she feels between her inner and outer nature:

Where the road sloped down she ran, disturbing stones, her body quite agitated as it accompanied her, but her inner self by now joyfully serene. The anomaly of that relationship never failed to mystify, and she stopped again to consider. For a variety of reasons, very little of her secret, actual nature had been disclosed to other human beings.[109]

In this early part of the book, White emphasizes that the elderly spinster's capacity to 'see' nature in her property is not to be confused with its strictly physical or legal properties. Imagination is characteristically, and *prima facie* paradoxically, allied with both the Delphic 'Know thyself' and the Orphic capacity to find attunement with nature. McGann and subsequent critics of English literature pilloried this 'Ideology'.

Yet what if there is real truth in Miss Hare's vision? Some famous words of Hölderlin express clearly the central thesis of this book:

---

108 William Wordsworth, *The Prelude*, VI, 594–603.
109 P. White, *Riders in the Chariot*, p. 11.

Nah ist
Und schwer zu fassen der Gott.[110]

The experience of God is neither to be construed in terms of a quasi-objective presence nor a purely figurative fiction. Imaginative apprehension of the Divine is pre-eminently the awareness of that reality which is pressing and proximate for the soul and yet hard to grasp or articulate in the categories appropriate for the physical domain. For human beings the tension between the material and the spiritual, between inward and outward worlds, is resolved in the imaginative vision of their underlying unity.

The imagination is the basis of the distinctive amphibious capacity of human beings to be both part of a natural environment and to transcend that same environment: we are organisms instinctively adapting to the world and interpreting it as reflective agents with memories and projections. The poignancy of secularisation in 'Modernity' is that it seems to rob us of the inherited architecture of spiritual reality, while imagination's freedom from stimulus and the peculiarly human yearning for transcendence continue to clash with the constraints of scientific naturalism.

110 Hölderlin, 'Patmos', p. 88.

2

The Creative Imagination

The imaginative animal

Man's chief difference from the brutes lies in the exuberant excess of his subjective propensities – his pre-eminence over them simply and solely in the number and in the fantastic and unnecessary character of his wants, physical, moral, aesthetic and intellectual. Had his whole life not been a quest for the superfluous, he would never have established himself as inexpugnably as he has done in the necessary. And from the consciousness of this he should draw the lesson that his wants are to be trusted; that even when their gratification seems farthest off, the uneasiness they occasion is still the best guide of his life, and will lead him to issues entirely beyond his present powers of reckoning. Prune down his extravagance, sober him, and you undo him. The appetite for immediate consistency at any cost, or what the logicians call the 'law of parsimony,'– which is nothing but the passion for conceiving the universe in the most labor-saving way, – will, if made the exclusive law of the mind, end by blighting the development of the intellect quite as much as that of the feelings or the will.[1]

William James is right to highlight the 'exuberant excess' of mankind's 'subjective propensities'. Many philosophers seem apt to bracket or dismiss the creative dimension of imagination. Yet this is to disregard a metaphysically intriguing fact about human beings. Human beings are not just creative in a way that bluejays, dolphins and bonobos are, but must be distinctively imaginative in order to interpret other complex rational agents: language users and members of specific historical cultures. I shall argue that this most inscrutable aspect of imagination, the creative, is the most significant. My thesis may be called the 'paradox of imagination'. Psychologically or morally, the imagination is a necessary route to reality. Strictly the paradox is that of empiricism – that it cannot do justice to experience, imagination being required in order to 'save the appearances'. But since crude empiricism is very pervasive in our culture, I shall use the word 'paradox' nonetheless. It is a paradox of empiricism that it cannot deal with experience because our experience is essentially imaginative. Our inner relation to circumstances is an inalienable element of consciousness. This inner relation is shaped

1 W. James, *The Will to Believe* (New York: Dover Books, 1956), pp. 131–2.

by memory – images of events and persons which pervade our perception – and primarily by the imagination. Once we start to pursue this general idea of the imagination, we find ourselves immediately confronted with questions concerning the mind and metaphysics. Imagination cannot be traced to verifiable phenomena or public behaviour. In imagining we can imagine a non-actual object, perhaps not present, not existing, perhaps not even capable of existence (Pegasus, the unicorn). The very extravagance of the human imagination presents a real problem for those philosophers who hold that the world is constituted exclusively by material items, and that philosophy should systematically ferret out bogus 'objects'. The sheer *inventiveness* of the mind, its boundless creative capacity, is the core sense of imagination: one which many philosophers – not just hard-headed physicalists wedded to biological naturalism or artificial intelligence – are loathe to contemplate.

The most obvious use of the word 'imagination' is linked to mental images – the employment of the mind's eye. Here the overlap with memory is striking. Another common usage of the term refers to propositional imagining, especially in counterfactual thought, where the mind entertains a range of possibilities or parallel worlds. This can range from quotidian 'What if . . . ?' thoughts concerning quite straightforward possibilities (e.g. What if I take the late train?) to much more complex counterfactual conditionals, e.g. what if Caesar had not crossed the Rubicon? Propositional imagination, that is, 'imagining that' in the sense of forming a hypothesis that p, does not require images. I can imagine that I will visit Athens in July without forming an image of the Acropolis. But this is not to deny that in consciousness inner pictures play an enormous and important role, and cannot be excluded from a serious account of our mental lives. The animal lives in the limited domain of immediate sensations; mankind experiences this sensory immediacy but also a much vaster domain populated by after-images from memory and projected fears and desires. Human beings are, as it were, amphibious. There is, of course, the being-in-the-world which we experience like any other animals. Yet there is the vast realm of the human imagination, which extends temporally and spatially far beyond immediate images and after-images of proximate objects. As Robert Burns in 'To a Mouse' exclaims:

> Still, thou art blest, compar'd wi' *me*
> The *present* only toucheth thee:
> > But Och! I *backward* cast my e'e
> On prospects drear!
> An' *forward*, tho' I canna *see*,
> I *guess* an' *fear!*[2]

These are states of mind that are akin to or copy beliefs, desires or perceptions but are not causally embedded in the environment in the

---

2 Robert Burns, *The Poems and Songs of Robert Burns*, ed. J. Kingsley, 3 vols (Oxford: Clarendon Press, 1968), vol. 1, p. 128.

mode of beliefs, desires or perceptions – 'the imagination is entertained with the promise of something more, and does not acquiesce in the present object of sense'.[3]

Vision is the most powerful mechanism we possess for obtaining information about the world and thus it is perhaps not surprising that the discussion of visual imagination should dominate. Yet this freedom from sense stimulus can be seen in aural imagination in relation to music. Nicholas Cook gives the following definition of a musical culture:

> a musical culture is, in essence, a repertoire of means for imagining music; it is the specific pattern of divergences between the experience of music on the one hand, and the images by which it is represented on the other, that gives a musical culture its identity.[4]

In this definition, Cook is positing a fruitful tension between the subjective experience and the representation of music. That is to say, there is necessarily a gap between the models and the reality of the unanalysable dimension of experience of music. For example, Cook claims that 'Audibility . . . is not everything in music' and 'One cannot reasonably demand that music must, by definition, yield all its meaning in perception'.[5] This is because the mind of the listener is irreducibly part of the music:

> If it is not possible to arrive at a satisfactory definition of music simply in terms of sound, this is probably because of the essential role that the listener, and more generally the environment in which the sound is heard, plays in the constitution of any event as a musical one.[6]

Hence it is not possible to 'perceive' audibility. Cook discusses scientific experiments in which tonal musical pieces were played to listeners who had not previously heard the compositions. These pieces had been deliberately altered so as to conclude in a false key. Any theory based upon a notion of music as possessing an essentially objective coherence which is, as it were, perceived would suggest that the listeners would pick up the error. However, these experiments showed that, surprisingly, even musically sophisticated listeners did not notice any difference – even unconsciously. This suggests that the appreciation of music is much more imaginative than any perceptual-cognitive account would grant. Certainly it seems unlikely that hearing is a complex mechanical response or reaction to external stimuli. Even the very sophisticated conceptual armoury of musical theory, concepts like pitch, chords, harmony, scale, key, consonance, etc., are insufficient tools for an exhaustive explanation of the phenomenon of music.

Yet it is not merely that human scanning equipment has greater scope than other creatures – that our thoughts range well beyond the

---

3 Edmund Burke, *A Philosophical Enquiry* (Oxford: Oxford University Press, 1990), p. 70.
4 N. Cook, *Music, Imagination and Culture* (Oxford: Clarendon Press, 1990), p. 4.
5 Ibid., p. 8.
6 Ibid., p. 11.

immediate physical habitat.[7] Nor is it just that we use language per se. Animals can use signs and signal to each other. However, only humans dwell in a world of imagination: the 'willing suspension of disbelief' of myths, sagas and legends, a narrative alternative world. This waking dream-world of mythology is an inalienable component of primitive mankind. The growth of science in various phases of human history, whether in the Athenian or French Enlightenment, has the effect of purging much mythical material, but human beings in such intellectually sophisticated and demythologized societies are left with rich mythic and symbolic residue in the cultural environment. We are self-understanding creatures and this symbolic residue pervades human culture. Heidegger's gnomic utterance 'Dichterisch wohnet der Mensch' is certainly true as an anthropological observation.[8] To try to explain human behaviour exclusively in terms of needs and socio-economic forces seems quite implausible given that art developed at a very early stage. The impulse for creativity seems just as deep a part of human nature as the technological drive to cope with and manipulate the immediate environment. Influential twentieth-century thinkers such as Carl Jung and Mircea Eliade have insisted that dreams of sleep, moods of reverie, day-dreams, make-believe, myths and legends constitute an important dimension of human awareness which inspires and sustains artistic creativity. So too, the symbolic-imaginative view of the world is just as much part of human life as the world of immediate sensory impressions. As the Platonic poet Thomas Traherne observes:

> Till that which vulgar sense
> Doth falsely call experience,
> Distinguish'd things:
> The ribbons, and the gaudy wings
> Of birds, the virtues, and the sins,
> That represented were in dreams by night
> As really my senses did delight,[9]

'Imagination' is also used to refer to imaginative representation, such as the child imagining a bush as a bear or the stick as a sword, or a doll as the baby. Such employment of symbols or tokens is clearly an integral part of human imaginative activity. This form of imagination is constituted by creative perception. It can go beyond elements of the perceived world and put them together as a construction: a winged horse or a centaur. There is also the important role of the imagination in executive functions of the mind: drawing upon past experiences as a basis for future decisions. Steve Mithen has explored the role of the imaginative capacities in human evolution and has coined the term

---

7 'Scanning equipment' should not be misunderstood as referring exclusively to the senses – animals often outstrip us in these.

8 M. Heidegger, *Poetry, Language, Thought*, tr. A. Hofstadter (New York: Harper and Row, 1972), p. 213.

9 Thomas Traherne, 'Dreams', §5, in *Selected Poems and Prose*, ed. A. Bredford (Harmondsworth: Penguin, 1991), p. 139

'cognitive fluidity' to express the creative shift between different semantic or cognitive fields.[10] Our ancestors on the savannah would have employed imagination, in the practical sense of doing things in novel ways, e.g. to search for new hunting grounds, develop tools, etc.

'Imagination' can have a cognitive sense referring to the employment of models, metaphors, or symbols which are legitimate elements of any rigorous and comprehensive account of rationality: religious beliefs often concern the unobservable, but so does science or ethics. Are there parallels between imagination in science, ethics and religion? One might surmise that the concept of imagination suggests Romantic arbitrariness. The imaginative capacity of human beings is a metaphysical problem. Why are we so different from the rest of the animal kingdom? Why are we concerned with right and wrong, truth and beauty? Religion and art are of particular concern because both try to articulate significance.

Whereas animals are parts of nature, human beings are separated from the natural realm. Even if we bracket questions of spirit, soul and language, it is evident that human beings are biologically unique because of the capacity to objectify the immediate environment as a 'world' in relation to human reflective subjectivity. The chasm between subject and object is not a Romantic delusion but, as James so eloquently says, is due to the 'exuberant excess' of mankind's subjective propensities, since we are not exhaustively determined by our instincts, and indeed suffer from an instinctual deficit which is compensated by cultural artefacts such as tools. This shows signs of limited imagination: there is evidence of tool use in *Homo habilis* two million years ago. Rob Foley has argued for an imaginative capacity linked to the evidence for greater brain size in hominids 300,000 years ago.[11] But imagination in the stronger sense seems to emerge with *Homo sapiens* about 150,000 to 100,000 years ago. The use of symbolism can be traced back to 70,000 to 50,000 BC. It is puzzling why there was a delay. Certainly a departure from the hunter-gatherer state in the Near East around 10,000 BC can be traced as part of a history of the imagination, associated with archaeological evidence of the attendant explosion of material culture and artefacts.

There are many naturalistic-reductionistic problems about imagination. It seems recalcitrant – it resists the conventional reductions of mental activity to behaviour or brain states. It seems difficult to give a causal explanation in relation to the environment or a defined biological purpose. It is intriguing to reflect upon the redundancy of such dramatic self-awareness from an evolutionary perspective. Richard Dawkins has a theory which is meant to accommodate this mysterious fact, and he does so with an ingenious attempt to explain culture on a broadly genetic model.[12] The theory of the 'meme', which is a unit of cultural transmission, represents 'that which is imitated' – including ideas,

---

10 S. Mithen, 'A Creative Explosion? The Theory of Mind, Language, and the Disembodied Mind of the Upper Palaeolithic', in S. Mithen (ed.), *Creativity in Human Evolution and Prehistory* (London: Routledge, 1998).

11 R. Foley, *Humans Before Humanity: An Evolutionary Perspective* (Oxford: Blackwell, 1995), pp. 160ff.

12 Richard Dawkins, *The Selfish Gene* (Oxford: Oxford University Press, 1989), pp. 189–201.

values and narratives. Evolution operates not for individual species but for genes and memes, which are mental entities, both of these needing to find an ecological location and reproduce. Some memes are very powerful replicators. For Dawkins, some (especially religion) are destructive parasites, spreading from one host to the next, according to the pattern of the co-evolution of host and virus. Dan Sperber has used the model of cultural transmission as a mental epidemic.[13] These are strictly Darwinistic theories. The only really creative force at work is the corrosive power of Darwin's dangerous idea – adaptation as the evolutionary algorithm and the destruction of variations. Yet it does not answer the question as to why we are so different from other higher primates. Great apes are more inventive than other apes but such inventiveness is far removed from human instances of imagination.

Benjamin Jowett observed that imagination distinguished man from animals:

> In the lower stages of civilisation, Imagination, more than Reason, distinguishes men from animals; and to banish art would be to banish thought, to banish language, to banish the expression of all truth.[14]

Yet our instinctive frailties as human beings are compensated by the imagination. For the deeply Darwinistic Nietzsche, man is the 'sick animal' (Anti-Christ) because of his capacity for pathological imagination.[15] The gap between instinct and action in human beings is bridged by culture, including cultural artefacts like clothes, tools, weapons, houses. Of all the animal kingdom, we have the weakest instincts. Our children correspondingly are vastly more vulnerable than the offspring of other species and require the long period of attention and support of childhood. The need to form lasting bonds to outlive the infancy and childhood of vulnerable offspring is doubtless the biological ground of monogamous marriage. But the *institutions* of marriage, kin, clan and society are social realities permeated by the imagination. The Franco-Greek philosopher and psychotherapist Cornelius Castoriadis speaks of the 'actual imaginary' to distinguish these structures from private mental images or make-believe. He points out that in the twentieth century the 'imagined' nation was a more real and powerful force in the lives of millions, as they died for their countries, than the instinct of self-preservation![16]

13 D. Sperber, *Explaining Culture: A Naturalistic Approach* (Oxford: Blackwell, 1996); S. Blackmore, *The Meme Machine* (Oxford: Oxford University Press, 1999).
14 B. Jowett, *Dialogues of Plato*, (Oxford: Clarendon Press, 1984), p. clxiv.
15 F. Nietzsche, 'The Anti-Christ', §3 of Nietzsche, *Twilight of the Idols, The Anti-Christ*, tr. R. J. Hollingdale (Harmondsworth: Penguin, 1981) p. 116.
16 C. Cornelius, *The Imaginary Institution of Society*, tr. K. Blamey (Cambridge: Polity, 1997), p. 148.

The Child is father of the Man

We can raise an epistemological question: does imagining generate *knowledge*? It would seem that there is empirical evidence that imagination in children's play is important for the proper psychological functioning of the adult in later life. Lord Macaulay in his first *Edinburgh Review* essay, 'Milton' (1825), writes:

> . . . of all people children are the most imaginative. They abandon themselves without reserve to every illusion . . . No man . . . is ever affected by Hamlet or Lear as a little girl is affected by the story of poor Red Riding Hood . . . she weeps, she trembles . . . Such is the despotism of the imagination over uncultivated minds.[17]

Macaulay is failing to recognize the legitimate role of imagination in children. Presumably counterfactual reasoning is supported by make-believe in the shift from the habitual to the make-believe state. Paul Harris has argued that children use pretence in order to explore the reality of their physical environment and other human agents. Pretence is evinced in very young children (12 months) and develops into the common make-believe of children's games. Harris sees imagination as a sophisticated organ for tracking facts: children, it seems, tend to internalize play between age 5 and 8 through school.[18] This provides the child thus endowed with a certain autonomy (inner speech and images), daydreams and fantasy, while being socialized and complying with school pressures: 'This human capacity for tolerating ambiguities and playing and manipulating them in a miniaturized private world of thought allows children to sustain the inevitable disappointments and tragedies of growing up.'[19]

Bruno Bettelheim has argued that the period of middle childhood also provides the opportunity to imagine other lives, particularly through heroic tales and romances. This is a genetic issue concerning the role of play in childhood. It would seem that imaginative activities are important for the proper development of the child.

In particular, Bettelheim has eloquently defended fairy stories as a unique children's art form – one which children understand readily since it addresses their needs through the imagination.[20] Whereas a fable is clearly moralizing, the fairy tale often leaves its message implicit. Nevertheless fairy tales provide guidance and reassurance for children facing the anxieties and bewildering turmoil of life when small and vulnerable, and importantly serves to externalize frustrations and fears, i.e. the wicked stepmother can represent an aspect of the real mother that

---

17 T. B. Macaulay, 'Milton', *Edinburgh Review*, 42. 74 (August 1825), pp. 308–9.
18 P. Harris, *The Work of the Imagination* (Oxford: Blackwell, 2000), pp. 186–90.
19 J. Singer, 'Imagination', in *Encyclopedia of Creativity*, ed. M. A. Runco and S. R. Pritzker (San Diego: Academic Press, 1999), vol. 2, p. 22.
20 B. Bettelheim, *The Uses of Enchantment: The Meaning and Importance of Fairy Tales* (Harmondsworth: Penguin, 1978).

the child cannot confront rationally. Bettelheim's goal is to show that in order for the child to gain the confidence and integrity of self to confront reality as an adult, the exploration of fears and anxieties through the childhood imagination in fairy stories is immensely important. In particular, fairy tales share a common motif of a trial and adventure which can be overcome successfully. The mixture of danger and excitement, combined with implicit ethical guidance and the reassuring 'happily ever after', constitutes a salutary exhortation to the child's conscious and unconscious that growth and independence are a welcome and exciting challenge. Fairy tales may often be unsavoury to more clinical and rationalistic contemporary minds because of their frequent savagery; yet they, unlike gloomy myths, tend to be optimistic and uplifting, thus providing a positive basis for the child's inner relation to adolescence and adult life. Whatever reservations one might have regarding the Freudian interpretation of specific fairy tales, Bettelheim's point that fairy tales are an important motor for the inner growth of the individual is very convincing, as is its correlate that individuals who fail to acquire a certain confidence in facing the challenges of reality adumbrated imaginatively in fairy tales often retreat into sterile fantasies in adult life.

Perception, art and creativity

The image of the mind as a theatre has prima facie attractions. An important question is the relation between perception and imagination, where the role and nature of 'images' is quite central. Ryle's theory of imagination as principally propositional pretending, and his expulsion of mental images, is an instance of a sophisticated theory banishing rather mundane facts of common human experience. Indeed, it seems to me to rival in sheer implausibility Norman Malcolm's claim that we do not have experiences in dreams.[21]

Sometimes philosophers present their activity as a conceptual preamble or prolegomenon to the work of science – a bit of preliminary housekeeping before the real scientific work is done. Philosophy by definition lacks experimental methods. Many philosophers who scoff at the subject matter of theology are loath to admit that the position of almost all philosophy is in virtually as precarious a state. Even a behaviourist philosopher like Ryle or a reductionist like Dennett appeals to non-experimental considerations. Why not hand the job over to the experimental psychologists or the neurophysiologists?

The concept of image is of particular interest: how 'visual' are mental images? Classical British empiricism conceived of mental contents in primarily visual terms and the problems of this have been much

---

21 G. Ryle, *The Concept of Mind* (London: Penguin, 1949), pp. 232–63; N. Malcolm, *Dreaming* (London: Routledge and Kegan Paul, 1976).

discussed, not least by phenomenologists like Sartre.[22] If one looks at a tree and forms a mental image of it, how are these two operations related? Hume regarded mental images as distinct from perceptions on the basis of their inferior vivacity. They are both visual experiences but they can be distinguished by their intensity. This is problematic. It is not phenomenologically obvious that mental imagery is less vivacious than perception: it may be very intense. But mental imagery seems dependent upon the will in a manner quite distinct from perceptual experience. I have to summon up the mental image of a tree, while the tree in the court seems (*pace* Berkeley!) to resist any subjection to the will of the perceiver.[23]

Surprisingly, perhaps, cognitive science has produced empirical support for the importance of images. There is a correlation between the particular qualities of a given item and the reaction time required to answer questions about it,[24] so that if under clinical conditions subjects are asked, say, about the number of windows in a building, their response time seems clearly linked to an internal scanning mechanism. That is to say, the subjects of the experiment look with the mental eye. Since eyes transmit information to the brain through the visual cortex, one might reasonably say that the brain is the organ of vision.[25]

Recent work on the right- and left-hand sides of the brain supports the importance of mental imagery. The left side is occupied with language and logic, the right with images and creative activity generally.[26] Activating the logical, analytic, verbal side of the brain seems to diminish creativity. In the medical condition of lupus there is loss of the mind's eye – visual memory and imagination.

Common sense tells us that to perceive an item in the world is to encounter reality and to form the appropriate belief that *p*. To remember *p* is to recall a truly existing item as opposed to a fantastical object like Pegasus. To imagine *p*, unlike perceiving or remembering *p*, the mind represents the non-actual, the unreal. Some reflection reveals problems with this account. Memory must be selective. Otherwise, the mind of any agent would be bombarded with unwanted memory-images. Even those images that are recalled from what Augustine calls the 'vast, immeasurable sanctuary' of memory are subject to imaginative re-vision, and this is a reason why the accuracy of memory is often in doubt.[27] Imagination is that power of the mind through which the materials of sensation become persisting objects of the perceived world. It is also the power through which our environment becomes shaped and moulded

22 J.-P. Sartre, *L'Imaginaire: psychologie-phénoménologique de l'imagination* (Paris: Gallimard, 1940).
23 C. McGinn, *Mindsight: Image, Dream, Meaning* (Cambridge, Mass.: Harvard University Press, 2004), p. 12.
24 E. T. H. Brann, *The World of the Imagination: Sum and Substance* (Lanham, Md: Rowman and Littlefield, 1991), pp. 211–90.
25 McGinn, *Mindsight*, pp. 43ff.
26 R. A. Finke, T. B. Ward and S. M. Smith, *Creative Cognition: Theory, Research, and Application* (Cambridge, Mass.: MIT Press, 1996), pp. 25ff.
27 Augustine, *Confessions*, X, 9.

by the human mind, an 'active sagacity in the soul', to use the fine phrase of Henry More.[28] The fact that a two-year-old child can identify kinds of objects is an instance of the working of the imagination. Shoes or cups, say, come in very different shapes, colours and sizes and yet a normal child can happily identify these myriad items as belonging to a class.

Imagination is traditionally seen as on the boundary between sensation and thought. Collingwood argues that sensation is 'not entirely unfree; it is the spontaneous activity of the living and sentient organism'; but the freedom of imagination extends beyond the freedom of sensation but not as far as the freedom of the intellect. Collingwood is attacking the empiricist idea that the world is a construct out of sense data or *sensa*.[29] Paraphrasing Glendower to Hotspur, Collingwood exclaims: 'They speak like men accustomed to call spirits from the vasty deep, who feel sure that they will come'.[30]

Imagination in its most basic function unifies experience by forging the elements of sensation derived from the environment into a set of stable objects. Though imagination is not a freedom of choice, it evinces a freedom beyond sensation.[31] 'The activity of consciousness . . . converts impression into idea, that is crude sensation into imagination'.[32] This is the important point made by Collingwood on the imagination as intermediate between feeling and intellect: 'the point at which the activity of thought makes contact with the merely psychic life of feeling'.[33] Collingwood, like Kant and Coleridge, proposes that perception is an active and synthesizing operation. Recent work in neurology supports this philosophical claim that the mind necessarily imposes unity upon the flux of appearances. When the mind attributes a single colour to an apple on a tree, the wavelength composition of the light reflected from the same apple varies according to the surrounding light conditions, such as the time of day or climatic conditions. Yet the mind has no problem discarding the differences in order to reidentify the same object.[34] Crucial is the idea that for a rational, self-aware agent specific feelings must be modified by consciousness. Collingwood avers that 'attention is in no sense a response to stimulus. It takes no orders from sensation. Consciousness, master in its own house, dominates feeling';[35] 'Regarded as names for a certain kind or level of experience, the words consciousness and imagination are synonymous'[36]; 'At the level of consciousness, the feelings are dominated by the self that owns them.'[37]

28 Henry More, *Antidote Against Atheism*, I.v.2.
29 R. C. Collingwood, *The Principles of Art* (Oxford: Clarendon Press, 1938), pp. 195, 214.
30 Ibid., p. 211, paraphrasing Shakespeare's *Henry IV: Part 1*, III.i.42.
31 Ibid., p. 197.
32 Ibid., p. 215.
33 Ibid., p. 171.
34 See S. Zeki, *Inner Vision: An Exploration of Art and the Brain* (Oxford: Oxford University Press, 1999), pp. 5–6.
35 Collingwood, *The Principles of Art*, p. 207.
36 Ibid., p. 215.
37 Ibid., p. 208.

Tears at a funeral or laughter at a party express the feelings of a self-conscious agent, part of a society of self-conscious agents.

Collingwood's employment of the concepts of imagination as halfway between intellect and sensation is part of his insistence that, notwithstanding classical empiricism from Locke to Russell, experience requires interpretation, and such interpretation is underdetermined by data. Imagination is the principle of active synthesis of sensation into conscious experience: in Collingwood's language, 'imagination is thus the new form which feeling takes when transformed by the activity of consciousness'.[38] The link between the spontaneous, hence free and non-mechanical, activity of the mind in its imaginative interpretation of experience finds eloquent expression in Coleridge's much-quoted distinction between imagination and fancy:

> The IMAGINATION then I consider either as primary, or secondary. The primary IMAGINATION I hold to be the living Power and prime Agent of all human Perception, and as a repetition in the finite mind of the eternal act of creation in the infinite I AM. The secondary I consider as an echo of the former, co-existing with the conscious will, yet still as identical with the primary in the *kind* of its agency, and differing only in *degree*, and in the mode of its operation. It dissolves, diffuses, dissipates, in order to re-create; or where this process is rendered impossible, yet still at all events it struggles to idealize and to unify. It is essentially *vital*, even as all objects (*as* objects) are essentially fixed and dead.
>
> FANCY, on the contrary, has no other counters to play with, but fixities and definites. The Fancy is indeed no other than a mode of Memory emancipated from the order of time and space; and blended with, and modified by that empirical phenomenon of the will, which we express by the word CHOICE. But equally with the ordinary memory it must receive all its materials ready made from the law of association.[39]

Coleridge distinguishes between 'fancy' and primary and secondary 'imagination'. Imagination is based upon the freedom or spontaneity of the mind's control over its images or contents. Primary imagination is simply the Kantian idea of 'apperception'. Fancy is rather the passive mechanism of association of images. The great medieval Parisian philosopher Albertus Magnus took up a distinction in Avicenna (980–1037) between the (*vis*) *phantastica* and the (*vis*) *imaginativa*. C. S. Lewis notes that Coleridge reverses the relation of the two.[40] It is in this context that Coleridge announces that it dawned upon him that 'fancy' and 'imagination' are 'two distinct and widely different faculties'. Although, as he admits, *imaginatio* is the most obvious translation of *phantasia*, he wishes to distinguish between the two, and believes that this distinction

---

38 Ibid., p. 215.
39 Coleridge, *Biographia Literaria*, vol. I, pp. 304–5.
40 C. S. Lewis, *The Discarded Image* (Cambridge: Cambridge University Press, 1964), pp. 162ff.

can furnish a torch of guidance to the philosophical critic, and ultimately to the poet himself.[41]

George Watson has convincingly argued that Coleridge erroneously believed that the distinction was novel.[42] Yet before Coleridge, fancy was associated with error. Coleridge's point is that fancy is 'an aggregative and associative power' whereas imagination is the 'shaping and modifying power'. Fancy and imagination are different ways of dealing with the mind's materials. The imagination is more primordial and inscrutable. One might say that it is both lower and higher than fancy. It is higher because it is linked to the divine madness delineated so memorably by Plato in the *Phaedrus*: 'repetition in the finite mind of the eternal act of creation in the infinite I AM'. 'Our way is to become like God', says Augustine.[43] Yet it is also 'essentially vital', the primordial and organic 'living Power and prime Agent of all human Perception'. It is a point where human self-consciousness merges with its subconscious roots in the vegetative soul, such that Coleridge can both exclaim 'How much of man lies below his consciousness!'[44] and exalt the point where the human soul can enjoy communion with the Divine, as Wordsworth claims in *The Prelude*:

To hold communion with the invisible world
Such minds are truly from the Deity[45]

Another important element is the unifying aspect of the imagination: 'The poet . . . brings the whole soul of man into activity . . . He diffuses a tone and spirit of unity, that blends and (as it were) fuses each into each, by that synthetic and magical power, to which we have exclusively appropriate the name of imagination.'[46] Whereas the 'aggregative and associative power' of fancy accumulates items and constructs an artificial whole, imagination forges an entire new fabric. The other important aspect of imagination which Coleridge emphasizes is freedom. Fancy is, in contrast, mechanical.

Coleridge inherits two distinct theories of the imagination within the English philosophical tradition. Coleridge's own sympathies will become clear in the following quotation: 'it is worthy of notice . . . (that) the system of idealism may be traced to sources equally remote with the former, or materialism; and Berkeley can boast an ancestry at least as venerable as Gassendi or Hobbes.'[47] Berkeley regards the mind as 'active being . . . which exercises diverse operations as willing, imagining, remembering'

---

41 S. T. Coleridge, *Biographia Literaria*, vol. 1, ed. J. Engell and W. J. Bate (Princeton, NJ: Princeton University Press, 1983), p. 85.
42 G. Watson, 'Contributions to a Dictionary of Critical Terms: Imagination and Fancy', in *Essays in Criticism*, 3 (1953), pp. 202–14.
43 Augustine, *City of God* IX, 17.
44 S. T. Coleridge, *Notebooks*, vol. 1 (Princeton, NJ: Princeton University Press, 1957), §1554.
45 Wordsworth, *The Prelude*, XIII, 105–6.
46 Coleridge, *Biographia Literaria*, vol. 2, pp. 15–16.
47 Coleridge, *Biographia Literaria*, vol. 1, p. 90.

on the tools of the mind: the ideas.[48] Regarding these ideas as inert images, 'A little attention will discover to us that the very being of an idea implies passiveness and inertness in it, insomuch that it is impossible for an idea to do anything, or, strictly speaking, to be the cause of anything'.[49] In a famous passage Berkeley notes:

> I find I can excite ideas in my mind at pleasure, and vary and shift the scene as oft as I think fit. It is no more than willing, and straightaway this or that idea arises in my fancy: and by the same power it is obliterated and makes way for another.[50]

In his *Philosophical Commentaries,* Berkeley observes: 'The Spirit the Active thing that which is Soul & God is the Will alone. The Ideas are effects impotent things'.[51] Berkeley's theory of the imagination is dominated by the idea of the conscious and creative control which the mind can employ. The capacity of the imagination to create and deploy images at will is, for Berkeley, a matter of great metaphysical and theological significance: 'Why may we not conceive it possible for God to create things out of Nothing. Certainly we our selves create in some wise whenever we imagine.' [52]

Hobbes, by way of contrast, sees the will as being excited by images:

> When a body is once in motion, it moveth, unless something else hinder it, externally . . . so also it happeneth in that motion, which is made in the internal parts of a man, then, when he Sees, Dreams, etc. For after the object is removed or the eye shut, wee still retain an image of the thing seen, though more obscure than when we see it. And this is it, the Latins call *Imagination,* from the image made in seeing; and apply the same, though improperly, to all the other senses. But the Greeks call it *Fancy;* which signifies *apparence,* and is as proper to one sense as to another . . . IMAGINATION therefore is nothing but *decaying sense;* and is found in men, and many other living Creatures, as well sleeping, as waking.[53]

Imagination in Berkeley is linked to the deep and irreducible fact of the will, whereas the will, for Hobbes, is merely an instance of the broader machinery of motive and attraction, and thought is ultimately constituted by a series of motions in the brain. The will is determined by the images of the mind.[54] Coleridge places Hobbes, quite rightly, in a tradition going back to Aristotle in which the imagination consists

---

48 George Berkeley, *Principles of Human Knowledge,* §2 , In *Philosophical Works,* ed. M. Ayers (London: Dent, 1993), p. 89.
49 Ibid., §25; *Philosophical Works,* p. 98.
50 Ibid., §28; *Philosophical Works,* p. 99.
51 George Berkeley, *Philosophical Commentaries,* §712; *Philosophical Works,* p. 392.
52 Ibid., §830; *Philosophical Works,* p. 406.
53 Thomas Hobbes, *Leviathan,* I.ii.3 ed. W. G. Pogson Smith (Oxford: Clarendon Press, 1958), p. 13.
54 Ibid., I.ii.3; p. 19: 'All Fancies are motions within us, reliques of those made in the Sense'. For a useful discussion, see A. Hannay, *Mental Images: A Defence* (London: George Allen and Unwin, 1971), pp. 237ff.

primarily of 'after-images'. The imagination is a form of faded perceptual experience: decaying sense – or as Coleridge puts it, *'after-consciousness'*.[55]

Hobbes and Berkeley represent two extreme and unsatisfactory accounts of the imagination. Hobbes seems to leave out the evident fact of its spontaneous and creative component. Berkeley, in going to the other extreme, seems to neglect the sub- or semi-conscious aspect of the imagination. The differences between Hobbes and Berkeley on the nature of the imagination resolve into a difference between an excessively active and an excessively passive view of mental activity.[56] One might speculate that the theological concerns of both men contribute to the basic difference in their view of the mind.

George Watson suggests that Coleridge's theory is a 'magnificent derelict, often studied and never employed'.[57] He suggests that we either understand it correctly and use it accordingly, or revert to the ancient priority of imagination over fancy. I suggest that a tripartite division is useful. 'Imagination' can denote the creative *nisus* towards unity, 'fancy' the mechanical association of mental representation, and 'fantasy' the capacity for delusion and escapism.

Consider Coleridge's much-discussed distinction between fancy as 'an aggregative and associative power' and imagination as a 'shaping and modifying power'. The imagination is linked to the unconscious as well as to the will. The imagination is more primordial and inscrutable than fancy. Fancy is a 'mode of Memory emancipated from the order of time and space'. This is the capacity of the mind to represent and combine remembered images. As such the term 'fancy' is not meant pejoratively; fancy is not bad as such, and can have a perfectly respectable and indeed necessary function. It is hard to see how we could negotiate and adapt to the world without the capacity to use memory in this way. Empiricists, from Aristotle to Hobbes, are correct to emphasize the importance of memory employed to such ends, but are wrong to identify this with the imagination in its most important meaning. Imagination is more than the mere reconstitution of items of memory into the new set of relations: it is the fusing power that produces a new unity.[58] The 'synthetic and magical power' of imagination is both higher and, as it were, lower than fancy. Imagination is more closely bound to the primordial unconscious power of the soul and to divine inspiration than the mundane fancy. The activity of the fancy is more narrowly instrumental: it furnishes the means by which certain images, 'fixities and definites', are modified through choice for certain ends. The creative imagination is not an agency of expedience or contrivance but the light and energy of soul as it relishes truth: knowledge 'wedded' to feeling. The concept of expression is linked to the deeply Romantic-Coleridgean idea of genius. In human beings, pre-eminently the artist of genius, unconscious nature becomes aware of itself as Spirit, in articulate self-awareness. In artistic expres-

---

55 Coleridge, *Biographia Literaria*, vol. 1, p.103.
56 See the fine discussion by Hannay, in *Mental Images*, pp. 237ff.
57 Watson, 'Contributions', p. 213.
58 Coleridge, *Biographia Literaria*, vol. 1, p. 304.

sion, Spirit manifests nature as slumbering spirit: the intelligible fabric of the natural world becomes transparent. Hence Genius is able to make the external internal and the internal external, 'to make nature thought and thought nature'.[59]

Coleridge's point, however, is that the relatively unproblematic mechanical mental capacity of fancy should not be confused with the vastly more mysterious, vital and creative imagination, which endeavours to see reality as a whole. The artistic imagination experiments with parts in order to create a new and beautiful whole, the attainment of which requires moral effort. The creation of a work of art as a world *sui generis* cannot be intelligibly reduced to simple mechanisms of addition and comparison. The poet 'diffuses a tone, and spirit of unity, that blends, and (as it were) *fuses*, each into each, by that synthetic and magical power, to which we have exclusively appropriated the name of imagination'.[60] One might compare Collingwood's emphasis on seeing parts as a whole, a capacity that belongs most distinctively to imagination. As Coleridge declares: the 'poet, described in *ideal* perfection, brings the whole soul of man into activity'.[61] Here the artistic imagination is not the unshackled expression of emotional forces or the mere receptivity of sensibility; it is a discipline and an endeavour to realize one's being. Art for Coleridge is not a skill or craft that creates certain emotions, nor is it the production of certain artefacts; it is rather the imaginative communication with another rational soul, the '*compact* between the poet and his reader', poetry making us poets.[62] Collingwood writes in *The Principles of Art*: 'As Coleridge puts it, we know a man for a poet by the fact that he makes us poets. We know that he is expressing his emotions by the fact that he is enabling us to express ours.'[63]

Collingwood claims that 'Every utterance and every gesture that each one of us makes is a work of art'. [64] Coleridge in 'Dejection' claims that 'we receive but what we give'.[65] If this seems fanciful, one might consider the work of the eminent psychoanalyst Donald Winnicott. In Winnicott's view, since 'objectivity' is always in relation to a subject, and 'objective perception' has to be considered as involving an element of subjectivity, a 'creative apperception' enables the subject to appreciate and relish the meaningfulness of living.[66]

---

59 S. T. Coleridge, 'On Poesy or Art', in *Biographia Literaria*, vol. 2, ed. J. Shawcross (Oxford: Clarendon Press, 1907), p. 258.
60 Coleridge, *Biographia Literaria*, vol. II, p. 16.
61 *Ibid.* vol. 2, p. 15–16.
62 Ibid., p. 65.
63 Collingwood, *The Principles of Art*, p. 118.
64 Ibid., p. 285.
65 Coleridge, *Poems*, p. 281.
66 D. Winnicott, *Playing and Reality* (Harmondsworth: Penguin, 1974), pp. 63ff. Enid Balint employs the term 'imaginative perception' for the inner meaning. See E. Balint, *Before I Was I: Psychoanalysis and the Imagination*, ed. J. Mitchell and M. Parsons (London: Free Association Books, 1993).

Unlike Freud – who linked creativity to unconscious and childhood conflicts and compensation for frustrated drives – Winnicott sees the artist re-presenting the world in novel ways as linked to that creativity which is defining for human existence: 'The creativity that concerns me here is a universal. It belongs to being alive.'[67] Authenticity is contrasted with the 'false self' or ego forged by mere 'compliance' with the subject's environment.[68] Winnicott is interested in the search for the self and the conditions required for success. Winnicott identifies these conditions of creativity with the 'approach of the individual to external reality'.[69] Through play the particular child or adult is able to become creative and to use the whole personality, and an individual discovers authentic selfhood through such creativity. He observes:

> It is not of course that anyone will ever be able to explain the creative impulse, and it is unlikely that anyone would ever want to do so; but the link can be made, and usefully made, between creative living and living itself, and the reasons can be studied why it is that creative living can be lost and why the individual's feeling that life is real or meaningful can disappear.[70]

Two significantly distinct aspects of specifically human existence are love and work. Both presuppose culture, technology and minimal social structures. The use of tools for agriculture, manufacture, trade, etc. are prerequisites for work by *Homo sapiens*, and there has been exponential growth at various crucial stages of human development as traced by anthropologists. Yet the English word 'work' can be used both for the toil of human existence and the creative 'works' of poetry and music that are so distinctively human and evident in the cave paintings of 50,000 years ago. The myth of Genesis reflects the sense of the burden of work, the poetry of the Psalms the work of praise through human creation. The creative dimension of human work is linked to the social forms connected to physical procreation. Freud is extreme in his view of the artist's work as based upon compensation but the bond between artistic creativity and the sexual *eros* is much documented in myth, biography and psychology. Creativity is a decisive characteristic of human life, whether evinced in the cave paintings of 50,000 BC, the monuments of the ancient Near East, the sculpture of Phidias, or the roads and architecture of the Roman Empire. And humans usually can shape a family life, far removed from 'mating' in the animal kingdom, a life which forms a basic social and political unit. Freud may have been rather extreme in his view of the discontents created by civilization but he is quite right to signal the great gap between the instinctual and the social imaginary, the codes and rituals of a civilization. His own scientific naturalism perhaps blinded him to the extent to which civilization is 'natural' to man since we lack the instinctual powers of the rest of the animal kingdom, and the fact that

67 Winnicott, *Playing and Reality*, p. 79.
68 Ibid., p. 76.
69 Ibid., p. 79.
70 Ibid., p. 81.

this instinctual weakness induces and encourages a creativity in human life which marks us off from that of other mammals in kind and not merely in degree. Freud's explanation of civilization is essentially utilitarian: the rules and taboos of society regarding monogamy, incest, etc. are in conflict, he believes, with instinctual pleasure but they serve to protect its members from pain. Yet this is too mechanical an explanation of human society. The shift from the hunter-gatherer society to more advanced civilization has been a poetic activity: a making or shaping (*poeien*) of the environment. The transformation of nature into a habitable world, into towns, agriculture, commerce, etc., is also the conferring of order and meaning. It is derived from a deep need to find meaning and this is connected to the imagination.

The fact that both work and love can be the source of torment and misery, that work and love can be bondage and suffering for human beings, is another index of the gap between the human race and the rest of the animal kingdom. The tragic labour of Sisyphus or the tormented and deceptive love of King Lear give imaginative expression to the specifically human condition. The supreme occidental myth of Adam and Eve after the expulsion from Paradise (and the *ora et labora* of the Christian community) gives poignant expression to the ambiguities of love and work. Yet a sense of vocation through creative work and the formative power of love reveals a significant distinction between brute existence and the imaginative creativity requisite for human flourishing.

Varieties of imagining

Some thinkers assert that there is no single nuclear 'imaginative' operation of the mind, constituting 'the busy and boundless Fancy of man'.[71] Gilbert Ryle, for example, rejects the idea of a special faculty of the imagination 'occupying itself single-mindedly in fancied viewings and hearings'.[72] Naturally, we should avoid imbroglio, and philosophers like Ryle can point to confusion unconsciously created by the improper use of language. Perhaps there is no more of a problem with imagination than with other important philosophical concepts. Consider 'nature', for example. Nature can be thought of as the opposite of 'art', or 'supernature' or 'law' or 'convention'. 'Nature' is a philosophical concept with a long history. Does it matter that a concept is hard to define? It is very difficult to find a satisfactory definition of tragedy and yet it is a useful and meaningful term. It is, for example, intelligible and comprehensible to classify *Oedipus Rex* or *Othello* as a tragedy. Ryle's reductive agenda was linked to an implausibly rigid view of category differences as the root of philosophical errors. He wanted to root out confusions caused by the failure to respect the differences between mental and physical predicates, especially the reification of mental predicates, which

---

71 John Locke, *An Essay Concerning Human Understanding*, II.i.2, ed. P. Nidditch (Oxford: Clarendon Press, 1975), p. 104.
72 G. Ryle, *The Concept of Mind* (London: Penguin, 1949), p. 243.

obscured the fact that describing the mind of a person is, according to Ryle, just a manner of describing a body and its dispositions. Thus to speak of mind and body as if these were separate items is a category mistake akin to talking of Oxford University as if it could be distinguished from the colleges, faculties, people and buildings that constitute it. This argument assumes the Procrustean view that concepts properly belong to rigidly separated categories and seems to deny the conceptual and categorical *fluidity* that characterizes language. Those who wish to maintain the idea of an immaterial self, for example, may wish to distinguish between occasions when we cannot properly replace talk of body with talk of soul, and occasions when we can. The boundless inward region of imagination resists external verification. It is concerned with meanings and possibilities rather than verifiable actions and functions.

On a crude empiricist model of the mind, the imagination is the faculty that produces fanciful (i.e. non-existent) objects from memory and should be rigorously distinguished from knowledge obtained from sense impressions. On a crass Romantic view, imagination is a royal road to reality, a specially privileged faculty of aesthetic vision. Imagination, on this view, is the highest form of knowledge. These would both be versions of a faculty theory.

This suggests that it is helpful to speak of imagination as a faculty or 'system' within the mind. A number of researchers have developed an interest in the functioning of the brain and how exceptional or unusual neurophysiological features are associated with reduced or enhanced imaginative activity. The brain can be damaged or impaired and yet the mind can function. Autism is an interesting instance of high intelligence in human agents linked with a failure of imaginative insight into the lives of others. As a result, autists are socially dysfunctional, many severely so.[73] Those suffering from autistic-spectrum disorder (perhaps autism is a family of conditions or problems) have an unusually powerful grasp of mechanical and causal relations. In childhood they do not show interest in stories, and failure to play or make-believe is regarded as a clinical symptom of autism. Tests have shown that while autistic children can draw existing objects in the world, they are incapable of fashioning fantastical hybrids.[74] Problems of understanding the minds of other people are well documented through clinical tests. Conversely, it has been suggested that the hyperactive imagination can be linked to psychosis and depressive disorders. Schizophrenia would seem like a good instance of an overactive imagination. Nettle has argued that the capacities relevant for creativity or what he calls 'strong imagination'[75]

73 G. Currie and I. Ravenscroft, *Recreative Mind: Imagination in Philosophy and Psychology* (Oxford: Clarendon Press, 2003), pp. 134–60.

74 I. Roth, 'Imagination' in *The Oxford Companion to the Mind* (Oxford: Oxford University Press, 2005) pp. 443–7.

75 Quoting from Shakespeare's *A Midsummer Night's Dream*, V.i.19.

can, and do, generate psychological illness.[76] Madness, on Nettle's account, is not an aberration of nature or culture but rooted in the same dimension of human nature responsible for great creativity. Madness, for Nettle, is the price humanity pays for the highly advantageous evolutionary trait of creativity.

Hence one might isolate two extremes. One is the crude faculty view, regarding imagination as an independent activity of the mind. The other is the 'no nuclear operation', but that term covers diverse activities with loose family resemblances.

Coleridge provides a remarkably sane middle way. He regards imagination as a mental power that can be *distinguished* but not divided from other mental powers. For the purposes of illustration, we may isolate the particular role of imagination while recognizing it as an inseparable element in the mind's unified activity. Yet to distinguish imagination from sensation or understanding is not to divide it from them:

> The office of philosophical *disquisition* consists in just *distinction*; while it is the privilege of the philosopher to perceive himself constantly aware, that distinction is not division. In order to obtain adequate notions of any truth, we must intellectually separate its distinguishable parts; and this is the technical *process* of philosophy. But having so done, we must then restore them in our conceptions to the unity, in which they actually co-exist; and this is the *result* of philosophy.[77]

The imagination is involved in the activity of the whole person. It is ubiquitous in mental processes and yet for the purpose of philosophical reflection can be isolated from memory or perception.

What do the different senses of imagination have in common? Etymology is significant in answering this question. 'To imagine' is derived from the latin *imaginari* and closely related to *imago* – 'copy' or 'likeness' – and cognate with *imitatio*. Imagination provides, in other words, a likeness of reality. In more recent philosophical discussion the word 'simulation' is used by thinkers who believe that understanding other minds is a matter of imaginative empathy with others rather than theoretical inference. Hence we simulate, from the Latin *similis*, 'like'. Currie and Ravenscroft provide a neat account of this simulation in imaginative activity:

> Imaginative projection involves the capacity to have, and in good measure to control the having of states that are not perceptions or beliefs or decisions or experiences of movements of one's body, but which are in various ways like those states – like them in ways that enable the states possessed through imagination to mimic and,

---

76 D. Nettle, *Strong Imagination* (Oxford: Oxford University Press, 2001), pp. 10ff. Ironically, for Nettle's argument, the judicious and prudent Shakespeare seems himself one of the greatest counter-examples to the thesis that 'Great wits are sure to madness near allied'.
77 Coleridge, *Biographia Literaria*, vol. II, p. 11.

relative to certain purposes, to substitute for perceptions, beliefs, decisions, and experiences of movements.[78]

The spectrum of such copying of reality is vast. It is a tendency of the human mind to form analogies, to spring from likeness to likeness. This is also related to a liberation from the immediate context and environment. Imagination can break through environment, instinct and custom. It presupposes freedom from sensory stimulus.

As Emily Dickinson wrote:

The Possible's slow fuse is lit
By the Imagination.[79]

Imagination as the *tertium quid*

What is the relationship between mind and world? Imagination belongs to the realm of conscious experience and cannot be reduced to forms of behaviour. The bearing of 'inner' to 'outer' processes is the stuff of dispute and cavil. Externalists want to argue that the mind extends into the world and is in part constituted by features of the environment which play the appropriate role in cognition. There is no reason, on this view, why information should not be considered as belief even if outside the skull of a knower. Cognitive capacities can be embodied in material items in the environment of the knower. Some philosophers oppose the idea that the distinctively mental is internal. The use of a pen and paper or a computer to write, as well as various other physical items or computational artefacts, are not, as it were, supplements to mind, but the very extension of mind itself. Philosophers like Andy Clark think of these as physical extensions of mind or 'external scaffolding'.[80] Hence beliefs are partially constituted by items in the environment of the subject. His example is that of a man with Alzheimer's who uses a notebook to remind himself of the way to the museum. Indeed, for Clark, the self is 'an extended system' – a combination of physical organism and the extended features of the environment – thus breaking down established divisions between perception and action.

Yet the phenomenology of imagination shows that mind cannot be identified with its implementation in the physical objects of its surroundings.

The mind is its own place, and in itself
Can make a Heaven of Hell, a Hell of Heaven.[81]

At the same time the human mind can range far beyond its physical environment:

---

78 G. Currie and I. Ravenscroft, *Recreative Mind*, p. 11.
79 E. Dickinson, *Poems*, ed. T. H. Johnson (Cambridge, Mass.: Belknap Press, 1955), vol. 3, p. 1146.
80 A. Clark, *Being There: Putting Brain, Body and World Together Again* (Cambridge, Mass.: MIT Press, 1997), pp. 45–6.
81 Milton, *Paradise Lost*, I, 254–55.

What we know is indeed an infinitely small part of what has been; but it is all that is left to us now; and by it we can still escape in imagination from the decree passed against each one of us at his birth, that he should not issue forth from his narrow space of years, with its little circle, that looks so large, of modern thoughts and sights and sounds.[82]→

This is nonsense to the strict naturalist, for whom self-consciousness must be a puzzling by-product of the evolutionary process which can only impede rather than enhance the prospects for survival in creatures who are so apt to dwell upon their miseries and imperfections. As the paradigmatically introspective Hamlet exclaims:

> O God! I could be bounded in a nut-shell, and count myself a King of infinite space, were it not that I have bad dreams.[83]

Such cognitive science is a good example of how a modern theorist models mind upon scientific studies of mind – on the basis of artificial intelligence, computer modelling and evolutionary psychology. Here the idea is that mind is essentially scanning equipment, and the environment plays a central role in the constitution of beliefs. Hence the externalist thinks we should break down any intuitive division between beliefs 'in the head' and the outside world.

However, it is not clear that the sophistication of a material culture mirrors its imaginative activity. As Coleridge observes: 'In Egypt, Palestine, Greece and India the analysis of the mind had reached its noon and manhood, while experimental research was still in its dawn and infancy.'[84] Indeed, it is not clear that Plato's dialogues are inferior to contemporary peer-reviewed journals in philosophy, or even to the major monographs of the twentieth century, nor the playwrights of ancient Athens inferior to those of modern Europe. Enlightenment critics like Gibbon were often inclined to blame this decline on Christianity, but in the twenty-first century this seems like wishful thinking.

The human imagination possesses a mediating power, or liminal quality. It provides a refuge of irreducible individuality and a part of subjective consciousness and yet draws upon the shapes and forms of physical objects. The imagination is uniquely characterized by a tension between the inner and the outer, thought and sense; this tension is unavoidable, and imagination hovers between the manifestation of the inner through the outer and yet the inscrutable private part of consciousness that creatively represents experiences, states of affairs in the theatre of consciousness, remains unmediated. Evidently language is required for elaborate and rich communication between two rational beings. Observation of the body and the existence of rules for a language provide necessary but not sufficient conditions for understanding. But

---

82 G. M. Trevelyan, *England Under the Stuarts* (London: Methuen & Co., 1904), pp. 516–17.
83 William Shakespeare, *Hamlet*, II.ii.1.
84 Coleridge, *Biographia Literaria*, vol. 1, p. 91.

communication through language is different in kind from non-linguistic behaviour:

> O Hamlet, speak no more;
> Thou turn'st mine eyes into my very soul.[85]

Arguments against the knowledge we have of our own minds and other minds often rely upon dubious premises such as the verificationist principle that to have a thought is in principle being able to know that a thought is true, or perhaps the principle that one cannot understand without reflexive awareness of that understanding. We may only experience the outward behaviour, gestures and sounds emitted by other human beings, but we instinctively hypostasize. That is, we assume some integrating principle lying behind the observable action – a persisting person; a self or soul – rather for the same reasons of intellectual economy as we perceive objects as persisting unities rather than transient phenomena of our senses. The Buddhist may warn us of the spiritual dangers of this practice but it is an uncontroversial assumption in habitual dealings with other agents. The non-reducibility of the inner to the outer is demonstrated by the fact that we know that the behaviour of the most courteous newcomer may be deceptive and we encourage our children and vulnerable friends to beware of well-behaved strangers. We form beliefs about the interior states of other human agents on the assumption that human beings share beliefs and sensations that are, *ceteris paribus*, largely similar to our own. Our own first-person experiences and privileged access to our first-person mental states must be the basis for this extrapolation to the minds of others. Iris Murdoch begins her *Metaphysics as a Guide to Morals* with the claim that

> The idea of a self contained unity or limited whole is a fundamental instinctive concept. We see parts of things, we intuit whole things.[86]

This seems correct when dealing with human beings. The error of Cartesianism is to present the *cogito* as theoretically autonomous, whereas the self requires mediation through a context and relations with other selves. But Cartesianism preserves the common-sense intuition that a substantial part of human identity eludes physiology, society and circumstance. And it is this sense of the human soul underlying the variations of culture, race and creed that founds the proper task of the humanities – of intelligent and critical empathy with the great cultures of the past:

> Men do mightily wrong themselves when they refuse to be present in all ages: and neglect to see the beauty of all kingdoms,[87]

Collingwood distinguishes crafts like the blacksmith or the tailor, whereby the craftsman knows what he is doing with the hammer and

---

85 Shakespeare, *Hamlet*, III.iv.79.
86 I. Murdoch, *Metaphysics as a Guide to Morals* (London: Chatto and Windus, 1992), p. 1.
87 Thomas Traherne, *Centuries of Meditations*, I, 85, ed. B. Dobell (London: P. J. and A. E. Dobell, 1927), p. 62.

the anvil or the needle and the materials – imposing form upon a certain matter in order to achieve a specific end – from arts, where the artist characteristically does not know what he is creating until it finds expression. The unconscious is made conscious of itself through the creative imagination. As Coleridge observes:

> the sense of musical delight, with the power of producing it, is a gift of imagination; and this together with the power of reducing multitude into unity of effect, and modifying a series of thoughts by some one predominant thought or feeling, may be cultivated and improved, but can never be learnt. It is in these that 'poeta nascitur non fit'.[88]

In *The Principles of Art*, first published in 1938, Collingwood argues that art is the manifestation and realization of that which is 'in the head' of the artist. The piece of marble or the paint on the canvas is not strictly the work of art. This view is at odds with the dominant philosophical-aesthetic positions of the twentieth century, which tended to define art in external terms: whether functionalist accounts, which defined art in terms of particular social ends or purposes; or procedural accounts, which defined art in terms of the methods employed in the public domain or institutions to furnish the work with meaning. Even Gadamer's polemic against aesthetics can be seen as a rejection of a Romantic tradition of art being inherently 'in the mind'.[89]

Collingwood asserts that the imagination is ubiquitous: 'Regarded as names for a certain kind or level of experience, the words consciousness and imagination are synonymous'.[90] This is an anti-empiricist polemic that he shares with Coleridge and Kant. Perception of an object always involves more than sense data: it involves the imagining of properties which are not disclosed to the senses, or noticing, i.e. looking at or attending to, what is seen. Hence there is a continuity between the imaginative component in habitual perceptual experience and in artistic vision. With a Ruskinian flourish, Collingwood observes: 'Only a person who paints well can see well; and conversely: only a person who sees well can paint well.'[91] He suggests that 'one paints a thing in order to see it':

> This seeing refers not to sensation but to awareness. Awareness presupposes sensation but involves self consciousness and the power of the mind itself. Rather than the power of the sensation on the mind (imagine here a raw pain), the mind is asserting itself upon the data of experience, not as a group of unrelated items but as 'a single indivisible unity'.[92]

88 Coleridge, *Biographia Literaria*, vol. 2, p. 20.
89 H. G. Gadamer, *Wahrheit und Methode* (Tübingen: Mohr Siebeck, 1990), pp. 48ff.
90 Collingwood, *The Principles of Art*, p. 215.
91 Ibid., p. 304.
92 Ibid., p. 223.

For both Coleridge and Collingwood there is an analogous relationship between art and religion because of the ineluctable role of imaginative creativity in both domains and the non-mechanical nature of such creativity. There are no rules which can exhaustively define the truly artistic activity. Secondly, true art is imaginative and is thus 'in the head' of both artist and audience because art is a seeing or hearing of the invisible or inaudible. Its power lies in that which it evokes through its materials, not in the materials themselves. Significance is attributed to material objects as signs and in this way imagination yokes the interior and the exterior. That which Coleridge affirms of art – 'to make the external internal, the internal external', blending the subjective and objective, is a primordial human need.[93] It shows how the world is saturated by mind – the head and the heart, inner and outer. The poet is not arguing for certain propositions but communicating experience – that which 'calls the whole soul of man into activity'.[94]

A poem provides a good example of this mediation of the inward with the outward that is characteristic of the imagination. The poem, in Coleridge's terminology, is a *tertium quid* between pure meaning or intention and objectivity. A poem can be admired for its formal qualities but it is not just a thing but a message. Yet nor is it, like a telegram, merely message. There is a dialectical relationship between meaning and its expression. The articulation of meaning requires specific forms, but those forms serve to convey the meaning. To appreciate a great poem, say, is a reaction to the vision of the poet as expressed in the poem. Meaning is closely linked to the transfer of intention and the understanding of this intention: the communion of *souls* as opposed to the communication of animals. Meaning in language presupposes exchange between persons rather than things. The expression, the formal shape of the artistic object, is a necessary condition of this communication. But the words on the page will not function as poetry without the reader's capacity to enter into the world of the poet. It has been well observed by Panofsky and others that the Gothic cathedral, with its elaborate *biblia pauperum* and symbolic structure pointing to heavenly light, articulates the ideas of medieval Western Christendom with the intricacy of St Thomas's *Summa*. Someone looking at the Gothic cathedral of Chartres as a mechanical feat, but with no appreciation of Christian theology (and perhaps even no appreciation of Neoplatonism), will not understand the building. The building will be ultimately as mysterious as the cities and monuments of Roman Britain were to the heathen Anglo-Saxons.

This is contrary to the views of Wimsatt and Beardsley on the intentional fallacy, or indeed the views of Freud or Marx, who took art to express the neurosis or class consciousness of the author.[95] Yet one might reflect upon the analogy of conversation. The meaning of certain utterances depends crucially upon what one knows about the personality

93 Coleridge, 'On Poesy and Art', in *Biographia Literaria*, vol. 2, p. 258.
94 Coleridge, *Biographia*, II, p. 16.
95 See S. Burke, *Authorship from Plato to the Postmodern: A Reader* (Edinburgh: Edinburgh University Press, 2000).

and opinion of the speakers. So too in art. It clearly makes a difference to the appreciation of *Middlemarch* to realize that George Eliot was the translator of one of the most significant radical theological texts of the nineteenth century: Strauss's *Das Leben Jesu*.

Mindedness, self-understanding and imaginative irreducibility

There are reasons for maintaining the irreducibility of thoughts and actions.[96] The normative quality of beliefs about goodness, truth or beauty is very puzzling from a naturalistic perspective. There is a significant asymmetry between the prediction of natural objects and reasoning about persons. How can science describe the process by which one judges an act reasonable or polite? Yet society clearly depends upon the existence of binding norms of behaviour. Socrates remarks in the *Phaedo* on the night before his execution that the contrast between instinct and duty poses a severe problem for the naturalist: 'I fancy these sinews and bones would have been in the neighbourhood of Megara or Boeotia long ago . . . if I did not think it was more just and honourable to submit to whatever penalty my country orders rather than take to my heels and run away.'[97] He is reflecting on a fact of human agency which resists quasi-scientific explanation in terms of aversion and inclinations.

Though traditionally psychological or rationalistic, recent atheism has taken on a particularly 'scientific' turn. Quite widespread is the 'reductionist materialist atheist', who looks at the physiological-neurological roots of religion. Such critics think we have been genetically determined to form certain beliefs. Some commentators even speculate about a link between visions and the neurological basis of epilepsy.[98]

Yet physicalism has problems. The relation between the nervous system and human consciousness is very mysterious. The brain is a necessary condition of consciousness in the finite world, but there is a gap between necessary and sufficient conditions. If thought processes are brain processes, and we should turn to examine more closely the visual cortex at the back of the brain or the aural cortex, it is puzzling that the properties of the thoughts and the chunks of the brain seem to differ so radically. Identity on Leibniz's Law means possessing the same properties. However, there are manifest problems in describing *thoughts* in material terms. Any brain is spatially located, but that is not obvious with the thought that 'the cricket season has started nicely'. An important component about beliefs is truth or falsity, but how can brain states be true or false? Sensations are hard to describe as brain states in a non-question-begging manner. Clearly, the physical description of pain employs talk of 'c-fibres' but the properties of pain – specific feeling of

---

96 T. Nagel, 'What is it Like to Be a Bat?', in *Mortal Questions* (Cambridge: Cambridge University Press, 1979), pp. 165–80; C. Taylor, 'Self-interpreting Animals', in *Human Agency and Language; Philosophical Papers*, vol. 1 (Cambridge: Cambridge University Press, 1985), pp. 45–76.
97 Plato, *Phaedo* 99a.
98 See e.g. M. A. Persinger, *Neuropsychological Bases of God Beliefs* (New York: Praeger, 1987).

intense physical discomfort – hardly apply to brain states. Furthermore, one is aware of one's own states of mind, e.g. anxiety or calm, elation or fatigue (*pace* Freud), while ignorant of the chemical workings of the brain within one's skull.

There seems to be some intuitive plausibility in trying to match a specific mental state with a physical process. After all, too much coffee or alcohol and conscious states are clearly affected. Yet the neuronal connections differ between the brains of two fruit flies. The exponential explosion of combinations of neurophysiological elements in the human case (30 billion nerve cells in the human brain, unique wiring in the womb, the particular developmental process of each brain) means that many neurophysiologists are very sceptical of the ambitions of physicalism. Damasio observes that an individual's life and specific experiences affect the cortical brain circuits operative in creative imaginings. Given the problems with explaining conscious experience neurophysiologically in the instance of discrete perceptual experiences, a fortiori the imagination will produce greatly enhanced (and presumably insuperable) complexities.[99] If an individual's memory and contingent history shape their neurophysiology, a complete and exhaustive explanation of the mental in terms of the physical will be impossible. But imagination does bring in the memory and thereby history of each individual. One might consider Proust's extraordinary account of the sensory experience of a madeleine dipped in tea that provoked a flood of images of his childhood in Combray.

Because of self-consciousness, there cannot be a science of thoughts and beliefs. The self-conscious usage of concepts resists lawlike explanations from the outside. Take a couple of surprisingly bold and unpredictable actions. Wilberforce's decision to campaign against slavery and Hannibal's decision to cross the Alps depended upon their respective beliefs about the authority of Scripture or Rome's threat to Carthage. There is quite good documentary evidence about these beliefs, and historians can tell us much about Wilberforce's evangelical Christianity or Hannibal's hostility to Rome. To understand their actions, we need to consider and engage with their mental worlds. Furthermore, this enterprise is holistic. Cultures and languages require interpetation. It is also the endeavour to understand the intentions, the minds, of human agents in so far as we can imaginatively engage in them. That is, we imaginatively re-create their thoughts and intentions in order to gain historical insight. If it is by historical thinking that we rethink and so rediscover the thought of Hammurabi or Solon, it is in the same way that we discover the thought of a friend who writes us a letter, or a stranger who crosses the street.[100]

We can understand this just as we can understand (if not approve of) Tamberlaine – because of Vico's *verum–factum* principle. In the humanities we know what we human beings have constructed – that is, when

99 A. R. Damasio, 'Some Notes on Imagination and Creativity', in K. H. Pfenninger and
    V. Shubik, *The Origins of Creativity* (Oxford: Oxford University Press, 2001).
100 Collingwood, *The Principles of Art*, p. 219.

we look at the Lion's Gate in Mycenae we can imaginatively engage with that archaic world and feel the curse of Agamemnon. At the Colosseum we can hear 'Ave, Caesar, morituri te salutant!' or the screams of the martyrs. The interpretation of historical events on the basis of fragmentary records – buildings, testimonies – is a search, but *making sense* of the past requires imaginative engagement closely cognate to the appreciation of fiction. To understand actions is to gain insight into the values and principles, motives and beliefs of the agents.

One becomes aware of one's desires through the imagination (these may be quite complex and barely understood desires). But conversely the imagination can shape one's desires. Education is the most obvious instance. Plato clearly thought that art should be censored because of this power of the imagination to affect motives and patterns of behaviour. Admiration for Achilles clearly fuelled Alexander the Great's ambition for conquest. It is poetry that supplies the why and wherefore of human behaviour, not 'science'.

The irreducibility of the normative in these areas of language or behaviour is a powerful argument in the hands of the proponents of hermeneutical philosophy. I share the view of Vico, Dilthey, Alasdair MacIntyre and Charles Taylor that it is futile to analyse central concepts of human spirit and agency without reference to the historical context from which the contemporary discussion emerges: 'Let us call this essential feature of agents the "significance feature". Then the crucial difference between men and machines is that the former have it while the latter lack it.'[101] The remarkable attainments and successes of natural science do not equip it with the resources to explain everything, We need not reject moral or aesthetic reflection or introspection because they cannot be reduced to physics. The physical description of the world ignores self-awareness: Know Thyself! This self-knowledge is as non-material individuals – the body is a necessary but not sufficient condition of self-awareness. How can we explore the mind except from within? It is through the arts that we can explore our self-awareness/consciousness. We are not merely creatures which can reason discursively about facts but are also self-conscious free agents who can apprehend values. The sublime, visceral might and yet delicious delicacy of genius, such as Milton or Bach, draws upon the most solemn and imaginative peregrinations of the human spirit. The violin concerto is just the sound waves generated by the friction of horsehair and catgut; the epic poem is just marks on the page. And yet the physical movements of the violinist or the printed signs can convey the thoughts and mood of a composer about an object of value (a person lost, a landscape loved) and awaken similar emotions or moods in the audience.

Charles Taylor observes that human beings are self-understanding creatures who exist in implicit frameworks. These frameworks are not explicit theories and are often not even recognized. Sometimes the contemporary framework is obscured by the experience of emancipation from some past framework; sometimes the framework consists of a

101 Taylor, *Human Agency and Language*, p. 197.

mixture of differing (even incompatible) inherited frameworks. Taylor thinks that contemporary culture is distinguished by a tension between the Enlightenment confidence in scientific reason and Romantic individualism and expressivism.

Taylor explores how Western societies developed through various frameworks, such as the honour code to Romantic expressivism. Such frameworks are cultural and linguistic. The world of an Englishman is not just radically different from that of a tribal South Asian, say. It is frequently unintelligible to a Frenchman, despite geographical, linguistic and historical affinities and kinship – because we are the products of different histories. The point should not be overstated, nor the absurd inference drawn that no genuine communication is possible; but naturalists tend to ignore such considerations altogether or dismiss them as insignificant, treating the mind as an abstract, naked instrument. There is an irreducibly imaginative component to our perception of the world. This is because we are agents, not merely spectators of the world. We necessarily perceive the world with an implicit imaginative framework. The real issue is the capacity to understand other minds. This means accepting both the irreducible reality of subjectivity and the capacity to engage with other minds: empathy or *Einfühlung*. Since the Romantic era, the most eminent European poet has doubtless been Shakespeare – not merely a poet in the technical sense, the master of English blank verse, but the single most potent creator of an imaginary universe, the poet who, for the great European nations and North America, most closely resembles Homer's impact in the ancient world, in the universal and archetypal legacy of Shakespeare's oeuvre. Throughout this work I will return to Shakespearean themes, not out of misplaced bardolatry, but in recognition of his ineluctable presence in the Western imaginary.

Verstehen is not an easy concept to understand. It means comprehension. The term goes back to Dilthey, who proclaimed that 'nature we explain, man we understand'. A widespread Anglo-Saxon paradigm of comprehension is that of possessing capacities, such as Ryle's celebrated tenet that manifest intelligent actions are not indications of mental events but rather constitute them.[102] John Searle's famous Chinese room argument is a powerful rebuttal of any simplistic identification of overt capacities with understanding. If a person wholly ignorant of Chinese is locked in a room and provided with Chinese characters and English instructions telling him what to do with the characters, which he follows to the letter, a Chinaman outside the room might think that the person within the room understands Chinese, which of course he does not. The ability to handle the characters correctly in this thought experiment has no relevance to whether he understands the language.[103] *Verstehen* must be more than correct overt function. This is obvious to anyone with a humanistic education but not at all obvious to many scientists or to those

102 Ryle, *The Concept of Mind*, pp. 26ff.
103 J. Searle, *Minds, Brains and Science: The 1984 Reith Lectures* (Harmondsworth: Penguin, 1984).

philosophers who pander to scientism. Consider the familiar problems of translation. Imagine trying to translate the English word 'whimsy' into contemporary German or Italian. Being 'whimsical' is part of the cultural imaginary of England: it is not that 'capriccioso' or 'seltsam' miss part of the resonance of the word 'whimsy', but that they are utterly inadequate for the task. To understand the word 'whimsy' is to appreciate a unique and distinctive dimension of English life and culture. Philosophers who find the *Verstehen* tradition attractive are usually disillusioned with the common tendency to assimilate psychological concepts to those of the natural sciences.

Collaboration, dialogue and exchange of ideas in a civilized society resist strict lawlike explanations. Whitehead maintained that the 'creation of the world of civilized order is the victory of persuasion over force'.[104] Knowledge of one's own inner states and those of others requires both historical memory and imaginative insight. Such knowledge is sui generis and cannot be assimilated to experimental methods or be available to computers, however sophisticated. That is why, as we shall see later in the chapter, Collingwood was correct to insist that art proper, as opposed to what he calls magical or amusement art, is a form of knowledge. And this is a knowledge evident not just in art but in rational activities relating to intention and agency such as historical criticism, historical research or legal reasoning. The psychological, the social and the historical present problems more akin to the interpretation of a text than experimentation in physics or chemistry.

Some philosophers of imagination, notably Bachelard, drive a wedge between the private and poetic imaginings and the objective rigour of science. This alternative is deeply unsatisfying. There is, as Basil Mitchell rightly argues, a *continuum* of rational disciplines from physics and chemistry through the biological sciences to the humanities and metaphysics. And it is clear that wonder can inspire the imagination both to operate creatively and to illuminate the structures of reality. There is evidence of an aboriginal power in images summoned by scientific or poetic genius. We might consider Einstein's image of a rider on a beam of light carrying a mirror and his development of relativity theory, or Kekulé's dream of the snake and his discovery of the benzene ring, or the chemist Mendeléev's resolving the problem of the periodic table through a dream of cards in a game of patience. Such examples of the role of creative imagination in the strict sense of ruminating on pregnant images in scientific discovery should discourage crude dichotomies, which are often lazily parasitic upon the nineteenth-century English coinage of 'science' as the distinct and superior domain of knowledge.

Yet the standard contrast between religion and science is usually attended by two misconceptions:

1. The first error consists in the conviction that scientific questions admit of a precise decision procedure whereas religious questions do

104 A. N. Whitehead, *Adventures of Ideas* (Cambridge: Cambridge University Press, 1933), p. 31.

not: scientific laws are certain, physical measurement is exact, and there is a clearly marked boundary between scientific and ordinary thought. The scientific inference to best explanation often requires imaginative judgements concerning background information or the selection of data. Furthermore, a botanist engaged in fieldwork employs his or her eyes to note colours, even if these are secondary qualities.[105]

2.   The second error consists in the conviction that science deals with literal truth, religion with myth and metaphor; like poetry, it is a matter of how one feels – it has nothing to do with truth.

Basil Mitchell observes:

To say that the human sciences and the humanities are inherently controversial is to recognize that, although a given position may in fact be rationally preferable to its rivals, this is rarely obvious . . . The issues in dispute are complex, highly ramified, and calling for trained judgement and sympathetic imagination. The resolution of any individual problem can rarely be achieved simply by inspecting the evidence provided by the present case. There will always be an immense background of theory, related to earlier observations, which cannot in practice be made wholly explicit, but which guides the thinking of the disputants.[106]

Mitchell is appealing to a notion of intuition in the sense of non-rigorous or informal reasoning. Personal judgement and imaginative assent form part of a theory of rationality between the extremes of an exclusively rule-based conception of reasoning and a fideism which surrenders the claim of rationality to the hard sciences.

The hermeneutical tradition is correct to emphasize that human beings are, in Charles Taylor's phrase, 'self-understanding creatures', but it pays too high a price by cutting us off from nature. The 'text' is divorced from the book of nature. In this sense the hermeneutics of Gadamer is as alienating as the positivism it wishes to oppose. The hermeneutical tradition is correct to emphasize the irreducibility of human self-understanding (*Verstehen*) to the methodology of the natural sciences. But it shuts down the metaphysical question just as effectively as positivism. I would prefer to locate these 'irreducibilities' within a metaphysical framework.

Mark Wynn, in his excellent book *Emotional Experience and Religious Understanding*, argues that affectively toned experience can involve something like a 'perception' of values. He draws on McDowell's critique of the attempt to view values as spread onto the world – especially McDowell's reflections upon disanalogies between secondary qualities

105 H. Jeffreys, *Scientific Inference* (Cambridge: Cambridge University Press, 1931), p. 183. I am very grateful to George Watson for pointing me to this work.
106 B. Mitchell, *Faith and Criticism* (Oxford: Clarendon Press, 1994), p. 25.

and values.[107] This view of nature as inherently devoid of value is itself a product of a certain period in Western thought. Primary qualities such as structure, size and shape are properties of the real, objective world, and colour or warmth belong to the subjective appropriation of the objective world. By way of analogy, beauty and goodness may be viewed as spread on the objective world of facts by the observer.

Wynn is quite properly raising the question of the relationship of the emotions to truth, and how imaginative insight into a dimension of reality may be occluded by a certain naturalistic view of experimental science. Yet Wynn is attaching himself to a dubious ally, since McDowell resists naturalism views through redefining 'reality'. McDowell is inspired by a neo-Kantian anti-realist desire to envisage the content of experience as conceptually suffused, whereas Wynn is concerned to argue for a more strident conception of the real, including a dimension, that of God, which utterly eludes our concepts, and, indeed, even our emotions and imaginations. McDowell's project only makes values more accessible at the cost of a metaphysical revisionism which Wynn cannot consistently accept. This is because McDowell's position depends upon the radical inseparability of concept and intuition, conceptual scheme and content. If the world depends upon us in such a radical way, our emotions must be part of what constitutes the world. The theist, like Wynn, believes that the world is dependent upon the radical and gracious love of God; however, he also thinks that the atheist could be correct, and that the world is devoid of inherent value. Thus some emotions for the theist, particularly self-giving love, can reflect reality in a profound way. Yet this is not because the world is of our making. On the contrary: it is the realization that the world is no *factum brutum* but gift. Thus Wynn and McDowell agree that emotions can play a cognitive role, but for such radically different reasons that Wynn's appeal to McDowell is ultimately unconvincing. The surface similarity masks radical divergence at depth.[108]

McDowell provides a good example of a certain Kantian view: the mind is an unavoidable component of the world. He sees his position as lying between a 'bald naturalism' which interprets human behaviour in terms of prediction, and 'rampant Platonism' which removes meaning, value and reason from nature. His Kantianism means distinguishing between the 'realm of law', i.e. the domain of natural science, and the 'space of reasons':

> In being initiated into a language, a human being is introduced into something that already embodies putatively rational linkages between concepts, putatively constitutive of the layout of the space of reasons, before she comes on the scene. This is a picture of initiation into the space of reasons as an already going concern; there is no problem about how something describable in those terms

---

107 M. Wynn, *Emotional Experience and Religious Understanding* (Cambridge: Cambridge University Press, 2005), ch. 1.
108 Thanks to Geoff Dumbreck for discussion of this.

could emancipate a human individual from a merely animal mode of living into being a fully-fledged subject, open to the world . . . A natural language . . . serves as a repository of tradition, a store of historically accumulated wisdom about what is a reason for what.[109]

Coleridge makes the same point, if more eloquently, when he observes that 'language is the armoury of the human mind; and at once contains the trophies of its past, and the weapons of its future conquests',[110] and like McDowell sees the 'advantages which language alone' presents to the instructor 'of impressing modes of intellectual energy so constantly . . . as to secure the formation of a second nature'.[111]

McDowell takes over Gadamer's distinction between an environment which is proper to animals, and a world of *Bildung* which is the context for human beings. But McDowell's dualism is not without its problems. John Haldane has remarked that the gap which McDowell proposes is both too great and unsustainable. If the difference between human and beast is *Bildung* via culture, where does the latter come from? If culture comes from nature, does this not raise certain questions about the specific and unique nature which was able to generate human beings? How can that which should be *explained* in causal terms give rise to that which is susceptible only to *understanding*? Language and its progeny in human thought and culture is a fact just as remarkable as the Cambrian explosion.

I argue for a much stronger view of objectivity and causality than an anti-realist like McDowell, while denying that objectivity and causality should be defined by the canons of methodological naturalism. Characteristically, the proponent of *Verstehen* will reply that the metaphysical questions presuppose an illicit assumption: that the mind is akin to a mirror of nature and that science is an accurate representation of the world's intrinsic nature. In fact, once we divest ourselves of this metaphor we can see that knowledge is much better understood in terms of a non-vicious circularity. Our attempts to explain or understand are always from within a particular lived context and certain ineluctable presuppositions. The Platonic theist will want to say that our assumed and discussed values may be wrong and that the deepest values – truth, beauty and goodness – are part of the fabric of the universe, and persist whether or not they are realized in particular human societies. Theism is not in competition with experimental science, but with the idea that empirical scientific method provides the only access to reality. The theist characteristically holds that the awareness of truth, beauty and goodness deserves due attention, and indeed the scientific project collapses when these components are rigidly discounted as non-scientific.

On the other hand, Dilthey's strategy is that of a cease-fire between *Geist* and *Natur*, or rather a peace in which the vanquished *Geist* is given comfortable terms of surrender. Dilthey himself regarded his project as

---

109 J. McDowell, *Mind and World* (Cambridge, Mass.: Harvard University Press, 1994), pp. 125, 126.
110 Coleridge, *Biographia Literaria*, vol. 2, pp. 30–1.
111 Ibid., p. 144.

empirical. He saw himself as an empiricist 'siding with Hume, J.S. Mill and the positivists against metaphysicians like Plato or Hegel'.[112] Richard Rorty is a particularly good instance of preaching Diltheyian hermeneutics while maintaining a particularly stark naturalism:

> Every speech, thought, theory, poem, composition and philosophy will turn out to be completely predictable in purely naturalistic terms. Some atoms-and-the-void account of micro-processes within individual human beings will permit the prediction of every sound or inscription which will ever be uttered. There are no ghosts.[113]

If Rorty is claiming that all thought is the product of physiological facts which will enable us to attain rigid and exhaustive prediction, he is open to the objection that this will eliminate the possibility of rational debate or truth. The theist who denies such a theory is subject to exactly the same mechanisms which have produced the ideas of the Rortian determinist. But the theist can retort that this destroys the idea of truth for the naturalist as much as for his or her opponent.

Verstehen and the closing of the book of nature

Darwin enabled modern secular culture to heave a great collective sigh of relief, by apparently providing a way to eliminate purpose, meaning and design as fundamental features of the world. Instead they become epiphenomena, explained incidentally by the operation of the non-teleological laws of physics on the materials of which we and our environments are all composed.[114]

There is a powerful link between imaginability and intelligibility. As a regulative principle we need to consider the world limpid and not utterly opaque if it is to be an arena within which we perceive certain truths. Otherwise 'knowledge' consists merely in manipulating the phenomena encountered. It is difficult for us to imagine a world which radically rebuffs our attempts to find order and meaning in it.[115] Such a world would be too outlandish. Yet how can hairless apes, whose emergence as intelligent and rational creatures is the accidental product of evolution, 'have access to universally valid methods of objective thought?'[116] Theories like Newton's theory of gravity or, a fortiori, Einstein's general theory of relativity describe the world with astonishing accuracy,

---

112 H. P. Rickman, *Wilhelm Dilthey: Pioneer of the Human Studies* (London: Elek, 1979), p. 21.
113 R. Rorty, *Philosophy and the Mirror of Nature* (Oxford: Blackwell, 1980), p. 387.
114 T. Nagel, *The Last Word* (New York: Oxford University Press, 1997), p. 131.
115 See E. Craig, 'Arithmetic and Fact', in *Essays in Analysis: Essays by Students of Casimir Lewy*, ed. I. Hacking (Cambridge: Cambridge University Press, 1985), pp. 89–112.
116 Nagel, *Mortal Questions*, p. 4.

employing highly complex mathematics. Are these mathematical theories, which enable a description of reality with such precision, mere
approximations which human beings project upon an essentially surd
universe? Or is it not more plausible to posit mathematical realism? This
can explain why the human mind can imagine and discover hidden
mathematical patterns and laws in the universe – because the universe
has an intelligible structure and the human mind has a capacity to reflect
this intelligible edifice.[117] The naturalist, by way of contrast, faces a
circulus vitiosus if positing a constructivist account of mathematical
entities: assuming minds are merely emergent properties of brains, the
laws of neurophysiology depend upon the highly sophisticated mathematics which presupposes brains.

This has implications not merely for the status of mathematics but
also for the mind. For it is the conscious mind that formulates the laws of
the universe in a Newton or an Einstein. On the materialistic hypothesis
the elementary particles of physics exhaust the ultimate constituents of
the universe. But if we have reasons for positing mathematical entities,
why should the mental not be admitted into the furniture of the
universe? After all, the matter that the common-sense, no-nonsense
materialist invokes looks increasingly puzzling (and immaterial!) once
science gets to the level of electrons, quarks and gluons and the solid
objects of the world evaporate into the paradoxical behaviour of
quantum components.

Rorty argues that philosophical or scientific objectivism is an ana-
chronistic product of theism, the view that the world is a divine artefact,
'the work of someone who has something in mind, who Himself spoke
some language in which He described his project'.[118] Furthermore, only
'if we have in mind . . . some picture of the universe as either itself a
person or as created by a person, can we make any sense of the idea that
the world has an intrinsic nature'.[119] Many prominent twentieth-century
thinkers reflected upon the apparently Faustian pact of the modern mind
– the gain in the material power of science but the loss of a spiritual
dimension in the wake of the French Revolution, Darwin, etc. The big
shift in the understanding of nature is away from a concept of nature as
concealing or pointing to some reality other than itself. The popularity of
the cosmological and teleological arguments for the existence of God
prior to David Hume's *Dialogues* is a witness to this.

Bertrand Russell, in his essay 'The Free Man's Worship', presents the
world as indifferent to human interests and ideals, and the appropriate
human response as being to maintain one's sense of integrity and
independence before this alien universe.[120] One can clearly see the
lineage between Hume's *Dialogues Concerning Natural Religion* and
Russell. Yet ironically, such a heroic defiance, the steely-eyed resignation

---

117 R. Penrose, *The Road to Reality* (London: Jonathan Cape, 2004), pp. 7–23.
118 R. Rorty, 'The Contingency of Language', *London Review of Books*, 17 April 1986, p. 6.
119 Ibid.
120 B. Russell, 'The Free Man's Workshop', in *A Free Man's Workshop and other Essays*
     (London: Unwin, 1976), p. 18: 'Brief and powerless is Man's Life, on him and all his race
     the slow, sure doom falls pitiless and dark.'

Russell seems to advocate, seems to precipitate a striking divorce between mankind and the universe which has produced intelligent persons. The attempt to discover meaning – and indeed self-conscious reflection of the kind which is capable of heroic defiance like that of Russell – may be an index of the world's significance. Humankind is not a mere spectator: the *real* world includes reflective human beings, and presumably the latter is a key to the meaning of the former.[121] Simon Conway Morris argues on the basis of evolutionary palaeobiology for the 'inevitability' of human life on this planet and the extreme unlikelihood of anything akin to it existing or arising in the rest of the universe.[122] He argues, using varied evidence from distinct branches of biology, that the various evolutionary patterns have a tendency to *converge* and that human beings are not accidents. If the clock were to be put back, a planet like ours would again produce intelligence like ours. This position is clearly counter to the views of a palaeontologist like Stephen J. Gould who sees life as a gigantic accident – or even the fervent nihilism of Richard Dawkins from the perspective of theoretical biology, with his celebrated view of evolution as a 'blind watchmaker' fumbling in the dark.[123] As Wordsworth exclaims in the '1814 Preface' to *The Excursion*:

How exquisitely the individual Mind
(And the progressive powers perhaps no less
Of the whole species) to the external World
Is fitted: – and how exquisitely too – . . .
The external world is fitted to the mind.[124]

If this universe is only 10 billion years old and in a state of entropy, it is puzzling that it can generate eternal and immutable laws at all, and even more puzzling that that human beings, as products of evolution, aspire to know more than mere approximations of truth but abiding and universal principles. Conway Morris' theory of convergence is not so far removed Plato's and Parmenides' momentous distinction between Being and Becoming and reveals a fundamental optimism about both the mind of mankind and the ultimate structure of the universe. William James says exactly this in *The Will to Believe*:

Is it not sheer dogmatic folly to say that our inner interests can have no real connection with the forces that the hidden world may contain? . . . Take science itself! Without an imperious inner demand on our part for ideal logical harmonies, we should never have attained to proving that such harmonies lie hidden between all the chinks and interstices of the crude natural world. Hardly a law has

---

121 H. H. Farmer, *God and Men* (London: Nisbet and Co., 1948), p. 37.
122 S. C. Morris, *Life's Solution: Inevitable Humans in a Lonely Universe* (Cambridge: Cambridge University Press, 2003), p. 15.
123 S. J. Gould, *Wonderful Life: The Burgess Shale and the Nature of History* (London: Vintage, 2000); R. Dawkins, *The Blind Watchmaker* (London: Penguin, 2000). I am grateful to Chloë Cyrus Kent for this point.
124 William Wordsworth, *Complete Poetical Works*, ed. E. de Selincourt (Oxford: Clarendon Press, 1936), p. 590.

been established in science, hardly a fact ascertained, which was not first sought after, often with sweat and blood, to gratify an inner need.[125]

James, perhaps curiously for a 'pragmatist', is insisting that we must assume a certain transparency of reality in order for knowledge to be intelligible as genuine *comprehension* and not mere manipulation. We must assume that harmonies hidden behind the 'chinks and interstices' can be imagined, that our powers and the inmost nature of reality are congenial. Otherwise, the 'imperious inner demand' could not be satisfied. That is to say that our subjectivity is key to unlocking an otherwise impenetrable habitat.[126]

James draws upon the Romantic vision of imagination rooted in the view of subjectivity which goes back to Augustine, for whom God is 'interior intimo meo et superior summo meo',[127] and to Plotinus, for whom 'we are each of us the intelligible world'[128] and hence can mirror the Divine. Here we have the emphatically Platonic sense of the soul's natural destiny as the return to its immaterial home. Coleridge liked to quote the line from Plotinus, 'Never could the eye have beheld the sun, had not its own essence been soliform'[129]: the human soul must constitute a point of contact with the Divine, and it is the immanence of the transcendent Divine source in the soul which becomes supremely manifest in genius, whether scientific or literary.

Fantasy, suffering and inspiration

'Phantasy' or 'fantasy' has its etymological roots in φαίνεσθαι (to show or appear) and is cognate with φαινόμενον (phenomenon). Plato's cave (εἰκᾰσία) is used to express bondage to illusion or fantasy. But creativity has a negative side – the unparalleled power of images in contemporary society through technology like television and the internet. Roger Scruton writes:

> The ennobling power of the imagination lies in this: that it re-orders the world, and re-orders our feelings in response to it. Fantasy, by contrast, is frequently degrading . . . Where imagination offers glimpses of the sacred, fantasy offers sacrilege and profanation.[130]

Selfishness, anxiety, cruelty, fanaticism and superstition are products of fantasy. In fantasy we collude with the 'facts' of a fallen world. Fantasy creates a substitute domain for the empirical world in which bad desires and passions can be gratified, and is frequently marked by a poverty of

125 James, *The Will to Believe.*, p. 55.
126 We shall omit consideration of whether quantum physics provides a rebuttal of this 'imperious inner demand'.
127 Augustine, *Confessions* III.6.11.
128 Plotinus, *Enneads* III.4.3.22.
129 Coleridge, *Biographia Literaria*, vol. 1, p. 115.
130 R. Scruton, *An Intelligent Person's Guide to Modern Culture* (London: Duckworth, 1998), p. 55.

imaginative possibilities. Various forms of psychological disorders can be viewed as bondage to false images of self and others. Imagination is, in contrast, a source of real freedom through the purification and re-channelling of desire, or what Murdoch terms 'a distinction between egoistic *fantasy* and liberated truth-seeking creative *imagination*'.[131] The latter requires the existence of beauty for its inspiration. For the Christian, and *ceteris paribus* the Platonist, that beauty only exists properly in God.

Serious art has a metaphysical dimension. It is on the basis of this high view of art that Collingwood distinguishes art from craft. Collingwood is determined to distinguish between what counts as art per se and what does not, and then to distinguish between good and bad art. This is very much the Ruskinian legacy in Collingwood: to separate genuine art from that which is bogus, and great art from the rest. The defining characteristic of art is inextricably normative:

> What the artist is trying to do is to express a given emotion. To express it and to express it well, are the same thing. To express it badly is not one way of expressing it . . . it is failing to express it. A bad work of art is an activity in which the agent tries to express a given emotion, but fails. This is the difference between bad art and art falsely so called . . . In art falsely so called there is no attempt at expression; there is only an attempt (whether successful or not) to do something else.[132]

Bad art is the denial or 'repression' of feelings: the 'corruption of consciousness'. Here Collingwood refers to Freud's language of repression and projection as the disowning of aspects of one's conscious experience and attributing them to other agents. He links this to Spinoza's ideal of self-mastery through transforming passive into active emotions in his *Ethics*. It was Spinoza who best delineated 'the conception of the truthful consciousness and its importance as a foundation for a healthy mental life'.[133] For:

> Art is not a luxury, and bad art is not a thing we can afford to tolerate. To know ourselves is the foundation of all life that develops beyond the mere psychical level of experience . . . Every utterance and every gesture that each one of us makes is a work of art. It is important to each one of us that in making them, however much he deceives others, he should not deceive himself. If he deceives himself in this matter, he has sown in himself a seed which, unless he roots it up again, may grow into any kind of wickedness, any kind of mental disease, any kind of stupidity and folly and insanity. Bad art, the corrupt consciousness, is the true *radix malorum*.[134]

131 I. Murdoch, *Metaphysics as a Guide to Morals* (London: Penguin, 1993), p. 321.
132 Collingwood, *The Principles of Art*, p. 282.
133 Ibid., p. 219.
134 Ibid., pp. 284–5.

This theory of art is linked to Collingwood's theory of 'the decay of our civilisation' and his view that most of what passes for art in a decadent civilization is mere amusement.[135] Yet it is also true that Coleridge and Collingwood are quite adamant that art does far more than merely *express* subjective emotions. This becomes clear in Coleridge's view of the imagination as 'a repetition in the finite mind of the eternal act of creation in the infinite I AM' and hence as imitating the divine mimesis.[136] It is also clear in Collingwood, with the closing words of *The Principles of Art* in his discussion of Eliot's *The Waste Land*, a passage of Ruskinian solemnity and hierophantic tone:

> The artist must prophesy not in the sense that he foretells things to come, but in the sense that he tells his audience, at risk of their displeasure, the secrets of their own hearts. His business as an artist is to speak out, to make a clean breast. But what he has to utter is not, as the individualistic theory of art would have us think, his own secrets. As spokesman of his community, the secrets he must utter are theirs. The reason why they need him is that no community knows its own heart; and by failing in this knowledge a community altogether deceives itself on the one subject concerning which ignorance means death. For the evils which come from that ignorance the poet as prophet suggests no remedy, because he has already given one. The remedy is the poem itself. Art is the community's medicine for the worst disease of mind, the corruption of consciousness.[137]

It is also clear from this passage that Collingwood's expressivism entails neither non-cognitivism nor individualism in aesthetics. Art provides knowledge of the most vital kind: self-knowledge. The artist tells his audience 'the secrets of their own hearts'. And this knowledge is the self-knowledge of the community. To understand an artwork on this model is to share a vision and to be transformed by it. As Coleridge insisted: 'The postulate of philosophy and at the same time the test of philosophic capacity, is no other than the heaven-descended KNOW THYSELF!'[138] Because art is not just a mirror of the mind, a *speculum mentis*, but of the soul, a *speculum animae*, the imagination can be a vehicle of self-transcendence.

Pope's that which was 'oft thought but ne'er so well expressed' does not do justice to this dimension. Poetry can make one reconsider the world – it can have a transforming effect. Consider the Ancient Mariner. His journey transformed his perception of reality – that which he sees upon his return he sees anew. And through the poem we are supposed to share that renewed vision. Wordsworth's 'Tintern Abbey' articulates this explicitly:

---

135 Ibid., p. 332.
136 Coleridge, *Biographia Literaria*, vol. I, p. 304.
137 Collingwood, *The Principles of Art*, p. 336.
138 Coleridge, *Biographia Literaria*, vol. I, p. 252.

For I have learned
To look on nature, not as in the hour
Of thoughtless youth; but hearing oftentimes
The still, sad music of humanity,
Nor harsh nor grating, though of ample power
To chasten and subdue.[139]

The poet interprets his experience as having a transforming effect upon his vision of reality.

Richard Dawkins begins *Climbing Mount Improbable* by recounting an anecdote concerning a literary lecture on figs, apparently an elegant and recondite performance, describing the symbolism and figurative meaning of figs: all of which provoked him to reflect upon the superiority of the biological, the 'true' story of the fig, as opposed to such fanciful whimsies.[140] One of the important contributions of reflection upon the work of imagination rests upon the fact of experience 'from within', rather than the universal and abstract perspective of natural science, and the ineluctably emotional and dramatic nature of this lived experience. And of course art and music are among the most powerful expressions of the experience of the *Lebenswelt*. Moreover, the rich content of self-awareness emerges in the spiritual drama of human life: the most potent expression of this drama is the imagination of the poet. Poetry is more primordial than science because it is the expression of nature's vision of itself at its highest level. It is prior not merely in time, but as Vico and Hamann insisted, because of the abysmal ground of the longings of the human heart. The greatest poets explore and make articulate through images and analogies our often mute intimations of invisible reality, and my project is inextricably linked to this poetic and philosophical imagination. In this capacity the poets and religious seers are momentous vehicles of revelation. Human beings are different from other species because in human beings nature becomes self-conscious and aware that it exists. The reality of human self-consciousness is nature seeing and articulating itself.

In the previous chapter we saw how, for Coleridge, imagination is both *lower* (more primordial) and *higher* than discursive intelligence. It is that dimension of the mind that is linked to the roots of our personal being and points to communion with the great 'I AM THAT I AM' of Exodus 3.14. The creativity and freedom that is definitive for human life points to the ultimate question, which is why is there something rather than nothing: God's own self-diffusive, creative love. Imagination, I argue, is the index of humanity made in the image of God. Better to think of human consciousness as inherently creative processing of the environment. Imagination is the mind's *freedom* from stimulus; this freedom is linked to a vocation for a soul, and the calling of the soul is linked to its image. This paradox also applies, I argue, more controversially, to the aesthetic and the religious spheres.

139 Wordsworth, 'Lines Composed a Few Miles above Tintern Abbey', ll. 88–93.
140 R. Dawkins, *Climbing Mount Improbable* (London: Penguin, 1996), p. 1.

Imagination is the index of our amphibious nature. We are animals, and our bodies are very important components in our minds – hence even the power of the image of the mind is located *in* the body. Yet the most somatic images can be a sign of the human capacity for transcendence. The capacity for transcendence is linked to an ontology of the 'image' or 'icon' in which the sensible cosmos is viewed as a *likeness* of the intelligible reality which is its source. The imagination itself is an instance of that force of the Divine within humanity, awoken by heavenly *eros*, which arouses the longing to return to the divine origin:

> If I am right, thou shouldst no more wonder at thy ascent than at a stream falling from a mountain height to the foot; it would be a wonder in thee if, freed from hindrance, thou hadst remained below, as on earth would be stillness in living flame.[141]

This is the Neoplatonic tenet that when the soul is liberated from evil it ascends quite naturally to the Good: *omnium in deum tendunt et recurrunt.* This metaphor of the natural place of the soul in God or its gravitation towards the One is employed by Christian theologians of Neoplatonic provenance such as Eriugena and Eckhart.[142] The doctrine of indwelling divine power was not a gloomy determinism. It was precisely on account of this conviction of the immanence of the divine in the human soul that the Florentine Platonists believed that the *artes liberales* are properly so called because they *free* and thereby enlarge the mind through the awakening and inspiring light of divine presence.

141 Dante, *Paradiso* I, 136–41, in *Dante: The Divine Comedy*, tr. J. D. Sinclair (Oxford: Oxford University Press, 1939).
142 W. Beierwaltes, *Platonismus und Idealismus* (Frankfurt: Klostermann, 1972), p. 63.

3

The Experience of God: Poetry, Enchantment and the Mood of Ecstatic Imagination

It is a fact of human nature, that men can live and die by the help of a sort of faith that goes without a single dogma or definition. The bare assurance that this natural order is not ultimate but a mere sign or vision, the external staging of a many-storied universe, in which spiritual forces have the last word and are eternal, this bare assurance is to such men enough to make life seem worth living in spite of every contrary presumption suggested by its circumstances on the natural plane.[1]

In this chapter I wish to focus upon the work of two very distinguished contemporary philosophers who have applied themselves to the question of religious experience. William Alston has produced a very powerful critique of familiar objections to religious experience which condemn such experience for features it fails to share with sense experience (the double standard) or insist unreasonably that religious experience should embody the same features as a sense experience (epistemological imperialism). But he argues for the parity of what he calls 'Christian mystical experience' with sensory experience. This raises the obvious objection that he underestimates the limitations of human finite experience of the Divine and the manifold possibilities for delusion. Denys Turner goes to the other extreme in denying the validity of religious experience at all. The first philosopher overemphasizes the transcendence of the Divine, so that the experience of God is reduced to the experience of divine absence. The second philosopher stresses the immanence of the Divine to the virtual exclusion of its transcendence. It seems to me that the truth lies between these two extremes. I argue that both fail to do justice to the Platonic conviction that the mind must ascend to God 'through a glass darkly'. I wish to present as an alternative the Romantic model. Wordsworth defines imagination as 'Reason in its most exalted *mood*'. The context of this definition shows that Wordsworth is linking imagination with a form of religious experience:

I was only then
Contented when with bliss ineffable
I felt the sentiment of Being spread
O'er all that moves and all that seemeth still
O'er all, that, lost beyond the reach of thought

1 W. James, *The Will to Believe* (New York: Dover Books, 1956), pp. 56–7.

79

And human knowledge, to the human eye
Invisible, yet liveth to the heart,
O'er all that leaps, and runs, and shouts, and sings,
Or beats the gladsome air, o'er all that glides
Beneath the wave, yea, in the wave itself
And mighty depth of waters. Wonder not
If such my transports were; for in all things
I saw one life, and felt that it was joy.
One song they sang, and it was audible,
Most audible then when the fleshly ear,
O'ercome by grosser prelude of that strain,
Forgot its functions, and slept undisturbed.[2]

The mood of joy is the feeling of the 'sentiment of Being': the perception of nature as a sacrament of the creative divine mind. Coleridge's finest poetry was written when he was very young, and he notes:

But now afflictions bow me down to earth:
Nor care I that they rob me of my mirth;
　　　But oh! each visitation
Suspends what nature gave me at my birth,
　　　My shaping spirit of Imagination.[3]

Wordsworth's *Prelude* is addressed to a large degree to his 'Dearest Friend' Coleridge, and in this extraordinary poem he produces a definition of the imagination as that 'clearest insight' and 'amplitude of mind' which is 'Reason in her most exalted mood'. Wordsworth's linking of imagination to religious experience flourished in the context of his symbiotic friendship with Coleridge, as the latter acknowledges:

It was the union of deep feeling with profound thought; the fine balance of truth in observing with the imaginative faculty in modifying the objects observed; and above all the original gift of spreading the tone, the *atmosphere*, and with it the depth and height of the ideal world around forms, incidents and situations, of which, for the common view, custom had bedimmed all the lustre, had dried up the sparkle and the dew drops.[4]

Since Nature expresses the *art* of the creator, the artistic sensibility can be inspired by contact with nature, and aroused to a transcendental mood which grasps the unity which precedes and transcends the conceptual structures of the world of the primary imagination. Hence Coleridge's description of

balancing & reconciling of opposite or discordant qualities . . . the sense of novelty & freshness with old or customary Objects, a more than usual State of Emotion with more than usual Order, Self-

2　William Wordsworth, *The Prelude*, II, 418–34.
3　S. T. Coleridge, 'Dejection: An Ode', VI. 82–6, *Poems*, p. 282.
4　S. T. Coleridge, *Biographia Literaria*, vol. 1, ed. J. Engell and W. J. Bate (Princeton, NJ: Princeton University Press, 1983), p. 80.

possession & Judgment with Enthusiasm and vehement Feeling . . . the sense of musical delight with the power . . . to reduce multitude into Unity or Effect, or by means of Passion to modify a series of Thoughts by some one predominant Thought or Feeling.[5]

Here we have the depiction of conscious states of awareness with soteriological significance. Within the Indic tradition in the *bhagavadgita* we have the epiphany of Krishna to Arjuna on the battlefield in his 'supreme divine form'.

And Arjuna saw in that form countless visions of wonder . . . If the light of a thousand suns suddenly arose in the sky, that splendour might be compared to the radiance of the Supreme Spirit. And Arjuna saw in that radiance the whole universe in its variety, standing in a vast unity in the body of the God of gods. Trembling with awe and wonder, Arjuna bowed his head, and joining his hands in adoration he thus spoke to his God . . . I see the splendour of an infinite beauty which illumines the whole universe. It is thee! with thy crown and sceptre and circle. How difficult thou art to see! But I see thee: as fire, as the sun, blinding, incomprehensible.[6]

This is greatly akin to Rudolf Otto's account of 'the Holy', experienced as *mysterium tremendum et fascinans*. The Holy is constituted by an inscrutable otherness; it ignites a sense of awe, even fear and self-disgust, and it enthrals through the love which it excites.

One of the great expressions of Plato's religious imagination is the *Phaedrus*. Beauty can awaken the soul to its true destiny because of its intense experiential power. Compared with beauty, justice is too abstract and dull to excite – it lacks the gripping, luminous immediacy of beauty. Plato employs the language of awe to express a sense of holiness – itself rather similar to that of Rudolf Otto:

Few indeed are left that can still remember much: but when these discern some likeness of the things yonder, they are amazed, and no longer masters of themselves, and know not what is come upon them by reason of their perception being dim.[7]

That is to say, 'they don't understand their experience' (τὸ πάθος ἀγνοοῦσι). Perhaps Plato is merely employing the conventional language of the mysteries, and we should not readily assume that he is referring to actual religious experiences. However, the Platonic tradition took up this experiential component in Plato. Émile Bréhier, in his classic work *La Philosophie de Plotin*, states: 'C'est trop peu de dire que Plotin a le sentiment du monde intelligible: c'est plutot chez lui sensation.'[8] The outstanding Cambridge Platonist John Smith (1618–1652), a contempor-

---

5 See S. T. Coleridge, *Lectures 1808–1819: On Literature*, vol. 1, ed. R. A. Foakes (Princeton, NJ: Princeton University Press, 1987), pp. 245, 241.
6 *The Bhagavad Gita*, XI, 10–17, tr. Juan Mascaró (London: Penguin, 2003), pp. 53–4.
7 Plato, *Phaedrus* 250b, tr. R. Hackforth (Cambridge: Cambridge University Press, 1952), p. 93.
8 É. Bréhier, *La Philosophie de Plotin* (Paris: Vrin, 1961), p. xii.

ary of Cudworth, shares this sentiment: 'That mind which is not touched by an inward sense of Divine Wisdom, cannot estimate the true worth of it'.[9] Smith refers explicitly to Plato's *Phaedrus* 316 and the Platonic preference for 'Impressions of truth which are made upon the men's Souls above all outward Writings, which he therefore compares to dead pictures'. Smith specifies 'Divinity' as a 'Divine Life' rather than a 'Divine science; it being something to be understood by a Spiritual Sensation, then by any Verbal description . . . as the Greek Philosopher hath well observed.'[10]

John Stewart writes:

> The essential charm of all Poetry for the sake of which in the last resort it exists, lies in its power of inducing, satisfying, and regulating what may be called Transcendental Feeling, especially that form of Transcendental Feeling which manifests itself as a solemn sense of Timeless Being – of 'That which was, and is, and ever shall be' overshadowing us with its presence.[11]

This feeling can be induced by natural beauty or sublimity. One might think of the mountains in Wordsworth's *Prelude:*

> Of that imaginative impulse sent
> From these majestic floods – these shining cliffs
> The untransmuted shapes of many worlds,
> Cerulian ether's pure inhabitants,
> These forests unapproachable by death,
> That shall endure as long as man endures[12]

William James reflected upon the 'gleaming moments' of Wordsworth. James was influenced by the Romantics in his critique of the British empiricist conception of 'experience', which he believed was not adequately radical. The 'will to believe' is part not of a Pascalian wager, but of theory about the disclosure of reality. For in classical empiricism one element is excluded: the spiritual side of human experience. And yet as philosophers, James thinks, we should take such spiritual experience seriously as revealing truths about both human nature and the world. With an impoverished concept of experience, one will produce an inadequate conception of reality. Yet James has a particular interest in mystical experiences, which he defines as:

1. ineffable, i.e. unspeakable.
2. noetic: these experiences seem to constitute real and new insight.
3. transient: they cannot be maintained for long periods.
4. passive: the experient has the sense of being in the presence of a superior and powerful reality.[13]

---

9 J. Smith, *Select Discourses*, p. 377.
10 Ibid., p. 2.
11 J. A. Stewart, *The Myths of Plato* (London: Centaur, 1960), p. 46.
12 Wordsworth, *The Prelude*, VI, 462–7.
13 W. James, *Varieties of Religious Experience* (Harmondsworth: Penguin, 1985), pp. 380–1.

In an early poem, 'The Eolian Harp', Coleridge exclaims:

> And what if all of animated nature
> Be but organic Harps diversely framed,
> That tremble into thought, as o'er them sweeps
> Plastic and vast, one intellectual Breeze,
> At once the Soul of each, and God of all.[14]

The Aeolian harp is the harp of Orpheus, which was played on the wind after his death.[15] It was a fashionable piece of garden furniture in the eighteenth century, an instrument which produces notes when the wind blows upon it. As such, it is a striking image of the creative, semi-conscious aspect of the mind. Wordsworth says in *The Prelude*:

> The mind of man is fram'd even like the breath
> And harmony of music. There is a dark
> Invisible workmanship that reconciles
> Discordant elements, and makes them move
> In one society.[16]

Since nature gives voice to the harmony of the creator, humans will be transformed through attunement with the 'intellectual breeze' of God. The attunement of the soul is integration of thought and sensibility, which is rooted in the heart. Cordial attunement, with its roots in the Augustinian mystical tradition, is very much the object of Wordsworth when he refers to

> that blessed mood,
> In which the burthen of the mystery,
> In which the heavy and the weary weight
> Of all this unintelligible world
> Is Lighten'd.[17]

For Coleridge, engagement with the ideal world evokes the solemn mood of wonder of having been in the presence of eternity:

> The Poet is not only the man made to solve the riddle of the Universe, but he is also the man who feels where it is not solved and which continually awakens his feelings being of the same feeling. What is old and worn out, not in itself, but from the dimness of the intellectual eye brought on by worldly passions he makes new: he pours upon it the dew that glistens and blows round us the breeze which cooled us in childhood.[18]

14 S. T. Coleridge, 'The Eolian Harp', ll. 44–8, *Poems*, p. 53.
15 Coleridge, *Biographia Literaria*, vol. 1, p. 117.
16 Wordsworth, *The Prelude*, I, 351–5.
17 William Wordsworth, 'Lines Composed a Few Miles above Tintern Abbey', ll. 37–41.
18 Coleridge, *Lectures 1808–1819*, vol. I, p. 327.

The incommensurability thesis

Denys Turner has produced a superbly learned and pungently polemical theory about religious experience. Not least on account of this, I wish to consider Turner's central claim or what we might call the 'incommensurability thesis' about 'religious experience'. I do not wish to, and indeed cannot, consider this claim from the perspective of the medieval historian. I wish to consider the incommensurability thesis as a position in the philosophy of religion and contemporary theology. Turner presents his work as 'philosophical history of some theological metaphors'. However, I think that 'theological history of philosophical metaphors' is more accurate: he concentrates on those of interiority, ascent, light–darkness and of 'oneness with God'.[19] His works, *The Darkness of God: Negativity in Christian Mysticism* and *Faith, Reason and the Existence of God*, have provoked much discussion. Tied to Turner's incommensurability thesis is the deeply postmodern fascination with figurative language: '*metaphors* of negativity' which are 'interpenetrated by a high Neoplatonic *dialectics* of negativity'[20]. These symbols are temporal and spatial, but refer to that highest reality which lies beyond space and time. The imaginative form in which we conceive such transcendent truths must have a dynamic and substantial relation to the spiritual truths they are expressing, but they are clearly very unlike phenomenal facts of the scientific or everyday kind.

Medieval mysticism is more concerned with the incommensurability of God than with human experiences. According to Turner, rather than being part of a perennial experience of the presence or absence of the Divine, that mysticism should be understood as the opposition to any appeal to 'religious experience' on the basis of divine transcendence, the God who is beyond both affirmation and denial. Turner distinguishes between the 'first-order language' of the experience of negativity and the 'second-order language' of the negativity of experience. The real incommensurability of God is revealed by the second-order language, in which 'the darkness of the apophatic is glimpsed'[21] and God is seen as beyond both the affirmations and denials of first-order language.

Turner's thesis is that the medieval mystics are properly understood as critics of 'mysticism', where mysticism is defined as the cultivation of 'a certain kind of experience'.[22] Just as much as Nicholas Lash in his classic work *Easter in Ordinary*, Turner wishes to criticize the fascination with extraordinary experiences. The great mystics were not pointing to ecstatic experiences beyond an interior spiritual perception and apprehension of the divine essence, but were offering a critique of just such an enterprise. The search for such experiences is a delusion, since it assumes that one can go beyond language and matter – beyond, that is, the

---

19 D. Turner, *The Darkness of God: Negativity in Christian Mysticism* (Cambridge: Cambridge University Press, 1995), p. 1.
20 Ibid., p. 7.
21 Ibid., p. 33.
22 Ibid., p. 4.

created realm. This pursuit of experience is founded upon the fallacy of assuming commensurability between God and beings.

The notion of mystical 'experience' as special or ecstatic experiences is due to the distinctively 'modern' mentality which, Turner claims in a most memorable phrase, 'abhors the experiential vacuum of the apophatic'.[23] 'Experientialism' for Turner is the 'positivism' of Christian spirituality. It is the 'displacement of a sense of the negativity of all religious experience with the pursuit of achieving *negative experiences*. Rather than the classical medieval *absence* of experience, modern nineteenth century "positivism" replaced this with an interior *experience* of absence'.[24] In *Faith, Reason and the Existence of God*, Turner states:

> The onto-theologian, therefore, in making Being into God, makes Being, and so God, into *a* being, and into the supreme object of metaphysics, and so on, the 'Aristotelian' conception of metaphysics, into a sort of all-embracing quasi-substance. And this is aptly named onto-theology because it both makes 'Being' into God and, thereby, reduces God to *a* being.[25]

In other words, since the natural theologian believes that God's existence is demonstrable by reason alone, and thus that there must be some sort of 'ontological continuity' between man and God, there must be some common conception of 'Being' that we share with God.

Fortunately, according to Turner, Thomas Aquinas can avoid the stigma of 'onto-theology' in that he holds that such reason-based 'proofs' of God's existence can only operate 'within and as presupposing the context of faith'.[26] Thomas clearly recognizes the limits of man's knowledge, that is, how much he cannot know. Turner presents the position of St Thomas as follows:

> Thomas's severe apophaticism and his equally apparent confidence in the theological capacity of reason to know God is reconciled in his view of rational proof as demonstrating, precisely, the existence of an unknowable mystery of creation . . . for the 'five ways' are intended to show both that we can speak truly of God and that all such talk falls radically short of him.[27]

We can observe God's effects in the world, through 'design', beauty, change, motion, and so on. This means that we can *know* that he exists, but at the same time, we must always be aware of our position as creatures, for as creatures, the divine mystery of Trinity and Incarnation, that is, of God, will elude us. Turner brings Thomas into proximity with Pseudo-Dionysius's explication of the names of God in *The Divine Names*, and his belief that humankind *must* talk about God; yet even this

---

23 Ibid., p. 259.
24 Ibid., p. 7.
25 D. Turner, *Faith, Reason and the Existence of God* (Cambridge: Cambridge University Press, 2004), p. 28.
26 Ibid., p. 14.
27 Ibid., p. 48.

ultimately brings out the paradox that in this speaking there can be no 'referring' to God in any positive sense – not even negation. Neither affirmation nor negation ultimately apply to him:

> As the mind ascends through the hierarchy of language, it moves therefore, from that which is most distinct from God, to that which is progressively less obviously so, from the more 'unlike' to the more 'like' . . . But the progression by which we eliminate what God can be compared with must also be the progressive elimination of everything with which God can be contrasted . . . Therefore, as comparisons fall away, so must contrasts . . . Hence, as we move from complexity to simplicity, from the multiplicity of creatures to the oneness of their cause, from differentiation to lack of differentiation, we must encounter, and then transcend the last differentiation of all: *the difference itself between similarity and difference.*[28]

This is why one ends up 'talking' about God in paradox, as language must ultimately break down when 'speaking' of him. Thus, he is neither 'light' nor 'dark', but, rather, 'brilliant darkness', for neither he, nor the degree of his transcendence, can be captured by language; ultimately, he cannot be conceptualized by humanity:

> In the *Divine Names* I have shown the sense in which God is described as good, existent, life . . . and whatever other things pertain to the conceptual names for God . . . [But] The fact is that the more we take flight upward, the more our words are confined to the ideas we are capable of forming; so that now as we plunge into that darkness which is beyond intellect, we shall find ourselves not simply running short of words but actually speechless and unknowing . . . since it will finally be at one with him who is indescribable.[29]

It seems, therefore, that in terms of natural theology and negative theology, although at a 'lower level' of understanding, one may see the world as indicating, and thus establishing, the existence of God. This is ultimately a matter of faith, which is why there is no need for real conflict between natural theology and faith either, as, indeed, faith seems to imply that we are allowed some access to God through reason, because it is, after all, believed to be God-given, and can 'talk' about God to this extent. In order to gain a deeper understanding of God, or at least of what the idea of God means, humanity must recognize that negative theology, necessarily 'ending' in paradox, is the only answer, as we cannot even understand the very infinity with which God transcends us; and, if we cannot even know how different we are from God, we certainly cannot know God. Theology boils down to the old question 'Why is there something rather than nothing?' Our awareness of contingency seems to contrast with, even depend upon, the intuition of necessary being.

---

28 Turner, *Darkness*, pp. 44–5.
29 Pseudo-Dionysius, *The Mystical Theology*, 1033b–c; *The Complete Works*, tr. C. Luibheid (New York: Paulist Press, 1987), p. 139.

Radical apophaticism?

The stark apophaticism of Turner's theology leads to some very counter-intuitive readings of the history of thought. It is particularly puzzling when Turner writes the following about the speculative Dominican, Eckhart:

> It is, then, very far from being an implication of Eckhart's doctrine of the divine element in the soul that the mystic is required to choose between that divine element and the created human. Indeed, the implication of Eckhart's doctrine as a whole is the reverse: that a spirituality or mysticism constructed upon the necessity of any such choice, whether between spirit and flesh, body and soul, interiority and exteriority, above all between God and creation, is a symptom not of the absoluteness of the claims of the divine over/against the human, but of a sin-induced false consciousness which is unable to see the divine *except* as over/against the human.[30]

This might make sense in a Spinozistic metaphysics, where mind and matter are properties of a basic substance which is itself neither. A dual-aspect theorist like Spinoza can remain neutral between body and soul, exteriority or interiority, but this cannot be true of a Platonist. Indeed, Eckhart privileges the immaterial. He says, for example, that 'aliquid est liberum, quia immune a materia',[31] which is precisely what Plotinus says: 'The immaterial is free'.[32]

The unity of the universe for Eckhart cannot be based upon the contiguity of extended items. A non-material principle of unity must be immaterially present in material objects and constitute the unifying power of the whole. The universe is thus an image of a transcendent, immaterial unity. Hume claims in his *Treatise* that the uniting principle among our internal perceptions is as unintelligible as that among external objects,[33] whereas the Platonist sees images of the Divine Spirit in nature and in souls leading to that perfection which is transcendent simplicity and the source of the many. The idea that God is radically 'other' in Eckhart depends upon the view that a spiritual God is not determined in the manner of all material objects. Without material limits, the supreme being can be present immediately and everywhere.[34] Eckhart is explicit that it is due to the supreme identity of the great I AM that we can speak paradoxically of the 'negation of the negation'. This has a practical component because the Platonic mystic sees human sympathy as a guide to truth and also illusion as inspired by selfishness

---

30 Turner, *Darkness*, p. 147.
31 Eckhart, *Die Lateinischen Werke*, ed. J. Koch (Stuttgart: Kohlhammer, 1936), vol. 5, p. 61, ll. 5ff.
32 Plotinus, *Enneads* VI. 8.6.26.
33 David Hume, *A Treatise of Human Nature*, I.iii.15.
34 'unde deus non est pars aliquid universi, sed aliquid extra aut potius prius et superius universo et propter hoc ipsi nulla privatio aut negatio convenit, sed propria est sibi, et sibi oli, negatio negationis, quae est medulla et apex purissimae affirmationis, secundum illud: "ego sum qui sum"': Eckhart, *Die Lateinischen Werke*, vol. 3, p. 175, ll. 3ff.

and sensuality. 'Interiority' is the principle that, for example, physico-chemical material processes are themselves expressions of a reality which is the non-spatial and non-temporal mind of God, whose closest analogue is the reflective human mind and ultimately and more properly the human soul. 'What particular privilege has this little agitation of the brain which we call thought, that we must thus make it the model of the whole universe?' says Hume's Philo.[35] Yet God is a Spirit with whom finite human spirit can enjoy communion, and the soul is the fountain of the creative imagination. As Plotinus writes,

> Let there be, then, in the soul a shining imagination of a sphere, having everything within it either moving or standing still, or something moving and another standing still. Keep this, and apprehend another, taking away the mass: take away also the places, and the mental picture of matter in yourself, and do not try to apprehend another sphere smaller in mass than the original one, but calling on the god who made that of which you have the mental picture, pray to him to come.[36]

Plotinus is contemplating through thought experiments the non-material omnipresence of the One, both recommending and rejecting images of intelligible reality. He suggests the invocation of the shining imagination of a sphere (φωτεινή τις φαντασία σφαίρας) and then its removal (ἄφελε), removing not just the mass and space but even the image or representation itself (φάντασμα). Here we find Plotinus practising negative theology with the creative imagination.

Plotinus uses an argument from the unity of perception to buttress his dualism of the material and immaterial realms. The unity of the body is constituted, Plotinus observes, by the spatial continuity of divisible chunks of matter. In conscious awareness, however, the soul is capable of perceiving different parts of the body. It is not a part of the soul perceiving; the soul is present as a whole in its awareness of bodily parts.[37] This presence of unity in different parts distinguishes the soul as an ontological item from bodies. This is a position in Plotinus that is distinctive for his treatment of the second and third hypostases. The World-soul is present to the physical cosmos in its parts as a whole. These are aspects which Augustine could not accept, but it seems to me evident that book X of *On the Trinity* is hard to grasp without understanding such a Platonic argument about the unique nature of the part–whole relation that distinguishes the soul from the body. This is not to denigrate the specific genius of Augustine but to make a point that he owed much to the 'books of the Platonists', as he himself insists in book VII of the *Confessions*. Nor is this an arcane and obsolete argument.

35 David Hume, *Dialogues Concerning Natural Religion*, part II, ed. J. C. A. Gaskin (Oxford: Clarendon Press, 1993), p. 50.
36 Plotinus, *Enneads* V.8.9.1–2. See John Dillon's discussion of this passage in his superb essay 'Plotinus and the Transcendental Imagination', in J. P. Mackey (ed.), *Religious Imagination* (Edinburgh: Edinburgh University Press, 1986), pp. 55–64.
37 Plotinus, *Enneads* IV.7.6.3ff.

Thomas Nagel observes that contemporary discussions about mind–body relations demand a proper understanding of the 'part–whole relation' with regard to attributing a state of unified perception to a composite physical entity.[38]

The problem is not limited to the soul but extends also to God, on account of the particular form of monotheism preferred by the Platonists and transmitted to Augustine and Eckhart. That form of monotheism was a *via media* between the unrelenting transcendence of the God of Aristotle and the materialism and pantheism of the Stoics. The (Neo) Platonists agreed with Aristotle that God is spiritual and not corporeal. But they wanted a God who is also immanent and providential like the Stoic deity; the non-spatial omnipresence of the One is a central tenet of Plotinus.[39] Hence the God 'whose centre is everywhere and his circumference nowhere'. Platonists could not be committed to the kind of radical apophaticism which Turner proposes – a theology beyond affirmation and denial. Both the spiritual and the providential nature of the Godhead were claims that the Platonists were committed to as metaphysical truths.

And quite apart from historical questions about the great dead philosophers, I do not see how any tenable theism can afford to dispense with these principles either. It is very difficult to see how Turner thinks that an apophatic theologian can preserve the characteristic attributes of the God of theism, such as goodness or personhood. I am inclined to agree with Cudworth that such radical apophaticism is a 'mysterious kind of Atheism'.[40] It is particularly puzzling if one holds to the tenet that divine love is not a contingent attribute of God, but belongs to God's essence. Clearly 'inwardness', 'ascent', 'light–darkness' and even 'union' are not meant literally in the sense in which these concepts are applied to quotidian phenomena: e.g. the pearl inside the oyster, climbing stairs, lighting a candle in a dark room, or welding two disparate pieces of iron into one. Yet in each case the image is *not* a mere metaphor. The image symbolizes a spiritual or immaterial law. If we consider the visions, it can be argued that they presuppose such a monistic hierarchy of being. Plato's vivid description of aesthetic-erotic experiences at the *Symposium* banquet presupposes the inferiority of sensual to intelligible beauty, just as the biblical visions of Isaiah or Ezekiel presuppose the frailty and inadequacy of the prophet. Even the theophany in Job presupposes his suffering and his sense of natural justice. In our unreflective judgements about illness we can see that the notion of the bad presupposes the good, or is parasitic upon it. The bad is not the criterion of the good, but the other way around. Hence the importance, within the Platonic tradition and in its Christian forms, of the claim that we can know God's essence as good. This is why the Platonists have difficulty with the Cartesian notion that God decides what is good *ex simplici voluntate*.

---

38 T. Nagel, *The View from Nowhere* (New York: Oxford University Press, 1986), p. 51.
39 Plotinus, *Enneads* V.9.
40 Ralph Cudworth, *The True Intellectual System of the Universe* (Royston, 1678), p. 585.

Augustine seems a very odd enthusiasm for the postmodern theologians: interiority plays such a central role in his thought, not least in his theorizing about the Trinity. This is not just a matter of verbal correspondences with Descartes, but also of the view of mind/soul and unity that he picks up (largely) from Plotinus, and the broader commitments of a Platonist against Stoic or Peripatetic theories. In fact, this is a central Neoplatonic tenet. It is precisely the immateriality of the soul which is the basis of its capacity to *re-flect* upon itself. Hence when Turner exclaims that 'the language of interiority is, at this level of generality, neutral as to any epistemology whatsoever . . . Even an out and out materialist can happily use it',[41] his words cannot apply to a Neoplatonist, for whom the doctrine of reversion is inextricably linked to the immateriality of the soul and the objects of its rapt contemplation. As John Smith reminds us, Plotinus insists in *Ennead* I.6 that 'as the Eye cannot behold the Sun . . . unless it be sunlike . . . so neither can the Soul of man behold God . . . unless it be *Godlike*'.[42]

Divine uniqueness

The Neoplatonist thinks that we cannot speak of God. This is not, however, for the Gnostic reason that God is radically and incommensurably beyond our apprehension but for the solid Platonic-Aristotelian reason of divine uniqueness: 'It is his uniqueness and not only his hiddenness, which prevents our saying anything perfectly exact about him, except that he is himself.' In the *Theaetetus*, Plato refers to the monist Parmenides as 'venerable and awesome'.[43] Plato refers to the Good beyond Being in the *Republic*, and in a late lecture Aristotle identifies Good with Unity.[44] Aristotle also speaks of the One and the Indefinite dyad.[45] Aristotle rejects this hypostasizing of the Parmenidean-Pythagorean-Platonic strand – for Aristotle, unity is not an entity beyond concrete unities. The One means 'continuous' or 'the whole', the 'individual' or the 'universal'. These are all one because they are indivisible.[46]

In Neoplatonism the second part of Plato's *Parmenides* was interpreted as providing an ontology in which the three hypostases become a descending hierarchy of unity. Incorporeal reality has three levels: One, Intellect and Soul, the latter two like concentric circles around the One. The ineffable 'One' or 'Good' becomes the transcendent principle of all being.[47] Plotinus pursues the Platonic-Pythagorean principle of a supreme transcendent unity that resists any positive predication and adds his own doctrine of ecstasy. This is the super-rational apprehension

41 Turner, *Darkness*, p. 91.
42 John Smith, *Select Discourses* (London, 1660), p. 2.
43 Plato, *Theaetetus* 183.
44 Plato, *Republic* 509; Aristotle, *Metaphysics* 1088b35–1089a6.
45 Aristotle, *Metaphysics* 988a6–10.
46 Aristotle, *Metaphysics* 1052a–1056b.
47 Plotinus, *Enneads* VI.9.5.30.

of the transcendent One. Following the tenet of Empedocles that 'like can only be known by like', Plotinus posits a capacity for an intuitive awareness of the supreme unity within the human mind – the experience of the ineffable. This is not the metaphysical horror generated by neo-Kantian epistemological limits, expressed so memorably by Kolakowski,[48] but the creative dialectic of the desire to attain union and knowledge of the One, while retaining the knowledge of the necessary separation. Incomprehensible to the discursive intellect, the supreme principle is nevertheless knowable: Coleridge liked to quote the line from Plotinus: 'Never could the eye have beheld the sun, had not its own essence been soliform.'[49] The human soul must constitute a point of contact with the One, which constitutes both an impasse and a stimulus for philosophical advance. In this manner God is a reality who is immanent and active in all creatures through continual creative power. He is the foundation of an intelligible uni-verse as opposed to a heap of unrelated things. God does not have composite parts which he could gain or lose: he is immaterial. Yet he guarantees the uniformity of explanation – i.e. the inference from *hic et nunc* to other parts of the universe.

Yet what is meant by unity? Is it a mathematical unity – numerical simplicity as absence of multiplicity? Is this the correct paradigm for thinking about the unity of the Godhead? Yet what of the unity of a work of art or the organic unity of an animal? Such a unity is – as it were – complex. The higher we move in the domain of living creatures, the more complex the unity. The amoeba is close to an arithmetical unity, in that it is one cell possessing one nucleus, and from sponges to more advanced metazoans (like flies or mice) we encounter increased grades of bodily organization which mirror an increase in the underlying genomic complexity. Observed advances in genomic complexity and morpho-logical diversity, however, have arisen through the interaction of integrated individuals with their environments over time. Each species defines a population of individual beings united by certain common characteristics (e.g. ability to breed). Consider the increase in complexity but also in integrating *identity* in a fly, a mouse, and a human being. In a human being there is the complex physical structure (body plan) but also the volitional agent, the character over time, the conscious selfhood of the agent, all contributing to personal identity. The first unity, the body plan, is more readily understandable. But perhaps we should be thinking of unity *as* unity by virtue of its unifying power. The paradigm would be the unification of the heterogeneous elements in human personality.

If the degree of unity should be measured on a scale of the intensity of unifying power, divine unity should be thought of as a *dynamic* unity or identity. All the unities of our experience, from the single-cell pollen grain to the unity of an artwork, the human self, the body politic, are imperfect shadows of the perfect divine unity. As the great seventeenth-century Oxford Platonist, Thomas Jackson, asserts:

48 L. Kolakowski, *Metaphysical Horror* (Oxford: Blackwell, 1988).
49 See e.g. Coleridge, *Biographia Literaria*, vol. 1, p. 115.

As an Orthodoxall principle of true Divinitie . . . [the] Multitude of
things visible, is but the multiplied shadow of invisible, independent
unitie: things sensible, or by imagination numerable, are but so
many severall representations of his incomprehensible being, who *is
one*, not as one is part of multitude, yet most truly One, because
indivisible and unmultipliable, as wanting nothing . . . most truly
One.[50]

Pantheism

The problem with Turner's account becomes evident when one compares
Neoplatonic mysticism with a pantheistic sense of deity. Let us take
pantheism to be the religious conviction or philosophical theory of the
identity of God and the universe and the denial of the personality and
transcendence of God. Pantheists reject a division between a creator and
the created world. But they also maintain that the rejection of a creator
allows room for a religious attitude. The discussion of Plotinus
concerning parts and whole, and the difference between soul and body
on this basis, makes sense in the context of polemics against Stoic
pantheistic materialism. The Stoics attempt to explain how a material
logos can pervade the physical universe; on this view it is a mixture akin,
as Chrysippus says, to 'the wine cast into the sea'.[51]

Let us pass over the fragments of Stoic theology and take Spinoza as a
clear modern instance of pantheism. As with Plotinus, Spinoza has a
fully articulated philosophical theology. Spinoza thinks that, strictly
speaking, only one substance can exist. It must be a completely
independent cause of itself, eternal and infinite, and this substance is
called 'God'. Spinoza thought that God's infinity entailed pantheism,
since there can be no beings *outside* God or Nature, *Deus sive natura*. God
is not a transcendent or personal being – and he does not will or choose
the modes which appear under the attributes of thought or extension.
The singular divine substance produces the modes necessarily. Necessity
is a very important component of Spinoza's thought: the remedy for evils
is to realize that they are necessary, and that there is no alternative to
their happening. All human acts are determined; but they can be
accompanied by rational insight or by irrational impulses. The difference
between bondage and freedom is between states of being where the
agent is subject to passive emotions which induce 'servitude', and the
rational insight into necessity which transforms emotions from passive to
active.

For Spinoza, salvation is insight. The intellectual love of God is the joy
of viewing reality as a totality. This is certainly not survival of the
individual soul. We might compare this with Plotinus, who believes in
the existence of forms of individuals – not only generic forms like Man

---

50 Thomas Jackson, *A Treatise of the Divine Essence and Attributes* (London, 1628), pp. 27–8.
51 A. A. Long and D. N. Sedley, *The Hellenistic Philosophers* (Cambridge: Cambridge
    University Press, 1987) vol. 1, p. 290.

but the souls of particular human beings.[52] Plotinus's monism does not mean the extinction of individuality[53] but the realization of the true self – which is 'the One in us'.[54] This shows the value of personality for Plotinus, and he also explores self-consciousness in a way alien to Plato or Aristotle. Through the mediation of Augustine he forges modern subjectivity.

One can also compare Plotinus and Spinoza over their use of the idea of *causa sui*. Self-constitution is a conceptual truth for a pantheist. If the world is identical with the Divine, then the creator creates himself with the creation of the world. Plotinus wants to emphasize the autonomy of the One. The One is not the product of fate or chance but of free will. Plotinus is the first philosopher to identify thought and being with will. The One of Plotinus is distinguished from all 'difference'. He is what he is absolutely – he is entirely self-constituted (αἴτιον ἑαυτοῦ).[55]

The One is what he wills and he wills himself (ἑαυτό τε θέλει).[56] The upshot is the entire and radical self-sufficiency of the One. Note that this is not pantheism or nihilism. Difference is produced by the goodness, plenitude and dynamic unity of the transcendent One. For Plotinus, the One is not the first of a series but the transcendent ground of all causes; not just *actus purus* but *causa sui*. The One is the power of all or to all (δύναμις πάντων); not the most rudimentary but the richest (Hegel would say most 'concrete') form of Unity.

Indeed, it is precisely the emphasis upon *transcendence* within the Platonic tradition which leads to a strong emphasis upon experience and a distrust of pure reflection. This may seem paradoxical because one is perhaps prima facie inclined to think of the Platonist as the philosopher dwelling upon the abstract realm of ideas in opposition to the empirically minded Aristotelian. But the Platonic conviction that the Good is 'beyond Being' leads to a scepticism with respect to dogmatic metaphysical speculation:

> To seek our Divinity meerly in Books and Writings, is to *seek the living among the dead*: we do but in vain seek God many times in these, where his Truth too often is not so much enshrined, as *entomb'd*: no; *intra te quaere Deum*, seek for God within thine own soul; he is best discerned . . . as *Plotinus* phraseth it, by an *Intellectual touch* of him . . . the soul itself hath its sense as well as the Body[57]

However, I will now consider a very different theory – that of William Alston.

52 Plotinus, *Enneads* V.7.
53 Ibid., I.1.7.16ff.
54 Ibid., III.8.9.23.
55 Ibid., VI.8.14.41.
56 Ibid., VI.8.13.21.
57 Smith, *Discourses*, p. 3.

The perception of God?

William Alston, in his seminal work *Perceiving God*, is not arguing that the existence of God is the best explanation for phenomena called 'religious experience' but that people do, in fact, see God, and in this way are justified in their belief. Underlying this proposal is a direct realism (though certainly not a naïve realism) about sense perception. The experience of God involves a presentation, or appearance, to the perceiver. This amounts to the claim that sometimes those people who think they are perceiving God are indeed seeing the Deity, are confronted with the givenness of the object. Hence Alston radically rejects projects such as those of John Hick, for whom the perception of all objects, including God, is mediated conceptually. Much of the epistemology of the book is directed against broadly Kantian theories of perception, in contrast with his own 'Theory of Appearing', in which an object X appearing in a particular mode is fundamental and unanalysable. Although much of the polemic of *Perceiving God* is directed at Kantianism of various kinds, I wish to claim that the sense of the ineffability of the Divine in the Christian mystical tradition itself is a more obvious objection to Alston's theory.

Alston employs two examples to make an important epistemological distinction:

A) In a barn we notice straw moving. We assume that a mouse is under the straw. The hypothesis that there is a mouse here is the best explanation for the movement. This is explanatory support.

B) The mouse becomes part of our experiential field.[58]

Religious experience can support faith in the first manner. For example, the Holy Spirit can be explanatory support for faith, as the workings of the Holy Spirit can explain the lives of inspired individuals. Yet though this is an important argument for the rationality of religious belief, Alston's concern is rather with the support of faith through direct perception, in which God becomes part of the perceptual field of the senses, as with the visions of Isaiah or Ezekiel. The individual perceives God: a deity who shows himself, and not merely his effects.

Another kind of distinction is between immediate and mediate perception. 'The whole earth is full of God's glory'[59] would be an example of mediate perception. But this is not Alston's interest: he is concerned with immediate perception of God, for which he uses the term 'mystical perception'. In the first chapter of *Perceiving God* he uses examples from Teresa of Avila, Henry Suso and some modern accounts. Alston sees three characteristics in these phenomena:

1. The vision of God is a matter of experiential awareness, a presentation rather than imagination or memory. The texts show

---

58 W. Alston, *Perceiving God* (Ithaca, NY: Cornell University Press, 1995), p. 287.
59 Isaiah 6.3.

that God is present to the observer like objects in our field of consciousness. There is a difference as to whether I perceive an actual house or whether I imagine such an object.
2. This vision is a direct awareness. It is like the direct awareness of a person – not like the awareness of that person in a mirror or television screen.
3. It is the awareness of God (not cherubs, angels, etc. or other parts of the celestial furniture).

Alston wishes to develop a general concept of perception which can include mystical perception: non-sensory perception can be construed as another 'species of the same genus'. This 'generic identity of structure' is an important claim: the experiential cognition of the Deity possesses *the same basic structure* as sense perception in the physical world. Mystical perception is a source of justification for what Alston calls M-beliefs (beliefs about perceivable attributes and activities of God which are based on seeing the Deity).

Thus Alston's claim is that there are cases in which a person takes himself or herself to be aware of God; these are genuine experiential cognitions of the Divine and they have the same basic structure as sense perception of the physical environment.

In the second stage of the argument, Alston sets out an account of epistemic justification. He is an externalist: justification requires objectively adequate grounds but it does not require that the knower has reflective, i.e. internal, access to these grounds. He also discusses how relatively important experience and background beliefs are in the justification of perceptual beliefs. Alston, as a robust empiricist, is inclined to give greater weight to purely experiential beliefs than most philosophers, and while accepting that sometimes justification of perceptual beliefs requires justification of background beliefs, he argues for a considerable domain of immediately justified perceptual beliefs. One is justified in believing p when that belief has an objective basis which is conducive to truth.

Sense perception

The third stage of Alston's case considers the typical attempts to show that perceptual beliefs are reliable. He argues that the leading attempts to justify perceptual belief (Descartes, verificationism, transcendental arguments, etc.) are all vitiated by circularity or implausibility. If non-circular arguments fail, why should SP (sensory perception) be more trustworthy than the horoscope? The answer to this question is provided in Alston's own attempt to give an account of the justification of sense perception through 'doxastic practices'. He argues that it is rational to engage in a socially established 'doxastic practice' which we have no adequate reason for regarding as unreliable. We have to engage in some doxastic practice and there are no non-circular ways of differentiating reliable and unreliable doxastic practices. A doxastic practice can be attributed self-support in terms of its ability to predict events. Alston does not think of experience as an explanation of data, but as analogous to the evidential support we have for the existence of the physical world. It is not a matter of gathering data in the form of sensory experiences and then claiming they are best explained by supposing they are due to the action of the physical world upon us. It is rather that we take ourselves to be aware in these experiences of the physical world. No explanatory issues are involved here, and by analogy a theist claims to be *aware* of God.

Alston is comparing the experiential support for theism to our experiential support for belief in the physical world, not to experiential support for beliefs in particular items such as a tree. We do not consult experience to determine whether God is there, like seeing whether the table in the shop window is still there, just as we don't look to see whether the physical world is still there. The assumption that there is a physical world is constitutive of the doxastic practice of forming particular beliefs about specific items (this is perceptual practice). Similarly, the abstract belief in God's existence is the basis of forming particular beliefs about the divine presence and activity in our lives (theistic practice). In both cases the question of the rationality of the particular belief is ultimately the question of the rationality of the practice. In both cases it is quite impossible to use particular experiences to justify the rationality of the practice.

Alston concentrates upon doxastic practices or practical rationality rather than strictly upon principles of justification or the adequacy of grounds. Rather in the manner of Wittgenstein's *On Certainty*, which argues that there can be no appeal beyond those practices to which we are committed, Alston contends that theory presupposes a form of life. Alston admits the circularity. Although he cannot prove that SP (sense perception) or MP (mystical perception) is reliable, he believes he can show that it is rational to take them to be reliable. Such practices are irreducibly plural: each practice has distinctive methods of justification. Here it should be emphasized that Alston uses Wittgensteinian ideas and arguments in a resolutely realist manner: doxastic practices produce epistemic but not metaphysical criteria.[60]

Doxastic practices enjoy a prima facie rationality in the sense that the belief that SP is reliable is subject to overriders. There may be some other reason to think the belief false, or the ground of the belief may not exert its expected force: one discovers that a witness in a law case has ulterior motives for testimony, etc. New developments in science can override beliefs previously held firmly. In such ways prima facie rationality can be subverted.

Alston concludes that it is rational to engage in a practice which is socially established, produces beliefs which are free from significant internal and external contradictions, and can offer real self-support in the sense of being fruitful. Sense perception can support its own claims in the sense that by employing SP and memory and practices of inference we can make useful predictions and control certain events. Such supporting

---

60 Alston, *Perceiving God*, pp. 165ff.

mechanisms are not free from epistemic circularity since one is pre-supposing the validity of SP, but assuming the reliability of the practice, Alston's 'self-support' can nevertheless provide further evidence of the reliability which is at stake.

Christian mystical perception and the analogy of sense perception

Brian Hebblethwaite has pointed to the affinity between Alston and Bishop Joseph Butler in his *Analogy of Religion* (1736), where this Hanoverian bishop subjected natural knowledge of God to a critique and concluded that natural theology was as opaque and bizarre as revealed theology, and indeed that we can form an analogy of the latter on the basis of the mysterious and opaque nature of the former.[61] Alston is exploiting the problems of justifying SP as the basis for a defence of, and an analogy with, MP.

On the basis of mystical perception, Alston considers mystical belief-formation as a socially embedded doxastic practice. This is one of the striking aspects of Alston's account: that he approaches the issue of religious experience from the perspective of the community rather than from that of the individual. This means that Alston has to choose one particular community, that of Christianity, designating this practice as CMP (Christian Mystical Practice), and then proceeding to consider the major problems which might disqualify CMP from being considered as a socially established doxastic practice.

The rationality of theistic belief in so far as it has an experiential base depends upon the rationality of a doxastic practice, what Alston calls theistic practice. But how do we decide whether theistic practice is rational?

The first point is that a basic practice cannot be justified in a non-circular manner, by using only the output of other practices. The most important consideration in deciding on the rationality of a doxastic practice is its reliablity, the extent to which it can yield true rather than false beliefs. But if the practice in question, P, is our basic access to the subject matter, we will have no independent way of comparing P's deliveries with the real facts of the matter, so as to determine the accuracy of P. In order to support this judgement, Alston produces a survey of attempts to establish from the outside the reliability or otherwise of basic doxastic practices like sense perception and intro-spection. Thus we should not suppose that unless we can establish the reliability of theistic practice on the basis of premises taken from other practices we will have to deem it irrational. If we imposed that requirement, we would also have to jettison sense perception, rational intuition, induction, etc. And how could we justify making this demand of theistic practice alone?

61 B. Hebblethwaite, review of W. Alston, *Perceiving God*, *Modern Theology*, Jan. 1994, pp. 117ff.

How can one assess the rational status of a basic doxastic practice? The obvious alternative is to look at its internal coherence, ways in which it might be self-supporting. This can be illustrated by some of the ways in which perceptual practice might be self-supporting. Engaging in the practice we discover that:

1. perceptual beliefs formed by a subject at a time can be confirmed by other subjects or by the same subject at other times, and
2. by relying on its inputs as a basis for reasoning, we can discover regularities, thereby putting us in a position to anticipate the course of events and exercise control over them.

This is a circular argument; it is only by relying on the outputs of the practice that we get our reasons for thinking that the practice exhibits these features. But there are ways in which perceptual practice supports itself from the inside: they are fruits of the practice which encourage us to engage in it and to take it seriously as a source of information. And this self-support is not a trivial matter: it is conceivable that perceptual beliefs and related beliefs might not hang together in this way.

It is clear that the critic of Alston can object that theistic practice does not evince this kind of self-support. Practice does not, after all, put us in a position to predict God's behaviour. Nor is intersubjective corroboration possible: the community of practitioners is much less extensive. And within that community there are no definite criteria of identification. These differences have been taken to discredit theism conclusively. But according to Alston this is epistemic imperialism, as much so as the requirement that the reliability of theistic practice be established in other practices, or the requirement that the existence of God be shown to be the best explanation of theistic experience: it is the imperialism which takes the mode of self-support exhibited by perceptual practice to be the standard for all doxastic practices.

Alston considers a number of reasons for considering CMP to be unreliable, involving naturalistic explanations of mystical experience. He also considers whether there are conflicts between CMP and other practices such as natural science, history and naturalistic metaphysics. He rejects the idea that Christianity conflicts with science per se or with critical historical research: the essential conflict is with a kind of naturalistic-materialistic metaphysics.

Alston argues that there is no reason to suppose that a practice engaged in by only some part of the population is less likely to be a source of truth than one in which we all engage. Here he adduces the examples of theoretical physics or wine-tasting: these are paradigms of such non-universal practices. It quite arbitrary to foist this objection on mystical perception and not physicists or connoisseurs of the grape.

Therefore, in denigrating CMP for not matching up to SP, some critics of religious experience are employing the standards of one doxastic practice as normative for another doxastic practice. Furthermore, such critics are inclined to employ an arbitrary double standard in that they require from one practice standards of justification from which other practices are exempt.

Does the analogy with perception work, or is the vision a metaphor?

On Alston's account, CMP satisfies conditions for rational acceptance because it

1. is a practice which is socially established,
2. is free from massive internal and external contradiction, and
3. demonstrates a degree of self-support.

The classic Western formulation of the idea of perceiving God is produced by Plato. Socrates prays, has ecstasies and is a contemplative figure. Plato develops his conception of the vision of God or of the Good in the context of his description of the life of Socrates as a midwife to reflection, as opposed to the unreflective acceptance of – as it were – merely 'doxastic' practices. Festugière, in his classic work *Contemplation et vie contemplative selon Platon* of 1936, observed that the Fathers of the Christian Church, when they began to reflect upon their mystical experience, tended to Platonize.[62] I wish first of all to make some observations of a historical nature relating to this fact.

Alston clearly wishes to be attentive to the traditions of the Christian community. I do not believe that my observations about the Platonic metaphysics embedded in CMP are necessarily conclusive: *magis Plato amicus magis amica veritas*. Nor would I wish to be committed to attacking the validity of Alston's position by reflecting on the genesis of Christian beliefs in a pagan Hellenistic context. I simply wish to reflect upon the basic paradox that the Platonic and the Christian mystical tradition are both employing the language of sight to express the invisible. The Platonic dialectic leads to a principle which transcends intellection: it is seized as presence through vision. Festugière writes of 'un sentiment de présence, un contact avec L'Être saisi dans son existence. Cette saisie dépasse et le langage et l'intellection. L'objet vu est au delà de l'oὐσία. Il est ineffable'.[63] Vision is a metaphor used paradoxically by those anti-empiricist philosophers who want to emancipate us from the 'despotism of the eye' in order to emphasize that aspect of intelligible knowledge which distinguishes it from the merely doxastic and yet is analogous to seeing: the immediate comprehension of the inner essence or the idea. I am not at all sure that 'seeing' in this sense can fulfil the criteria listed by Alston.

Despite Alston's emphasis upon the importance of community for mystical practice, mystical vision is subject to varied social and institutional proscriptions because of its highly potent nature. If a person

---

62 A. J. Festugière, *Contemplation et vie contemplative selon Platon*, 2nd edn (Paris: Vrin, 1950), p. 5.
63 Ibid.

claims direct knowledge of God, this is traditionally far from welcome in religious communities. He or she is often persecuted: consider Socrates, John the Baptist, Joan of Arc, George Fox or Martin Luther King. Within the philosophical tradition, the rapture of the vision (and what William James might call its pathological character) is denoted by the symbol of the winged or celestial chariot. Parmenides' κοῦρος is taken up to the heavens in a chariot to discourse with the Goddess. Plato employs a cognate image in his *Phaedrus*: the beautiful myth of the soul as a heavenly charioteer who contemplates the ideas before falling into embodiment. (A glance at the work of Gershom Scholem reveals that in the Jewish mystical tradition this image of the chariot is central to Merkabah mysticism.) And the image expresses the danger and the excitement of the journey. (Festugière's Greek motto to his book can be translated 'Because the venture is beautiful'.) Orthodox institutional theologies are often critical of theophanies and visions. What Alston presents as healthy internal critique within CMP may not do justice to the potentially dangerous, disruptive and subversive force of claims of immediate knowledge of the Divine. With characteristic caution, Thomas Aquinas restricts the vision of God to saints and angels even though he considers the possibility of a few who might through ecstasy or *raptus* attain that vision in this life.[64]

Another disanalogy between Alston's position and traditional Christian Platonism is that Alston is chastising the religious sceptic for judging one domain by the standards of a quite different domain. But the tendency in the mystical tradition itself is against such pluralism, and is closely linked to the Platonic conception of dialectic. This consists in driving a wedge between thought and sense. To this extent Plato concedes sceptical claims with regard to sensory experience in order to attain certainty at the intelligible level. In the *Phaedo*, Socrates is presented as arguing that sense experience does not furnish the mind with truths but can suggest them. To think means to employ judgements which extend beyond sensation; however, to know means more than just thinking: it is to provide justification which extends beyond mere agreement of the kind which crafty orators can obtain.[65] Famously Plato in the *Timaeus* distinguishes between the pure realm of 'what is' and the actual sensual realm of 'becoming'.[66] The dialectic of the *Republic* proceeds by examining hypotheses as principles of reality until one arrives at self-luminous or self-evident principles. Thus the structure of Plato's thinking employs sceptical arguments in a totally different way from that of Alston. Whereas Alston employs sceptical arguments to show that the mystical vision can enjoy some of the relative immunity from critique enjoyed by sensory perception, Plato builds his mystical ascent upon the very inadequacy of the realm of sensory experience. As half-real, nature symbolizes an invisible, non-sensuous reality: God. Rather than admitting a plurality of epistemic practices, Plato sees the

64 Aquinas *Summa contra Gentiles* III.52–3.
65 Plato, *Phaedo* 76ff.
66 Plato, *Timaeus* 27–9.

inadequacies of sense perception as generating an ascent of the mind towards a principle which can provide a guarantee of knowledge.

And Plato's mysticism has its rational foundations. In his view, mathematics is much more stable in its results than empirical experience. That is why Parmenides, Plato and Descartes held sense perception in such low esteem. Sense perception, though a useful guide to the physical environment, does not rank as high as it might – there are many respects in which it is imperfect. There are contradictions; and although there are regularities, if we are to trust contemporary science, our basic perceptual beliefs badly misrepresent the basic character of objects: most perceivers assume physical objects to have intrinsic colours, and to look as if they are solid when in fact they are largely particles in empty space. If perceptual practice has these limitations or even distortions, why should we adhere so slavishly to its canons?

The philosophical mystic will usually recognize degrees of reality. For the Christian Platonic tradition, the one true being is God and all other beings participate in this supreme being. As finite beings are limited, they are only partially real. God is the only entirely adequate object of intellection. But knowledge of true being is impossible *quoad nos*, and God can only be known through limited manifestations:

> The source of this [that is, the ecclesiastical/'man's'] hierarchy is the font of life, the being of goodness, the one cause of everything, namely, the Trinity which in goodness bestows being and well-being on everything . . . It has bestowed hierarchy as a gift to ensure the salvation and divinization of every being endowed with reason and intelligence.[67]

God 'assimilates them [that is, human beings] as much as they are able, to his own light'.[68] It is through 'hierarchy', that is our varying degrees of participation in God's 'Being', that one becomes more 'like' God, and so can work towards union with him. Denys Turner observes that, whereas for Pseudo-Dionysius, 'hierarchy was both an ontological structure and a rule of governance of the universe', in secular society 'we have no systematically hierarchical conception of either'.[69] For us, things either exist or they do not; there is no real idea of things being more or less existent, depending on how much or little they resemble God. But it is not clear that we should accept Turner's pessimism about the intelligibility of hierarchy so readily. We have a notion of reality as a continuum of increasing reality ranging from the greatest prime number and the square circle, which are logically impossible, to silver mountains, which are only contingently impossible. Hallucinations, dreams, delusions, illusions, shadows, rainbows, material objects, fundamental laws of science are part of a 'great chain of being' of increasing reality. We also possess ideals of unity, and explanatory power is a very convincing mark of reality. Because it is reasonable to seek a unified system of explanation,

---

67 Pseudo-Dionysius, *The Ecclesiastical Hierarchy*, 373d, 376b; *The Complete Works*.
68 Ibid., 372b.
69 Turner, *Darkness*, p. 28.

and to think that we have one, it is natural to think that we have a correspondingly *unified* order of reality, in which ultimate reality is that in terms of which everything is explained. Divine actuality precedes potentiality. If there are real intelligible patterns in the world – i.e. traces of *sameness/identity* in *different/manifold* items – then there must be a real mind prior to finite discoveries of these patterns.[70] Or – as in that later Platonist, Descartes – knowledge requires the existence of the divine mind. Essence and existence co-inhere uniquely in God. With any other item we can ask whether it has an instantiation. If a perfect transcendent being exists, then it exists necessarily. This is not the same as the ontological argument. Perfect knowledge might entitle one to grasp the indubitable existence of God, but we human beings have finite capacities.

Mystical practice

It seems very odd to present visions which are often expressed in paradoxical terms as 'free' from massive internal and external conflicts. God is described by many mystics as a *coincidentia oppositorum*, and writers such as Nicholas of Cusa can use a term like *docta ignorantia* to highlight the conflict between the mystical vision and the eye of the 'flesh'. It is not just that the mystic does not care about avoiding contradictions of these kinds: he even seems to revel in them. Perhaps this does not matter. Alston makes the important point that we should not confuse knowledge with our capacity to articulate it,[71] and perhaps that is just paradigmatically so with mystical perception.

One of the great changes which the Enlightenment has brought about is in our attitude to the authority of tradition. And this has as much to do with the eclipse of theology as the key narrative which occurred during the Enlightenment. Of course we accept much of our beliefs in geography, physics, science, etc. on the basis of testimony: we are convinced of the competence of the people who are describing their experience, and, *pace* extreme versions of the 'sociology of knowledge' approach, the ideological component is rather minimal. But where human interests and ideals are more obviously concerned, we know that the capacity for delusion and manipulation is considerable. A better analogy than the natural sciences would be politics. We know that highly intelligent people in the twentieth century admired fascism or communism, well after the evils of both became obvious. Plato, who has been represented as a forerunner of modern totalitarianism, presents Socrates as a 'lover of knowledge' and knowledge is defined in contradistinction to opinion. The Platonic definition of knowledge in opposition to belief is determined to a large degree by Plato's revulsion against rhetoric and the Sophistic view that knowledge is just opinion. Plato clearly thought that this had contributed to the death of his master. The excessively strict

---

70 S. Clark, *The Mysteries of Religion: An Introduction to Philosophy through Religion* (Oxford: Blackwell, 1986), p. 75.
71 Alston, *Perceiving God*, p. 38.

nature of the Platonic concept of knowledge is doubtless rooted in Plato's perception of the religious and political significance of the execution of a visionary. That is why it is so un-Platonic to appeal to doxastic practices. William James has numerous examples of the mystical principle that a man must die to the unreal life before he can be born into real life.[72] The believer must be delivered from the illusions of everyday life, its fake consolations and its spurious distractions. The authority of the saints is not a corroboration of our lives. The pattern of the mystical life is a good example. It consists of the radical dissolution of one's habitual self and its doxastic practices and the subsequent reconstruction of a real self. The same applies to one's belief-forming procedures.

The 'cultured despisers' of Christianity will object to CMP on ethical grounds. Why did Christianity not stop slavery; why did it pursue wars of religion, persecute heretics? The emphasis upon personal and individual religious experience which is stressed powerfully by William James has been much maligned as subjectivistic and elitist. But James argues in his *Varieties of Religious Experience* that the bad in religion usually results from confusing genuine religious experience with the cruelty of the mob: 'the best fruits of religious experience are the best things that history has to show'.[73] He insists: 'I beseech you never to confound the phenomena of mere tribal or corporate psychology which it presents with those manifestations of the purely interior life.'[74] James is adamant that

> personal religion will prove itself more fundamental than either theology or ecclesiasticism. Churches, when once established, live at second hand upon tradition; but the *founders* of every church owed their power originally to the fact of their direct personal communion with the divine. Not only the superhuman founders, the Christ, the Buddha, Mahomet, but all the originators of Christian sects have been in this case; – so personal religion should still seem the primordial thing, even to those who continue to esteem it incomplete.[75]

Perhaps the importance of 'mystical perception' within a religion such as Christianity is to keep the prophetic component alive and to attack the complacency and worldliness which afflicts any socially established religion. But the forces which sustain a religion must include more widespread sense or experience of the Divine than the rapture of the mystic, and Alston's attempt to employ the latter as a model for the former is very counter-intuitive.

On Turner's account, the mystical theologian cannot allow any standard that is external to the life of faith. The revived apophaticism of Turner's account is linked to a strident doctrine about the primacy of *practice*. The medieval mystical tradition is a tradition of doing theology which cannot be separated from Christian practice:

---

72 James, *Varieties of Religious Experience*, pp. 166, 363, 488.
73 Ibid., p. 259.
74 Ibid., p. 338.
75 Ibid., p. 30.

God is found in the negation of experience and in the negation of the
negation so that everything is denied and nothing is abandoned, so
that all things lead to a God who is beyond what they lead to, by
means of ways which are the active practice of the denial of ways.[76]

The medieval tradition of 'mysticism' as interpreted by Turner is
properly an element within the 'ordinary practice' of 'the Christian life' –
worship, liturgy and sacraments. This is a practice embodied in a life. I
agree that experiences of the divine presence require interpretation and
critical awareness, and that traditionally religious communities employ
tests for establishing their validity, and that the experiences of great
visionaries cannot be understood without reference to the traditions,
documents, canons, etc. of their communities. One can draw useful
analogies with moral or aesthetic judgement. A moral agent needs to
cultivate discrimination as much as the seeker of beauty, and this usually
requires training and the aid of experts. If the critique of religious
experience produces excessively strict criteria of valid experiences, this
may serve to subvert aesthetic or ethical discriminations. But I cannot
help but be struck by the irony that a major player in Turner's story,
Eckhart, was condemned to death by his community. For all his
enthusiasm for the active Martha, I suspect Eckhart in Avignon would
have been less sanguine about the practice of 'the Christian life' than
Turner's account will permit.

Apophaticism and metaphor?

In the wake of Freud and Marx, there is increased awareness about the
links between adolescence, conversion and the irrational component in
the human subconscious. Do not genetic accounts of religious beliefs
render appeals to the validity of special experiences a forlorn and
hopeless exercise? But if religious experiences exhibit analogies with
romantic-sexual longings or fears of powerful natural items, this hardly
warrants the reduction of religious experience to various forms of
psychic excitement of a purely natural kind. In fact, if one believes in an
author of the cosmos, one would expect nature, the starry heavens and
the moral law, to point back to its author.

This is the real problem with any appeal to religious experience – the
fact that it may be a deluded or mistaken modification of sexual impulses
or atavistic memories. Turner's incommensurability thesis renders the
medieval mystics *ex definitione* immune from the fear that their experiences of the presence of God were inauthentic. This entails an
incommensurability between different epochs of human thought and
culture. We, according to Turner, are able to recover this genuine
medieval apophatic anti-mysticism because postmodernism constitutes a
'revival of that awareness of the "deconstructive" potential of human
thought and language which so characterized classic medieval apophati-

76 Turner, *Darkness*, p. 272.

cism'. Turner is arguing for a convergence of 'medieval and contemporary apophaticisms',[77] for this providential convergence of pre-modern and postmodern apophaticism is the key. Postmodernism is notoriously sceptical about what really can be known and offers a contemporary cloud of unknowing: pre-modernism offers the radically unknowable God. If God is radically unknown, there is a dimension to all his creation which is unknown – the whole of creation is 'self-subverting, centred upon an unknowable reality'.[78]

But just how plausible is this dialectically ingenious immunization of the medieval mind from the fear of delusion? Is it not much more probable that the despair and anxiety of medieval mystics had its real basis in a sense of alienation from God which was motivated by deep and serious doubts? However much one learns about the different specific conditions of medieval (or any very distant and alien) culture, we continue to esteem great dead writers because of what we share in common humanity and what we can learn from their perception of it. It is hard to avoid attributing to their treatises the perennial questions of the human condition. Turner's account has the effect of limiting the question about the validity of such experiences to a misguided question posed by 'modernity', which presumably we postmoderns can renounce as the misguided 'psychologistic positivism' that the medievals never knew. It is doubtless consoling to think that the medievals were untroubled by those experiences of doubt which characterize modern culture. But I hardly think it likely.

The major weakness of Alston's project, on the other hand, is his employment of the language of perception. He avoids the word 'experience' because it is too vague.[79] Here he is joining a chorus of writers who dislike the term. For reasons that cannot be pursued now, I think that the difficulties surrounding the idea of experience are no greater than those of many other central philosophical notions, and in the religious context this point is fairly clear. There is a dimension of the reflective human experience of reality in which many have a sense of contact with a numinous or sacred domain. This experience is closely related to, but not identical with, a widespread sense of the ethical. Such an experience may not be definable, but Alston himself has many powerful objections to the prejudice against the unanalysable.[80] But though 'experience' is a very wide term, 'perception' is far too specific. In concentrating upon 'putative direct awareness of God',[81] Alston is trying to employ very marginal experiences to corroborate the general acceptability of religious beliefs. The visionary tradition – in both its philosophical and its less reflective forms – provides (very enigmatic) answers to questions which are rooted in universal human experiences: contingency, pain, wonder, fear of death, etc. Hence the visions of the

---

77 Ibid., p. 8.
78 Ibid., p. 271.
79 Alston, *Perceiving God*, p. 34.
80 Ibid., p. 38.
81 Ibid., p. 35.

poets and the prophets can be enormously meaningful to those of us who cannot leap into the celestial chariot and see the mind of God. We can understand these visions because of an innate sense of the sacred which human beings widely share, inchoately and in ways very difficult to articulate, but which often find expression through the visionaries. That is to say, the elevated and perhaps pathological visions of the few can have significance for the many not because of the acceptance of testimony, but because of the *animal religiosum*.

Xenophanes observed that oxen would create deities in their own image. Plato's theology is the beginning of a very long and sophisticated series of answers to that charge of anthropomorphism, of which Aristotle and Thomas are a part. But Plato bequeathed a paradoxical legacy in his idea that mankind has an innate longing for a vision of the Good which eludes our physical perception: in the *Phaedrus*, the being with which knowledge is concerned is without colour, without form, intangible, and can only be seen by the pilot of the soul.[82] Within the Platonic tradition, which for Augustine was his essential path into the Christian Church, 'seeing' is an analogy for human access to a transcendent spiritual reality because the physical realm is an image or symbol of true reality, and we have to see through this physical image as in a glass darkly.

The harp of Orpheus and religious affections

Axioms in philosophy are not axioms until they are proved on our pulses[83]

I wish to propose a position very different from either Turner's or Alston's. I wish to claim that the perception involved is more complex and involves emotion and imagination. I wish to consider the classic theory of Romantic aesthetics – that of art as *Einbildungskraft*, as the power-of-forming-into-one the *infinite* and the *finite*. The effect of such art is characteristic – the creation of a mood of enchantment. An individual agent's perspective is formed by images of reality which decisively affect perception. Emotions and imagination necessarily shape the perception of the objective world. They are clearly linked in phobias. Hence we should avoid any facile dichotomy between imagination and emotion. It is clear that we can understand an idea emotionally: images can help produce a portrait of life, as Keats memorably says of the axioms of philosophy and our pulses. Objects and events are not real until there is some corresponding emotional experience. Poetry is not ornament, but the vehicle and stimulus for imaginative insight.

82 Plato, *Phaedrus* 247.
83 John Keats, *The Letters of John Keats: 1814–1821*, ed H. E. Rollins, 2 vols (Cambridge, Mass.: Harvard University Press, 1958), p. 279.

Mark Wynn employs John Deigh's work on pre-conceptual awareness of the world – between 'being sensible of something' and 'having a concept of it'.[84] Deigh notes that at this pre-conceptual level, which adult human agents share with higher animals and children, the affective element is very powerful and the affects constitute a 'mode of perception which operates independently of any conceptual articulation of the world's character'.[85] In an affectively toned perception, one cannot isolate an affect independent of perception or thought. Wynn uses Deigh's example of scariness as an immediate apprehension, as opposed to the inference that an object or agent is dangerous. This is an affective response independent of any conceptual structure. However, Wynn also considers cases where a conceptual comprehension is enriched by an affective sensitivity. Certain fears, for example, can be deepened by this 'affectively toned appreciation' of the threat or hazard, which has a content that cannot be cashed out in a feeling-neutral manner or even articulated conceptually. Understanding the hazard means having the right affects. Both models, pre-conceptual awareness and extending the conceptual through affect, can be viewed as ways of seeing the inalienably cognitive dimension of many emotions and the necessary role of the emotions in knowledge. But Wynn notes that an 'affective complex' may suggest certain boundaries within which the mind may interpret the world.[86] Here Wynn draws upon the work of de Sousa and his proposal that the emotions help to direct the mind to those items which deserve attention – they can be seen to 'light up features of the environment'.[87] Further, Wynn gives an example of the cognitive role of emotions, drawn from music. Here an affectively toned anticipation may point to a (not yet experienced) resolution. The expectancy is a sort of yearning for resolution based upon a pre-conceptual awareness of a tension. Someone not trained in music can nevertheless have an affective intimation of the resolution. Wynn links his discussion of these philosophical arguments with literature culled from cognitive science about the importance of non-propositional awareness – felt responses which, though not discursive, are rational. Damasio has shown that agents who are deficient in the pre-frontal cortex cannot imagine emotionally. They possess the cognitive capacity but lack the emotional knowledge which is vital for practical decision-making: Damasio has a striking instance of a patient who could not decide on which day in the week he should make an appointment.[88]

Wynn draws upon contemporary reflection about the emotions in order to attack a stark dualism of a thought components and affective state. According to such a model, the thought is objective and mirrors certain facts, whereas the attendant affective state represents a merely subjective experience. Wynn presents a case for the subtle interdepend-

---

84 M. Wynn, *Emotional Experience and Religious Understanding: Integrating Perception, Conception and Feeling* (Cambridge: Cambridge University Press, 2005), pp. 93–8.
85 Ibid., p. 94.
86 Ibid., pp. 97ff.
87 Ibid., p. 104.
88 Quoted ibid., p. 115.

ence of feeling, perception and understanding. His aim is to show that perception and thought are best understood as suffused by feeling and that this has considerable consequences for our understanding of religious belief. Yet the theories which Wynn draws upon are egocentric – the enhancing of the individual agent's interests and needs is the *raison d'être* of rehabilitating the emotions within a broad cognitive framework. Yet a deep religious impulse runs contrary to this – religion is often perceived as liberating the self from selfishness. Buddhism is a clear instance, but many forms of Christianity also emphasize the overcoming of self-will as the cardinal point of faith.[89] Even Schleiermacher's sense of absolute dependence, on which Wynn draws, is explicitly not a theory about the enhancement of self.

Secondly, Wynn is perhaps too dismissive of moods, which seem an obvious candidate for the feeling of totality which he is interested in exploring. Emotions tend to be specific, moods more general. Fear usually has an object; anxiety is more diffuse. Wynn is looking for 'an affective state which is targeted more explicitly at the world'.[90] Moods seem inextricably tied to our subjective dispositions rather than any objective facts about the world. However, as William James notes,

> In like manner an enraptured man and a dreary feeling man are not simply aware of their subjective states; if they were, the force of their feelings would all evaporate. Both believe there is outward cause why they should feel as they do: either, 'It is a glad world! how good life is!' or, 'What a loathsome tedium is existence!'[91]

Moods can be seen as candidates for human emotional experience of the world, in which moods reveal an otherwise hidden dimension of the world rather in the way in which senses reveal particular objects. Consider further the conviction of William James that religion is 'a man's total reaction upon life':

> so why not say that any total reaction upon life is a religion? Total reactions are different from casual reactions, and total attitudes are different from usual or professional attitudes. To get at them you must go behind the foreground of existence and reach down to that curious sense of the whole residual cosmos as an everlasting presence, intimate or alien, terrible or amusing, lovable or odious, which in some degree every one possesses. This sense of the world's presence, appealing as it does to our particular individual temperament, makes us either strenuous or careless, devout or blasphemous, gloomy or exultant, about life at large; and our reaction, involuntary and inarticulate and often half unconscious as it is, is the completest of all our answers to the question 'What is the character of this universe in which we dwell?'[92]

89 See Ralph Cudworth, *A Sermon Preached Before the Honourable House of Commons, March 31, 1647* (New York: Facsimile Text Society, 1930), pp. 21ff.
90 Wynn, *Emotional Experience*, p. 62.
91 James, *The Will to Believe*, p. 83.
92 James, *Varieties of Religious Experience*, p. 35.

When he is describing such deep responses to the presence of the universe, James uses the ideas of the 'field of consciousness' or the 'entire wave of consciousness'. Some fields are narrow and some are wide:

> Usually when we have a wide field we rejoice, for we then see masses of truth together, and often get glimpses of relations which we divine rather than see, for they shoot beyond the field into still remoter regions of objectivity, regions which we seem rather to be about to perceive than to perceive actually. At other times, of drowsiness, illness, or fatigue, our fields may be narrow almost to a point, and we find ourselves correspondingly oppressed and contracted.[93]

James notes that it is impossible to outline the wave or field with any definiteness – the margin is indeterminate. And the fringe or marginal elements are in some respects more significant than the actual sensory items which the classical empiricism of Locke, Berkeley or Hume tend to emphasize. James uses the concept of 'mood' to describe such indeterminate fringes of consciousness, and the use of the word 'moods' to describe such phenomena. The 'will to believe' is not part of a crude Pascalian wager, but part of a theory about the disclosure of reality.

At this point I wish to draw on the work of John Stewart (1846–1933) and his theory of the transcendental feeling that appears in discursive conscious reflection but does not originate in it.[94] The transcendental feeling is a sense of pre-conceptual connection with the rest of nature – 'at once the solemn sense of Timeless Being – of "That which was, and is, and ever shall be" overshadowing us – and the conviction that life is good.'[95] He links this feeling to the 'vegetative part' of the soul,

> which made from the first, and still silently makes, the assumption on which our whole rational life of conduct and science rest – the assumption that Life is worth living. No arguments which reason can bring for, or against, this ultimate truth are relevant; for Reason cannot stir without assuming the very thing which these arguments seek to prove or disprove. 'Live thy Life' is the Categorical Imperative addressed by Nature to each of her creatures according to its kind.[96]

Is this the belief in the inherent value of life experienced ecstatically as the apprehension of *eternity* sustaining and suffusing the fleeting realm of becoming? Stewart argues that the human sense of the impending nature of death would sap human energy if it were not for that part of the soul which extends beyond conscious awareness and discursive rationality, what Stewart calls the 'vegetative soul', that 'without sense of past or future or self, silently holds on to Life, in the implicit faith that it is

---

93 Ibid., p. 231.
94 Stewart, *The Myths of Plato*, p. 67.
95 Ibid., p. 66.
96 Ibid., p. 64.

worth living – that there is a Cosmos in which it is good to be'.[97] Stewart calls this feeling 'transcendental' since it is a condition rather than a consequence of certain experiences.

> Transcendental feeling may be said to be a normal experience of our conscious life: it is not an experience occasionally cropping up alongside of other experiences, but a feeling which accompanies all the experiences of our conscious life – that 'sweet hope', in the strength of which we take the trouble to see after the particular achievements which make up the waking life of conduct and science.[98]

It is a not a specific object of experience nor does it supervene upon conscious states, but upon a fundamental mode of experience – of a transcendent, harmonious unity which is seen to be more deeply rooted than it is in discursive reflection. Yet it is also tied to the sense of having seen the mysteries.[99] Wordsworth in 'Tintern Abbey' speaks of the

> blessed mood,
> In which the burden of the mystery,
> In which the heavy and the weary weight
> Of all this unintelligible world,
> Is lightened: – that serene and blessed mood
> In which the affections gently lead us on, –
> Until, the breath of this corporeal frame
> And even the motion of our human blood
> Almost suspended, we are laid asleep
> In body, and become a living soul:
> While with an eye made quiet by the power
> Of harmony, and the deep power of joy,
> We see into the life of things.[100]

This contemplative 'serene and blessed mood' of which Wordsworth speaks is thrust at the rational egoism of Hobbes and Hume. On the latter theory, action just is self-motivated desire. Quite apart from the problems of calculation, it is unclear that human beings do act in terms of specific desires. Much human behaviour is less rational than this: habits, customs, duties – and even many familiar pleasures – may not fit into the self-motivated desire model. Kinship and quasi-tribal loyalties constitute a good part of the well-being and happiness of most human beings and yet fit poorly into any schemes of rational preference. Attending a cricket match or sharing in the games of children may have such components. The 'enjoyment' cannot be calculated: it is a part and by-product of being able to act in ways and with people that we care about. Yet at a more serious level, the rational preference theory fails to account for more serious kinds of motivation. Some moods are required

---

97 Ibid., p. 66.
98 Ibid., p. 66–7.
99 Ibid., p. 47.
100 William Wordsworth, 'Lines Composed a Few Miles above Tintern Abbey', ll. 37–48.

in order to galvanize and inspire the agent to acts of personal sacrifice or great endeavours, and the power of imagination, about which Wordsworth is so eloquent in 'Tintern Abbey' and *The Prelude*, is precisely the inspiring mood of contemplative vision.

Martin Heidegger developed a complex and powerful theory of moods or *Stimmungen* in *Being and Time*.[101] He rejects the traditional philosophical terminology of feeling or affects because of its associations with the merely subjective. Rather, he speaks of the 'state' or 'situation' or 'finding oneself in a certain condition' (*Befindlichkeit*). Depression and joy, anxiety and good cheer, boredom and enthusiasm are affective states of *Dasein* (being there) in the world. Such moods are pre-theoretical in the sense that they filter all particular experiences and theoretical relations to the world, and are more 'primordial' than objective knowledge of specific items. Moods are distinguishable from emotions by not being directed to a specific intentional object. They are not, Heidegger wishes to claim, simply subjective reflections of individual minds, but serve to disclose features of the world:

> A mood assails us. It comes neither from 'outside' nor from 'inside', but arises out of Being-in-the-world, as a way of such Being . . . Having a mood is not related to the psychical . . . and is not itself an inner condition which then reaches forth in an enigmatical way and puts its mark on Things and persons.[102]

Moods comprise both self and world, and Heidegger takes this phenomenon as an index of a more 'primordial' state than reflective consciousness, which re-presents the world.[103] Heidegger's use of the concept of a pre-theoretical mood can be traced back to Schleiermacher and his primordial and pre-theoretical 'intuition of the universe' which is closely associated with feeling, as opposed to reason or will.[104]

Whatever I do, I always find myself in a particular mood. Moods are modes of self-awareness characteristic of human beings. One's being is experienced through the filter of certain moods that, according to Heidegger, disclose one's being prior to the actual exercise of the will. A mood discloses one's being in a particular way for the will. The will is thus parasitic upon being affected in certain ways which are experienced in moods.[105] Heidegger is appealing to a pre-reflective immediacy of experience or encounter in *Dasein* which is prior to theoretical observa-

---

101 See M. Heidegger, *Sein und Zeit*, §29, The theory is also developed in various other works throughout his œuvre. See, for example, *Das Wesen der Wahrheit* and *Einführung in die Metaphysik*. I am grateful to Sophie von Wulffen for discussion of this topic..
102 M. Heidegger, *Being and Time* (Oxford: Blackwell, 1962), §29, p. 176.
103 For a remarkably lucid commentary, see H. L. Dreyfus, *Being-in-the-World: A Commentary on Heidegger's 'Being and Time', Division I* (Cambridge, Mass.: MIT Press, 1999). Moods on this account are antecedent to any abstract gulf between knowing subject and an objective world.
104 M. Trowitzsch, *Zeit zur Ewigkeit: Beiträge zum Zeitverständnis in der "Glaubenslehre" Schleiermachers* (Munich: Chr. Kaiser, 1976), pp. 117ff.
105 E. Tugendhat, *Self-consciousness and Self-determination* (Cambridge, Mass.: MIT Press, 1986), p. 187.

tion. One finds oneself disposed. This is a level of facticity which Heidegger sees missing in Cartesian accounts such as Husserl's.

Die Stimmungen leads to 'das abgründige Daß des Daseins' (the abysmal surd of *Dasein*).[106] But the analysis of *Being and Time*, which dwells upon the mood of anxiety as a *Grundbefindlichkeit* (basic manner of finding oneself in a state), relates to the complete state of our existence and, indeed, the 'whence' of our being.[107] Such a *Grundbefindlichkeit* illuminates our being in the world, and (in Heidegger's quasi-soteriology) culminates in the 'resoluteness' of authentic existence: 'die unheimlichkeit der Welt, in der radikalen Befindlichkeit des "Nicht-zuhause-seins" ' (uncanniness of the world, in the radical sense of 'not being at home'). Heidegger is playing upon the etymology of *Erschlossenheit* (disclosure) and *Entschlossenheit* (resoluteness) as literally the *un-locking* of a realm which has been hidden by convention and everyday preoccupations. Truth discloses itself in situations of attunement.[108] The movement of *Dasein* from anxiety to resoluteness discloses something about Being itself[109] : Das Stimmt in German means 'It's true'.

Heidegger's debt to Romanticism is deep. Speaking of Descartes, he writes:

> The seemingly new beginning which Descartes proposed for philosophizing has revealed itself as the implantation of a baleful prejudice, which has kept later generations from making any thematic ontological analytic of the 'mind' ‹Gemütes› such as would take the question of Being as a clue and would at the same time come to grips critically with the traditional ancient ontology.[110]

John Macquarrie translates 'Analytik des ‹Gemütes›' as 'the analytic of the "Mind" ', with 'Mind' in inverted commas: mind, disposition or character. *Gemüt* is cognate with *Mut* (courage) and the English word 'mood'. *Gemüt* conveys the sense of the interior-personal core of a human being and the affective-conative aspect rather than the purely or exclusively cognitive.[111] *Contra* Denys Turner, its conceptual provenance

---

106 P.-L. Coriando, *Affektenlehre und Phänomenologie der Stimmungen: Wege einer Ontologie und Ethik der Stimmungen* (Frankfurt: Klostermann, 2002), pp. 124ff.

107 The affinity with Heidegger's Marburg colleague Rudolf Otto's 'creaturely feeling', and via Otto to Schleiermacher, is not coincidental. Another Marburger, Tillich, spoke of 'ultimate concern'.

108 See J. Cottingham, *Philosophy and the Good Life* (Cambridge: Cambridge University Press, 2005), p. 107.

109 Hence Heidegger's vehement rejection of Sartre's claim that existentialism is a form of humanism.

110 J. Macquarrie and E. Robinson, trs, *Being and Time* (Oxford: Blackwell, 1980), p. 46. 'Der scheinbare Neuanfang des Philosophierens enthüllt sich als die Pflanzung eines verhängnisvollen Voruteils, auf dessen Grunde die Folgezeit eine thematische ontologische Analytik des ‹Gemütes› am Leitfaden der Seinsfrage und zugleich als kritische Auseinandersetzung mit der uberkommenen antiken Ontologie verabsäumte.' M. Heidegger, *Sein und Zeit* (Tubingen: Max Niemeyer, 1993), p. 25.

111 The intimations of the mind are often described in the Christian tradition through the language of the heart or *cor*. The central place for this concept is Augustine and especially his repeated appeal to Isaiah 7.9: 'Unless ye believe, ye shall not understand': *On the Trinity* IX.1.1 *et al.*

is in medieval German mysticism (Eckhart and from there to Boehme) and Romanticism (Schlegel, Novalis and Tieck).[112]

For the great Romantics, the artist represents the proper attunement of mind and world, freedom and nature. I use the musical analogy deliberately. The German word *Stimmung* has a Pythagorean provenance.[113] In the *Biographia* Coleridge defines the poetic imagination as the capacity to see the universal in the particular, to endow with feeling and empathetic attunement. Imagination can create certain emotions. Imagination has a role in the promotion of life – it can be therapeutic.

We need not try to sustain any commitment to the details of the bizarre realized eschatology of Heidegger's existential ontology to extract the idea of affectively toned or tuned disclosure of the world, which poetry, art and an imaginative communion with nature can induce. There is an analogy with the poets. In situations of extreme suffering the human mind can be shaken out of complacency into a heightened receptivity and awareness of reality. If mood is unlike the perception of an object or specific sensation, it is not the mind which grasps (in the sense of articulate discursive reflection) but the mind which is itself grasped – a pre-theoretical state of awareness.[114] A psychotic has lost any grasp on reality, but all human minds are attuned to reality by their own psychic images and experiences. Much of this attunement is pre-theoretical. Symbols ignite emotional energies and powers which are not entirely comprehended.[115] Put in another way, the mind is not a *tabula rasa*: it must be attuned and open to truth before it can properly form true beliefs. Whereas metaphors can be articulated, symbols point to that which eludes conceptualization. In the case of the symbol, it is the mood which conveys meaning rather than the narrative.

Wordsworth in his seminal poem 'Intimations of Immortality from Recollections of Early Childhood' speaks of the experience of the world being 'Apparelled in celestial light'. Such intimations are – *contra* Turner – of the presence rather than the absence of deity, and the exalted mood of reason is mediated through the imaginative power of symbols. It is to these symbols that we must now turn.

---

112 'Gemüt', in *Historisches Wörterbuch der Philosophie*, ed. Joachim Ritter (Darmstadt: Wissenschaftliche Buchgesellschaft, 1974), vol. 3, pp. 258–64.

113 See L. Spitzer, *Classical and Christian Ideas of World Harmony: Prolegomena to an Interpretation of the Word 'Stimmung'* (Baltimore: Johns Hopkins University Press, 1960).

114 S. Mulhall, 'Can There Be an Epistemology of Moods?', in A. O'Hear (ed.), *Verstehen and Humane Understanding* (Cambridge: Cambridge University Press, 1996), pp. 191–210.

115 Dan Sperber discusses emotions in relation to religion with his interesting concept of 'mood memories' in *Rethinking Symbolism*, tr. A. L. Morton (Cambridge: Cambridge University Press, 1975), p. 115. Symbols cannot be equated with a set of signs, or a language waiting to be decoded. He contrasts encyclopaedic and symbolic knowledge. The first is linked to the left brain hemisphere, being linguistic and rational. Symbolic knowledge differs from propositional (left-hemisphere-based) knowledge.

4

Religion: Fantasy or Legitimate Longing?

O what a thing is thought!
Which seems a dream; yea, seemeth nought,
Yet doth the mind
Affect as much as what we find
Most near and true! Sure men are blind,
And can't the forcible reality
Of things that secret are within them see.[1]

In the last chapter I sketched a broadly Romantic view of religious experience as affective rather than cognitive, an ecstatic mood of apprehending eternal deity, in opposition to both Turner's rejection of the very notion of religious experience and Alston's misleading perceptual model of such an experience. Thus the Platonic account of the imaginative experience of transcendence set out in the first two chapters was defended against alternative contemporary accounts, but with a somewhat negative or critical emphasis. In this chapter I wish to set forth a more positive story, more specifically a version of a neo-Romantic theory inspired by Coleridge and Schelling. In particular I shall outline a defence of a robustly Romantic theory of religion. This includes the Romantic distinction between symbol and allegory, and a theory of the mythological on the basis of Coleridge's concept of the 'tautegorical'. The Coleridge–Schelling option obviates the critiques that assume the Hegelian–Feuerbachian concept of the imagination. It is within the context of this Romantic legacy that I discuss more recent figures. My deployment of Jung and Corbin will not be designed to support a religious universalism, but rather to function as a prologemenon to a theory of special revelation. This is the point of the central distinction between the symbolic and the figurative or the tautegorical and the allegorical, and my concluding discussion of Walter Benjamin and Paul de Man should reinforce precisely the theological dimension of the theory of the symbol as opposed to allegory.

The Romantics developed highly influential theories about the religious psyche, and I shall explore a central source of such reflections as they have shaped much recent thought about religion. Carl Jung envisaged the religious imagination as a way of crossing the borders between the unconscious and the conscious and as a healing process.

---

1 Thomas Traherne, 'Dreams', ll. 43–9; *Selected Poems and Prose*, ed. A. Bradford (Harmondsworth: Penguin, 1991), p. 139.

Mircea Eliade saw modern man as alienated from the symbolic inheritance of the past, and the religious imagination as the means of reawakening ancient but forgotten symbols and thereby reinvesting the world with the sacral significance which it has lost through the disenchantment process of modernity. Mankind is not just *homo faber* but *homo religiosus*. Jung writes as a psychologist, Eliade as a theorist of religion. Both have a deep and specific debt to Romanticism in thinking that we detect the sacred in the profane.

Theories of religion and the tautegorical imaginary

One might speak of two major types of theory of religion. The first we might call the Enlightenment model, the second the Romantic. The first is the strict rationalistic view. A science of religion views the phenomenon of 'religion' as a pre-scientific (and usually false) theory about the world. Durkheim's *Elementary Forms of the Religious Life* and Frazer's *The Golden Bough* are classic examples of this kind of Enlightenment-style theory: much empirical, anthropological evidence is amassed and naturalistic reasons are provided for the beliefs and practices proposed. This theory draws upon progressivist strands in Enlightenment thought. Religion, far from being a *desiderium naturale*, is a naturalistically explicable phenomenon, if not a kind of parasitic disease, which is gradually waning among more sophisticated cultures but shows a remarkable tenacity in the ill-educated margins of such societies and in less cultivated civilizations.

The general problem with the first kind of theory is that it consigns all religion to error of varying levels of crassness. Evolutionary psychology has tried to reduce Christianity to its genetic role; cognitive psychology tries to explain religion as a ritualized *memoria technica*. For example, Pascal Boyer argues that, with evolutionary biology and cognitive psychology, we can explain religion properly for the first time as the application of basic inferential processes to imaginary agents: ancestors or gods. Although religion is culturally universal, it is parasitic upon more basic and diverse mental capacities. There is no religious instinct as such but only different domains, some of which our evolutionary history has favoured, and from which religion – as an item of the cultural imagination, like fiction, can be viewed as the cumulation of relatively inconsiderable breaches of inferential explanations.[2] These theories have the general character of viewing religion as essentially practical: a method of coping with an unknown and frightening world, akin to magic. If that is correct, and religious beliefs are as preposterous as its critics claim, the persistence of religious belief is rather puzzling. Since evolution presumably favours those organisms capable of forming correct beliefs in reacting to their environment, the extravagant and erroneous religious beliefs of human beings present a puzzle for

---

2 P. Boyer, *Religion Explained: The Evolutionary Origins of Religious Thought* (New York: Basic Books, 2001).

evolutionary theory. Although products of evolution, human beings seem strikingly unique and the religious drive seems a distinctly human characteristic. As Whichcote remarks, ' "a man" is not to be defined with Plato as *"Animal rationale"*, i.e. a rational creature" but as *"Animal religiosum"*, a religious creature'.[3] Yet, far from placing *Homo sapiens* at an advantage, the religious drive would seem to make the species uniquely inept. As Kolakowski observes:

> If religious belief is simply the result of our wish to control the world, it is hard to see why so purely a technical attitude could have involved the human imagination in such aberrations as the search for hidden and technically useless meanings in empirical phenomena, or how and why the idea of the sacred was formed.[4]

The alternative model, of Romantic provenance, challenges the rationalist model as far too crude to encompass – far less explain – the phenomenon of the sacred. Religion is *sui generis,* and the Enlightenment view fails to account for the symbolic aspects of religion. I shall refer to this position as the Coleridge–Schelling view.[5] In order to explore this view, we need to consider the questions of symbol and mythology with the key concept of the 'tautegorical'. A symbol is tautegorical on this view because it cannot be translated into something other, but is *itself.* Whereas an allegorical narrative presupposes a one-to-one correspondence between the described subject and the intended other, a symbol is self-contained and resists translation into anything other than itself. As the great French scholar of Islam, Henri Corbin, writes:

> The symbol is not an artificially constructed sign; it flowers in the soul spontaneously to announce something that cannot be expressed otherwise; it is the unique expression of the thing symbolized as of a reality that thus becomes transparent to the soul, but which in itself transcends all expression. Allegory is a more or less artificial figuration of generalities or abstractions that are perfectly cognizable or expressible in other ways.[6]

An allegory is primarily intellectual and transitive; symbol is more immediate and intransitive. The meaning of the allegory can be articulated and is finite; the symbol is not exactly inexplicable, but it is inscrutable and infinite in its meaning. It is this Coleridge–Schelling concept of the symbol as 'tautegorical' and not allegorical which we shall explore.

3 B. Whichcote, *Some Select Notions* (London, 1685), pp. 85–6.
4 L. Kolakowski, 'The Revenge of the Sacred in the Secular', in *Modernity on Endless Trial* (Chicago: University of Chicago Press, 1990), pp. 64–5.
5 Our emphasis upon English and German Romanticism can be justified by the fact that French Romanticism was not much concerned with symbol until later.
6 H. Corbin, *Avicenne et le récit visionnaire* (Lagrasse, France: Verdier, 1999), pp. 43–4.

Tautegory and Romantic mythology

The Romantic idea of the religious symbol was closely linked to burgeoning eighteenth-century theories of mythology. Karl Philipp Moritz (1756–1793) saw mythology as poetic. Gottfried Hermann (1772–1848) interpreted myth as having philosophical significance and Friedrich Creuzer (1771–1858) in his seminal work, first published as *Symbolik und Mythologie der alten Volker* (1819–23), argued that mythology is a divine illumination in the soul of man.[7] But it is really Schelling who developed the most detailed metaphysical account of mythology among the German idealists/Romantics, and his legacy was powerfully felt in the twentieth century. Coleridge managed to give expression to the rejection of an allegorical approach to myth – a tendency in Schelling's own thought about mythology which Schelling had been developing for several years, and which only comes into clear expression in his lecture *Über die Gottheiten von Samothrake* of 1815. Coleridge might be seen to be intuiting and articulating Schelling's own intellectual temper. On the other hand, Schelling was continuously wrestling with the same problems: myth, nature, art and the absolute. He never found an adequate form in which to articulate a 'system' of philosophy, which was the ambition of the day. His earliest work was as the youthful genius in the Tübinger Stift conjuring over the myth of Genesis and Plato's *Timaeus*. One is reminded of Coleridge as the young Bluecoat boy of Christ's Hospital described so memorably by Charles Lamb:

> Come back into memory, like as thou wert in the dayspring of thy fancies. . . How I have seen the casual passer through the Cloisters stand still, entranced with admiration (while he weighed the disproportion between the *speech* and the garb of the young Mirandula), to hear thee unfold, in thy deep and sweet intonations, the mysteries of Jamblichus, or Plotinus (for even in those years thou waxedst not pale at such philosophic draughts), or reciting Homer in his Greek, or Pindar – while the walls of the old GreyFriars re-echoed to the accents of the inspired *charity boy!*[8]

The achievement of both writers was fragmentary and clouded by controversy, both over their personal lives and regarding their integrity as writers. Yet both have subsequently exerted an enormously rich influence upon subsequent generations.

It is sometimes suggested that Schelling is a protean figure who moved from an early Fichtean position to *Naturphilosophie*, his Identity Philosophy (*Identitätsphilosophie*), and then a final phase under the gnoseological-theosophical influence of Baader; yet there is much continuity in Schelling's œuvre. The concept which most powerfully and acutely expresses Schelling's philosophy of mythology, and the

---

7 See E. Benz, 'Theogony and Transformation in Schelling', in J. Campbell (ed.), *Man and Transformation*, (Princeton, NJ: Princeton University Press, 1964), p. 206.

8 Quoted in R. Holmes, *Coleridge: Early Visions* (London: Hodder and Stoughton, 1989), p. 32.

concept which was used by his successors in the twentieth century such as Corbin and Cassirer, was that of the symbol as 'tautegory', and this term was borrowed from Coleridge.

Schelling was fascinated by mythology from the very beginning of his thought. His earliest attempt, in his Master's dissertation, 'Antiquissimi de prima malorum humanorum origine philosophematis Gen. III explicandi tentamen criticum et philosophicum' (1792), showed signs of rationalism. In his philosophy of art mythology, the substance of art is constituted by the ideas which are bodied forth in the shape of the gods. Mythology provides the stuff of art. Art, however, as the locus in which the infinite is manifested in the finite, becomes theophanic – that is, showing the Divine. In Schelling's lectures on the philosophy of art the theophanic dimension of art is sublimated as the theogonic aspect of mythology comes to the fore. The later Schelling does not discuss art explicitly, but it is clear that for him the myths are themselves expressed through poetry and other arts. His late idea that myth is an index or protocol of the Divine has a clear relation to both his early (Tübingen) work on myth and his reflections upon art during the period of his collaboration with the great Romantics.

The exact relationship between Coleridge and Schelling is deeply intriguing. The later work of Schelling on the nature of mythology was met with incomprehension and ridicule. Kierkegaard famously thought Schelling drivelled on intolerably.[9] Schelling is not attributing faint praise to Coleridge as one who understood his work while his own countrymen were either ignorant or hostile towards his endeavours, but instead is expressing a deep and grateful affinity. Coleridge's account of the Prometheus myth is as a hieroglyphic tale, a synthesis of poesy and philosophy.[10] It is close to Schelling's view of myth as the primordial and ineluctable reflection and unfolding of the nature of the human spirit. Coleridge shares with Schelling the sense of a historical and providential dimension to myth and also the broader link with Christian revelation. Unlike Kierkegaard (or his more recent followers like Auerbach), Coleridge wishes to emphasize continuity between Christian and pagan culture. Whereas Kierkegaard uses Agamemnon as a foil to Abraham the Knight of Faith in *Fear and Trembling*, Coleridge develops a Christian inclusivism, like Schelling, which sees mythology as a part of a broader process of revelation and salvation. It is no accident that Schelling and Coleridge were both writing at a time of great missionary activity, and the increasing facility of communication between cultures two hundred years later enhances the attraction of such universalism.

Furthermore, Coleridge is a unique figure in the Anglo-Saxon world. Blake developed his own idiosyncratic mythology out of biblical, apocalyptic, and Neoplatonic elements, but does not produce such sophisticated reflection upon mythology. Also, Coleridge exhibits a fascinating link with the German tradition. The distinguished Scots

9 See X. Tilliette, *Schelling Biographie* (Stuttgart: Klett-Cotta, 1989), p. 404.
10 S. T. Coleridge, *Shorter Works and Fragments* (Princeton, NJ: Princeton University Press, 1995), vol. II, p. 1267.

theologian Thomas Erskine of Linlathen wrote in a letter of a meeting with Schelling:

> Schelling is here – I know him and like him very well, but cannot get much out of him – he says he is here to drink the waters, and not to make out propositions, and that he must avoid everything that would trouble his head . . . I spoke to Schelling about Carlyle – he said he could not tolerate his style . . . he thought a good deal of Coleridge, he spoke of him as a great genius.[11]

On the other hand, it is clear that Schelling continued to influence Coleridge long after 1818. Coleridge's interest in myth, though worked out in an independent spirit, reveals a deep interest and respect for Schelling's thought.

Prometheus and the deities of Samothrace

In 1825, Coleridge lectured to the Royal Society of Literature 'On the Prometheus of Aeschylus'. It is Coleridge's most important study of mythology. The text has a tripartite structure. The lecture begins with a broadly anthropological account of myth, starting from the controversies surrounding the deciphering of hieroglyphics, explaining Egyptian religion as pantheism in the process of degenerating into polytheism. It then moves on to an exposition of Coleridge's theistic metaphysics, including the relations of the histories of the Phoenicians, Hebrews and Greeks to their respective metaphysical systems, nature and spirit, law and idea. The third and final section is the largely allegorical – and somewhat mechanical – application of (Coleridge's own) metaphysics to Aeschylus's play *Prometheus*, in which Zeus represents 'law' and Prometheus 'idea'.

Coleridge claims that 'The earliest Greeks took up the religious and lyrical poetry of the Hebrews' from the prophets via the Phoenicians.[12] The Hebrew tradition represents the childlike obedience to the eternal I AM; the Greek mind developed philosophy as its distinctive achievement in the historical development of man towards truth. And (here the Platonist Coleridge is revealed) philosophy revolved around the question of self-consciousness; 'Great minds turned inward on the fact of the *diversity* between Man and beast; a superiority of *kind*'.[13] The poets in Greece could serve as a means of preserving the original insight of monotheism from decaying into pantheism and polytheism, unlike the Hebrews, who possessed revelation to preserve them, and the Egyptians, who had collapsed into pantheism by the time of Moses:

---

11 T. Erskine, letter to Jane Stirling, 31 August 1846, quoted in D. Horrocks, *Laws of the Spiritual Order: Innovation and Reconstruction in the Soteriology of Thomas Erskine of Linlathen* (Nottingham: Paternoster Press, 2004), p. 229.
12 Coleridge, *Shorter Works*, vol. II, p. 1265.
13 Ibid., p. 1266.

What proof have you of the fact of any connection between the Greek drama and either the mysteries or the philosophy of Greece? What proof that it was the office of the tragic poet, under a disguise of the sacerdotal religion, mixed with the legendary or popular belief, to reveal so much of the mysteries interpreted by philosophy, as would counteract the demoralising effects of the state religion, without compromising the tranquility of the state itself, or weakening that paramount reverence, without which a republic (such, I mean, as the republics of ancient Greece were) could not exist.[14]

The *Prometheus* of Aeschylus was, according to Coleridge's account, the adaptation of the 'secret doctrines of the mysteries' as an 'antidote to the debasing influences of the religion of the state'.[15] The myth of Prometheus in Aeschylus's 'stupendous poem' represents primarily the *gift* of reason – as 'unapproachable and unmodifiable by the animal basis'.[16] This is the *Deus in nobis*:[17]

In the Greek we see already the dawn of approaching manhood. The substance, the stuff is philosophy, the *form* only is poetry. The Prometheus is a philosopheme and tautegorikon.[18]

Coleridge wishes to explore the continuity between the Hellenic and the Hebrew traditions, and indeed the dialectical interdependence of the two, although he holds quite strictly to belief in primordial monotheism. Schelling distinguishes between relative and absolute monotheism in his *Philosophy of Mythology*.[19] However, in his earlier *Deities* he seems to reject the primordial monotheism theory (which he associates with Warburton).

Schelling's *Deities of Samothrace* presents a very different picture of the relationship between the Greeks and the Hebrews. Schelling explores linguistic affinities between Greek, Hebrew and Phoenician in order to show that the Samathrocean deities both exhibit affinities with the symbolism of the ancient Near East and point to the central themes of the Eleusinian mysteries.[20] Unlike the clear priority of Hebrew scripture in Coleridge, the Bible becomes a prudent restriction ('weiseste Einschränkung') of an older and richer system of thought. Hence for Schelling there are traces in Scripture of ideas which can be found in greater detail in other traditions (especially Greek mythology), even if for providential reasons Hebrew scripture was best suited for the victory of the idea of a providential, transcendent God.[21] Schelling's view is that the

---

14 Ibid., p. 1264.
15 Ibid., p. 1277.
16 Ibid., p. 1281.
17 Compare Nicholas of Cusa: 'deus et creatura, absolutum et contractum.': *De docta ignorantia* 192, 7.
18 Coleridge, *Shorter Works*, vol. II, pp. 1267–8.
19 E. A. Beach, *The Potencies of God(s): Schelling's Philosophy of Mythology* (Albany: SUNY Press , 1994), p. 188.
20 See R. F. Brown, *Schelling's Treatise on "The Deities of Samothrace"* (Missoula, Mont.: Scholars Press, 1974).
21 Ibid., p. 25.

gradual disclosure of truth in myths is part of a progressive unfolding of the Godhead, and throughout Schelling's work on mythology the Greeks provide the cipher for all other mythologies. Paralleling his greater emphasis upon divine immanence, Schelling places far greater weight upon the continuing and incremental process of the historical enhancement of the human consciousness as divine disclosure through mythology. Mythology is the protocol of a developing divine revelation, whereas Coleridge sees the myth as giving expression to a revelation which is instantaneous rather than cumulative or incremental.[22] Prometheus represents the giving of Reason to mankind as a divine gift. This, I think, is Schelling's point when he remarks that Coleridge understands tautegory as a philosopheme, i.e. bodying forth a philosophical principle or truth. For Coleridge, this truth is essentially timeless, whereas for Schelling the symbols represent diachronic divine disclosure. Schelling is quite right to flag up the differences. Yet he was clearly much indebted to Coleridge for the term 'tautegory', whatever their specific metaphysical/theological disagreements. In his *Historical Critical Introduction to the Philosophy of Mythology* Schelling writes:

> Mythology is not allegorical, it is tautegorical. The gods are really existing beings, which are not some other things, which mean not something other, but just what they are.[23]

He notes that this is borrowed from the 'well known Coleridge', the 'first English scholar to have understood and creatively employed German poetry and thought, especially philosophy'.[24] Schelling found the expression in the remarkable (*wunderlich*) essay on Prometheus. It delighted Schelling how Coleridge had understood Schelling's own text *On the Deities of Samothrace*, whose philosophical signifiacance was little understood or completely misunderstood in Germany. It seems as if Coleridge had found a term which expressed an idea which Schelling had been labouring to articulate for several years. Benjamin Jowett spoke to Schelling about Coleridge, and Schelling remarked that Coleridge 'had expressed many things better than he could himself, that in one word he had comprised a whole essay, saying that mythology was not allegorical but tautegorical.'[25]

---

22 I am very grateful to Jeff Einboden for this observation.
23 'Die Mythologie ist nicht allegorisch, sie ist tautegorisch. Die Götter sind ihr wirklich existierende Wesen, die nicht etwas anders sind, etwas anderes bedeuten, sondern nur das bedeuten, was sie sind.': F. W. J. Schelling, *Ausgewälte Schriften Philosophie der Mythologie*, in vol. 5, pt 1 (Frankfurt: Surkamp, 1985), p. 205.
24 Schelling, *Ausgewählte Schriften*, vol. 5, p. 206.
25 Quoted in Coleridge, *Lay Sermons* (Princeton, NJ: Princeton University Press, 1972), p. 30 n. 3. In the 1847 edition of *Biographia Literaria*, edited by Sara Coleridge, she relates that Schelling said 'I have read what he has written with great pleasure, and I took occasion in my lectures to vindicate him from the charge, which has been brought against him, of plagiarising from me: and I said that it was rather I who owed much to him, and that, in the Essay on Prometheus, Coleridge in his remark, that "Mythology was not allegorical but tautegorical" had concentrated in a striking expression (*in einem schlagenden Ausdruck*) what I had been labouring to represent with much toil and trouble': pp. xxxviii–xxxix.

Because Mythology is not artificial but natural, indeed developed under conditions of necessity, content and form, stuff and appearance cannot be divided. The representations are not in another form but appear in just this (specific) form.

Since consciousness does not choose or discover the representations, mythology develops as such, and in a different sense, in so far as it expresses Itself. In consequence of the necessity, with which the content of the representations are formed, mythology has a real and doctrinal meaning: because of the necessity, with which the form develops, it is really, i.e. everything is to be understood as expressing itself, not as if something *other* were thought or something *other* were said.[26]

The basic mistake was to view myths as saying something 'other' than themselves, whether this 'other' be legends or histories of great men, or personifications of natural forces, or moral truths, etc. Schelling's argumentative strategy is to reverse the naturalist or the euhemerist stance. In his late *Philosophy of Mythology*, he explains the physical or historical events in terms of the spiritual experience, rather than explaining the latter via the former. He does not doubt, for example, the enormous significance of such items as seasons or stars on the development of religious ideas. But he doubted that these items per se could explain the religious instinct in a non-question-begging manner. Rather, it is the a priori religious instinct which best explains the construal of inanimate objects or remarkable personalities as 'gods' or as vehicles of spiritual realities: 'A reversed euhemerism is the correct view'.[27] The mistake of the naturalists is to interpret the higher as pointing to the lower. The correct approach is to see the sensible or lower reality as pointing to the higher spiritual truth. But the point is not just that we have an activity of the psyche which cannot be readily explained in biological or materialistic terms and which is an index of spiritual and immaterial facts; the question is also one of the order of explanation. The myth does not proceed from the material fact, but shapes how the psyche experiences the biological, historical or material facts. It is not history that

---

26 'Weil die Mythologie nicht ein künstlich, sondern ein natürlich, ja unter der gegebenen Voraussetzung mit Notwendigkeit Entstandenes ist, lassen sich in ihr nicht Inhalt und Form, Stoff und Einkleidung unterscheiden. Die Vorstellungen sind nicht erst in einer andern Form vorhanden, sondern sie entstehen nur in und also zugleich auch mit dieser Form. Ein solches organisches Werden war früher von uns in diesem Vortrag schon einmal gefordert, aber das Princip des Processes, wodurch es allein erklärbar wird, war nicht gefunden.

Weil das Bewußtsein weder die Vorstellungen selbst, noch deren Ausdruck wählt oder erfindet, so entsteht die Mythologie gleich als solche, und in seinem andern Sinn, als indem sie sich ausspricht. Zufolge der Notwendigkeit, mit welcher sich der Inhalt der Vorstellungen erzeugt, hat die Mythologie von Anfang an reelle und also doctrinelle Bedeutung; zufolge der Nothwendigkeit, mit welcher auch die Form entsteht, ist sie durchaus eigentlich, d.h. es ist alles in ihr so zu vertsehen wie sie es ausspricht, nicht als ob etwas anderes gebracht, etwas anderes gefragt ware': Schelling, *Philosphy der Mythologie*, p. 205.

27 Schelling, *Philosphie der Mythologie*, p. 243.

determines the mythology of a people, but the mythology which determines the history.

Not only is this account of mythology tied to a universal account of human consciousness but also to a theory of encounter with the divine presence in history, a confrontation with supernatural agency. God is not the product of human fantasy, as in Hume's natural theory of religion, but the human mind is imprinted and forged by its primordial (and ongoing) encounter with the 'unprethinkable' (*unvordenklich*) divine reality. Hence mythology is not an index merely of human consciousness but of Being itself. Here is the question of ontology. If the only *real* facts are those of natural science, and if the only values are competing interests of competing egos, then mythology looks entirely antiquated. But if virtue and vice, good and evil, justice and tyranny relate to the fabric of the universe, moral and spiritual facts are as much a part of the universe as particles and waves. This should not surprise us: Schelling's idealism becomes evident in his attempt to see the history of mythology and religion as a process of divine economy – an account of *Geist*. Coleridge differed on this point – he insisted that such a theogony compromised divine perfection; but his sympathy for Schelling's metaphysical ambitions was deep and provides the context for his criticisms.

Schelling's specific arguments against the naturalists are often very convincing. He rejects the idea that the original purpose of myth could have been the conveyance of metaphysical-ethical ideas as an esoteric content. Nor is it likely that myths were really quasi-scientific explanations. This would assume a huge gulf between the makers of myths and the population at large, but would also make deeply mysterious the acceptance of myths by the people. Schelling argued that the sheer force of myth was explicable only in terms of an objective necessity. They were not merely the products of invention, since this would render their universal power utterly mysterious. As Beach observes: 'no function of human conscious life which was subject to the free decisions of intelligence and will could ever have produced the irresistible hold myths have exercised on whole people and cultures'.[28] To use Schelling's neat example, Persephone does not symbolize the planting and growth of crops but the crops symbolize Persephone.[29] The archetypal imaginative structure forms an irreducible pattern for events in the world. Hence the evidently historical figure of Alexander was shaped profoundly by the poetic figure of Achilles. Thus history conformed to an imaginative archetype, and hence nature 'imitated' art.

Christianity and myth

Yet since it was Hegel, rather than Schelling, who was the *spiritus rector* of so much modern theology, we can see the Hegelian legacy in much of

28 Beach, *The Potencies of God(s)*, p. 38.
29 Schelling, *Philosophie der Mythologie*, pp. 639ff.

the historical-critical work on, say, the Christian Bible in the nineteenth and twentieth centuries. One might note that Bultmann's existentialism grew out of a dialectical Lutheranism and his view that the mythological language in the Bible is a cloak for the kerygma. His seminal 1941 essay 'Neues Testament und Mythologie: Das Problem der Entmythologisierung der neutestamentlichen Verkündigung' had roots in Bultmann's proximity to Heidegger in Marburg (1923–8). The legacy of *Lebensphilosophie* of a Heideggerian stamp and a scientific positivism (not always conscious) drives Bultmann to an untenable dualism between the imaginative cloak and the genuine core of the gospel.

There are two major problems with Bultmann's proposal, and they are closely linked to his positivism and *Lebensphilosophie*. First, Bultmann seems to rule out of court as unscientific a providential and active deity. He is captive to just the same naturalistic assumption, i.e. that 'nature' is itself a closed system, which shaped the rationalists of the Enlightenment and the neo-Hegelians. Science provides laws of nature and special divine action would contravene these laws. Yet such a position is hardly verifiable scientifically, and must be a philosophical viewpoint – as many acute thinkers from C. S. Lewis to Alvin Plantinga have observed. The affinity between Bultmann and Spinoza is striking – biblical criticism and the metaphysics of a closed naturalistic universe converge on each other.

Secondly, if we demythologize Christianity, it is not at all clear what is left of the religion of the descendant of David, who returns as king to Jerusalem, who enters the Temple and is crucified by the Romans, to say nothing of the sacrificial Lamb who is also the Christus Victor who defeats Satan. The personal encounter with the Divine Word which Bultmann perceives as the core of Christianity is either simply a version of Heidegger's own decisionism, or if not explicable in philosophical-existentialist terms, it is – as Kolakowski observes – just as mythological as the story Bultmann wishes to dispense with.[30]

Yet the Christian gospel is presented as a cosmic drama, the story of the Messiah who through his sacrifice will renew the Temple of Jerusalem and thereby overcome the powers of darkness.[31] A typical bad argument against the reality of Jesus of Nazareth is that because the history contains archetypal or mythic elements, these cannot be historical. History may reflect myth, but that does not necessarily invalidate the factual component. The stories of the Corsican who rose to be Emperor of the French and master of Europe, the Georgian who became the most powerful and brutal of the Tsars, and the Austrian subaltern who founded a Third German Empire, are full of mythic elements, but it does not mean that there are no facts of the matter – no Napoleon, Stalin or Hitler. They all have in common the 'Parsifal' motif of the sacred task and astonishing, mysterious charisma and power of the outsider who fulfils it. 'God redeemed the corrupt making creatures, men, in a way fitting to this aspect, as to others, of their strange nature', says

30 Kolakowski, 'The Illusion of Demythologization', in *Modernity on Endless Trial*, p. 105.
31 G. Graham, *Evil and Christian Ethics* (Cambridge: Cambridge University Press, 2001), pp. 29–73.

J. R. R. Tolkien.[32] He observes that 'History often resembles "Myth" because they are both ultimately of the same stuff.'[33] Tolkien believes that each myth partakes in the greater story of salvation through Christ. Tolkien, unlike Bultmann, presents Christianity unabashedly in its eschatological-apocalyptic mode, and discusses the relationship between fairy tales and the gospel in terms of the Great Eucatastrophe or good turn. The salvation of the gospel is the primary story which 'embraces all the essence of fairy stories': the happy ending of the fairy story 'may be a far off gleam or echo of *evangelium* in the real world'.[34]

He states explicitly that *The Lord of the Rings* is 'a fundamentally religious and Catholic work . . . the religious element is absorbed into the story and the symbolism'.[35] However, the work should not, Tolkien says, be understood allegorically.[36] 'As for any meaning or "message", it has in the intention of the author none. It is neither allegorical nor topical . . . I cordially dislike allegory in all its manifestations'.[37] However 'it [myth] is at its best when it is presented by a poet who feels rather than makes explicit what his theme portends . . . for myth is alive at once and in all its parts, and dies before it can be dissected.'[38] That said, Tolkien clearly thinks that an effective story draws its power from underlying truths which it can represent. The Gospels contain a fairy story, the essence of fairy stories: 'this story has entered History and the primary world; the desire and the aspiration of sub-creation has been raised to the fulfilment of Creation. The Birth of Christ is the eucatastrophe of Man's history. The resurrection is the eucatastrophe of the story of the Incarnation'.[39] Christianity is presented by Tolkien as a story which has entered history, a myth which has become fact. A good story is suffused with that structure of ultimate reality which is paradigmatically expressed in the gospel. Genuine and rich fiction has a truth component, though partly veiled in the symbolic form. In this manner literature participates in man's communion with the Divine.

Perhaps the mythic dimension of Christianity is less of an obstacle than Bultmann supposed. Perhaps the surprising persistence of Christianity as a phenomenon in Western culture, as well as in much of the rest of the world, lies in its capacity to address with the imagination, through symbols and narrative, those archetypal aspects of human experience which lie beyond the merely instrumental, and indeed are often submerged beneath consciousness. Ernst Benz writes: 'Schelling's approach to mythology takes on a special significance in the light of

---

32 J. R. R. Tolkien, *Tree and Leaf* (London: George Allen and Unwin, 1970), p. 62.
33 Ibid., p. 31.
34 Ibid., p. 62.
35 H. Carpenter, *The Letters of J. R. R. Tolkien* (London: George Allen and Unwin, 1981), p. 172.
36 See C. Moseley, *J. R. R. Tolkien* (Plymouth: Northcote, 1997), pp. 76–7.
37 J. R. R. Tolkien, *The Lord of the Rings* (London: HarperCollins, 1968), p. 11.
38 J. R. R. Tolkien, *The Monsters and the Critics*, ed. M. Drout (Arizona: Tempe, 2002), pp. 14–15.
39 Ibid., p. 62.

this rediscovery of myth by modern psychology.'[40] On the account offered above, the study of mythology becomes not so much an exploration of the minds of particular poets or subcultures as human consciousness itself. The great theorist of religions Eliade writes:

> The psychologists . . . have shown us how much the dramas of the modern world proceed from a profound disequilibrium of the psyche, individual as well as collective, brought about largely by a progressive sterilisation of the imagination. To "have imagination" is to enjoy a richness of interior life, an uninterrupted and spontaneous flow of images. But spontaneity does not mean arbitrary invention. Etymologically, "imagination" is related to both *imago* – a representation or imitation – and *imitor*, to imitate or reproduce. And for once, etymology is in accord with both psychological realities and spiritual truth. The imagination *imitates* the exemplary models – the Images – reproduces, reactualises and repeats them without end. To have imagination is to see the world in its totality, for the power and the mission of images is to *show* all that remains refractory to the concept: hence the disfavour and failure of the man "without imagination"; he is cut off from the deeper reality of life and from his own soul.[41]

Rather than being reduced to the denuded existentialist gauntlet, the soul confronted with the stark and denuded decision of faith, Christianity is better considered in all its imaginative panoply. Rather than myth being a bar to its proper comprehension, perhaps the mythological elements provide an apologetic bridgehead – a point of contact with archetypal experiences and images in which revelation proper can perform its transforming work. As C. S. Lewis wrote:

> We must not be ashamed of the mythical radiance resting on our theology. We must not be nervous about 'parallels' and 'Pagan-Christs'; they *ought* to be there – it would be a stumbling-block if they weren't. We must not . . . withhold our imaginative welcome. If God chooses to be mythopoeic – and is not the sky itself a myth? – shall we refuse to be mythopathic? For this is the marriage of heaven and earth.[42]

Imagination and the unconscious

Carl Jung saw the primary work of imagination as being primarily disclosed in dream symbols. In such a way the imagination provides a symbolic mediation between the conscious and unconscious life. Jung

---

40 E. Benz, 'Theogony and Transformation in Friedrich Wilhelm Joseph Schelling', in *Man and Transformation*, p. 209.
41 M. Eliade, *Images and Symbols: Studies in Religious Symbolism* (Princeton, NJ: Princeton University Press, 1991), p. 20.
42 C. S. Lewis, 'Myth Became Fact', in *God in the Dock: Essays on Theology*, ed. W. Hooper (London: Fount, 1998), p. 67.

drew upon the interest in myths and dreams in the Romantic period evident in writers such as Creuzer, Carus and von Schubert. I wish to concentrate upon Jung's employment of archetypes because it is at once very suggestive but rather lacking in historical and conceptual rigour. One can draw much out of Jungian reflections without any deep commitment to the methodology or some of the basic tenets.[43]

Freud's emphasis upon mythological elements in the subconscious – the Oedipus complex is striking – demonstrates that myth reflects an experience of humanity, and he sees the subconscious as condensing psychic conflicts into symbolic form which finds expression in myths, dreams and fairy tales. The 'discovery' of the unconscious around 1900 was embedded in various philosophical interests and assumptions which are clearly traceable to the Enlightenment tradition, which pursues neo-Darwinian, late-nineteenth-century naturalism.[44] Dreams are interpreted in terms of instincts, and the repression of instinctual forces, the resultant disturbances of consciousness, and the mythic elements are remnants of an earlier phase of human development. Dreams depict those secrets which are otherwise hidden from consciousness, the chaos which is hidden by the order of the conscious mind. Yet Freud did provide ammunition against the dissolution of the soul. One need only consider the bitter opposition between behaviourism, which saw religion as merely conditioned behaviour, and psychoanalysis in the mid-twentieth century to see why Freud was regarded as a crypto-Romantic by the positivists. Religion is neurosis for Freud, but it is a part of the interior life. Visions and dreams play a significant role in most great religions; and Freud plausibly emphasized the importance of images and dreams in the development of the psyche. In as much as the contents of the mind are shaped by a mixture of conscious and unconscious influences, some of which extend to early childhood, the various experiences of the psyche have a shaping influence upon the temper and disposition of the ego via certain patterns. These patterns structure the encounter with both present and future. But the pattern may be shaped by traumas lodged in childhood memories or semi-conscious or subconscious experiences which can lead to dysfunction in adult life. The therapist's task is thus to help bring to the ego's consciousness patterns which it can reinterpret and thus experience anew. Hence the mature ego need not be locked into patterns of behaviour which were shaped by the needs of the dependent and fragile infant. The repatterning process can thus be a route to liberation.

Between 1910 and 1920, Jung developed a much broader model, much more deeply indebted to the Romantic tradition, in which religious images are construed as potent and unavoidable realities of the uncon-

---

43 For a critical Christian appreciation of Jung, see V. White, *God and the Unconscious* (London: Harvill, 1952).

44 De Quincey first used the word 'subconscious' in print in 1823 – perhaps prompted by conversation with Coleridge, who uses it in *The Notebooks of Samuel Taylor Coleridge*, ed. K. Coburn (Princeton, NJ: Princeton University Press, 1971–2002), vol. 2, p. 2915. See also 'how much lies below consciousness' (ibid., vol. 1, p. 1554) and the 'mysterious gradations of consciousness'(ibid., vol. 3, p. 3362).

scious mind. He developed a theory of these patterns of the collective unconscious as 'archetypes'. The archetypal symbol is the bodying forth of the pattern in a particular form, e.g. the archetypal pattern of evil takes on the shape of the devil or a witch. The archetypes find expression in visual or image form rather than verbally. The archetypes have a clear Platonic/Neoplatonic provenance.[45] Claire Douglas notes the 'Romantic philosophers who played a crucial role in the formation of Jung's theories', and makes special mention of Schelling.[46] In Jung's model, the symbolic realm has its own autonomy and necessity – a priori, irreducible to instinctual naturalistic forces, and collective. The symbolic domain is not primarily the unconscious of an individual but that of the group or the race. Myths are 'first and foremost psychic phenomena that reveal the nature of the soul.'[47] Consciousness can tap a vast symbolic reservoir of myth and symbols which Jung interpreted as forming a subconscious language.[48] Jung's critique of Freud follows basically Schelling's path. Freud is trying to explain behaviour in terms of individual relations of human beings and their instincts. Hence he explores the history of individual patients and considers how this history might be related to the instinctual drives grounded in their sexuality. Jung thinks that this is far too narrow and employs a much broader vista, one which includes cultural, historical and archetypal dimensions. Rather than seeing the father–son relationship as a complex of aggression and guilt, Jung sees the tension between father and son as part of a broader need for the process of individuation and drama of deliverance in which the son emancipates himself from the father, a pattern which can be observed in countless fairy tales or myths because, in the terminology of Jung, our psyches contain instances of those contents of the collective unconscious which he calls archetypes. The biological relationship (father–son) is understood in terms of a spiritual/immaterial reality. Jung is much more positive towards archaic consciousness. Freud sees the conscious ego as trapped between the competing pressures of the id and the superego at the personal level and the draconian demands of civilization on the other. For Freud, the dark and dangerous id needs to be explored and illuminated, and this illumination requires the rational evaluation and critique of those compromises of civilization, of which religion is a particularly baneful instance. Yet for Jung, it is precisely the loss of the archaic and the religious which explains man's current malaise. The complexes are remnants of a primordial state of mind but are a healthy part of the psyche. Rather than a crude primitive

45 Albeit indirectly. The immediate sources would seem to be the *Corpus Hermeticum* and the Church Fathers.
46 C. Douglas, 'The Historical Context of Analytical Psychology', in P. Young-Isendrath and T. Dawson (eds), *The Cambridge Companion to Jung* (Cambridge: Cambridge University Press, 1997), pp. 22–3. Jung's dependence on Friedrich Creuzer is documented in his autobiography, *Memories, Dreams, Reflections* (New Pantheon, 1961), p. 163.
47 Benz, 'Theogony and Transformation', p. 208.
48 P. Pietikäinen, *C. G. Jung and the Psychology of Symbolic Forms* (Helsinki: Finnish Academy of Science and Letters, 1999).

and infantile legacy which should be overcome, this is the holy place or sanctum of the soul, part of the Promethean fire.

We began by considering the Enlightenment model of religion in contrast with the Romantic model. Jung is more sympathetic to the Romantic model of 'religion', and clearly bears the influence of the Schelling–Coleridge legacy. The Weimar period witnessed a striking revival of interest in Schelling: Otto, Jaspers, Tillich, Cassirer, Benjamin and Heidegger were all deeply influenced by this remarkable Schelling renaissance.[49]

The influence of the Schelling–Coleridge account of symbol was felt deeply in the twentieth century in the context of the distinguished group of scholars known as Eranos.[50] Steven M. Wasserstrom has produced a very thorough account of these seminal theorists of religion of the twentieth century. The creator of this group was Olga Fröbe-Kapteyn, who possessed a house outside Ascona at the magnificent location of Lago Maggiore, fand invited Jung in 1933. The word Eranos, suggested by Rudolf Otto, means feast, and each guest had to make a contribution to the banquet.[51] Between 1949 and 1976, Mircea Eliade, Gershom Scholem, Henry Corbin and Carl Jung all lectured at Eranos. All these figures were concerned about the disenchantment of Western civilization as a result of secularization and felt acutely the 'Age of Anxiety' of post-First World War Europe. Twentieth-century civilization was perceived as decadent and desiccated: alienated from its symbolic inheritance; deracinated from its spiritual sources; and starved by a dreary materialism and a vulgar obsession with technological advance.

Corbin argues that the strict link between symbol and symbolized differentiates symbol from allegory. He is explicit that the image of the Jerusalem Temple is not allegorical but tautegorical – it shares an identity with that which it expresses. Corbin, like Eliade and Jung, used Schelling's legacy to give a more satisfactory account of the numinous power of religion than those reductionistic narratives which translate religion into something 'other'. But Corbin insists that 'the *imago* is the form in which both the *one* and the *other* integrally manifest themselves. This privileged imaginal form can also be called *tautegorical'*.[52] In this way the Romantic/Platonic concepts of myth and symbol enjoyed a fertile and explicit *Nachleben*.

Yet this presents a challenge to the traditional theologian. The reality of theology is recognized, but it is interpreted as an entirely 'internal' reality relating to psychic powers. God is a reality for the psyche and the health of the psyche depends upon the symbolic system. Such a view of religion is far more easily reconcilable with Buddhism, for instance, than with the

49 Heidegger's Schelling lectures were given in Sommersemester 1936 and repeated during the war. See M. Heidegger, *Schellings Abhandlung über das Wesen der menschlichen Freiheit*, ed. H. Feick (Tübingen: Max Niemeyer, 1971).
50 S. Wasserstrom, *Religion After Religion: Gershom Scholem, Mircea Eliade, and Henry Corbin at Eranos* (Princeton, NJ: Princeton University Press, 1999).
51 See ibid., p. 36.
52 Corbin, 'The Imago Templi in Confrontation with Secular Norms', in *Temple and Contemplation* (London: KPI, 1986), p. 38.

monotheistic faiths.[53] The Eranos group – Jung, Eliade, Corbin, Scholem and others – performed a great service by pleading for the resurrection of the spiritual dimension, and in this respect were great inheritors of the Romantic tradition. But a central question remains. Is this ultimately a question of exploration, or transcendence, of the self? Is the Mundus Imaginalis of Corbin a shield in the face of the excessive light of the transcendent Deity, or a means of protection from the meaninglessness of the world after the death of God? The Coleridge–Schelling position challenges the view that the 'mythic' has been superseded by the rise of experimental science, and denies that a naturalistic construal of science can explain those elemental experiences of human beings which are expressed by the poets. The soaring lyricism of Plato's *Phaedrus* is a fine instance of this aesthetic religious impulse. John Stewart observes:

> The visions of the mythopoeic fancy are received by the Self of ordinary consciousness with a strange surmise of the existence, in another world, of another Self which, while it reveals itself in these visions, has a deep secret which it will not disclose. It is good that a man should thus be made to feel in his heart how small a part of him his head is – that the Scientific Understanding should be reminded that it is not the Reason – the Part, that it is not the *whole* Man. Herein chiefly lies the present value of Myth (or of its equivalent, Poetry, Music or whatever else) for civilised man.[54]

Stewart's words capture Jung's theory of the process of individuation through the means of intuitions and dreams. Perhaps one might say that this is the point of the mania of the *Phaedrus* (and a fortiori the *Ion*) – that art is parasitic upon levels of the mind which often elude the conscious rational intellect, both for the creator and the audience. The artist can give expression to that invisible and dynamic domain of the unconscious forces within the generic human soul. Linked to this mythic sense of a transcendent homeland is the corresponding feeling that the physical cosmos is a place of exile:

> Earth fills her lap with pleasures of her own:
> Yearnings she hath in her own natural kind,
> And e'en with something of a mother's mind,
> And no unworthy aim,
> The homely nurse doth all she can
> To make her foster-child, her Inmate Man,
> Forget the glories he hath known,
> And that imperial palace whence he came.[55]

---

53 J. Hillman, *Re-Visioning Psychology* (New York: Harper and Row, 1975), pp. 200–15, and 'Plotinus, Ficino, and Vico as Precursors of Archetypal Psychology', in *Loose Ends: Primary Papers in Archetypal Psychology* (Dallas: Spring, 1978). See also T. Moore, *The Planets Within: Marsilio Ficino's Astrological Psychology'* (Lewisburg, Pa.: Bucknell University Press, 1982).
54 J. A. Stewart, *The Myths of Plato* (London: Centaur Press, 1960), p. 29.
55 William Wordsworth, 'Ode: Intimations of Immortality', ll. 78–85.

On such a metaphysical view, human beings are, in their natural, unreflective state, 'asleep'. Our relationship with eternal truth is expressed in a number of myths of sleep and waking, remembering and forgetting, expressed vividly by Wordsworth's 'Our birth is but a sleep and a forgetting'. But, of course, such a picture has enormous philosophical and theological ramifications.

Symbol, allegory and the divine spark

Coleridge speaks of the symbol as tautegorical and as a *philosopheme*: a philosophical axiom or truth. Wherever we find the problem of the relation of *mythos* and *logos* discussed, we can suspect Platonic influence. The idea of a revelatory dimension of the imagination is cognate. The *presence* of the symbol points to that which is otherwise *absent*. In this Jung was quite candid about his debt to Friedrich Creuzer, and in the theory of the universal, archetypal and numinous power of symbol we possess a clear link through Creuzer's seminal and momentous work of symbolism in Mythology between Jung and modern analytic psychology and the Neoplatonic tradition that Creuzer so admired.

The interest in myth goes back from the Romantics through Plethon to Proclus and to Plato. Plato developed his own myths, and in the *Phaedrus* Socrates is presented as dismissive of rationalistic explanations of myth as 'ingenious and laboured'. Socrates says that he has no time for such work and has to attend to the Delphic imperative 'Know Thyself'.[56] Plato uses myths which have no ritual context and are supposed to convey a spiritual, interior reality. These highly visual images of a transcendent, invisible reality are instances and products of Plato's own poetic imagination.

Myths characteristically bridge the heavenly (intelligible) and terrestial (sensible) domains in so far as myths employ vivid and concrete earthly images to body forth transcendent reality. Perhaps we can find *logos* in *mythos* if myth is the suitable expression of the presence of the transcendent *logos* in the finite-earthly context: in the imagination, through the symbol, the realities of the spiritual world become present in the material. Coleridge makes the metaphysical presuppositions quite explicit:

> *This*, to mark the pre-existence, in order of thought, of the Nous, as spiritual, both to the objects of sense, and to their products, formed as it were, by the precipitation, or if I may dare adopt the bold language of Leibnitz, by the coagulation of spirit. In other words, this derivation of the spark from above, and from a God anterior to the Jovial dynasty (i.e. to the submersion of spirits in material forms), was intended to mark the *transcendency* of the Nous, the contra-distinctive faculty of man, as timeless, . . . and in this *negative* sense eternal.[57]

56 Plato, *Phaedrus* 230.
57 Coleridge, *Shorter Works*, pp. 1268–9.

And Creuzer, the seminal and indefatigable Romantic researcher of the 'symbolic', writes:

> Here the inexpressible prevails, in so far as it seeks expression, at last the earthly form, through the too weak vessel for the infinite power of its being, it bursts it. Thus the clarity of vision itself is destroyed and one is left only with a speechless awe. We have described the utmost form, and name the symbolic of this kind mystical.[58]

By 'mystical' or 'mystery', Creuzer does mean in opposition to truth, but a transcendent truth expressed in an inferior medium. Creuzer does not wish to exempt the symbolic-religious from considerations of truth. On the contrary, he wants to avoid the crass confusion of truth with a positivistic concept of knowledge. He, after all, is the first translator of Plotinus into German. The metaphysical principle here is that of Plotinus, that the material is within the spiritual, and that matter is thus a particular density or 'thickening' of spirit. Leibniz and Henry More express the Plotinian idea with the notion of the *coagulum spiritus* or, as Henry More writes, the 'conspissation or coaguzlation' of spirit.[59] This metaphysical construal of mind and matter finds trenchant expression in More's rather rough-cast but vigorous poetry:

> And what is done in this Terrestriall starre
> The same is done in every Orb beside.
> Each flaming Circle that we see from farre
> Is but a knot in *Pysches* garment tide.
> From that lax shadow cast throughout the wide
> And endless world, that low'st projection
> Of universal life each thing deriv'd
> What e're appeareth in corporeal fashion;
> For body's but this spirit, fixt, grosse by conspissation.[60]

Matter is the concentration of spirit – like ice is a solidification of water.[61] Hence the spiritual in man is not the by-product of a random material process, but the index of the transcendent precondition of all material reality. Nor is spirit contained 'within' matter – matter is included 'in' spirit.[62] For Plotinus, this idea of matter as spirit transformed rests upon

---

58 'Hier waltet das Unausprechliche vor, das, indem er Ausdruck sucht, zuletzt die Irdische Form, als eine zu schwaches Gefaess, durch die unendliche Gewalt seines Wesens zersprengen wird. Hiermit ist sofort die Klarheit des Schauens selbst vernichtet und es bleibt nur ein sprachloses Erstaunen übrig. Wir haben hiermit das extrem bezeichnet und nennen die Symbolik dieses Charakters die mystische.': E., Howald, *Creuzers Symbolik: Eine Auswahl in Dokumente* (Tübingen: J. C. B. Mohr, 1926), p. 67.
59 Henry More, *A Platonick Song of the Soul*, ed. A. Jacob (Lewisburg, Pa: Bucknell University Press, 1998), p. 611.
60 Ibid., p. 409.
61 The image is that of Owen Barfield in his essay 'Matter, Imagination and Spirit', *Journal of the American Academy of Religion*, 42 (1974), pp. 621–9.
62 Cf. Coleridge, *Biographia Literaria*, 17, vol.2, p. 17, where he rewrites Davies so that imagination 'turns / bodies to spirit by sublimation strange'. I owe this point to James Vigus.

the premise that matter has no formative power, and Henry More concurs:

And that which conspissate active is;
Wherefore not matter but some living sprite
Of nimble nature.[63]

We cannot think of spirit without the material forms in which we encounter it in the world; yet we should avoid the error of thinking of spirit in quasi-physical terms – perhaps akin to a gas. But the mind's habitual commerce with the material realm is necessarily spiritual: as conscious subjects, human beings perceive objects as items in their field of awareness. One does not have to subscribe to Berkeley to accept that, in a minimal sense at least, material objects are objects to a subject who perceives them as such. The 'view from nowhere', to use Nagel's famous phrase, is a goal of science but is not a readily attainable or sometimes even desirable perspective. Yet the concentration upon perception as 'the point of view', and matter as the objective realm of describable 'facts', sets up an opposition between mind and matter, subject and object. Matter looks like the negation of mind and vice versa:

Thought! Surely thoughts are true,
They please as much as things can do:
Nay, things are dead,
And in themselves are severed
From souls; nor can they fill the head
Without our thoughts. Thoughts are the real things
From whence all joy, from whence all sorrow springs.[64]

The materialist tries to reduce consciousness to matter and the idealist tries to reduce matter to mind. The Cartesian distinction between *res extensa* and *res cogitans* expresses sharply a duality which haunts modern thought in particular, but which goes back to Plato, and his division between the intelligible and the sensible.

Matter is, for the Platonist, both the product of spirit and the opposite of spirit; and it is the special prerogative of the symbol to articulate both the opposition of matter and spirit and their ultimate unity. That symbols proper are tautegorical (i.e. expressing the same subject but with a difference) in contradistinction from metaphors and similitudes, which are always allegorical (i.e. expressing a different subject but with a resemblance), requires this metaphysical underpinning.[65] The imagination is seen as the divine spark or presence in human beings: the vehicle of illumination, inspiration and divine communication.

Hans Georg Gadamer in his famous chapter in *Wahrheit und Methode* on the subjectivization of aesthetics argues that the prioritizing of symbol over allegory develops with the emergence of *Erlebniskunst*. Gadamer

63 More, *A Platonick Song of the Soul*, p. 409.
64 Traherne, (Dreams ll. 50–6), *Selected Poems and Prose*, p. 139.
65 Coleridge, *Shorter Works*, II, p. 1268. For Henry Corbin's use of the term, see *Temple and Contemplation* (London and New York: KPI, 1986), pp. 267, 305–8.

presents symbol and allegory in radical opposition – as art is to non-art. But for Coleridge, symbol and allegory are not opposed but distinct. He speaks of the symbol of Prometheus and the allegory of the Tree of Good and Evil. Coleridge is not denigrating allegory; on the contrary, Scripture clearly has precedence over pagan thought in Coleridge. However, they operate in different ways, as do reason and understanding, or imagination and fancy. The symbol is endlessly fertile and suggestive, whereas the meaning of allegory is rapidly exhausted. In the symbol, we have a cluster of related 'meanings', and its power rests in the sum of the variety of connotations rather than in one specific definable meaning. For example, the symbol of light conveys the productive bestowing of illumination without exhaustion or depletion of the source, but also joy; awe; insight; warmth; sustenance. There is a continuum between the nature and effects of the symbol (e.g. the sun) and the object symbolized (God). The symbol presupposes a vital link between meaning and Being: between the visible and invisible coincidence between image and substance – partaking of the 'Reality which it renders intelligible; and while it enunciates the whole, abides itself as a living part in that Unity, of which it is the representative.'[66] It is an immediate image and vehicle of the divine presence, whereas the allegory is at a greater remove from its object. It is typically an 'instrument of instruction'.[67]

The great Victorian divine B. F. Westcott observes:

> in the allegory the thought is grasped first and by itself, and is then arranged in a particular dress. In the myth, thought and form come into being together: the thought is the vital principle which shapes the form; the form is the sensuous image which displays the thought. The allegory is the conscious work of an individual fashioning the image of a truth which he has seized. The myth is the unconscious growth of a common mind, which witnesses to the fundamental laws by which its development is ruled.[68]

Though myth is opaque and does not disclose its truths directly, Westcott's central thought is that truth is seen 'in the myth, and not separated from it. The representation is the actual apprehension of the reality'.[69] Myths involve a claim to an 'inherent communion with a divine and suprasensuous world'. Speaking of the magnificent *Phaedrus* myth, Westcott observes that

> Plato sketches in a few ineffaceable lines what he holds to be the divine lineaments of the soul, seen in its power to hold fellowship with GOD and apprehend absolute truth. It may fall from the heights of heaven which it has been privileged to climb, but even so the transitory images of earthly things are for it potential symbols, and memorials of glories which it has seen; and in its degradation it

66 Coleridge, *Lay Sermons* p. 30.
67 Coleridge, *Shorter Works*, p. 1268.
68 B. F. Westcott, 'The Myths of Plato', in *Essays in the History of the Religious Thought of the West* (London: Macmillan, 1891), p. 4.
69 Ibid.

yet can feel that the way of return to supra-celestial joy is not finally closed.[70]

The critique of symbol and the rehabilitation of allegory from Benjamin to de Man

Such a Platonic metaphysics of the 'presence' of the infinite in the finite has provoked fierce criticism in the hands of the post-structuralist theorists and their mentors. Martin Heidegger in *Der Ursprung des Kunstwerkes* sneers contemptuously at the apparently common and long-standing approach to art through allegory and symbol:

> It is probably superfluous and confusing to inquire because the work of art goes beyond the materials to something other. This other constitutes the artistic. The work of art is a constructed object but it expresses something other than itself, ἄλλο ἀγορεύει. The work makes the other known, it reveals the other: it is allegory. With the finished object in the work of art something else is brought together. 'Bring together' in Greek means συμβάλλειν. The work is symbol. Allegory and symbol have provided for a long time the parameters for envisaging an art work.[71]

Heidegger seems strangely unaware of the Schelling–Coleridge contrast between tautegory and allegory. However, his Weimar contemporary Walter Benjamin's magnificent essay, *Ursprung des deutschen Trauerspiels* (1925), contains a detailed account of the Romantic view of symbol in relation to allegory.[72] We shall mainly reflect upon Paul de Man's nominalist critique of the symbol. Both de Man and Benjamin were experts on the Romantic tradition and both realized that Schelling and the Romantic thinkers generally were articulating a problem which is a distinctive mark of the Platonic tradition: the relation between *mythos* and *logos*.[73]

Benjamin, of course, has provided a profound stimulus for much post-structuralist thought – and like Heidegger, Benjamin was writing in an age of anxiety – the antinomian, apocalyptic, Gnostic atmosphere of interwar Germany. Wohlin observes that this mood of 'extreme devalu-

---

70 Ibid., p. 31.
71 'Vermutlich wird es überflüssig und verwirrend, dem nachzufragen, weil das Kunstwerk über das Dinghafte hinaus noch etwas anderes ist. Dieses Andere, was daran ist, macht das Künstlerische aus. Das Kunstwerk its zwar ein angefertigtes Ding, aber es sagt noch etwas anderes als das bloße Ding selbst ist ἄλλο ἀγορεύει. Das Werk macht mit Anderem öffentlich bekannt, es offenbart Anderes; es ist Allegorie. Mit dem angefertigten Ding wird im Kunstwerk noch etwas Anderes zusammengebracht. Zusammenbringen heißt griechisch συμβάλλειν. Das Werk ist symbol. Allegorie und Symbol geben die Rahmenvorstellungen her, in deren Blickbahn sich seit langem die Kennzeichnung des Kunstwerkes bewegt': M. Heidegger, *Der Ursprung des Kunstwerkes* (Stuttgart: Reclam, 1967), p. 10.
72 W. Benjamin, *Ursprung des deutschen Trauerspiels* (Frankfurt am Main: Suhrkamp, 1963).
73 L. Brisson, *How Philosophers Saved Myths: Allegorical Interpretation and Classical Mythology* (Chicago: University of Chicago Press, 2004), pp. 5–8, 56–106.

ation of the empirical world' in the mood of *Lebensphilosophie* and Expressionism in the early twentieth century mirrored the Baroque critique of the optimism of the Renaissance and its worldliness.[74] Benjamin turned from his early studies of Romanticism, with its optimistic aesthetics and its longing for the absolute and for human perfectibility, to the darker age of allegorical German *Trauerspiel*: the drama of sorrow/grief. Here the *Trauerspiel* is viewed as a labour of 'mortification', as destructive and dialectical: it diminishes the over-weening ambition and pretension to symbolic plenitude in Renaissance aesthetics: 'Der falsche Schein der Totalität geht aus.'[75] The Baroque allegory is fragmentary and ruined. However, allegory in its very ruin points dialectically beyond destruction to redemption. The image of an absolutely fallen world is inverted into the allegory of resurrection: death's head becomes an angel's countenance.[76] One might, in the English context, think of the elaborate pessimism of John Bunyan's *Pilgrim's Progress* as an analogy to the Lutheran Baroque allegory which Benjamin discusses. The sense of transcendence in German Baroque Lutheranism melancholy provided this genre with its own authentic aesthetics. The extravagance of the allegorist is justified by a vast gulf between meanings of words and objects.[77] The picture of the symbol is replaced by the allegoric script wherein there is a mystical hope – the natural world is a set of signs wherein the finitude and futility of the world, and the need for redemption, is revealed. Allegory is thus linked to rejection of mimesis and exaltation of subjective existence – as powerfully expressed by contemporaries such as Proust, Joyce, Breton and even Heidegger's *Analytik des Daseins* which, despite all his protestations to the contrary, revolves around *Dasein* as *Existenz-Sorge*, time, death, etc.[78] One could plausibly see the excessive scepticism of post-structuralism, the programme of deconstruction, as grounded in the destruction of mimesis in the interwar period – a movement close in spirit to Bultmann's demythologizing programme.[79]

Paul de Man, in his seminal paper 'The Rhetoric of Temporality', writes:

Since the assertion of a radical priority of the subject over objective nature is not easily compatible with the poetic praxis of the romantic

---

74 There was a deeply Platonic element in Benjamin – reinforced, perhaps, by Baudelaire and the Cabbala – via friendship with Scholem, but any such Platonism was of a deeply apophatic sort. See G. Scholem, *Walter Benjamin: The Story of a Friendship* (London: Faber and Faber, 1982).

75 Benjamin, *Ursprung*, p. 154.

76 R. Wohlin, *Walter Benjamin: An Aesthetic of Redemption* (New York: Columbia University Press, 1982), p. 71.

77 J. Roberts, *Walter Benjamin* (London: Macmillan, 1982), pp. 140ff.

78 Wohlin, *Walter Benjamin*, p. 75.

79 Cf. F. Burwick, *Mimesis and its Romantic Representations* (University Park, Pa: Pennsylvania State University, 2001).

poets, who all gave a great deal of importance to the presence of nature, a certain degree of confusion ensues.[80]

Perhaps, but the confusion is de Man's. The Neoplatonic legacy, in both Traherne and Wordsworth, is such that *both* nature and interiority-subjectivity are emphasized. Nature is, after all, a product of Soul for Plotinus. That is the reason why the attention to the outward is accompanied by greater inwardness: imagination, reverie or memory help furnish a more faithful observation of nature, 'the one life within us and abroad'. Paul de Man notes correctly that for Coleridge the emphasis is upon the 'translucence' of the symbol, and that both symbol and allegory 'have a common origin beyond the world of matter . . . a transcendental source'.[81] Both are in fact 'oblique' designations of this source, even if one depends upon a synecdoche (symbol) and the other upon an arbitrary convention (allegory). de Man uses this to argue that the great Coleridgean distinction in fact collapses. However, de Man launches a direct attack upon this view of the symbol as 'tenacious self-mystification':

> The supremacy of the symbol, conceived as an expression of unity between the representative and semantic function of language, becomes a commonplace that underlies literary taste, literary criticism, and literary history. The supremacy of the symbol still functions as the basis of recent French and English studies of the romantic and post-romantic eras, to such an extent that allegory is frequently considered as an anachronism and dismissed as non-poetic.[82]

On his account, Romanticism was not about the 'dialectical relationship between subject and object', but 'the temporal relationships that exist within a system of allegorical signs' – i.e. the self 'seen in its authentically temporal predicament'.[83] He asserts that 'the prevalence of allegory always corresponds to the unveiling of an authentically temporal destiny.'[84]

Paul de Man refers in this seminal essay to Walter Benjamin's attempt to see artworks as hieroglyphs of a (redeemed) life in his *Ursprung des deutschen Trauerspiels*. de Man's own exaltation of allegory as the aporetic mode of the serial and temporal in opposition to the (quasi-or pseudo-Romantic) totalizing fusion of subject and object in the symbol is a part of his own Nietzschean-inspired preference for open-ended aesthetic possibilities. Whereas the symbol postulates the possibility of an identity or identification with a supersensible totality, allegory designates primarily a distance. The interpretation of allegory is dependent upon an arbitrary signifier. It presupposes a code, whereas a symbol requires

---

80 P. de Man, 'The Rhetoric of Temporality', in *Blindness and Insight*, 2nd edn (London: Methuen and Co., 1983), p. 196.
81 Ibid., p. 192.
82 Ibid., pp. 189–90.
83 Ibid., p. 208.
84 Ibid., p. 206.

presence. It is the opposition of the script and the image. Thus the *vertical* axis of Platonic metaphysics is replaced by the *horizontal* secular and historical, infinitely deferrable signs of allegory. de Man pursues Benjamin's argument for the priority of allegory – with the aim of destroying the idea that the literary text is a vehicle for conveying truths. He wants to replace this essentially Platonic model with the idea that the literary text need not refer to anything beyond its boundaries. Allegory becomes a good aid to the appreciation of the arbitrary nature of the sign:

> it remains necessary, if there is to be allegory, that the allegorical sign refers to another sign that precedes it. The meaning constituted by the allegorical sign can then consist only in the *repetition* (in the Kierkegaardian sense of the term) of a previous sign with which it can never coincide, since it is the essence of this previous sign to be pure anteriority . . . Whereas the symbol postulates the possibility of an identity or identification, allegory designates primarily a distance in relation to its own origin, and renouncing the nostalgia and the desire to coincide, it establishes its language in the void of this temporal difference.[85]

de Man assaults the Romantic view of the symbol, calling it 'an act of ontological bad faith', and it is striking that he uses a religious vocabulary in his critique. Of course, de Man is quite correct in his conviction that, lying behind the idea of the symbol in the strong Platonic sense of conveying *truths* and not mere figurative illustrations, is the conviction that matter can body forth the immaterial – it can become an *image* and give authentic expression to the spiritual.[86] Conversely, the imagination is the means by which the human mind can apprehend the reality beyond the images. de Man quotes Wordsworth's famous lines:

> I was often unable to think of external things as having external existence, and I communed with all that I saw as something not apart from, but inherent in, my own immaterial nature.[87]

It is quite baffling, however, why de Man can think that the distinction between allegory and symbol is of 'secondary importance'.[88] It is through Coleridge's insistence that an *ontological* link between symbol and the reality symbolized becomes transparent in the image that his Platonism is most evident. But that does not mean that Coleridge wishes to denigrate allegory as a means of conveying spiritual realities. He merely wishes to expound a different relationship between the means of expression and the objects of that expression. The mistake of the materialist is to confuse the dependence of spirit upon matter for its *expression* with the *ontological* dependence of spirit upon matter. This is

---

85 Ibid., p. 207.
86 See Barfield, 'Matter, Imagination and Spirit', p. 625.
87 de Man, 'Rhetoric', p. 196. The passage can be found in Wordsworth, *Poetical Works*, ed. E. de Selincourt and H. Darbishire (Oxford: Clarendon Press, 1940–7), vol. 4, p. 463.
88 de Man, 'Rhetoric', p. 193.

the mistake of *'cum hoc: ergo, propter hoc'*.[89] Even worse is the identification of the sum of reality with the perceptible – this is the despotism of the eye. Much of the densest material in the *Biographia Literaria* is aimed at the ideas of the spiritual being caused by the material or the identification of reality with sense perception, and defends the 'preexistence, in order of thought, of the Nous, as spiritual, both to the objects of sense and to their products'.[90]

The legacy of the tautegorical: religion as *sui generis*

Paul Ricœur posits a decisive rupture in occidental culture between the sacred and the secular in the nineteenth century with the impact of the critique of religion in Marx, Nietzsche and Freud as a form of false consciousness. Most of these were hybrid versions of the Enlightenment and Romantic traditions. Ricœur claims that the sum of this critique is that 'Religion has a meaning that remains unknown to the believer by virtue of a specific act of dissimulation which conceals its true origin from the investigation of consciousness.'[91] This is the challenge of projectivist and positivistic critiques of religious beliefs as destructive fantasy. Freud claims that religion is infantile neurosis and Marx claims that religion is servicing the requirements of the ruling elite. As Garrett Green observes, the critique of religion in Marx, Nietzsche and Freud has its roots in Feuerbach's theory of the religious 'imagination' via its employment of the Hegelian concept of *Vorstellung*.[92] If the critique of religion in Marx, Nietzsche and Freud has its roots in a particular version of Hegel's theory of imagination through the mediation of Feuerbach, one should not forget Strauss and his impact upon historical criticism. Strauss's own itinerary from Hegelianism to Darwinian positivism is an intriguing index of nineteeth-century intellectual history: the attempt to reduce the supernatural to the naturalistic, a project which has its roots in Reimarus. Hegel's view that the imaginative content of *Vorstellung* could be *translated* into the purely conceptual *Begriff* should not be misunderstood in narrowly rationalistic terms. Yet the *Linkshegelianer* were largely of a reductionistic temper. If one combines such reductionism with the deep and (quite un-Hegelian) pessimism of Schopenhauer (or Spinoza), one has the *dysvangelists* of the nineteenth century and their attendant *Kulturpessimismus* reinforced by Darwin. The result is the view that religious symbols and myths can be translated into another language or medium. Freud thinks this is infantile neurosis, Marx the opium of the people, and Nietzsche the resentment of the priestly caste. Freud and Marx see the sacred as a smokescreen for very profane interests: class interests, repressed sexuality or the will to power. Freud, for example,

89 Coleridge, *Biographia Literaria*, vol. 1, p. 142.
90 Coleridge, *Shorter Works*, p. 1268.
91 P. Ricœur, 'Religion, Atheism and Faith', in *The Conflict of Interpretations: Essays in Hermeneutics*, ed. D. Ihde (Evanston, Ill.: Northwestern University Press, 1974), p. 442.
92 G. Green, *Theology, Hermeneutics, and Imagination: The Crisis of Interpretation at the End of Modernity* (Cambridge: Cambridge University Press, 2000) pp. 83ff.

understands spiritual drives as masking carnal impulses, even if many of these are locked into early childhood. The sacred camouflages profane interests.

We have contrasted this theory with the Coleridge–Schelling view. This is a powerful Romantic tradition which sees the reductionist account as a reversal of the correct relations. These Romantics insisted that the profane should be seen as disclosing the sacred. The symbol, in particular, is a vivid and instantaneous disclosure of a higher truth in a lower medium. The symbolic form is not, however, an accidental cloak – or, indeed, a perversion of the core meaning of the symbol. Rather, the form is a necessary correlate of the content. Hegel claims that 'Der Gedanke und die Reflexion hat die schöne Kunst überflügelt.'[93] This means not just that art is inferior to religion and philosophy, but that art, and a fortiori imaginative expression, is at an end. Schelling's counter-claim is that the image (*Bild-Vorstellung*) is not merely an inferior stage on the way to the concept (*Begriff*) but a necessary condition for the latter's expression. Hence Schelling provides a very different answer to the ancient question of the relation between *logos* and *mythos*. Westcott rightly observed that Plato's myths were not 'for him poetic fancies, but representations of momentous truths'.[94] The formula of Beierwaltes concerning Plato – 'Mythos gründet im Logos; Logos lebt im Mythos' – expresses neatly Schelling's critique of the rationalistic demythologizing – even iconoclastic – tendency in Hegel.[95]

What should by now be obvious is the egregious error of the claim that the Romantic view of religion is by definition non-cognitivist.[96] The Romantic appeal to symbol is only non-cognitivist if it identifies knowledge with the capacity for articulation, but there are good reasons for maintaining that our knowledge often exceeds any formal description. The allegory is a form of knowledge by description, the symbol of knowledge by acquaintance. The point of the appeal to symbol in Schelling and Coleridge is not to discover a *non*-rational foundation for religion (as Penner puts it) but to discover the rational in the apparently irrational: *logos* in *mythos*. This endeavour, whether for Platonists or idealists, is closely linked to the underlying metaphysics and the rejection of empiricism.

For the motto of *The Ancient Mariner*, Coleridge quotes the Cambridge Platonist and Fellow of Clare College Thomas Burnet: 'I readily believe that there are more invisible than visible things in the universe'. And unlike any other members of the animal kingdom, human beings are consciously and reflectively aware of the spiritual as such: as the law and

93 G. W. F. Hegel, *Vorlesung über Äesthetik* (Frankfurt am Main: Surkamp, 1986–9), vol. 1, p. 24.
94 Westcott, 'The Myths of Plato', p. 47.
95 W. Beierwaltes, 'Logos im Mythos: Marginalien zu Platon', in *Weite des Herzens, Weite des Lebens: Beiträge zum christsein in moderner Gesellschaft. Festschrift für Abt Odilo Lechner*, ed. M. Langer and A. Bilgri (Regensburg: Friedrich Pustet, 1989), p. 274.
96 Among those who commit this error is Hans Penner; see 'You Don't Read a Myth for Information', in N. K. Frankenberry (ed.), *Radical Interpretation in Religion* (Cambridge: Cambridge University Press, 2002), esp. pp. 162ff.

harmony which pervades the natural order and makes the truths of
natural science attainable, as the beauty of the natural, cultural and
ethical dimensions of human experience, and the belief in goodness
which inspires hope, faith and love. We need symbols and allegories
because we are amphibious. We dwell in the unavoidable tension
between the instinctual animal world and the spiritual domain expressed
by the *mythos* of Aeschylus in his *Prometheus* or the allegory of the Tree of
Knowledge in Genesis. Decision and action are far more complex for
human beings than for the rest of the animal kingdom because of the
relative lack of instinctual integration, and the integration of the
conscious self with the unconscious remains an extremely difficult task
throughout an entire life. It is primarily the symbol which helps
reintegrate the soul with the spiritual dimension of living 'in the
world' by representing transcendence in its immanent expression. In this
sense the etymology of symbol is fitting – it is that *sym-ballein* or
throwing together of the finite and the infinite.

Nietzsche thought that the desire for truth in this sense was the
expression of a pusillanimous failure of nerve. However, perhaps we
would have no awareness of imperfection if we already possessed
implicitly a sense of perfection. Hence the imagination raises philoso-
phico-theological questions of the immanence and transcendence of the
Divine: our very sense of our finitude is an index of our capacity to
transcend it. The Romantic position claims a bond between the
immanence of the imaginative vision and the transcendence of the
object signified. Language and knowledge are not themselves final and
transparent but are the opaque index of the existence an ultimate reality –
like the shadows in Plato's cave in book VII of the *Republic*. That is, there
must be an innate dimension – a universal and essentialist component –
which is quite explicit in the 'Logos in whom the whole human race
participates', as Justin Martyr claims.[97] Or as Clement of Alexandria
writes: 'Come, I will show you the Logos and the mysteries of the Logos;
and I will show them to you in the images which are entrusted to you.'[98]
This is the faith that we can rise from the visible to the invisible and that
the imagination, as the immediate source of our images, is a dim mirror
and index of the boundless plenitude of the infinite I AM.

97 Justin Martyr, *Protreptikos* XII.119.1.
98 *Clement de Alexandrie: le Protreptique* (Paris: Éditions du Cerf, 1976), p. 188.

5

The Problem of Metaphysics

All of us, I presume, more or less, are led beyond the region of ordinary facts. Some in one way and some in others, we seem to touch and have communion with what is beyond the visible world. In various manners we find something higher, which both supports and humbles, both chastens and transports us. And, with certain persons, the intellectual effort to understand the universe is a principal way of thus experiencing the Deity. No one, probably, who has not felt this, however differently he might describe it, has ever cared much for metaphysics.[1]

In this chapter I shall produce a qualified defence of Kant's ethical position. This is inspired by Donald MacKinnon's exploration of ethics as ultimately concerned with the metaphysical and imaginative foundations of the moral 'ought'. Ethics points to the metaphysics of morality, such as the nature of freedom and responsibility. But metaphysics cannot escape ethical considerations. As argued in the previous chapter, reflective, self-conscious creatures dwell amphibiously in two realms of being: the world shared with other sentient mammals and which can be described by the exact sciences, and the apprehension of value, which only human beings possess. MacKinnon dwells in particular upon Plato and Kant, philosophers in whom the ethical dimension of metaphysics looms particularly large.

Christian theologians have often found Plato's views on ethics deeply congenial and Kant, as a moralist, is deeply affected by Christianity. The mythological and apocalyptic dimension of the Christian gospel is significant here. It is hard to find anything distinctive about the content of Christian ethics; it is rather the apparently paradoxical framework which is decisive. In fact, the paradox is determined by the apocalyptic context, within which it is a greater evil to do than to suffer injustice or it is better to suffer for well-doing than for evil-doing. Hence 'Blessed are they who are persecuted for righteousness' sake'[2] is not a piece of psychological propaganda in the service of a growing sect in the Roman Empire but a paean to the good will.

The greatest poet of medieval Christendom explores this in his *Commedia*: for Dante, morality is not a matter of external observance or effects, but of *intention*. Sins of weakness are punished in the region of upper hell and deliberate sin is punished in lower hell. We find what Sinclair calls a descending scale 'from incontinence to treachery'.[3] The

---

1 F. H. Bradley, *Appearance and Reality* (Oxford, 1930), p. 5.
2 Matthew 5.10.
3 Dante, *Inferno*, tr. J. Sinclair (New York: Oxford University Press, 1999), p. 153.

path back to the good, moreover, requires recognition of the disorder of the soul and the steps of purgatory demand a gradual purification of the will. Sordello in Canto VII of *Purgatorio* explains to Virgil that they cannot ascend during and after the setting of the sun. The sun is an image of divine truth and Dante presents a picture of the spiritual necessity for clear vision as a precondition for the ascent of the soul.[4] Dante clearly believed in an eternal and immutable morality, the 'light given to you to know good and evil'.[5]

Kathleen Raine notes that poetry is the natural language of longing. The sexual imagery in the *Phaedrus* or the *Commedia* should be taken no more literally than the image of the hunt in Nicholas of Cusa's *De venatione sapientiae* or Giordano Bruno's use of the figure of Actaeon in *Gli Eroici Furori*. The eponymous Phaedrus refers to the myth of Boreas and Oreithyia, and Socrates says that he has no time for tedious (rationalistic) explanations of the kind offered by the Sophists. Rather, he needs to follow the Delphic injunction, 'Know Thyself'. Yet it is the myth of the chariot of the soul and love drawing the charioteer which provides the answer to the question. The soul's share in the Divine constitutes its true nature. As T. H. Green observes, this is 'the moral life as the fulfilment in the human spirit of some divine idea'.[6] This is the view which Aristotle attacks in Plato – that the goal of ethics is to become God-like.

Here we have the basis of the idealistic critique of biological or utilitarian theories of ethics. Ethics is not concerned primarily with questions of cooperation or public prosperity, but with the self-realization of the soul. Self-consciousness and the awareness of the divine (non-natural) component of that consciousness is the key to ethics. The argument is quite simple. The move from instincts and desires to awareness of the desire implies the subject's distinction of itself from specific objects of desire and *motives* for action. Hence the self-conscious subject is not merely a part of a set of natural causes and effects, but a free agent.[7] When the free agent contemplates the ideal of action, the awareness of the de facto imperfection in ethical judgement and action points to some absolute normative standard.

In their polemic against determinism, be it of the Stoic or more modern variety, both Plotinus and Kant produce a metaphysics of morals in which the true and properly free agent is identical with a principle of transcendent rationality. This true self is dislocated from its physical and causal matrix. William Barrett remarks justly that the Kantian good will, which wills to submit itself to the moral law, is a descendant of the *voluntas*, the will in St Augustine, which is restless until it rests in God.[8] The apprehension of the moral law is participation in the mind of God or what T. H. Green calls the 'reproduction . . . of an eternal consciousness'

4 See the argument of I. Brandeis, *The Ladder of Vision: A Study of Dante's Comedy* (London: Chatto and Windus, 1960), pp. 184–5.
5 Dante, *Purgatorio*, XVI, 75.
6 T. H. Green, *Prolegomena to Ethics* (Oxford: Clarendon Press, 1882), p. 216.
7 Ibid., pp. 213ff.
8 W. Barrett, *The Illusion of Technique* (New York: Doubleday, 1978), p. 247.

in finite consciousness,[9] or the *Deus in nobis*. The Cambridge Platonists develop this tenet as the doctrine of the ecstasy of experience, 'not as an occasional and temporary state of religious exaltation, but rather as habitual concentration of affection, will, and understanding upon God'.[10] This is the raising of the soul to the level of the Divine; the linking of ethics to ontology – or rather to a state of the soul. The presence of goodness is the 'true Efflux'[11] of divine sagacity, or the presence of God in the soul. The indwelling of the divine presence in the soul characteristic of Platonic and Neoplatonic mysticism is linked with the Pauline 'not I but Christ in me'.[12] It is a fusion of the Plotinian doctrine of experience with sanctification: 'Where the spirit of the Lord is, there is liberty. But we all, with open face beholding as in a glass the glory of the Lord, are changed into the same image from glory to glory, even as by the Spirit of the Lord'.[13]

The language of union with the Godhead, or deification, is often misinterpreted. One error is that of understanding the divine indwelling as the substitution of the Divine for the human. The other extreme is the view of a mere harmony of two mutually exclusive wills. If one takes the doctrine of the Logos seriously – if the Son of God is a genuinely cosmic principle – one is driven to some form of what Austin Farrer calls 'double agency', the doctrine that God acts in individuals without negating the integrity of those finite agents. The action of the agent is naturally intelligible, and the agent is not coerced, as it were, by the peremptory force of the divine will. However, the divine uniqueness means that the 'causal joint' of human and divine agency is by definition hidden. God is not a possible object of rational scrutiny in this sense:

> There is . . . a sense in which we can say that the world of finite intelligences, though distinct from God, is still, in its ideal nature, one with Him. That which God creates and by which He reveals the hidden treasures of His wisdom and love, is still not foreign to His own infinite life, but one with it. In the knowledge of the minds that know Him, in the self-surrender of the hearts that love Him, it is no paradox to affirm that He knows and loves Himself. As He is the origin and inspiration of every true thought and pure affection, of every experience in which we forget and rise above ourselves, so is He also of all these the end . . . In the language of Scripture – 'It is God that worketh in us to will and to do of His good pleasure'.[14]

---

9 Green, *Prolegomena*, p. 89.
10 J. A. Stewart, 'Cambridge Platonists', in *Encyclopedia of Religion and Ethics*, vol. III, ed. J. Hastings (Edinburgh: T. & T. Clark, 1910), pp. 168–9.
11 John Smith, *Select Discourses* (Cambridge, 1660), p. 2.
12 Galatians 2.20.
13 2 Corinthians 3.17–18.
14 J. Caird, *An Introduction to the Philosophy of Religion* (Glasgow: Maclehose, 1894), p. 245.

Mackinnon's paradox

The seminal twentieth-century Cambridge philosopher-theologian Donald MacKinnon published his Gifford Lectures as *The Problem of Metaphysics*. This title may be interpreted in two ways. Did he mean the genitive 'of' in the sense of the questions inherent within the field of metaphysics, or is he problematizing metaphysics itself? The answer is both. MacKinnon is writing in the context of the twentieth-century *critique* of metaphysics. And yet he is also wanting to present his view of the distinctive questions raised within legitimate metaphysical enquiry. He defines metaphysics in terms of a 'commerce with the transcendent'[15] and argues that ethics is inchoately such a commerce, albeit one in which we are continually thrusting against the very limits of language. Human life, as MacKinnon approvingly quotes Blondel, is 'metaphysics in action'.[16]

Plato represents for MacKinnon 'a kind of exemplary exposé of the approach to metaphysics by way of ethics, seeing and capturing the kind of ethical reflection that is all the time inchoately metaphysical'.[17] This was because for Plato 'what men ought to do, the way in which they ought to live their lives, sprang out of the way in which things are; in some sense . . . their lives *correspond* with the order of being and becoming'.[18] MacKinnon also discusses Kant's doctrine of the primacy of pure practical reason as the core of his metaphysical endeavours. For MacKinnon, Kant is a metaphysician himself in his defence of the primacy of pure practical reason, and his metaphysics is a metaphysics of morals. Kant's faith of the moralist leads from the phenomenal into the noumenal. Our concepts do not apply to the noumenal. He calls God, immortality and freedom 'ideas', and as spiritual beings we must assume as truths ideas which cannot be proven or articulated conceptually. MacKinnon develops an intriguing analogy with Plato in the *Republic* 'that the argument is not about some trivial matter but about what way one ought to live'.[19] There is, of course, a deep but intriguing ambiguity in Kant's notion of understanding our moral obligations as divine commands. It may be interpreted as an appeal to the *imagination* and the absolute nature of moral obligation. Kant is horrified by theological anthropomorphism of the typical divine command variety, yet clearly envisages the awe for the moral law as profoundly akin to the reverence for a transcendent, intelligible and sacred source of Being.

If divine commands are not seen as constituting external compulsion, but expressing the internal force of goodness, this sharply raises for MacKinnon the question of the tragic – in particular in the plays of

---

15 D. MacKinnon, *The Problem of Metaphysics* (London: Cambridge University Press, 1974), p. 39.

16 Ibid., p. 24.

17 Ibid., p. 30.

18 Ibid., p. 37; cf. p. 29: Plato defended 'the thesis that one form of life was highest, because it most corresponded with what was the case, because it most captured the likeness of the actual'.

19 Ibid., p. 29; see Plato, *Republic* 352d5.

Shakespeare. Plato's dialogues are dramas, and MacKinnon reflects upon Shakespeare's philosophical dramas. Tragedy reveals an intimation of depth and meaning in human life, albeit meaning thwarted or truncated by evil, which is at odds with strict naturalism. Yet this very same reality of evil frustrates any attempt to produce a metaphysical theodicy which tries to articulate and explain the inscrutable. Let us call this MacKinnon's paradox. Evil thwarts both strict naturalism and classic theodicy.

Many of the facts of our world are the result of fortune – notable errors, accidents or serendipity. Columbus sailed to the East Indies for cheap pepper and cloves in the wrong direction and discovered America. The ancient Epicureans considered the seemingly rational appearance of the world as the result of the 'fortuitous concourse' of atoms. The mindless algorithm of natural selection reinforces the old Epicurean outlook. If evolution is a 'mindless, purposeless algorithmic process',[20] fortune, not providence, rules our universe. If the universe is the product of fortune, vast quantities of struggle, pain and suffering are precisely what one would expect. How does one generate the sense of 'evil' without presupposing some prior standard of goodness?

The unfairness of the distribution of life's goods is egregious. This unfairness of the distribution of different national structures and resources is not very puzzling in evolutionary terms. Yet the sheer *urgency* and *absoluteness* of the idea of justice is rather remarkable: it is shocking that any human being has to endure tyranny or poverty. The technological advances of the twentieth century enabled tyrants to inflict suffering and injustice on a previously unparalleled scale – deportations, camps, genocide – from the plight of the Armenians to the Albanians. It is puzzling that our messy and impure world should generate the limpid purity of the idea of justice, particularly evident to small children, who are most apt to say 'It's not fair', but it is also intriguing that the concept of evil should be so deeply lodged in the minds of post-Darwinian thinkers.

That may just be a peculiarity of occidental culture, as Nietzsche, the advocate of an ethics beyond good and evil, proposes. But it is striking that so many crucial elements of our moral imagination should naturally extend beyond the bounds of kith and kin. Take, for example, slavery. Today, slavery is regarded as an intolerable institution, and yet for centuries, some of the most civilized and humane thinkers from St Paul to Jefferson condoned slavery. One of the greatest ancient philosophers, Epictetus (AD 55–135), was himself a slave. Conversely, in the twenty-first century there is much de facto slavery, often linked with child labour or prostitution. Bernard Williams, otherwise a sharp critic of absolutist conceptions of ethics, observes that there are strong pressures for the 'justice or injustice of past societies not merely to evaporate in the relativism of distance'.[21] Kant expresses a powerful intuition when he speaks of the awe which the sense of the sovereignty of obligation, of

---

20 D. Dennett, *Darwin's Dangerous Idea: Evolution and the Meanings of Life* (London: Penguin, 1995), p. 320.
21 B. Williams, *Ethics and the Limits of Philosophy* (London: Fontana, 1983), p. 166.

unconditional goodness, generates – as the sense of a gap between the empirical and pure practical reason. The sovereignty of obligation is supersensible: it cannot easily be deduced from any facts which we perceive in nature or, indeed, from much observable behaviour.

The biological and the economic perspective

One way of defusing the problem of evil is to take a radically naturalistic or utilitarian view of ethics. We might look at human beings from an anthropological standpoint. From this perspective, ethics is primarily a question of cooperation – how do human agents pool their resources? We might look at mankind from a biological perspective. If ethics is the description of how organisms like human beings behave and of our emotions about such behaviour, then ethics might just be an offshoot of biology. Human beings are organisms in the natural world: if ethics is concerned with calculating what we want, some rational decision procedure might be helpful. There is clearly a tradition which presents a thoroughly naturalistic view of human ethics as, at least theoretically, subject to rigorous scientific explanation. Human beings are studied in much the same fashion as birds, bees or ants. Sociobiology in particular is a clear example of such a 'scientific' approach to ethics, but Spinoza is also a good traditional example of a philosopher who wants to base ethics upon an understanding of the natural causes of action. Spinoza attacks the intuitive idea of freedom as in opposition to necessity, regarding that idea as the baneful product of the imagination; the true 'scientific' idea of freedom is genuine insight into necessity and the consequent transformation of the emotions from passive into active. But apart from such a stringent metaphysical theory as Spinoza's, there is little reason to think that biology might have any more to say about contemporary ethics than, say, Dante's *Commedia*, medieval cosmology or modern mathematics.

The naturalistic approach of Spinoza, Hume and their modern followers can be distinguished from the *economic* approach of utilitarianism. Here the emphasis is upon the public good and the maximization of quantifiable public benefits. The concern is less with human nature and its structure than with the enhancement of collective or social interests. Utilitarianism has exerted an enormous influence over economists and political and legal reforms; hence the charge of *hedonism* is clearly quite inadequate. Hedonists are rarely concerned with improving the living conditions and opportunities of their neighbours. However, the lack of an adequate concept of a person severely limits the theory. If the right action is to be judged by the calculation of the general happiness, the integrity of an individual's rights seems to have little place. In a quantitative analysis of ethical value, the unique moral agent seems inadequately accommodated.

It seems to me that here one also has a real problem for utilitarianism and for naturalistic ethics in general. If the greatest happiness principle is the measure for judging what is right or wrong, any exploration of the psyche is futile. It is an instance of an 'obsessive preoccupation with motive and intention'.[22] Yet Shakespeare's plays are an exploration of the public disorder created by the psyche – jealous, ambitious, prevaricating, vain – we can see in Othello, Macbeth, Hamlet or Lear, and in our own souls. The greatest pagan moralist (Plato) and the greatest moralist of the modern period (Kant) both employ residually mythic elements to express imaginatively the moral problem. Both moralists, otherwise relentless critics of obfuscation, employ quite consciously apocalyptic language to articulate man's ethical vocation, the true self. If we raise the general question 'What is metaphysics?' we may well turn back to Plato: *Platonism* is the recognition of world as *images*[23] and Platonic philosophy is the *ascent* from appearance to reality. In Kantian thought this is the elevation of man through duty above nature and constitutes his freedom from the mechanism of nature.[24] Kant's idea of the noumenal character beyond space and time has evident parallels within the Platonic tradition, e.g. Plotinus's doctrine of the 'upper soul'. However, Kant's grounding of moral philosophy upon a self outside any specific community, history, culture and language seems to most a vulnerable and counter-intuitive point of his theory. A chorus of recent distinguished writers have attacked the Kantian doctrine of obligation. Some recent writers, such as Bernard Williams or Alexander Nehemas, have been influenced by Nietzsche; Nussbaum by a naturalistic reading of Aristotle; Anscombe and MacIntyre by a more Thomistic Stagyrite. They all object to the inscrutable Kantian self which eludes conceptual definition. Kant, Williams argues, 'believed that all actions except those of moral principle were to be explained not only deterministically but in terms of egoistic hedonism. Only in acting from moral principle could we escape from being causally determined by the drive for pleasure, like animals'.[25]

Let me try to counter this view with the idea that the moral agent cannot be assessed by outward criteria but only by the inner state. At this point the idea of the free self merges into the soul. This can be nicely illustrated by Shakespeare, whose tragedies revolve around guilt and remorse rather than regret and shame. Hamlet faces his prophetic soul in the vision of his father's ghost. This illustrates the gap between conventional morality or prudential considerations and genuine obliga-tion. The others present could not see the ghost (just as only Macbeth sees Banquo and only Brutus sees Caesar's ghost and Gertrude cannot see old Hamlet). Kant says famously: 'The good will is not good because of what it effects or accomplishes – because of its fitness for attaining some proposed end: it is good through its willing alone, that is, good in itself.[26] Kant is claiming that contingent empirical factors are strangely irrelevant to moral agency. If we analyse the circumstances of any moral act in naturalistic terms, the domain of genuine freedom seems to

---

22 MacKinnon, *Problem of Metaphysics*, p. 92.
23 Plato, *Republic* 508; *Phaedrus* 250b.
24 Immanuel Kant, *Critique of Practical Reason*, A156.
25 Williams, *Ethics and the Limits of Philosophy*, p. 64.
26 Immanuel Kant, *The Moral Law*, tr. H. J. Paton (London: Hutchinson, 1981), p. 60.

evaporate: the psychological dispositions, temperament, prudence and skills of the agent; good or bad fortune in upbringing, education, culture; the chain of specific events leading up to any one decision (and beyond the control of the agent); and fortune in the way things turn out. And Kant starts his *Grundlegung zur Metaphysik der Sitten* by stating forthrightly that this is how the common-sense view of morality actually operates. We do not in fact praise or blame moral agents for factors over which they have little or no control. *Ought* implies *can*. That this common-sense view is a product of a certain Christian humanism and universalism which the aristocratically minded Aristotle would have rejected, or that this aristocratic, hierarchical Aristotelianism was quite congenial for feudal Europe, is a separate matter. Not all human beings can contribute to science or art, but all can be good. At this point, nature and morality converge.

Thomas Nagel has argued very persuasively that 'something in the idea of agency is incompatible with actions being events or people being things', but the gradual exposure of the external determinant of action means that there is nothing left which can be attributed to the 'responsible self', and we are left with nothing but a portion of a larger sequence of events, which can be deplored or celebrated, but not blamed or praised.[27] Nagel notes that moral assessment seems undermined in various ways. Personal qualities are clearly not chosen and one's accountability for basic dispositions is quite opaque. Clearly some human beings are much more inclined to melancholy than others. How can this be factored into the analysis of freedom? But circumstances are also very important for ethical evaluation, and here again we confront deep problems. Take the case of Brutus killing Caesar: the poignancy of those last reported words, 'et tu, mi Brute, tu quoque. Mi fili?', expresses vividly the horror of the act. Yet is Brutus to blame? How does he differ from George Washington, who would have been punished as a traitor had the revolutionary army been defeated, or Oliver Cromwell, who is regarded as either a vile regicide or a bold republican? The ultimate reputation and legacy of these three resolute opponents of tyranny is embedded in the historical contingencies which determined the success or failure of their resolutions.

First, the very range of choices of an agent in a liberal and tolerant society are very different from those available in highly formal, archaic societies, or those in a repressive totalitarian regime, but how do we compare, praise and blame without reference to such vast differences of culture, mores, etc.? Moreover, antecedent conditions seem to rest upon factors which greatly exceed any rational calculation or individual responsibility. The factors which lead to the noble and honourable Brutus slaying Caesar, the ambitions and jealousies which he does not share, nevertheless decisively affect his action. And of course the consequences of an action depend upon other variables which cannot be predicted or even measured. Mark Antony's visceral eloquence

---

27 T. Nagel, 'Moral Luck', in *Mortal Questions* (Cambridge: Cambridge University Press, 1979), p. 37.

unleashes an unexpected fury and the civil war which leads to the death of Brutus.

Freud has given imaginative shape to the rejection of autonomy as the idea of the will as the executive power of the rational subject. If consciousness is seen to be in the thrall of unconscious forces, the will is no longer the determining principle of the human agent, and the Kantian position that the human personality is defined by the moral will seems no longer tenable. However, as Nagel notes,

> We are unable to view ourselves simply as portions of the world, and from inside we have a rough idea of the boundary between what is us and what is not, what we do and what happens to us, what is our personality and what is an accidental handicap. We apply the same essentially internal conception of self to others. About ourselves we feel pride, shame, guilt, remorse – and agent regret. We do not regard our actions and our characters merely as fortunate or unfortunate episodes . . . We cannot *simply* take an external evaluative view of ourselves – of what we most essentially are . . . These acts remain ours.[28]

Nagel is surely correct about this. We cannot avoid the Kantian assumption that other human beings are free agents. We may use the psychoanalytic language of neurosis or complexes quite freely in detached conversation or reflection, but over decisive issues – love and death, war and peace, health and sickness and a host of less pressing, but nonetheless significant issues which affect us, where we are not just observers – it is almost impossible to use clinical language: we resent vices and praise virtues. Kant's interest lies in the *metaphysical* conditions of morality. He describes the sovereign power exerted by the moral principle as it is felt by a sensual and social being. The moral agent is subject to real needs and impulses. However, the ultimate identity of the agent is not morally defined by these. The defining component of the human moral agent lies in the capacity of being *more* than the sum of instincts, needs and society – the capacity to act out of reverence for the moral law and not merely in accordance with it. Hence Kant's concept of 'heteronomy' is not so much an absurdly rigoristic dismissal of altruistic behaviour towards friends and family per se but the rejection of ethical naturalism. Kant is attacking the *restriction* of ethical behaviour to those 'nearest and dearest': a restriction which is implied in any theory of ethics (like Hume's) based on sympathy. Autonomy proper means the ability to treat others as ends in themselves without external social pressures or instinctual propensity.

Intrapsychic virtue, or the difference between guilt and shame

A popular approach to ethics is linked to a revival of Aristotelianism and an emphasis upon the centrality of character traits or virtues. The central

28 Nagel, 'Moral Luck', p. 37.

ethical concepts are best explained, on this view, as deriving from qualities of virtuous agents. The founder of the revival of virtue ethics, Elizabeth Anscombe, famously argued that the concepts of moral obligation and moral duty 'ought to be jettisoned' as useless relics of an older kind of ethics in which moral authority rested in divine law.[29] The *societal* dimension looms large since the virtues practised in different communities will vary. Goods are then those preferences of good men. Yet virtue ethics is inadequate because it fails to address the need for ontology, i.e. conscience. Shakespeare can reveal the force of what Bishop Butler called that 'superior principle of reflection or conscience in every man, which . . . passes judgement upon himself'.[30] Macbeth and Hamlet are both epitomes of what Aristotle calls the μεγαλόψυχος, the great-souled man: visible achievements and status.[31] Macbeth in particular is a brave and ambitious man. But the audience can see into the inner life of these great men, and how each succumbs to a hidden, interior vice. Shakespeare the moralist dramatizes the inadequacy of the Aristotelian conception of the μεγαλόψυχος.

MacKinnon explores the example of imagination as an aid to truth in the biblical account of Nathan and David over Bathsheba and Uriah – as recounted in the parable of the lamb.[32] David's sexual greed and self-deception is presented in his attempt to offer his subject the opportunity to cover himself with military glory in the service of his monarch. MacKinnon writes:

> It is by means of his parable of the ewe lamb that Nathan first elicits from David his personal and royal condemnation of a comparable invented act of covetousness. Then when the king has said that such men as the thief of the poor man's ewe lamb deserve the supreme penalty Nathan directly identifies the king as the one whose guilt he has indirectly constrained him to acknowledge. Thus the king now grasps the principle he has violated . . . It shatters the veil of self-induced pretence whereby David has hidden from himself what he is about.[33]

One might see the parable as having a transforming effect analogous to that of the dream in Shakespeare. Dreams or parables represent the power of the imagination to effect transformation and renewal. Of course, common to Shakespeare and to Joseph Butler (and indeed to Kant) is the primacy of conscience.[34] The moral agent is not to be assessed by outward criteria but by the interior state. But therein lies the rub! To examine the interior life is to confront the capacity for self-deception, greed and cruelty which Kant exposes as 'radical evil'. We should

---

29 G. E. M. Anscombe, 'On Moral Philosophy', in *The Collected Philosophical Papers of G. E. M. Anscombe*, vol. 3, *Ethics, Religion and Politics* (Oxford: Blackwell, 1981), p. 27.
30 Joseph Butler, *Fifteen Sermons Preached at the Rolls Chapel*, II, 8.
31 Aristotle, *Nicomachean Ethics* 1124b.
32 2 Samuel 12.1–15.
33 MacKinnon, *The Problem of Metaphysics*, p. 92.
34 'Conscience' and 'consciousness' were virtually synonymous in the age of Shakespeare. See J. Bate, *The Genius of Shakespeare* (London: Picador, 1997), p. 257.

remember that Kant sees morality as a battle between good and evil.[35] Chastising the Stoics for failure to realize that the enemy is not folly but wickedness, he quotes Ephesians 6.12: 'For we wrestle not against flesh and blood, but against principalities, against powers, against rulers of the darkness of this world, against spiritual wickedness in high places'.[36]

Virtue ethics has performed a useful service in emphasizing the importance of the context of ethical beliefs. However, virtue ethics has the effect of separating ethics from ontology. If ethics is a matter of practising virtues *within* a community, we do not need a theory about how *what ought to be* is related to *what is the case*. Of course private ethics is an absurdity – the ethical Robinson Crusoe is not the true opposite of 'politics', since such a creature would be a ridiculous abstraction. But there is an important sense in which man made in the image of God is man in a perspective radically different from questions of habit, custom and behaviour within particular communities. English country folk may baulk at the rituals that produce halal meat, while happily accepting field sports as parts of rural English custom.

Jowett writes:

> The Greeks in the age of Plato admitted praise to be one of the chief incentives to moral virtue, and to most men the opinion of their fellows is a leading principle of action. Hence a certain element of seeming enters into all things; all or almost all desire to appear better than they are, that they may win the esteem or admiration of others. A man of ability can easily feign the language of piety or virtue; and there is an unconscious as well as a conscious hypocrisy which is the worst of the two.[37]

By 'unconscious hypocrisy' Jowett simply means the instinctive conformity to those pressures and norms exerted by the community. The figure of Socrates presents a visceral critique of the force of opinion and praise on mens' lives: to be and not to seem is the end of life. As Hamlet exclaims to Gertrude: 'seems, Madam! Nay, it is; I know not "seems"'.[38] Ethics is not primarily a matter of action but of *being*. The strenuous attempt at goodness is a pilgrimage; Hamlet, like Macbeth or Othello or Lear, is the image of a descent into evil. It is the exploration of the public disorder created by a sinful but not a depraved or wicked soul. The 'ought' of obligation expresses the supernatural within human beings – if goodness is an ultimate value which reveals the divine nature. The gap between the public and the private, which rests upon the fact that reflective, self-conscious human agents are 'pilgrims' and 'exiles' in whatever society, means that no account of ethics in terms of flourishing

---

35 See I. Murdoch, *Metaphysics as a Guide to Morals* (Harmondsworth: Penguin, 1992), p. 446.

36 I Kant, *Die Religion innerhalb des Grenzen der bloßen Vernuff*, p. 72. See also the excellent discussion in G. Graham, *Evil and Christian Ethics* (Cambridge: Cambridge University Press, 2001). pp. 74–118.

37 B. Jowett. *Select Passages from the Introductions to Plato*, ed. L. Campbell (London: John Murray, 1904), p. 85.

38 William Shakespeare, *Hamlet*, I.ii.76.

will suffice. Hamlet is a good illustration. The courtiers are outwardly deferential, yet this serves to reinforce his sense of inward alienation.

Shakespeare illustrates the manner in which conscience can prevail over natural, psychological and social forces. King David is successfully prosecuted from 'within'. And it is guilt, not mere shame, which convicts him. Wilberforce was able to overcome the weight of tradition and class interest to pursue the abolition of slavery. Joseph Butler argues: 'If the real nature of any creature leads him and is adapted to such and such purposes only or more than to any other, this is a reason to believe the Author of that nature intended it for those purposes.'[39] Conscience points to the intention of the author of the world, and hence is the 'candle of the Lord within' – a God-given guide.

Evidently, Butler's account will have no appeal to the secular mind, but at first glance he also appears to fall foul of the religious sensibility. Anscombe argues that Butler might sanction prejudice and wickedness – 'Butler exalts conscience, but appears ignorant that a man's conscience may tell him to do the vilest things'.[40] But this criticism rests on a misinterpretation. As Brian Hebblethwaite observes, bad action cannot be prompted by conscience per se, but only by the perverted sense of conscience.[41] Conscience as divinely implanted cannot err, but it can be overridden, ignored or suppressed. Consideration of the wider accusation that Butler presents an idolatrous substitute for divine law must be postponed until later in this chapter.

Even the fact that Macbeth can recognize his own descent points to the fact of conscience within the breast of the tyrant:

> I have supped full with horrors.
> Direness, familiar to my slaughterous thoughts,
> Cannot once start me.[42]

The force of conscience is one of right, not power: 'Had it strength, as it has right; had it power, as it has manifest authority; it would absolutely govern the world'.[43]

The Dostoyevsky syndrome and the teleological suspension of the ethical

A further approach is the existentialist espousal of authenticity despite, and in the context of, absurdity. Existential ethics goes to the other extreme from virtue ethics. The roots of existentialist ethics lie in Kierkegaard and his famous 'teleological suspension of the ethical' in

---

39 Butler, *Fifteen Sermons*, II, 1.
40 G. E. M. Anscombe, 'Modern Moral Philosophy', in *Ethics, Politics and Religion*, vol. 3 of *Collected Papers* (Oxford: Blackwell, 1981), p. 27.
41 B. Hebblethwaite, 'Butler on Conscience and Virtue', in C. Cunliffe (ed.), *Joseph Butler's Moral and Religious Thought: Tercentenary Essays* (Oxford: Clarendon Press, 1992), pp. 197–207.
42 William Shakespeare, *Macbeth*, V.v.13–15.
43 Butler, *Fifteen Sermons*, II, 14.

which the 'Knight of Faith' finds himself outside the domain of the ethical. Kierkegaard attempts to challenge the Kantian and Hegelian models of the moral life, which he saw as domesticating true religion on the Procrustean bed of universalist ethical and political considerations. The God of Abraham is not the God of the philosophers! The faith of Abraham represents a marked contrast with the abstract bourgeois sublimation of religion in Kant or Hegel. Abraham stands alone in an absolute relation to God without any mediation, and in a mood of infinite resignation he is prepared to sacrifice his dearest and most cherished son – without any crude or sublimated egotism. He is a heroic figure, in a living and not merely a formal relationship with God. It is in 'fear and trembling' that Abraham contemplates the 'teleological suspension of the ethical'. The position of Abraham is even more drastic than that of the hero of Greek tragedy. Agamemnon has at least the consolation that the sacrifice of his daughter is in conformity with the law of the state and can at least expect the respect of his fellows. But the breach of the ethical means that Abraham is bereft of any sympathy from others.

Kierkegaard famously distinguished between recollection and repetition as the contrast between the Platonic-idealistic attempt to comprehend reality and the 'truth of subjectivity'. This is what he meant when he said that life can only be understood backwards, but it must be lived forwards.[44] The upshot of the teleological suspension of the ethical seems to be the abrogation of Kantian universality in favour of a more Aristotelian vision of ethics as dealing with decisions on a relatively ad hoc basis (living forwards) and a more nominalist concept of God (i.e. 'His ways are not our ways', and 'Who are we to enquire?'). Throughout Kierkegaard's writings we find an aversion to the idea that God might conform to our expectations, the kernel of *Fear and Trembling*.

The standpoint of faith, having a higher *telos* than the ethical, is that in which the individual is recognized as higher than the universal: faith is the 'highest passion of an individual'. Kierkegaard does not deny the validity of the ethical; he sees it as a stage superior to the aesthetic but inferior to the religious. Yet how does this position then differ from Dostoyevsky's character Raskolnikov or Nietzsche's vision of an ethics *beyond* good and evil?

The case of Heidegger is fascinating. He claims:

The affirmation of 'eternal truths' – just as much as the mixing of the phenomenally based 'ideal nature' of *Dasein* with the idealized absolute subject – belong to the remaining vestiges of Christian theology within the philosophical debate.[45]

---

44 S. Kierkegaard, *Kierkegaard's Writings, VII: Philosophical Fragments* (Princeton, NJ: Princeton University Press, 1985), p. 80; cf. A. Hannay, *Kierkegaard* (London: Routledge and Kegan Paul, 1982), pp. 143–4.
45 'Die Behauptung "ewiger Wahrheiten" ebenso wie die Vermengung der phänomenal gegründeten "Idealität" des Daseins mit einem idealisierten absoluten Subjekt gehören zu den längst noch nicht radikal ausgetriebenen Resten von christlicher Theologie innerhalb der philosophischen Problematik': M. Heidegger, *Sein und Zeit* (Tübingen: Max Niemeyer, 1993), p. 229.

The analytic of existence should remove this hubristic illusion of eternal truth – and reinstate the truly finite nature of human consciousness in its being-towards-death. Such is the nihilism of the 'naked givenness in the nothing of the world' (*nackten Daß im Nichts der Welt*).[46] Or the analysis of guilt (*Schuld*) – that basic mode of nothingness (*Grundsein einer Nichtig- keit*).[47] *Dasein* can never get beyond its facticity (*Faktizität*). *Dasein* is condemned not just to the limits of the given thereness (*Da*) but to the brute *Daß*.[48] The religious tone is deep – and derived from Kierkegaard, Luther and Augustine, but without any metaphysical or religious resolution. Life is anxiety and care (*Sorge*). *Being and Time* was composed in the 1920s, a period marked by a mood of extreme subjectivism – whether in the novels of Proust and Joyce or the expressivism of the Blaue Reiter, or Breton's manifesto of Surrealism (1924) and the deep, almost Gnostic pessimism of the period after the First World War in German culture. It was a culture in which Kierkegaard, Nietzsche and Dostoyevsky exerted enormous influence – especially as an antinomian critique of bourgeois complacency and aridity. Heidegger's extreme 'subjectivism' in *Being and Time* is the iconoclastic denigration of the universal as 'das Man', the inauthenticity of 'they' who are lost in bourgeois conformity, as the expression of a vacuous idealism and priggish moralism. Heidegger's vitalism is also partly the expression of the Dionysian impulse of late-nineteenth-century German culture – of Nietzsche in particular, not least Nietzsche's quip that Kant's primacy of pure practical reason is a pale northern version of Platonism.[49] Plato thought art was not truth; Nietzsche thought art higher than truth. Perhaps Nietzsche's influence ushered in the aestheticizing of ethics: authenticity replaces obligation. For all his destabilizing of obligation through its teleological suspension, Kierkegaard recognizes the distinc- tion between the ethical and the aesthetic. In Nietzsche and his most influential twentieth-century disciples, Heidegger (possibility is higher than actuality) and the later Foucault (*le souci de soi*), the ethical becomes aesthetic. Self-expression replaces conscience.

Freudianism has enormous appeal because it appeases the dark aspect of human nature as 'repression'. It suggests that if we can understand, express and sublimate these pressures in an acceptable manner, we can accept ourselves. Hence Freudianism reinforces the Dionysian sanctifi- cation of primordial sub-ethical energy. Through what appears trivia to the conscious intellect (e.g. the Freudian slip) we gain access to the non- rational self or the id. Here Plato and Freud have deeply contrasting perspectives. The 'puritanical' aspect of Plato is most evident when he speaks devastatingly about the lower self:

> The sort that wakes us while we sleep, when the reasonable and humane part of us is asleep and its control relaxed, and our fierce bestial nature, full of food and drink, rouses itself and has its fling

46 Ibid., p. 276–77.
47 Ibid., p. 283.
48 Ibid., p. 284.
49 F. Nietzsche, *Twilight of the Idols*, How the Real World Finally Became a Myth, p. 40.

and tries to secure its own kind of satisfaction. As you know, there's nothing too bad for it and it's completely lost to all sense and shame. It doesn't shrink from attempting intercourse (as it supposes) with a mother or anyone else, man, beast or god, or from murder or eating forbidden food. There is, in fact, no folly nor shamelessness it will not commit.[50]

Iris Murdoch presents Freud as producing a vivid depiction of the life in the cave, and is intensely aware that the scope of Freud's libido resembles Platonic *eros*.[51] The sense of a lower self which characterizes Plato and most ancient moralists is much less sanguine than that of the psychoanalysts. In fact the violence of their language is startling. Plato speaks of the practice of death, St Paul about crucifying the old man. The lower self is not to be accommodated, integrated and sublimated but *mortified*.

The practice of death

Verily, verily I say to you, unless a grain of wheat falls into the earth and dies, it remains alone, but if it dies it bears much fruit.[52]

Heidegger's analytic of Existence and especially the concept of *Sorge* revolves around the Kierkegaardian anxiety about finitude and death. As such *Sorge* is the conscious reversal of the Stoic ideal of calm (ἀταραξία) and lying behind this Stoic doctrine the Platonic practice of death, based as it is on the doctrine of Ideas. In the *Symposium*, Socrates is depicted as falling into an absent-minded trance before entering the scene of the banquet. The servant calls Socrates to enter the house, but Aristodemus says, 'let him alone. It's a way he has. He goes apart sometimes and stands still wherever he happens to be.'[53] Festugière sees this account of the detached stillness of Socrates as the fount of much speculation in the Platonic school about the interiority of virtue – the concentration of the soul and its detachment from concerns of the body, and ultimately the intrapsychic ethics of the Platonists, especially as expressed in the *Phaedo*.[54] The goal of philosophy in the imperial period was to concentrate and retire, 'to draw itself together as a mollusk retracts and detaches at all points from its shell . . . and thus to retire from all

---

50 Plato, *Republic* 571c, tr. D. Lee in *Plato: The Republic* (Harmondsworth: Penguin, 1987) p. 392.
51 I. Murdoch, 'On "God" and "Good"', in *Existentialists and Mystics: Writings on Philosophy and Literature* (London: Chatto and Windus, 1997), pp. 341ff.
52 John 12.24.
53 Plato, *Symposium* 175a–b.
54 Plato, *Phaedo* 67c7, 83a6.

sense impressions.'[55] The soul in its highest state of contemplation of the Ideas is 'Pure and unmarked with this thing we now, fettered in the manner of an oyster, carry around and name body'.[56] The Greek puns upon the term for mark (σῆμα) and is a reference to the idea of the body (σῶμα) as the soul's tomb. Since there are eternal truths, the soul that can enjoy communion with such truths cannot suffer annihilation. This view is defended at some length in the *Phaedo*, but the *Phaedrus* describes mythically the process of universalization as a view from above whereby the sage becomes elevated above the pettiness and constraints of the particular perspective: a radical transformation of self. The beautiful story of the horses of the chariot bringing the charioteer to the outer circle of the heavens from which he can gaze upon eternal reality is linked to the description in the *Republic* of the philosopher who 'has greatness of mind and the breadth of vision to contemplate all time and all reality' so that he will not fear death.[57] Of the true philosopher 'only his body has taken residence in the city and can be found there, while his mind disdains all these matters, seeing them as petty and worthless, and wings its way everywhere, as Pindar says, "from beneath the earth to above the heavens"'.[58] The flight of the soul is the expression of the idea that the soul's object of contemplation determines its identity.

Far from being morbid, the philosophical significance of training for death is a spiritual exercise which consists in changing one's point of view. Through the disciplined use of imagination reflective agents can change from a vision of things dominated by the individual passions to a representation of the world governed by universality and objectivity of thought. This constitutes a conversion (μεταστροφή) brought about with the totality of the soul.[59] From the perspective of pure thought, things which are 'human, all too human' seem awfully puny. This is one of the fundamental themes of Platonic spiritual exercises.[60] The 'memento mori' was a central spiritual exercise in antique or medieval culture and the Western artistic tradition reflects this tradition in depictions of still life as images of transience, or more explicitly, in depictions of skulls. This spiritual exercise is an employment of the imagination to purify the desires of the agent in line with the dictates of conscience rather than of habit or inclination. The visualization of one's own death puts into perspective and exposes the futility of many of the cherished but paltry interests and obsessions of unreflective or semi-reflective life; it relativizes the concerns which gnaw at the reflective life. And it can release great energy. Once the mind is able to reflect upon the possibility of one's own non-existence, the luminous and irrefragable fact of Being as gift streams into one's consciousness: 'a sense sublime / Of something

55 A. J. Festugière, *Personal Religion among the Greeks* (Berkeley, Calif.: University of California Press, 1954), p. 59.
56 Plato, *Phaedrus*, 250c.
57 Plato, *Republic* 486a.
58 Plato, *Theaetetus* 174a, tr. R. Waterfield, Plato (Harmondsworth: Penguin, 1987), p. 69.
59 Plato, *Republic* 518.
60 P. Hadot, *Exercices spirituels et philosophie antique* (Paris: Albin Michel, 2002), p. 52.

far more deeply interfused', in the words of the greatest of all Romantic poets.[61]

Modern empiricists like to make the condescending claim that Plato, Leibniz and Heidegger were making the logical error of considering 'Being' as a referring noun and thus generating pseudo-questions and metaphysical muddles which could have been avoided with a rudimentary knowledge of quantifiers and other logical operators. But this is to misrepresent the spiritual dimension and practical implications of the question raised by the peculiar nature of self-consciousness. Self-awareness is not one item alongside others, or an object of possible identification or misidentification. The awareness of oneself as a human being is unlike the awareness of all other animals in that it is an awareness through imagination of our own finitude, and radical dependence upon those processes which enabled the universe, organic life and, ultimately, consciousness to emerge. In this sense the awareness of Being as such is hardly trivial. On the contrary, the earnest recognition of this fact may be a radically transformative experience in the life of a human being.

Iris Murdoch has argued eloquently that ethics is the attention to the real, a genuinely existing other, and the only path to this recognition is some form of negation of self. She writes:

> We are anxiety-ridden animals. Our minds are continually active, fabricating an anxious, usually self-preoccupied, often falsifying *veil* which partially conceals the world. Our states of consciousness differ in quality, our fantasies and reveries are not trivial and unimportant, they are profoundly connected with our energies and our ability to choose and act. And if quality of consciousness matters, then anything which alters consciousness in the direction of unselfishness, objectivity and realism is to be connected with virtue.[62]

She refers to 'a hint in Plato' from the *Phaedrus* by speaking of beauty as 'an occasion for unselfing'. In this passage, she maintains, Plato presents beauty as the 'only spiritual thing that we love by instinct' and hence that art can invite 'unpossessive contemplation' and resists absorption into the selfish life of the consciousness.[63]

One needs to consider the principle of life out of death. All life involves struggle, limitation and renunciation:

> Then was the truth received into my heart,
> That under heaviest sorrow earth can bring,
> Griefs bitterest of ourselves or of our kind,
> If from the affliction somewhere do not grow
> Honour which could not else have been, a faith,
> An elevation, and a sanctity,

---

61 W. Wordsworth, 'Lines Written a Few Miles above Tintern Abbey', ll. 95–6.
62 I. Murdoch, 'The Sovereignty of Good Over Other Concepts', in *Existentialists and Mystics*, p. 369.
63 Ibid.; see Plato, *Phaedrus* 250.

If new strength be not given, or old restored,
The blame is ours not Nature's.[64]

Wordsworth is claiming that a genuine moral agent is shaped through the confrontation with disappointment, regret and remorse. Suffering can be the stimulus and fuel real growth and transformation of the soul. It is usually not what happens to a human being but the nature of the response which is decisive. As William James observes, Christianity and Buddhism are religions of deliverance: 'the man must die to an unreal life before he can be born into the real life'.[65] James's reflection upon the proximity of Christian to oriental themes of emancipation from illusion can be buttressed by the persistence of this topic in the Shakespearean drama:

> We are such stuff
> As dreams are made on, and our little life
> Is rounded with a sleep.[66]

Shakespeare, whose sonnets are full of reflection upon transience and death, is drawing on the *memento mori* – that this life is at one level an 'insubstantial pageant', transient, fading and doomed to dissolution. Yet his greatest plays are reflections upon the momentous struggle between good and evil and the grandeur of the soul. A human being can transcend his or her circumstances – is not a poor player,

> That struts and frets his hour upon the stage,
> And then is heard no more.[67]

Human beings do not just undergo death like all other animals but are aware of it. Man is not just finite but knows his finitude; as Pascal says, 'un roseau qui pense l'univers'. And there must be the capacity for liberation from the care of *Dasein*. In Platonic-Phaedran mode, Schiller enthuses of the soul,

> But free from the ravages of time,
> . . .
> Would'st thou freely soar on her wings on high,
> Throw off earthly dread,
> Flee from narrow, stifling life
> Into the realm of the ideal![68]

---

64 W. Wordsworth, *The Prelude* (1805), X, 422–9.
65 W. James, *Varieties of Religious Experience* (Harmondsworth: Penguin, 1982), p. 165.
66 William Shakespeare, *The Tempest*, IV.i.156–8.
67 Shakespeare, *Macbeth*, V.v.24–5.
68 F. von Schiller, 'Das Ideal und das Leben', in *Sämtliche Werke*, ed. E. v. der Hellen (Stuttgart and Berlin: J. G. Cotta, 1904), vol. 1, p. 192.

Aber frei von jeder Zeitgewalt,

. . .
Wollt ihr hoch auf ihren Flügeln schweben,
Werft die Angst des Irdischen von euch,
Fliehet aus dem engen dumpfen Leben
In des Idealen Reich!

Heidegger has inherited Nietzsche's critique of Socrates as a decadent who opposed life and instinct with rationalism, universalism and the idea of life as an illness cured by death. The emphasis upon death as subjective possibility rather than as an external objective actuality is part of Heidegger's general resolve to reverse the inherited priority of actuality over possibility. The moods (especially anxiety in the face of death) reveal those possibilities of authentic existence which determine what we are. Hence *Dasein* shows the priority of possibility over actuality. Yet it has often been remarked that the absence of any sense of ultimate value leaves Heidegger with a pseudo-ethic without content. The 'resolve' of the end of *Being and Time* is compatible with almost any substantial ethical position whatsoever.

The apocalyptic solution to the paradox

Throughout this chapter, in my critique of biological, economic and theonomic ethical theories, I have sought to defend precisely the view which Bernard Williams calls a 'powerful misconception of life' – the 'Morality Project' or the 'Peculiar Institution' – and in particular the 'extravagant metaphysical luggage of the noumenal self'.[69] Kant, Williams argues,

> started from what in his view rational agents essentially *were*. He thought that the moral agent was, in a sense, a rational agent . . . [a] 'noumenal' self, outside time and causality, and thus distinct from the concrete, empirically determined person that one usually takes oneself to be . . . He did not believe that we could fully understand this conception, but we could see that it was possible and we could know that it was involved in both morality and rational action.[70]

Williams notes that Kant's view is 'in some ways like a religious conception . . . but also unlike any real religion.'[71] Williams exaggerates, but this could be either a compliment or a criticism. The imagination is necessary once we consider human life as a self-conscious subject and agent which requires residually mythic forms. The expression of the genuine self demands a vision of the soul's journey from its fall, purification and reunion with God. This use of imaginative, mythical language can result in apparent inconsistency. Plato's myth of Er in the *Republic* and the chariot myth in the *Phaedrus* imply that the quality of human lives depends upon factors outside the individual's control, namely actions in a previous existence, whereas Plato's insistence at the end of the *Republic* is upon the momentous reality of the moral struggle between the better and the worse in the soul. The role of a quasi-mythical

---

Cassirer quoted this passage against Heidegger. See E. Cassirer, *The Metaphysics of Symbolic Forms*, ed. J. M. Krois and D. P. Verene (New Haven, Conn.: Yale University Press, 1996), p. 204.
69 Williams, *Ethics and the Limits of Philosophy*, p. 65.
70 Ibid., p. 64.
71 Ibid., p. 195.

illud tempus in both Plato and Kant distinguishes them radically from the pragmatic-prudential ethics of Aristotle or Bentham. Good or bad consequences are quite irrelevant for an eternal and immutable morality. The practice of a community cannot form the norm for the principles of ethics: those principles by virtue of which an act is right or wrong. The symbolic or mythic nature of this eschatology is unavoidable – heaven and hell have no geography, and eternity no duration. Symbol, myth and poetry can partially convey truths about that realm of experience which science and discursive reason cannot attain. The image of the soul in the *Phaedrus* is that of the capacity to rise to the intelligible or to descend from it, and the myth is profoundly religious.[72] But it is a myth which expresses both a sense of exile and belonging in the world[73] – which affirms that both knowledge and moral advance are possible. It is the intimation of transcendent reality through aesthetic and ethical experience. Since the arch-rationalist Plato locates ideas in the super-sensible realm, these can only be known intermittently and inadequately: he is thrown back upon the use of myth and metaphor.

Appearance, reality and Shakespeare's true fiction

Coleridge observed that 'Plato was a poet of such excellence as would have stood all other competition but that of his being a philosopher'.[74] And Plato is a magnificent dramatist – especially in the masterpieces of the middle period. One might consider the elaborate framing of the *Symposium* – a party set in 416 BC. The dialogue was probably composed in 385 BC. Apollodorus is dependent upon a report from an eyewitness called Aristodemus. The *Phaedrus* is set between 411 and 404 BC, framed around a conversation between Socrates and the young man called Phaedrus. In the *Republic*, Plato employs the idea of a 'noble falsehood'. Jonathan Lear observes that 'if one wishes to communicate with people whose lives are dominated by illusion, one must speak the language of the illusory world in which they live'.[75] One construal of myth in Plato is as a philosophical truth expressed in narrative and accessible form, and Plato's poetic genius is evident in these great seminal myths of the soul chariot, the creation myth of the *Timaeus*, or the eschatological myth of Er.

Coleridge observed that 'From Shakespeare to Plato, from the philosophic poet to the poetic philosopher, the transition is easy'.[76] Shakespeare often puns on the relationship between art and reality. Consider again the famous speech in *The Tempest*:

---

72 Neoplatonist commentators designated the main topic of the *Phaedrus* as love, and saw it as a work of ethics. Cf. H. Bernard, *Hermeias von Alexandrian: Kommentar zu Platons 'Phaidros'* (Tübingen: Mohr Siebeck, 1997), pp. 86ff.
73 J. A. Stewart, *The Myths of Plato* (London: Centaur Press, 1960), p. 310.
74 S. T. Coleridge, *Philosophical Lectures* (London: Pilot Press, 1949), p. 158.
75 J. Lear, *Open Minded: Working Out the Logic of the Soul* (Cambridge, Mass.: Harvard University Press, 1999), p. 60.
76 S. T. Coleridge, *The Friend* (London: Routledge, 1969), vol. 1, p. 472.

Our revels now are ended. These our actors,
As I foretold you, were all spirits, and
Are melted into air, into thin air,
And, like the baseless fabric of this vision,
The cloud-capped towers, the gorgeous palaces,
The solemn temples, the great globe itself,
Yea, all which it inherit, shall dissolve;
And, like this insubstantial pageant faded,
Leave not a rack behind. We are such stuff
As dreams are made on, and our little life
Is rounded with a sleep.[77]

The analogy of human life as a play is a powerful theme in Stoic and Platonic reflection upon providence (e.g. Marcus Aurelius or Plotinus) and Shakespeare may have picked up the idea from his Renaissance milieu. But Shakespeare is also thinking of degrees of reality. If we think of consciousness as discursive reflection rather than the entire palette of intuitive and imaginative experience of which the 'rational' is a part, we are ironically subject to an illusion which can be exposed by comparative realities. Is the 'real world' that of the mobile phone, television and email, or the sky, the hills and the trees, or the particles/waves of fundamental physics, or the infinite, luxuriant and terrifying landscape of soul inhabited with ancient and archetypal images? Shakespeare repeatedly puns on the metaphysical question of the relation between reality and appearance, seriousness and play, and often presents a continuum of dream and life, imagination and reason:

If we shadows have offended,
Think but this, and all is mended:
That you have but slumbered here,
While these visions did appear;
And this weak and idle theme,
No more yielding but a dream,[78]

Yet this is precisely the Shakespeare who uses dream to reveal the depths of character, insight and knowledge: hence Puck's paean to sleep as the gateway to visions 'most rare'; the Athenian lovers find true love after sleep in the forest. And drama is used to reveal essential truths. It is through the play within the play that Hamlet comes to know the guilt of his stepfather: the mechanicals' play of Pyramus and Thisbe, taken as it is from Ovid's *Metamorphoses*, is a tragic inversion of the story of the play. It is Prospero who deciphers and reverses the dreamlike illusion. The magical island is the place where the treachery of the King of Naples and his courtiers, 'three men of sin' and 'unfit to live' amongst men, will be exposed and chastised. A. E. Taylor observes of the tragedies:

---

77 Shakespeare, *The Tempest*, IV.i.148–58.
78 William Shakespeare, *A Midsummer Night's Dream*, Epilogue 1–6.

Othello and Macbeth . . . are fighting for their lives in a battle where the stakes are Heaven and Hell, and it is because the battle is so grim and the stakes so fearful that we feel that the fight is being waged, not in fairy land, but in the real waking world of our common life.[79]

Notwithstanding Johnson's and Milton's disparaging reflections on Shakespeare's learning, in Shakespeare we have the sublime confidence of the late Renaissance poet – in the mould of Tasso or Sir Philip Sidney – who knows the truth of his art:

Fifteenth-century Florentine humanism . . . and the long shadow it casts across the ensuing century in the writings of Sidney and Shakespeare, is the first sustained and articulate theory of fiction in modern times: the first modern version of the view that fiction offers knowledge, even certain knowledge, and a knowledge clearer and more certain than life itself.[80]

Sidney's *A Defence of Poetry* argues that the arts are 'actors and players, as it were, or what nature will have set forth'.[81] The arts, for Sidney, represent or describe – albeit in an idealized form. The artist creates a world of 'gold' rather than the brass of the habitual environment of human beings. Watson observes that in many 'practical' matters, like the instructions for the use of a tool, the description is clearer or 'more golden' than its subject matter.[82] A map or a grammar represents by means of significant but illuminating modification. By analogy, the imaginative paradigms of literature imitate nature while deviating from it:

Of course the world shows no friend as constant as Pylades was to Orestes, as he argues, or any hero as virtuous as Aeneas: such ancient models of constancy and virtue are imaginary. But then if the world around us were as lucid as literature, the poet would have slight reason to exist, or none, and even slighter reason to be valued.[83]

And yet Shakespeare is also the poet of real characters, the 'Proteus', Coleridge famously said, who 'darts himself forth, and passes into all the forms of human character and passion'.[84] His characters change over time: they are not merely formal representatives or types, but recognizable as people transformed by events and experiences. Iris Murdoch vividly expressed this Coleridgean point about Shakespeare as a maker of real characters – 'free and eccentric personalities whose reality

---

79 A. E. Taylor, *The Faith of a Moralist* (London: Macmillan, 1930), vol. 1, p. 337.
80 G. Watson, *The Certainty of Literature: Essays in Polemic* (London: Harvester, 1989), pp. 113–14.
81 Sidney, *A Defence of Poetry*, p. 22.
82 Watson, *The Certainty of Literature*, pp. 110ff.
83 Ibid., p. 122.
84 S. T. Coleridge, *Biographia Literaria* (Princeton, NJ: Princeton University Press, 1983), vol. 2, p. 27.

Shakespeare has apprehended and displayed as something quite separate from himself. He is the most invisible of writers'.[85]

Human agents are, as Murdoch argues, very mysterious, but moral philosophers tend not to dwell on this. Any adequate moral philosophy must give some account of states of mind or dispositions of the soul, rather than propriety or prudence. Transformation, salvation and divine inspiration play an important role in the late romances of Shakespeare. Ferdinand concludes after the second song of Ariel,

> This is no mortal business, nor no sound
> That the earth owes.[86]

The attribution of divinity or divine inspiration is important to the late-Renaissance Shakespeare in all the romances, but especially the imaginative masterpiece of *The Tempest*. But this is not fanciful in any trivial sense. What is at stake is the state of souls of the protagonists. When Sebastian inquires about Antonio's conscience, Antonio replies:

> Ay, sir; where lies that?.
> I feel not
> This deity in my bosom.[87]

When, as moral agents, we judge others, we are projecting onto them an internal life akin to our own, and bracketing the differences. The real agent can be detected through imagination, since the circumstances or external factors cannot exhaust the core self. And this is where a brilliant artist like Shakespeare can explore the core self which transcends or eludes external criteria. Moreover, there is an obvious continuity between the creative imaginative activity of the great dramatist and the habitual use of the imagination in our lives. We need to employ imagination to understand others as coherent agents with a set of instincts and inclinations as well as values and goals in order to cooperate with them in a productive manner; and secondly we use imagination because of the awareness that overt behaviour may be deceptive and/or dangerous. The mugger may well pose as a beggar; the thief may pose as a random house visitor; Iago presents himself as the concerned friend of Othello. The imaginative capacity to envisage potential deception and danger has obvious utility. Yet we also can employ imagination in order to exercise a deeper insight into the interior lives of others. In friendship or love the capacity for complex imaginative judgement which far exceeds empirical evidence is ineluctable yet often intractable. Close family or friends may seem strangely unfathomable. Lear's preference for the flattery of Regan and Goneril over Cordelia's admirable but disturbing honesty is a fine depiction not only of the

---

85 I. Murdoch, 'The Sublime and the Beautiful Revisited,' in *Existentialists and Mystics*, p. 275. See the discussion in G. Watson, *Never Ones for Theory? England and the War of Ideas* (Cambridge: Lutterworth, 2000), pp. 103–10.
86 Shakespeare, *The Tempest*, I.ii.408–9.
87 Ibid., II.i.281–3. See *Titus Andronicus*: 'Yet, for I know thou art religious / And hast a thing within thee called conscience' (V.i.74–5).

ambiguities, delusion and deception which mark many close human relationships, but also of the difficulty of proper insight. Donald MacKinnon notes the interesting overlap between the parable of the prodigal son and the story of Lear. Perhaps one can sense the generosity of the father welcoming the prodigal son and his rebuke of the elder son merging into the indulgence of Shakespeare's Lear. MacKinnon observes: 'There is in the father of the parable the making of a Lear'.[88] As MacKinnon's erstwhile pupil Iris Murdoch notes: 'We use our imagination not to escape the world but to join it, and this exhilarates us because of the distance between our ordinary dulled consciousness and an apprehension of the real.'[89]

Faith or fate?

The paradigmatic Shakespeare play about self-knowledge is, of course, *Hamlet*. The eponymous protagonist struggles with his own doubts and prevarications and exclaims,

> The time is out of joint. O cursed spite
> That ever I was born to set it right![90]

It is little wonder that this figure, intensely reflective and yet destroying both himself and others dear to him, fascinated Freud. Rather as a therapist tries to discover roots of action of which the agent is ignorant, Shakespeare is quite candid about the cardinal importance of self-knowledge. Gonzalo in *The Tempest* recounts the chaos that ensued 'When no man was his own'.[91] But in Shakespeare it is not, as generally in the Greek tragedies, destiny or fate (i.e. chance) which destroys the individual. Rather, the individual is caught between the demands of conscience and the circumstances which frustrate the execution of that conscience:

> To die, to sleep –
> No more; and by a sleep to say we end
> The heartache and the thousand natural shocks
> That flesh is heir to – 'tis a consummation
> Devoutly to be wished. To die, to sleep.
> To sleep, perchance to dream.[92]

The sentiment expressed is a longing for the abdication of responsibility rather than the sense of inexorable fate. Hamlet has the intimation of a transcendence order intruding on the natural and human order.[93] However inscrutable the ultimate purpose of the universe may be, it is not fate:

88 MacKinnon, *The Problem of Metaphysics*, p. 137.
89 Murdoch, 'The Sovereignty of Good Over Other Concepts', p. 374.
90 Shakespeare, *Hamlet*, I.v.189–90.
91 Shakespeare, *The Tempest*, V.i.213.
92 Shakespeare, *Hamlet*, III.i.61–6.
93 MacKinnon, *The Problem of Metaphysics*, p. 169.

There's a divinity that shapes our ends,
Rough-hew them how we will[94]

This is to say that mankind as self-conscious is distinct from the animal kingdom, and that human self-consciousness represents the eternal self-consciousness of God. Shakespeare's Christian providentialist vision is also evident in the suggestion of growth out of chaos. Fortinbras arrives at Elsinore, and Malcolm at Dunsinane, to rebuild from the ruins.

MacKinnon, writing in the wake of two terrible world wars, returns to the intractable problem of evil. He restates Dostoyevsky's problem: why should even the pain and suffering of one child be acceptable to a good God? The twentieth century employed technology to perpetrate crimes of cruelty and barbarism on a scale previously unknown, but the kind of cruelty was evident previously. It is not clear that the concentration camps revealed anything new about the 'crooked timber of humanity'; but they haunt MacKinnon's work and his answer is deeply aporetic.

Consider Hume's conviction that 'there is no view of human life or of the condition of mankind from which, without the greatest violence, we can infer the moral attributes, or learn the divine benevolence'. The world is 'blind nature . . . pouring forth from her lap, without discernment or parental care, her maimed and abortive children'.[95] Kant would not object to the description per se, but to Hume's inference. Hume is inferring from *outward facts* to God's existence or absence. Kant is arguing from the *interior sense* of goodness as revealed in consciousness by conscience as distinct from prudence. This unveils a categorical moral law and the recognition of the binding nature of this law implies a creature capable of executing it, and not a mere mechanism. Kant does not rely upon any facile congruity between our aspirations and the way the world turns out, but upon an inner intuition of moral law. It is most unlikely that we should have epistemic access to the details of divine purposes in the world in any detail if God is a being who vastly transcends our cognitive capacities and our moral limitations.[96] But if one does hold to the objectivity of the moral law and to the idea that it cannot be frustrated, this drives one to the acceptance of an eschatological reconciliation between the source of nature and the source of morality in a transcendent, good God. Duty demands that we assume God's existence as a practical postulate, if not as a fact of speculative metaphysics.

---

94 *Hamlet.*, V.ii.10–11. James Vigus has remarked to me in conversation that these lines come from a speech describing the murder of Rosencrantz and Guildenstern. However, it seems part of Shakespeare's craft to place some of his most striking philosophical affirmations within incongruous contexts. Theseus's classic speech about 'Imagination' (*A Midsummer Night's Dream*, V.i.4–22) is a paradigm example.

95 David Hume, *Dialogues Concerning Natural Religion*, XI, in *David Hume: 'Dialogues' and 'Natural History of Religion'* (Oxford: Oxford University Press, 1993), p. 113.

96 See Stephen J. Wykstra on the condition of reasonable epistemic access in 'The Humean Obstacle to Evidential Arguments from Suffering: On Avoiding the Evils of "Appearance"', in M. M. Adams and R. M. Adams, *The Problem of Evil* (Oxford: Oxford University Press, 1990), pp. 138–60.

And this phenomenon requires explanation. This sense and awareness of the absoluteness of moral obligations and the guilt generated by the failure to fulfil these obligations distinguishes human beings from animals in kind and not merely in degree. The human sense of the gap between what *is* and what *ought to be* is not the refutation of theism, but its most powerful basis. In Plato this is the result of seeing the Good as the supreme principle of Being, and for Christian Platonists the structure of a reality is that of a hierarchy of levels of being, each presupposing the inferior level, and yet pointing to that which is higher, culminating in the creative divine will. On such a Platonic scheme, existence is secondary to goodness. In fact, one can say that existence is consequent upon value. Caird is reported as objecting to the phrase 'too good to be true': 'if anything is not true, he would say, it is because it is not good enough to be true'.

Caird is correct about God, but not about the world. The 'ought' of ethical obligation is only realized partially within the created order. The Spinozistic view that collapses the distinction between what 'is' and what 'ought to be' and denies the real challenge of evil in the world of human experience is a perspectival illusion. This is a wolf in sheep's clothing. In the finite world, evil is a distinct reality, just as substantial as goodness – only in the eternal realm of the divine mind are being and goodness identical. William James writes,

> It is indeed a remarkable fact that sufferings and hardships do not, as a rule, abate the love of life; they seem, on the contrary, to give it a keener zest. The sovereign source of melancholy is repletion. Need and struggle are what excite and inspire us.[97]

Material needs are usually a necessary but not sufficient condition of human happiness. Extreme asceticism and even martyrdom are facts of human nature which cannot be ignored. Indeed, some ascetics like the Buddha or Christ have exerted disproportionate influence over humanity. John Henry Newman is eloquent in his depiction of 'real apprehension' involving imagination and experience in opposition to merely notional cognition:

> To a mind . . . carefully formed upon the basis of its natural conscience, the world, both of nature and of man, does but give back a reflection of those truths about the One living God, which have been familiar to it from childhood. Good and evil meet us daily as we pass through life, and there are those who think it philosophical to act towards the manifestations of each with some sort of impartiality, as if evil had as much right to be there as good, or even better, as having more striking triumphs and a broader jurisdiction. And because the course of things is determined by fixed laws, they consider that those laws preclude the present agency of the Creator in the carrying out of particular issues. It is otherwise

97 W. James, 'Is Life Worth Living?', in *The Will to Believe and Other Essays in Popular Philosophy* (New York: Dover Books, 1956), p. 47.

with the theology of a religious imagination. It has a living hold on truths which are really to be found in the world, though they are not upon the surface. It is able to pronounce by anticipation, what it takes a long argument to prove – that good is the rule, and evil the exception. It is able to assume that, uniform as are the laws of nature, they are consistent with a particular Providence. It interprets what it sees around it by this previous inward teaching, as the true key of that maze of vast complicated disorder; and thus it gains a more and more consistent and luminous vision of God from the most unpromising materials. Thus conscience is a connecting principle between the creature and his Creator; and the firmest hold of theological truths is gained by habits of personal religion.[98]

Conscience, Newman argues, provides an imaginative access to reality which might otherwise be obscured or hidden. We need to be able to view the world as grounded in divine purpose, however inscrutable this may appear. This is not fideism, but the basis of the categorical imperative in opposition to hedonistic or pessimistic individualism. Cosmological pessimism is often disillusioned hedonism. Kant, like Plato, considers the moral life to be intrinsically religious because we are denizens of two realms, and our anxieties and conflicts of conscience are witness to this primordially religious intimation that our obligations are not questions of prudence or respectability but are based on the supreme value of goodness, and a deep sense of human inadequacy in the face of this supreme good. Kant and Plato present an essentially imaginative picture of human vocation. Life is a drama in which each individual has a choice of rising or descending. The ascent may not be as dramatic as the depiction in Plato's *Phaedrus* or the descent as grim as Shakespeare's tragic heroes, yet I cannot see how any approach which does not consider the imaginative dimension of human thought will be very useful in ethics. We possess certain ideals and aspirations which are irreducible to instinct and embedded in an organic history and culture:

Contentment is a sleepy thing!
If it in death alone must die,
A quiet mind is worse than poverty!
Unless it from enjoyment spring![99]

It may be objected that ethical obligations are only obligations to other finite agents and/or that any appeal to transcendence undermines the very *absoluteness* of what the moralist is trying to explain. Both Plato and Kant start from the sense of absolute obligation and draw religious *implications* from this. The argument does not depend upon the idea of God or even the Good. Both thinkers, moreover, hold to an overarching providential scheme, but this is hardly equivalent to a prudential

98 J. H. Newman, *An Essay in Aid of a Grammar of Assent* (Notre Dame, Ind.: University of Notre Dame Press, 1979), p. 106. C.f. J. Coulson, *Religion and Imagination 'In Aid of a Grammar of Assent'* (Oxford: Clarendon Press, 1981), pp. 46–83.

99 T. Traherne, 'Contentment is a Sleepy Thing', 1–4, *Selected Poems and Prose* (Harmondsworth: Penguin, 1991), p. 162.

supernaturalism. Neither produces a Pascalian wager for belief in the afterlife, but rather they provide a theory about a prior commitment to what *must* be: the ultimate identity of value and existence.

Ascent from the cave

The cave is often taken to offer but a bleak prospect for human life, but I think it is the most optimistic metaphor in Western Philosophy. Although our experience may be permeated by distorted images, they are ultimately distortions of something real.[100]

This central mythos of Plato's cave suggests that strenuous effort can attain real progress towards the ideal. Moreover, the political and epistemological project of the *Republic* presupposes the possibility of real freedom. Martha Nussbaum has emphasized the importance of the tragedians for Plato.[101] The Greeks thought of these as teachers, and would be far less inclined than we to attribute to the poets a merely ornamental function. Plato clearly believed that the pessimistic determinism of the tragic poets was an erroneous paradigm. The polemic of the Platonic school in figures such as Plotinus and Proclus against Stoic determinism is rooted in Plato's own rejection of fatalism.[102]

William James maintained that 'freedom was the one fact in human life where belief in the thing and the reality of the thing coincided'.[103] But it is a salutary fact expressed beautifully by St Paul that our immediate desires, wishes and actions conflict with the dictates of the rational will. The changing of one's habits is a good concrete example that it is possible to live according to imagination rather than memory and conditioning. A person who is in the grip of a destructive habit can employ imaginative ingenuity in providing stratagems to change the habit. But the change in *thought* precedes any isolated actions. The possible's slow fuse is lit by the imagination: the importance of discipline in self-formation is matched only by the indispensable role of imagination in providing inspiring images. As Barrett says, 'We can devise and set up circumstances for our own conditioning.'[104] People can transform old habits and inaugurate new ones through origination. And traditional religions provide rituals and practices which are powerful imaginative aids for transforming the will as the centre of the human self or personality.

---

100 J. Lear, *Open Minded*, p. 59.
101 M. Nussbaum, *The Fragility of Goodness: Luck and Ethics in Greek Tragedy and Philosophy* (Cambridge: Cambridge University Press, 1986).
102 See Plotinus, *Enneads* III.2, 3; Proclus, *Trois études sur la Providence* (Paris: Les Belles Lettres, 1977).
103 Quoted in W. Barrett, *The Illusion of Technique* (New York: Anchor Press, 1978), p. 329.
104 Ibid., p. 30.

Freud is in some respects closer to the pessimism of the poets than to Plato in his sense of the fragility of reason's hold on the id, and his own mission as a debunker of false pretensions. MacKinnon does not discuss the central model of the *ascent* in his fascinating (but often infuriatingly aporetic) account of Plato's ethics. Yet this is the great legacy of the Platonic tradition. One need only think of the image of ascent in Diotima's speech in the *Symposium* or the paradigmatic image of ascent in the chariot of the *Phaedrus*. Biblical exegesis of Jacob's ladder, Moses on Mount Sinai and St Paul's experience of the ascent of the mind to God are further instances of this paradigm of ethics as ascent. It is this model of ascent to the Divine through self-consciousness which is the key to ethics in Plato and the whole Platonic tradition. This model is fiercely opposed to the determinism of the Greek tragedians. Plato is not merely opposed to artists like Homer because they corrupt the public with their tales of immorality; the tragedians also subvert morality with their pessimism. The tragic view of 'Know Thyself' as 'nothing too much' is the opposite of Plato's view. For him 'Know Thyself' means 'Reverence Thyself'! It is to explore and actualize the best within: that which is divine. The poet-philosopher gives us in the *Phaedrus* an imaginative account of human nature as reflective subjectivity and how beauty can inspire the soul to rise up to intelligible goodness.

The figure of Beatrice illuminates this principle:

> As soon as I was on the threshold of my second age and I changed life he took himself from me and gave himself to another. When I had risen from the flesh to spirit and beauty and virtue had increased in me I was less dear to him and less welcome and he bent his steps in a way not true, following after false images of good which fulfil no promise; nor did it avail me to gain inspirations for him with which both in dream and other ways I called him back, so little did he heed them.[105]

The erotic form of the longing for Beatrice is closer to Plato than to Petrarch. It is grounded in the experience of transcendence: 'the inborn and perpetual Thirst for the godlike kingdom'.[106] Dante's own spiritual experience is a mirror of an eternal and immutable reality. The moral will is the core and fulcrum of the human soul: the perverse will of the *Inferno*, the longing of the *Purgatorio* and the contemplation of the *Paradiso* are imaginative apocalyptic depictions of a spiritual pilgrimage. All men and women have to undergo an inward pilgrimage which is quite distinct from the outward ceremonies, ritual behaviour, conventional mores and practices of the tribe. The pagan Platonists liked to use the *Odyssey* as an allegory of this inner journey and the author of the Epistle to the Hebrews employs the analogy of a race observed by the faithful and culminating in Christ.[107] The genius of Shakespeare in his major plays is to exploit imaginatively the fault lines between the inner

---

105 Dante, *Purgatorio*, XXX, 124–35.
106 Dante, *Paradiso*, II, 20.
107 Hebrews 12.1–2.

journey and the outer world. In tragedy, the breach between the two is clearly revealed, whereas in the romances there is resolution. Yet in Dante the visionary world impinges on the physical world. The capacity to hold together both the acute and 'worldly' observation of human finitude with a vivid sense of its ultimate and inevitable 'commerce with the transcendent' is not an accident of the Christian culture of the two men but an essential characteristic of the imagination of both poets.

Our capacity to employ conscience with imagination avoids the Scylla of reductive naturalism, on the one hand, and the Charybdis of theonomic positivism, on the other. To answer the demands of conscience is an autonomous exercise of human rationality, rather than the brute acceptance of an exterior code. But it is also the imaginative intimation of an order that transcends the immediate biological, social and economic circumstances of human life. In this sense Butler, far from positing an idolatrous substitute, is right to see conscience as the candle of the Lord.

6

Myths, Dreams and Other Stories

The man who likes stories is a kind of philosopher[1]

In the previous chapter I argued that the true 'drama' – as it were – of human living is not circumstance or fate but one's interior relation to events. Consideration of questions raised by Donald MacKinnon led to reflection upon the true fiction of Shakespeare and Dante. This, in turn, might be related to what Charles Taylor calls 'horizons of significance' for the ethical agent, and to recent developments in moral philosophy, in order to emphasize the importance of literature for ethics, such as in the work of Martha Nussbaum. Yet there seems something odd about the idea that reading novels might be a prerequisite for ethics. What about the good-natured non-literate or semi-literate? What evidence is there that the highly literate are better ethical agents? In this chapter I would like to disentangle the good thought from the bad. I want, in particular, to draw upon two literary figures who are deeply anti-modernist in their views of literature, lovers of romance and fairy tale, writing in an epoch of English literature dominated by a quite alien 'realistic' mood: J. R. R. Tolkien and C. S. Lewis. Behind this love of the genre of 'romance' lies an interest in myth, which links them both to Coleridge and Romanticism but also to the Platonic tradition more generally. C. S. Lewis exclaims in a poem:

> In England the romantic stream flows not
> From waterish Rousseau but from manly Scott,
> A right branch on the old European tree
> Of valour, truth, freedom, and courtesy,
> . . .
> It flows, I say from Scott; from Coleridge too.
> A bore? A sponge? A laudanum-addict? True;
> Yet Newman in that ruinous master saw
> One who restored our faculty for awe,
> Who rediscovered the soul's depth and height,
> Who pricked with needles of the eternal light
> An England at that time half numbed to death
> With Paley's, Bentham's, Malthus' wintry breath.[2]

I wish to argue that novels are parasitic upon a tradition of primordial story-telling: oral narratives, myths and legends. I also wish to suggest a

---

1 Aristotle, *Metaphysics* 982b18.
2 C. S. Lewis, 'To Roy Campbell', in *The Collected Poems of C. S. Lewis*, ed. W. Hooper (London: Fount, 1994), p. 80.

historical argument for the paradigmatic position of the novel in contemporary society. The greatest literary works in the Western canon – epic poem, drama (which seems to me evidently narrative – though this is debated) and novels – are great stories. Samuel Johnson described European literature as a series of footnotes to Homer's *Iliad* and *Odyssey*. The most elevated form of poetry was traditionally epic. Northrop Frye argues for the Bible as an epic form.[3] Virgil's *Aeneid* reinforced this primacy and Dante and Milton are the great Christian forms. *Paradise Lost* was the last great attempt to rise 'above the Aonian Mount'. Shelley says of Milton:

> He mingled . . . the elements of human nature as colours upon a single pallet, and arranged them . . . according to the laws of epic truth; that is, according to the laws of that principle by which a series of actions of the external universe and of intelligent and ethical beings is calculated to excite the sympathy of succeeding generations of mankind.[4]

The boundaries between the epic, the medieval or Renaissance romance, and the saga are fluid and I shall use the idea of story or *mythos* in relation to these cognate genres. Aristotle uses *mythos* in his poetics for narrative.[5] Sir Philip Sidney writes that the poet, with a tale forsooth he cometh unto you, with a tale which holdeth children from play, and old men from the chimney corner'.[6] He somewhat conventionally extols epic as the 'best and most accomplished kind of poetry' because it 'stirreth and instructeth the mind, so the lofty image of such worthies most inflameth the mind with desire to be worthy, and informs with counsel how to be worthy'.[7] The traditional pre-eminence of epic, from Homer and Virgil through Milton's *Paradise Lost* and Tasso's *Jerusalem Delivered*, was based on the idea of the spiritually edifying story. The great master of psychological observation in Western literature, Shakespeare, had no obvious successor in drama, but exerted a rich and powerful influence on the eighteenth-century novel.[8]

I wish to pursue Charles Taylor's suggestion in his magisterial *Sources of the Self* that Romanticism is a central source of contemporary intellectual culture.[9] The impact of novels is dependent upon the more primordial power of story. One finds one's own spiritual predicament in Dante, Shakespeare or Milton while being taken to the archaic domain of thirteenth-century Florence or the great age of English literature. I wish

3 N. Frye, *The Great Code: The Bible and Literature* (Toronto: Academic Press Canada, 1982).
4 P. B. Shelley, 'A Defence of Poetry', in *Shelley's Literary and Philosophical Criticism*, ed. J. Shawcross (London: Henry Frowde, 1909), p. 146.
5 Aristotle, *Poetics* 1450b1–3.
6 Sir Philip Sidney, *A Defence of Poetry*, 'Examination 1' (Oxford: Clarendon Press, 1966), p. 40.
7 Ibid., 'Examination 2', p. 47.
8 I owe this point to George Watson.
9 C. Taylor, *Sources of the Self: The Making of the Modern Identity* (Cambridge: Cambridge University Press, 1989), p. 461.

to try to give some account of the thrill and awe of engaging with certain forms of artistic representation.

Much has been made of narrative in structuralism and literary criticism. Not all narrative is fictional. Much historical narrative is emphatically not fictional. Yet with much literary criticism – under the influence of post-structuralism – the motive has been Protagorean: to develop an epistemic anti-realism. Philosophy, history and science are themselves narratives in a strong sense – knowledge is invention (or imagination) rather than discovery. Stanley Fish claims that discourse creates our reality.[10] I wish to push the question of narrative in a rather more Parmenidean direction. In conscious opposition to Derrida's claim that there is 'nothing outside the text', I shall insist that stories resist reduction to the text or words. The Romantics were quite correct to subordinate the literary vehicle to its message: story, rather like melody, is ineffable but nevertheless exerts prodigious force.

For some, this may evoke the idea of R. B. Braithwaite's famous version of expressivism, the theory that religion consists of imaginative stories which give expression to a certain way of life: 'A religious assertion, for me, is the assertion of an intention to carry out a certain behaviour policy, subsumable under a sufficiently general principle to be a moral one, together with the implicit or explicit statement, but not the assertion, of certain stories.'[11] For Braithwaite, stories are neither true nor false, but indicate the behaviour required by religion. But such an account is notoriously thin. How can the expression of certain attitudes sustain the weight of the doctrinal formulations of, say, credal Christianity? How can it explain the Trinitarian controversy of Nicaea and Constantinople between the homoousios party and the homooiousians, as Gibbon quipped, over the diphthong (between ὁμός and ὁμοῖς)?

One might say that whereas Braithwaite wants to explain religion in terms of stories, I wish to explain stories in terms of religion.

Make-believe and imagination

How easy is a bush suppos'd a bear![12]

Analytic philosophy has devoted much attention to the status of fictional objects. Much of this literature is influenced by discussion of Russell's Theory of Descriptions, in which ostensibly referring expressions like 'The present King of France is bald' are analysed as identifying

10 S. Fish,' 'How To Do Things with Austin and Searle', in *Is There a Text in This Class? The Authority of Interpretative Communities* (Cambridge, Mass.: Harvard University Press, 1980), pp. 242–3.

11 R. B. Braithwaite, 'An Empiricist View of the Nature of Religious Belief', in B. Mitchell (ed.), *The Philosophy of Religion* (Oxford: Oxford University Press, 1971), p. 89.

12 William Shakespeare, *A Midsummer Night's Dream*, V.i.22.

descriptions: predicative expressions, making assertions about existing entities as possessing particular properties. Russell's theory aims to explain how we can legitimately entertain thoughts about fictional or non-existent items without thereby being committed to their existence in some shadowy, quasi-Platonic domain. Hence, to use Russell's example, we can assert the baldness of the purported current Gallic monarch, though our assertion is simply false. Russell is using Frege's theory of reference for the purposes of a fairly typical British empiricist epistemology. Like Locke or Hume, Russell is concerned with how we can know objects, whether by mediate or immediate channels (acquaintance or description). Understanding a proposition (mathematics aside) means knowing the requisite spatio-temporal items which determine whether it is true or not. Most of the attacks on Russell have accused him of 'idealism' (since he fixes reference by mental items), but Russell was motivated by a reductive empiricism, and the desire to produce a sharp distinction between truth and fantasy or error.

In his seminal and highly influential work *Mimesis as Make Believe*, Kendall Walton tries to understand the aesthetic imagination. Walton develops a highly sophisticated theory of imagination employing the concept of 'make-believe' – modelled on children's games of make-believe. He suggests that human engagement in stories is a kind of make-believe which employs external props in imaginative activities. To engage in a work of art properly is to play a game of make-believe.

Various artforms count as representational because paintings or novels prompt the imagination to represent. What adults do with art is different in degree but not in kind from children's games. Just as a child uses a stick as a gun and can shoot at trees as if they were terrifying alien invaders, readers of an imaginative fiction place themselves within that fictional world. Walton distinguishes three roles that something can play in games of make-believe:

1. Prompters of imaginings – those elements in the game which cause thoughts by association. For instance, a tree stump provokes a young girl to think about a bear.[13]
2. Objects of imaginings – things imagined as something else, e.g. the plastic doll is imagined as a baby.
3. Props – 'generators of fictional truths, things which, by virtue of their nature or existence, make propositions fictional'.[14] Rather than simple imaginings, we have fictional truths within a highly specific realm of make-believe.

Hence the activity of aesthetic engagement is a game of adult make-believe.

'Prompters' need not be 'props', nor the other way around. Walton's explanation of representational art is that it is constituted by consciously produced props for games of make-believe. There is a normative

13 K. Walton, *Mimesis as Make Believe: On the Foundations of the Representational Arts* (Cambridge, Mass.: Harvard University Press, 1990), p. 22.
14 Ibid., p. 37.

component in that some imaginings are sanctioned, others not. However, Walton's account can be seen as broadly functionalist. A narrative is fictional within a socially agreed practice of deploying an object – within the context of make-believe. It is not the intention of the artist which is important but accepted usage within a community.

Walton's employment of childhood inclinations is plausible. Between two and five years of age, children develop a form of quite open playing or pretending which is commonly known as make-believe.[15] This seems to be internalized in later childhood and is presumably the precursor of adult daydreaming and fantasizing. Donald Winnicott has drawn attention to the phenomenon of transitional objects or imaginary friends.[16] Some children seem to require transitional objects to facilitate the move from total dependence upon parents to relative independence by holding fast to toys or soft materials, which on occasion may be treated as companions. Sometimes these companions are invisible, but named and given quite specific identities.

Although Walton provides a neat account of aesthetic representation, it is an oddly desiccated and parochial account of art, one which concentrates upon art's function in promoting the flourishing of individuals. While no one who has read Schiller, Huizinga or Gadamer will want to denigrate the concept of play,[17] there is also the earnest issue of engagement in an artwork. Gadamer famously criticizes the view of art as a primarily subjective experience or *Erlebnis*. Gadamer notes that it is characteristic of play that the players become absorbed and immersed in the game:

> All play is about being played. The charm of play, the fascination it exerts, lies in the fact that the play becomes lord over the players.[18]

Indeed, imaginative play constitutes an important part in a child's developing capacity to engage with and adapt to the world, to process and integrate information, to experience vicariously a range of emotions, to anticipate and accept events and patterns of behaviour. Autistic children seem to have either too little or too much imaginative capacity – and experience considerable difficulties in relating to the world. There is much evidence that games of make-believe and pretence may provide a basis for tolerating the pain and ambiguities of adult experience.[19] Much psychological research suggests a paradoxical link between imagination

15 See G. Currie and I. Ravenscroft, *Recreative Minds: Imagination in Philosophy and Psychology* (Oxford: Clarendon Press, 2002), pp. 134–60. Autistic children are a possible exception to this, although in relation to this field a considerable body of literature is developing. See below.

16 D. W. Winnicott, *Playing and Reality* (Harmondsworth: Penguin, 1980), p. 2.

17 See F. Schiller, *On the Aesthetic Education of Man*, ed. E. M. Wilkinson and L. A. Willoughby (Oxford: Clarendon Press, 1985); J. Huizinga, *Homo ludens: A Study of the Play-Element in Culture* (London: Routledge, 1998).

18 H. G. Gadamer, *Wahrheit und Methode* (Tübingen: Mohr-Siebeck, 1999), pp. 101–2: 'Alles Spielen ist ein Gespielt-werden. Der Reiz des Spieles, die Faszination, die es ausübt, besteht eben darin, daß das Spiel über den Spielenden Herr wird.'

19 A. Runco and S. R. Pritzker (eds), *The Encyclopedia of Creativity* (San Diego: Academic Press, 1999), pp. 20–1.

and the recognition of reality. This, of course, would be particularly paradoxical given the confines of old-fashioned stimulus–response psychology.

The philosophical question that Walton is trying to answer is the knotty paradox of 'fictional truth'. I wish to explore the paradox that the truest poetry is the 'most feigning'. Why is the most feigning the truest? Certainly, there seems something normative about genuine artistic activity. We enter into a world governed by certain laws and often suspend our disbelief.[20] Dante boldly asserted that he 'produced a true reality'.[21] This, in turn, raises the question posed by Aristotle in the *Poetics*: can poetry be truer than history? How come the creative imagination of the poet is able to provide knowledge about real life? If art is merely an extension of 'make-believe', why does it affect us so deeply? 'What's Hecuba to him, or he to Hecuba, / That he should weep for her?' says Hamlet of the tragic actor.[22] If art were experienced as mere ornament, the paradox of true fiction would not arise.

There is a remorselessly smug quality about Walton's account of artistic representation.[23] In contrast to Gadamer, who links play via tragedy to the most profound human concerns, Walton does not give an adequate account of the political, religious and psychological power of art: the sense that art touches human beings at the level of their deepest motivations and aspirations. Walton's account seems to leave out the inspirational potential in art, both for good and bad. Plato wished to ban the artists because he recognized a potential for inspiring good and evil in human beings. Art may serve grotesque, infantile and cruel fantasies. Aristotle recognizes the primordial power of art, but has a theory to explain why this can be productive and useful.

C. S. Lewis once remarked, playing on the biblical image of Ezekiel, that 'It is either in art or nowhere that the dry bones are made to live again.'[24] Lewis and Tolkien both argued that we are moved as mature spiritual beings by stories, and it is a mistake to think of stories as childish amusements or adult fantasies: they are our spiritual oxygen. Tolkien produces a defence of stories as answering to genuine and legitimate human needs. Tolkien's major point is that even fairy stories are not exclusively for children, nor can they be dismissed as infantile escapism or consolation for adults. Tolkien himself notes that in his case 'A real taste for fairy-stories was wakened by philology on the threshold

---

20 S. T. Coleridge, *Biographia Literaria*, ed. J. Engell and W. J. Bate (Princeton, NJ: Bollingen, 1983), vol. 2, p. 6.
21 See E. Auerbach, *Mimesis: The Representation of Reality in Western Literature* (Princeton, NJ: Princeton University Press, 1971), p. 554.
22 William Shakespeare, *Hamlet*, II.ii.548–9.
23 I owe this point to Jane Heal.
24 C. S. Lewis, 'The Anthropological Approach', in *English and Medieval Studies Presented to J. R. R. Tolkien on the Occasion of his Seventieth Birthday*, ed. N. Davis and C. L. Wrenn (London: Allen and Unwin, 1962), p. 223.

of manhood, and quickened to full life by war.'[25] Fairy tales are often about 'peril, sorrow and the shadow of death'.[26] If written with art, fairy tales offer fantasy, recovery, escape and consolation, which adults probably need more than children.

Art is the human process that produces (though not as its only or ultimate object) secondary belief. The term Tolkien uses is 'enchantment'. 'Enchantment' produces a secondary world into which both designer and spectator can enter. Magic, Tolkien argues, 'produces, or pretends to produce an alteration in the Primary World . . . it is not an art but a technique; its desire is *power* in this world, domination of things and wills'. Fantasy, by way of contrast, is different from the 'greed for self-centred power which is the mark of the mere Magician'.[27]

The task of creating the 'inner consistency of reality' is very difficult.[28] Tolkien describes the artist as a 'sub-creator'. The story-maker is a successful sub-creator of

> a Secondary World which your mind can enter. Inside it, what he relates is 'true': it accords with the laws of that world. You therefore believe it, while you are . . . inside. The moment disbelief arises, the spell is broken; the magic, or rather art, has failed. You are then out in the Primary World again, looking at the little abortive Secondary World from outside.[29]

Is Tolkien's theory of the artist as a sub-creator who produces a secondary realm of enchantment a basically Platonic theory about how the imagination is capable of providing knowledge? Coleridge speaks of the 'suspension of disbelief' rather than belief. Wordsworth asks in his *Preface to Poems of 1815* which term might designate 'that Faculty of which the Poet is "all compact"; he whose eye glances from earth to heaven, whose spiritual attributes body forth what his pen is prompt in turning to shape'.[30] Wordsworth is quoting Shakespeare:

> The poet's eye, in a fine frenzy rolling,
> Doth glance from heaven to earth, from earth to heaven,
> And as imagination bodies forth
> The forms of things unknown, the poet's pen
> Turns them to shapes, and gives to airy nothing
> A local habitation and a name.[31]

25 J. R. R. Tolkien, 'On Fairy Stories', in *Tree and Leaf* (London: George Allen and Unwin, 1975), p. 40.
26 Ibid., p. 42.
27 Ibid., p. 48–9.
28 Ibid., p. 45.
29 Ibid., p. 36.
30 William Wordsworth, *The Prelude* (1805 text), Preface §12; ed. E. de Selincourt and S. Gill, 2nd edn (Oxford: Oxford University Press, 1984), p. 753. *The Complete Poetical Works*, Dorothy Wordsworth noted of Coleridge 'more of "the poet's eye in a fine frenzy rolling" than I ever witnessed': quoted in S. Perry, *S. T. Coleridge: Interviews and Recollections* (Basingstoke: Palgrave, 2000), p. 45.
31 William Shakespeare, *A Midsummer Night's Dream*, V.i.12–17. See the discussion in Chapter 5 above.

Here the poet is seeing the intelligibles and giving imaginative expression to them, rather like Coleridge's own poet in 'Kubla Khan' who 'on honey-dew hath fed, / And drunk the milk of Paradise'.[32] Sidney, in his *Defence of Poetry*, defends the view of the Neoplatonic Florentine poet Christoforo Landino (and his master Ficino) that the mysteries of poetry are written by poets 'so beloved of the gods that whatsoever they write proceeds of a divine fury'.[33] He states that the 'figuring forth' or imaginative activity of the poet has been 'given divine commendation' unto poetry by Plato, the 'very inspiring of a divine force, far above man's wit'.[34] Sidney defined poetry as

> an art of imitation, for so Aristotle termeth it in the word μίμησις – that is to say, a representing, counterfeiting, or figuring forth – to speak metaphorically, a speaking picture – with this end, to teach and delight.[35]

Art is mimetic in the sense that it imitates reality not appearance, and being rather than becoming. 'There is no art delivered to mankind that hath not the works of nature as its principal object', Sidney claims, and lists astronomy, geometry, natural and moral philosophy, law, history, grammar, rhetoric and logic, medicine and metaphysics – since poetry is not less but more than these arts. However, the poet creates 'another nature', a world of gold, rather than the brass world of every day.[36] How can the artist describe and yet improve nature? The poet employs imagination to produce representations that highlight in order to describe or illustrate.[37] They capture their object, while transforming it. For Sidney the poet is not a mere servant of nature:

> he goeth hand in hand with nature, not enclosed within the narrow warrant of her gifts, but freely ranging only within the zodiac of his own wit.[38]

Sidney follows a Neoplatonic tenet when he argues that the poet is expounding his inner vision:

> the skill of each artificer standeth in that *idea* or fore-conceit of the work, and not in the work itself. And that the poet hath that *idea* is manifest, by delivering them forth in such excellency as he had imagined them.[39]

---

32 S. T. Coleridge, 'Kubla Khan', ll. 53–4, *Poems*, p. 168.
33 Sidney, *A Defence of Poetry*, 'Peroration', p. 75.
34 Ibid., 'Refutation: Four Charges, Charge 4', p. 60.
35 Ibid., 'Proposition: A Definition of Poetry', p. 25.
36 Ibid., 'What Poetry Is. Art and Nature', p. 23.
37 G. Watson, *The Certainty of Literature* (Hemel Hempstead: Harvester Wheatsheaf, 1989), pp. 110–12.
38 Sidney, *A Defence of Poetry*, 'What Poetry Is. Art and Nature', pp. 23–4.
39 Ibid., 'What Poetry Is. Art and Nature', p. 24.

Alfred Hitchcock was reported to complain about the dreariness of shooting scenes in his films because he had already seen them. Plotinus and Michelangelo would have understood.[40]

Though Shakespeare has often been depicted, from Ben Jonson to Voltaire, as the paradigm of untutored genius, he was *au courant* with Renaissance theories of art, and the supremely articulate voice in Elizabethan England of the Neoplatonic justification of art. Hence Scruton is correct to write, 'Shakespeare's plays are works of philosophy – philosophy not argued but shown.'[41] *A Midsummer Night's Dream* is particularly interesting in relation to the question of make-believe because it is consciously a fairy-tale drama. It was possibly written for the wedding of the Earl of Southhampton's mother – it has been speculated that the performance of the play within the play of the mechanicals for the marriage of Theseus and Hippolyta mirrors the performance by a company of actors in an aristocratic-courtly context. Shakespeare's Hamlet produces, as it were, *The Mousetrap*. Hamlet directs 'The Marriage of Gonzalo' and says explicitly,

> The play's the thing,
> Wherein I'll catch the conscience of the King.[42]

Though *Hamlet* and *A Midsummer Night's Dream* are evidently plays with an explicit play within a play, *The Tempest* contains the masque of Ceres, Iris and Juno, which celebrates the betrothal of Ferdinand and Miranda on the Island before their wedding in Naples. The play within the play is a device for presenting the hidden truth of the play.[43] It is a dramatically potent technique which Shakespeare learnt from the tragedies of Thomas Kyd. Yet it is also a highly appropriate artifice for a late-Renaissance artist concerned with the philosophical status of poetic representation.[44] The play within the play, which conveys a profound truth crucial for the overarching narrative, mirrors the high Renaissance view, so eloquently expressed by Sidney, of the golden world of poetry shedding light upon the brazen world of habitual experience. C. S. Lewis is thinking in a similar mode when he pronounces that

> The story does what no theorem can quite do. It may not be 'like real life' in the superficial sense: but it sets before us an image of what reality may be like at some more central region.[45]

Gadamer develops this thought in relation to Aristotle's famous account of tragedy. The spectator of tragedy is not experiencing a temporary

---

40 See A. Blunt, *Artistic Theory in Italy 1450–1600* (Oxford: Clarendon Press, 1978), pp. 58–81.
41 R. Scruton, *Gentle Regrets: Thoughts from a Life* (New York: Continuum, 2005), p. 9.
42 William Shakespeare, *Hamlet*, II.ii.606–7.
43 I am very grateful to Elizabeth Cormack for this and other reflections on Shakespeare's imagination.
44 Cf. F. Burwick, *Illusion and the Drama: Critical Theory of the Enlightenment and Romantic Era* (University Park, Pa: Pennsylvania State University Press, 1991).
45 C. S. Lewis, 'On Stories,' in *Of this and Other Worlds*, ed. W. Hooper (London: Collins, 1982) p. 39.

intoxicating fantasy from which he or she emerges and readjusts to reality. Rather, the experience of the tragedy is a confrontation with reality itself:

> The spectator is not in a state of aesthetic awareness, enjoying the art of the representation, but is in the communion of 'taking part'.[46]

Tolkien on fairy stories

Imaginations real are,
Unto my mind again repair:
Which makes my life a circle of delights;
A hidden sphere of obvious benefits:
An earnest sense that the actions of the just
Shall still revive, and flourish in the dust.[47]

The German Romantic Novalis stated that the fairy tale (*das Märchen*) is the 'canon' of poetry. 'Everything poetic', he enigmatically claimed, must be *märchenhaft* (must have the quality of fairy tale):

> It is only because of the weakness of our organs and of our contact with ourselves that we do not discover ourselves to be in a fairy world. All fairy tales are only dreams of that familiar world of home which is everywhere and nowhere. The higher powers in us, which one day will carry out our will like genies, are now muses that refresh us with sweet memories along this arduous path.[48]

Tolkien enquires why fairy stories have been restricted to the nursery. The reason, he maintains, is because of 'their arresting strangeness'.[49] But many people dislike being 'arrested'; they confuse fantasy and dreaming with mental disorders. But it is not just a question of dislike. The enchanted world often is perceived, as eighteenth-century novels were by critics during the Age of Sensibility, as indulgent escapism:

> creative Fantasy is founded upon the hard recognition that things are so in the world as it appears under the sun; on a recognition of fact, but not a slavery to it . . . If men really could not distinguish

---

46 Gadamer, *Wahrheit und Methode*, p. 126: 'Der Zuschauer verhält sich nicht in der Distanz des ästhetischen Bewußtseins, das die Kunst der Darstellung genießt, sondern in der Kommunion des Dabeiseins.'
47 Thomas Traherne,'The Review II', v.8–13, 'Poems of Felicity', in *Selected Poems and Prose*, ed. A. Bredford (Harmondsworth: Penguin, 1991), p. 153.
48 Novalis, *Philosophical Writings* (Albany, NY: State University of New York Press, 1997), p. 67.
49 Tolkien, *Tree and Leaf*, p. 44.

between frogs and men, fairy-stories about frog kings would not have arisen.[50]

Tolkien admits that fantasy can be abused, but *abusus non tollit usum* – the existence of abuse does not invalidate proper usage. 'Fantasy' is a human right, and is essentially derivative, because we are made in the image of a maker.[51] His defence of 'fantasy' (i.e. what we have otherwise referred to as 'imagination') involves three elements: 'recovery', 'escape' and 'consolation'. By 'recovery', Tolkien means the 're-gaining' of a correct perspective, a 'freshness of vision' which can remove the 'film of familiarity'. Simple things become more 'luminous' by the fantastical context: the very habitual and customary nature of human engagement with the world can deaden our awareness of its treasures. Fairy tales can reawaken our sense of wonder and appreciation of everyday objects and events: 'It was in fairy stories that I first divined the potency of the words and the wonder of the things, such as stone, and wood, and iron; tree and grass; house and fire; bread and wine.'[52] One might compare this with Coleridge presenting Wordsworth as awakening the mind from the lethargy of custom and pointing it to the 'inexhaustible treasure' hidden by 'the film of familiarity and selfish solicitude'.[53] Genius does not 'distort' what it represents, but is capable of showing 'many a vein and many a tint, which escape the eye of common observation, thus raising to the rank of gems, what had been often kicked away by the hurrying foot of the traveller on the dusty high road of custom'.[54]

The second point which Tolkien addresses is the challenge of the alleged escapism of fairy stories. What is wrong if a man is imprisoned and wishes to escape? This escape is sometimes confused with the flight of the deserter. The resistance of the patriot is preferable to the acquiescence of the collaborator. This can excuse any treachery – and 'glorify it'. In the tradition of Ruskin and Morris, Tolkien means escape from the ubiquitous ugliness of the modern world. What is meant by 'real life'? Is the car or the electric street lamp more 'real' than dragons or centaurs? It seems absurd to view machines as more real than the 'elm tree'.[55]

Finally, Tolkien justifies the function of consolation. He employs an argument about ugliness in a technological age of 'improved means to deteriorated ends'.[56] Lying behind Tolkien's reflections is the point that we find it difficult to link beauty and evil. In fairy tales it is hard to think of a dreadfully ugly castle or hall for a good king. But technological advances have blurred our perception. Here one senses the Platonic principle that 'Beauty is truth and truth is beauty'. If that beauty is not to be thought of as entirely random, one must postulate the ultimate governance of the world by ideals. But there are also questions of

50 Ibid., p. 50.
51 Ibid.
52 Ibid., p. 53.
53 Coleridge, *Biographia Literaria*, vol. 2, p. 7.
54 Ibid., vol. 2, pp. 148–9.
55 Tolkien, *Tree and Leaf*, p. 55.
56 Ibid., p. 57.

'hunger, pain, injustice, sorrow, death'. If fairy tales provide consolation in the face of such suffering, this is good. Like Ruskin or Morris, Tolkien argues for the legitimate desire to escape the evil and ugliness, noise, stench, ruthlessness and extravagance of the contemporary technological world. But this is to affirm life, not to deny it. We are surrounded by the ugly mechanical products of *homo faber* – our ancestors lacked the means of mechanization, and had a very different sense of the beauty of crafts.

The Romantic unconscious

Freud spoke of '[t]he stubborn denial of a psychical character to latent mental acts'.[57] Coleridge would not have been surprised: 'how much lies below [the] Consciousness'.[58] In *The Unconscious Before Freud* Lancelot Law Whyte discusses 'the concept of the unconscious mind . . . from Cudworth to Jung'.[59] Coleridge is clearly drawing upon the idea of an animated nature 'plastic and vast' from Cudworth's *Plastic Nature* and Cudworth's writings often suggest some 'acquaintance with the subconscious levels of human personality'.[60] Indeed, Cudworth likes to dwell upon the semi- or sub-conscious reaches of the mind in his critique of Descartes. Cudworth links dreams with creativity:

> There is also another more Interiour kind of *Plastick Power* in the Soul (if we may so call it) whereby it is Formative of its own Cogitations, which it self is not always Conscious of; as when in Sleep or Dreams, it frames Interlocutory Discourses betwixt it self and other Persons in a Long Series, with Coherent Sence and Apt Connexions, in which oftentimes it seems to be surprized with unexpected Answers and Reparties; though it self were all the while the Poet and Inventor of the whole Fable.[61]

Wordsworth exclaims:

>   my brain
> worked with a dim and undetermin'd sense
> Of unknown modes of being.
> . . .
> But huge and mighty Forms that do not live
> Like living men, mov'd slowly through the mind
> By day, and were a trouble of my dreams.[62]

57 S. Freud, *The Unconscious*, in *Complete Works*, vol. 14 (London: Hogarth Press, 1952), p. 168.
58 S. T. Coleridge, *Notebooks* (London: Routledge and Kegan Paul, 1957), vol. 1, § 1554.
59 L. L. Whyte, *The Unconscious Before Freud* (London: Friedmann, 1978), p. 11.
60 C. Raven, *Natural Religion and Christian Theology: Science and Religion* (Cambridge: Cambridge University Press), p. 117.
61 Ralph Cudworth, *The True Intellectual System of the Universe* (Royston, 1678), p. 161. Cudworth's important argument against Descartes for levels of consciousness and the importance of the conscious is derived directly from Plotinus. See H. J. Blumenthal, *Plotinus' Psychology* (The Hague: Nijhoff, 1971), pp. 95–7, and P. Merlan, *Monopsychism, Mysticism, Metaconsciousness* (The Hague. Nijhoff, 1963) pp. 55ff.
62 William Wordsworth, *The Prelude*, I, 419–20, 425–7.

In the *Biographia* Coleridge employs the following striking image of activity and passivity in the workings of the mind:

Most of my readers will have observed a small water-insect on the surface of rivulets, which throws a cinque-spotted shadow fringed with prismatic colours on the sunny bottom of the brook; and will have noticed, how the little animal *wins* its way up against the stream, by alternate pulses of active and passive motion, now resisting the current, now yielding to it in order to gather strength and a momentary *fulcrum* for a further propulsion. This is no unapt emblem of the mind's self experience in the act of thinking. There are evidently two powers at work, which relatively to each other are active and passive; and this is not possible without an intermediate faculty, which is at once both active and passive . . . In philosophical language, we must denominate this intermediate faculty in all its degrees and determinations, the IMAGINATION.[63]

Coleridge is thinking of self-consciousness as pointing to its own source in the unconscious and organic. Here he is considering the unconscious energy which underpins imaginative activity. He uses the remembering of names as an example of the creative tension between the involuntary and the voluntary.[64] Certain ideas or impulses seem to arise 'out of the blue'. This awareness of the subconscious is closely linked to observation about dreams. Coleridge observes that 'The passions of the Day as often originate in the Dream, as the Images of the Dream in the day.'[65] Hackforth, in his commentary on Plato's *Phaedrus*, notes that ἡνιοχεύειν (to act as a charioteer) is employed as a metaphor for the guiding and ruling aspect of the soul.[66] Yet the image of the mind as a charioteer controlling horses conveys equally the pre-theoretical component of the mind:

In every work of art there is a reconcilement of the external with the internal; the conscious is so impressed on the unconscious as to appear in it . . . he who combines the two is the man of genius; and for that reason he must partake of both. Hence this is the true exposition of the rule that the artist must first align himself from nature in order to return to her with full effect. Why this? Because if he were to begin by mere painful copying, he would produce masks only, not forms breathing life. He must out of his own mind create forms according to the severe laws of the intellect, in order to generate in himself that co-ordination of freedom and law . . . which assimilates him to nature, and enables him to understand her. He merely absents himself for a season from her, that his own spirit, which has the same ground with nature, may learn her unspoken language in its main radicals, before he approaches to her endless compositions of them . . . The artist must imitate that which is within

63 Coleridge, *Biographia Literaria*, vol. 1, pp. 124–5.
64 Ibid.; Coleridge, *Shorter Works*, p. 947.
65 Coleridge, *Notebooks*, vol. 3, §4409.
66 R. Hackforth, *Plato's Phaedrus* (Cambridge: Cambridge University Press, 1997), p. 77.

the thing, that which is active through form and figure, and discourses to us by symbols – the Natur-geist, or spirit of nature, as we unconsciously imitate those we love.[67]

The discussion of the conscious and the unconscious is part of the conviction that self-consciousness is not alien to nature. The artist, who gives the most articulate expression to self-consciousness, is a mirror into that world which has produced finite consciousness – not a soulless mechanism. Shakespeare, for all the Romantics, is the paradigm artist – the one who is supremely conscious and yet working according to forces beneath consciousness itself.

The question is: which is higher or lower? For Freud, creativity is a by-product of the ineluctable conflict between mankind and its environment. The artist is neurotic; art is compensation. Thomas Mann presents the artist in *Dr Faustus* and *Death in Venice*, under the influence of Freud, as sick. The vegetative soul is much lower than the intuitive intelligence in the scale of nature. But nature is itself the product of soul and points to the noetic cosmos – however imperfectly. For Freud, the unconscious does not point to any superior realm. Lancelot Law Whyte observes:

The springs of human nature lie in the unconscious, for it links the individual with the universal, or at least the organic. This is true, whether it is expressed as the union of the soul with the divine, or as the realm which links the moments of human awareness with the background of organic processes within which they emerge. But the fascination of the idea arises because it is felt to be the source of power, the home of the *élan* which moves us, the active principle which leads us to feel, to imagine, to judge, to think, and to act. This is more than mechanics or dynamics, or chance; it is a principle of biological surplus vigor, of potential order or organization continually coming into being as far as clash permits.[68]

Yet the depths of the mind point to the divine transcendence. The imagination points both above and below itself. William James claims that 'whatever it may be on its *farther* side, the "more" with which in religious experience we feel ourselves connected is on its *hither* side the subconscious continuation of our conscious life'.[69] It is of particular interest that Cudworth's brilliant contemporary John Smith uses the idea of 'Plastic Virtue, a Secret Energy' in a passage of great relevance to both the concept of nature and the *furor poeticus*:

the Mind of man is alwaies shaping it self into a conformity as much as may be to that which is his *End*; and the nearer it draws to it in the achievement thereof, the greater likeness it bears to it. There is a

---

67 Coleridge, *Biographia Literaria* vol. II, ed. J. T. Shawcross (Oxford: Oxford University Press, 1907)), p. 258.

68 Whyte, *The Unconscious Before Freud*, p. 70.

69 W. James, *Varieties of Religious Experience* (London: Longmans, Green and Co., 1902), p. 512; quoted in M. Wynn, *Emotional Experience and Religious Understanding: Integrating Perception, Conception and Feeling* (Cambridge: Cambridge University Press, 2005), p. 188.

Plastick Virtue, a Secret Energy issuing forth from that which the Mind propounds to itself as its *End* . . . the more the Soul directs it Self to God, the more it becomes God-like, deriving a print of that glory and beauty upon itself which it converseth with as it is excellently set forth by the Apostle, *But we all with open face, beholding as in a glass the glory of the Lord, are changed into the same image, from glory to glory.*[70]

John Cottingham has pointed to the pivotal challenge posed by the unconscious to the traditional philosophical project. Hume claims that reason is the slave of the passions, but he does not think there is any problem gaining access to these passions. Freud, however, challenges just this capacity 'to access the *materials* for appropriate deliberation'.[71] For Cottingham, what gives our lives direction is in an important sense beyond reason's capacity to regulate. Cottingham uses the example of the finding of a solution to an intellectual puzzle after sleep. The mind has been working, though unbeknown, presumably, to the waking self.[72] Cottingham points out that psychoanalytic theory has concentrated upon dream as a focus of interface between the creative forces within the unconscious and the reflective power of the conscious mind – yet clearly there is much more to mental activity proper than what can be produced by conscious concentration alone. Out of the depths of the materials of the unconscious are bodies which the conscious intellect shapes, structures and refines. Referring to Plato's Phaedran charioteer, Cottingham observes:

> There is an intense *anxiousness* that such [ratiocentric] models betray
> – the fear that unless reason remains fussily and tensely at the helm,
> our lives will lose direction. Yet even a moment's reflection should
> reveal that what gives our lives direction – the springs of human
> creativity, inventiveness and imagination – are in an important sense
> beyond reason's power wholly to encompass and regulate . . . Yet for
> all that, many try to cling to the image of themselves as thinking
> beings who are always 'in charge', who are somehow *directing* their
> thought processes from beginning to end.[73]

Cottingham suggests that we require a 'Full self-awareness' which 'must involve more than widening the scope of deliberative reasoning; it requires a new *kind* of understanding, one mediated not by the grasp of the controlling intellect, but by a responsiveness to the rhythms of the whole self'.[74]

Dreams must constitute a crucial element in 'responsiveness to the rhythms of the whole self'. Jung thinks that dreams constitute a resource as a guide to the psyche – they help in coping with forces of the inner life

---

70 John Smith, *Select Discourses* (London, 1660), pp. 405–6.
71 J. Cottingham, *Philosophy and the Good Life: Reason and the Passions in Greek, Cartesian and Psychoanalytic Ethics* (Cambridge: Cambridge University Press, 1998), p. 131.
72 Ibid., p. 164.
73 Ibid., pp. 163–4.
74 Ibid., p. 163.

and serve to integrate the personality. Without a spiritual base, human life becomes sterile and neurotic. Jung sees dreams as an important part of the 'individuation process' by which (through our dreams and intuitions) the ego discovers its hidden and holy ground.[75] And there is a history of dreams shaping history: the most striking instance is perhaps Constantine's *in hoc signo vinces* dream. Constantine saw a cross in the heavens in a dream before the decisive battle with his rival Maxentius in AD 312. He had the shields of his troops marked with the cross and was victorious. As a result he promulgated the 'Edict of Milan' in 313, which initiated the process that culminated in Christianity becoming the official religion of the Roman Empire. Christendom, according to tradition, has its founding vision in a dream.

Dreams as stories

Mankind owes a great debt to story-telling inspired by dreams. Other animals dream, presumably. Yet it is what human beings *do* with dreams that is of interest: the visions of the mythopoeic-mythopoetic fancy and their interpretation by ordinary consciousness. Dreams do not usually contain random and unconnected images but have narrative structure.[76] The Islamic philosopher Al-Ghazali linked dreams with mirrors and in medieval dream literature, as Steven Kruger notes, 'Often, mirror and dream serve as parallel or complementary modes of self knowledge'.[77] Kruger also observes that 'Dreams, fictions, and mirrors all involve "higher" and "lower" forces. Like dreams and poems, the mirror reaches both upward and downward, both into and beyond the individual self'.[78] The mirror motif has powerful Neoplatonic resonances throughout English poetry from Chaucer to Spenser, Shakespeare up to Milton.[79] True knowledge is to be found in self-knowledge. Yet self-knowledge should not usher in narcissistic and futile self-awareness but should reveal the transcendent reality which supports and suffuses the phenomenal realm. Athenian lovers find true love in the forest; Hamlet confronts his prophetic soul in the vision of the ghost. Ovid's collection of myths is called *Metamorphoses*. The mythical dreamworld in Shakespeare's *A Midsummer Night's Dream* is a place of *metamorphosis*. Therein dream is linked to supernatural enlightenment, regeneration and *self-knowledge*.

What is a dream? Hobbes defines dreams as 'imaginations of them that sleep'.[80] Dreams take the dreamer beyond the palpable objective

---

75 See K. Raine, *The Inner Journey of the Poet*, p. 24.
76 See C. McGinn, *Mindsight: Image, Dream, Meaning* (Cambridge, Mass.: Harvard University Press, 2004), pp. 84f.
77 S. Kruger, *Dreaming in the Middle Ages* (Cambridge: Cambridge University Press, 1992), p. 130.
78 Ibid., p. 137.
79 See e.g. M. B. Garber, *Dream in Shakespeare: From Metaphor to Metamorphosis* (New Haven, Conn., and London: Yale University Press, 1974).
80 Thomas Hobbes, *Leviathan*, I. ii (Oxford: Clarendon Press, 1958), p. 15.

existence of individual items and events. We have vivid experiences in this realm. This alone suggests that human existence cannot be captured in crude terms of stimulus and response to the material environment. There is an intriguing problem generated by various naturalistic or reductionistic programmes – especially the problem of evolutionary explanation. What is the biological purpose of dreams? It is not even clear that sleep has a very obvious biological function.[81] God could plant dreams as coded messages, but it is difficult to see dreams produced by the 'blind watchmaker' as possessing any useful causal effect upon an organism's relation to its environment. Dreams have no obvious adaptive function. Attempted explanations such as the rehearsal of threats[82] seem tenuous. Other theories are that dreams are just meaningless 'noise', or an intriguing by-product of evolution but with no direct adaptive function.

Contemporary culture is confronted with the following dilemma. Darwin seems to have rendered dreams meaningless, since it is very obscure how dream-thought can enhance biological fitness. At the same time, contemporary culture has been deeply influenced by the tenet of depth psychology that dreams, as the 'royal road to the unconscious', contain a level of meaning unavailable to the conscious mind. Just at the time when dreams were given a hitherto unimaginable prominence – in twentieth-century intellectual culture – their intelligibility was becoming increasingly problematic. Many naturalists think that Freud and Jung are 'obscurantists' because they think that dreams have meaning.[83]

Some philosophers, most notably Norman Malcolm, argue that since dreams take place during sleep there is no opportunity for verification – there are no *criteria* for whether the events of a dream occurred or not. Malcolm suggests that we link the dream to the process of recall rather than to any purported and unverifiable dream experience. Of course, he is correct to highlight the problem of the trustworthiness of such reports, like Freud's famous 'Maury's guillotine dream', in which the dreamer dreams about the French Revolution and his own beheading – triggered by a board falling on his neck. Here Freud proposed that the accident triggered a dream which existed in the shape of a mental narrative. The composition of the dream can thus be thought of as independent of memory or even of the occurrence of the dream. The repetition of the same dream-plot is considered evidence for such a theory.

However, the strict dislocation between dream and experience suggested by Freud and Malcolm is open to obvious objections. The experience of waking from a nightmare is so vivid, especially the sense of

---

81 Dreaming certainly seems critical for sustaining health. REM deprivation creates considerable disturbances. It is not clear why dreaming is critical in this way or how, indeed, the dreaming trait is produced.

82 A. Revonsuo, 'The Reinterpretation of Dreams: An Evolutionary Hypothesis of the Function of Dreaming', in *Sleep and Dreaming: Scientific Advances and Reconsiderations*, ed. E. F. Pace-Schott, M. Solms and M. Blagrove (New York: Cambridge University Press, 2003).

83 As noted by O. Flanagan, in *Dreaming Souls: Sleep, Dreams, and the Evolution of the Conscious Mind* (Oxford: Oxford University Press, 2000), p. 57.

escape from immediate terror, that it seems very draconian to render such experiences unintelligible. And it appears counter-intuitive to deny the experiential component of the dream in the sense of a mental occurrence which parallels neatly the physical occurrence. Imagine the experience of dreaming that one is falling from a cliff – to discover, upon waking, that one has fallen out of bed. The subject's experience of falling in the dream corresponds to the physical sensation of falling. Children frequently dream of urinating in conjunction with actual bedwetting; the emission of semen with erotic dreams presumably provides another instance. It seems odd to disqualify a priori the vivid subjective experience.

One might reflect upon dreams in a foreign tongue. I recall a dream in which the language was German. Upon waking, I was reflecting in English upon a German word which I had encountered in the dream. However, I could not remember the meaning of this word, and took recourse to a German–English dictionary. I looked up the word and the meaning given made perfect sense within the dream context. Here the conscious report in English is parasitic upon the memory of the *experience* in German. I recalled the word as a familiar phoneme, yet without knowledge of its meaning. The most economical explanation in such an instance is surely that the waking mind reflects upon the recalled experience of the sleeping mind.

Malcolm has philosophical reasons for driving a wedge between conscious thought and dreams. Dreams are sometimes extremely coherent while much conscious experience is irrational and disconnected – daydreams, random ideas, and powerful moods might all be examples. One might turn Malcolm's objection around and point to the intriguingly unverifiable nature of dreams as constituting much of their interest. Unless one writes down the contents of a dream soon after waking, the dream will be forgotten. Yet the mood of the dreams remains even if part of the narrative is lost.

Freud presents the *Oedipus Rex* of Sophocles in terms of the expression of unfulfilled childhood wishes. He finds in Sophocles material which can substantiate the evidence he had collected from reports concerning dreams. The mythic elements are remnants of an earlier phase of human development – but express instinctual drives and conflicts rooted in the unconscious. Thus linking dream with myth, Freud presents mythic material as an index of the psyche and a clue to its workings. The myth of Oedipus has a particular poignancy in its expression of the necessity of self-knowledge notwithstanding anguish. There is the phenomenon of anticipatory or prognostic dreams. It would seem that the subconscious can be aware of future contingencies – in particular impending crisis. One can imagine a scenario in which a man dreams of a friendly colleague as a predator. Let us further imagine that in fact the colleague is plotting against our dreamer in actual life. Only his overt charm and apparent warmth disguises quite malicious intent. It is conceivable that the subconscious is processing danger signals to which the conscious mind is oblivious. One might imagine a parallel in which a woman has sexual dreams about a man whom she heartily dislikes. The dreams may give expression to feelings and longings of which the conscious agent disapproves or dislikes.

Here there is an interesting analogy with psychoanalysis. The analyst exposes those truths which in a sense are already known. Men need more often to be reminded than instructed, said Dr Johnson, and the poet will typically remind his audience of those facts which they already know at some level. Dreams can be akin to riddles. They can have a content which is puzzling at the immediate level of narrative. Say a man dreams of being tongue-tied in a public context. This could be puzzling if the man is usually confident in public and on occasion eloquent. But the dream can give vent to a deeper anxiety about the communication. The dreamt stuttering may express the dreamer's sense of helplessness or inadequacy in communicating his or her views or position within a specific context. Or imagine a dream about crossing a road. The dreamer is riding a motorbike and trying to cross a busy road. While traversing the road, the rider discovers a passenger with a frightening face giving advice about the height of the seat. This can express a sense of bewildering possibilities at a life juncture and anxiety about advice and support structures.

Through apparent trivia we can gain insight into the spontaneous self. Speaking of Sophocles, Freud notes: 'While the poet, as he unravels the past, brings to light the guilt of Oedipus, he is at the same time compelling us to recognise our own inner minds.'[84] The Delphic oracle is very important in Freud's account of the tragedy. Reflective intelligence can be brought to bear upon those anxieties and images which are in the dormitory of the soul. Freud thought that dreaming was needed to protect sleep against unacceptable impulses from the unconscious – dreams are defence mechanisms of the organism. Dreams are interpreted in terms of instincts, and the analysis of the repression of instinctual forces, and the consequent disturbances of the conscious mind. Linked to his view of dreams as basically defensive, Freud saw creativity as overcoming traumatic experience, usually in childhood, and as essentially sublimation (most are creative when they cannot fulfil sexual needs). Jung, by way of contrast, saw dreams as not just defensive – defusing conflicts, disguising wishes, etc. – but also as potentially creative. Of course, he characteristically takes a more optimistic view of creativity as drawing upon these archaic and collective resources.

Dreams, awakening and mirrors

A Chinese sage dreamt he was a butterfly, and on waking could not tell whether he was a sage dreaming of being a butterfly or a butterfly dreaming of being a sage.[85] Pierre Hadot points out that Descartes' choice

---

84 S. Freud, *The Interpretation of Dreams*, vol. 1, tr. J. Strachey (Harmondsworth: Penguin, 1991), p. 365.

85 W. D. O'Flaherty, *Dreams, Illusions and Other Realities* (Chicago: University of Chicago Press, 1984), p. 250.

of title, *Meditations*, links him back to the ancient tradition of philosophy
as a spiritual exercise.[86] It is quite plausible to see Descartes' argument as
closely akin to exercises of detachment.[87] Reflection is designed to wean
the thinking self from unreflective assumptions about the deliverances of
the senses and turn instead to the sounder foundations of God and the
soul: Descartes insists in the Preface to the *Meditations* that the reader
must be prepared to meditate with the author.[88] Descartes' attempt to
ascertain authentic wakefulness (cf. mindfulness in the Buddhist tradition) has a venerable lineage. In the Islamic tradition this long and
dangerous journey from self to self is presented as the pilgrimage from
the West to the East, the latter representing the source of Light. Ancient
philosophers were worried about the apparent regress problem posed by
dreams. How do we know that we are awake or in the 'arms of
Morpheus'? The *Theaetetus* raises the question of how one can verify that
the knower is awake or sleeping.[89] In the crucial passage on the definition
of the philosopher, Socrates in the *Republic* asks, 'Isn't dreaming simply
the confusion between a resemblance and the reality which it resembles,
whether the dreamer be asleep?'[90] If we are like Plato's prisoners, much
of habitual quotidian consciousness is a state of drowsiness if not
slumber. The metaphor of the Cave suggests that we, in our natural state,
are 'asleep', and that knowledge is effectively liberation from illusion.[91]
This is an even stronger position than Descartes' move (employing
dreams and the malicious demon) from the general possibility of
cognitive failure to the possibility of universal cognitive failure.[92] Our
relationship with the eternal in Plato finds expression through a number
of myths of sleep and waking, remembering and forgetting. These are
images to express the insubstantiality of the visible cosmos in relation to
the intelligible world:

> We assume that tangible realities are 'more real' than abstractions,
> that Ideas are only idealized images . . . Our customary, fashionable
> world is a weird mixture of phenomenalistic empiricism and
> mathematical abstractionism. Philo and other Platonizing thinkers
> admitted that the intelligible world was 'more real', that it was the
> proximate cause of the phenomenal and ordinary world, while
> denying, implicitly, that such a cosmos was a complex merely of
> human abstract thoughts. The *cosmos noetos* . . . is the Unfallen
> Universe.[93]

86 P. Hadot, *Philosphy as a Way of Life: Spiritual Exercises from Socrates to Foucault*, tr.
   M. Chase (Oxford: Blackwell, 1995), p. 33.
87 See S. Clark, *God's World and the Great Awakening* (Oxford: Clarendon Press, 1990),
   pp. 155ff.
88 René Descartes, *Philosophical Writings of Descartes*, tr. J. Cottingham, R. Stoothoff and
   D. Murdoch (Cambridge: Cambridge University Press, 1984), vol. 2, p. 8.
89 Plato, *Theaetetus* 157–158e.
90 Plato, *Republic* 476c tr. H. D. P. Lee (Harmondsworth: Penguin, 1987), p. 209.
91 Raine, *The Inner Journey of the Poet*, p. 33.
92 See B. Williams, *Descartes: The Project of Pure Enquiry* (Harmondsworth: Penguin, 1978),
   pp. 51ff., 309–13.
93 Clark, *God's World*, p. 101.

Plotinus writes some lines of spiritual autobiography which tend to imply some genuine religious experience:

Often I have woken up out of the body to my self and have entered into myself, going out from all other things; I have seen a beauty wonderfully great and felt assurance that then most of all I belonged to the better part; I have actually lived the best life and come to identity with the divine . . . Then after that rest in the divine . . . I am puzzled how I ever came down, and how my soul has come to be in the body.[94]

But this suggests levels of reality – whereas the modern mind thinks of 'existence' as all or nothing, neatly represented by the existential quantifier in predicate logic. The natural order is a sign or vision, the external panoply of a universe in which spiritual forces are ultimate and eternal:

In waking up we find that what we had thought were real causal connections were only occasions or symbolical associations. If we can wake to immortality, to the eternal world, it is because that world is already the true cause of what is happening here.[95]

This is clearly the Wordsworthian feeling of transcendence:

Our birth is but a sleep and a forgetting:
The soul that rises with us, our life's Star,
Hath had elsewhere its setting,
And cometh from afar:
Not in entire forgetfulness,
And not in utter nakedness,
But trailing clouds of glory do we come
From God, who is our home.[96]

The significance of this appeal to the pre-existence of the soul within Wordsworth's poem is a complex issue.[97] However, the poem gives eloquent expression to the ancient Platonic notion of attaining truth as an awakening.

It is a platitude that the author of 'Kubla Khan' drew on dream materials. But dreams are also important for Wordsworth. We read of the

94 Plotinus, *Enneads* IV.8.1ff.
95 Clark, *God's World*, p. 168.
96 William Wordsworth, 'Intimations of Immortality', Excursion V, ll. 59–66.
97 Obviously the acceptance of *creatio ex nihilo* meant that Christian theologians had to conceive immortality rather differently from the pagan Platonists. Origen thought the soul pre-existed the body and that life in the body was a punishment. Augustine rejects this in *The City of God* (II, 23), but is somewhat ambiguous on the issue. Ficino argues for the pre-existence of the soul in Christian Platonic terms, and consciously adopts some arguments from Augustine. See M. A. Allen, *Platonism and the Origins of Modernity*, ed. D. Hedley and S. Hutton (Dordrecht: Springer, 2007), p. 34.

education of the Wanderer 'In dreams, in study, and in ardent thought'[98] and Wordsworth's recollections of the river Derwent:

And from his fords and shallows, sent a voice
That flow'd along my dreams[99]

Within *The Prelude* there is a very important recounting of the dream of a friend. While reading *Don Quixote* and thinking about the relation between geometric and poetic truth, the poet's friend falls asleep near a seaside cave and dreams of a desert and an Arab on a camel carrying a bright shell in one hand and a stone in the other hand. The stone represents Euclid's *Elements* (and the cognate knowledge) whereas the shell contains far more precious knowledge:

And, at the word,
The Stranger, said my friend continuing,
'Stretch'd forth the Shell towards me, with command
That I should hold it to my ear; I did so
And heard that instant in an unknown Tongue,
Which yet I understood, articulate sounds,
A loud prophetic blast of harmony,
An Ode, in passion utter'd, which foretold
Destruction to the Children of the Earth,
By deluge now at hand.'[100]

Here poetry is linked to prophecy and apocalypse, knowledge and wisdom.

In Plato we find a theory of inspired dreams linked to prophecy. Aristotle explains the phenomena in terms of physiology.[101] Sleep can be a 'gateway to visions most rare' (Bottom's dream in *A Midsummer Night's Dream*); *Piers Plowman* and *Pilgrim's Progress* are dream allegories.[102] In the medieval and Renaissance tradition that drew upon the dream vision, e.g. in Plato's myth of Er and Cicero's *Dream of Scipio*, dreams are a path to an invisible world – a realm beyond habitual space and time.

The *locus classicus* of biblical dreaming is perhaps Jacob's dream. Philo discusses Jacob's dream – 'a stairway set upon earth, and the top of it reached to heaven: and the angels of God were ascending and descending on it; and the Lord stood firmly upon it'[103] –

The dream shewed the Ruler of the angels set fast upon the stairway, even the Lord: for high up like a charioteer high over his chariot or a helmsman high over his ship must we conceive of Him that is standing over . . . all things seen and unseen: for having made the

98 Wordsworth, 'Intimations of Immortality', Excursion I, l. 301.
99 Wordsworth, *The Prelude*, I, 27–8.
100 Wordsworth, *The Prelude*, V, 90ff. (Oxford: Clarendon, 1970), p. 69.
101 P. C. Miller, *Dreams in Late Antiquity: Studies in the Imagination of a Culture* (Princeton, NJ: Princeton University Press, 1994) p. 44f.
102 Kruger, *Dreaming in the Middle Ages*.
103 Genesis 28.12–13.

whole universe to depend on and cling to Himself, He is the Charioteer of all that vast creation.[104]

Reverie

Arthur Koestler famously observed of the mind's interior terrain:

> The most fertile region seems to be the marshy shore, the borderline between sleep and full awakening – where the matrices of disciplined thought are already operating but have not yet sufficiently hardened to obstruct the dreamlike fluidity of imagination.[105]

In a dream the dreamer is, *nolens volens*, concentrating upon the images or events of the dream narrative. The daydreamer, by way of contrast, flits from the empirical world to the imagined world. The dreamer is captivated by the dream. But in daydreams the agent is aware of two worlds – empirical and imagined domains.[106] Similarly in poetry the reader is aware both of the real world and of being in another world:

> The "Universal of Poetry" is apprehended by us when, having entered at the beck of the Poet, our initiator, into the vast wonderland of the dream–consciousness, we presently return therefrom to the waking world of his interesting story, and see its particulars again with the eyes of *revenants* who now know their secret meaning[107]

T S. Eliot remarks that 'the poet is occupied with the frontiers of consciousness beyond which words fail, though meanings still exist'.[108] One might think, for example, of his *Waste Land* with its deep mythological resonances. We may reflect upon the possible influence of J. A. Stewart upon his erstwhile student Eliot. Through the descent into a pre- or semi-conceptual reverie, the mind can encounter verities of a higher world. In this sense, the way down is the way up.[109] Poetic language furnishes a dimension of symbolic depth which defies exact articulation. Poetry, in Eliot's fine phrase, is the 'raid on the inarticulate'.[110] The poetic deployment of symbols can paradoxically combine both the ancient/archaic dimension and that of a contemporary psychic reality. The poet's imagination can thus create in the 'patient's imagination' a sense of being both in and out of the empirical world. It is a state of dream consciousness which is not separated from the waking

---

104 Philo, *On Dreams, Philo*, tr. F. H. Colson and G. H. Whitaker (Cambridge, Mass.: Harvard University Press, 1968), vol. 5, p. 379.
105 A. Koestler, *Act of Creation* (London: Hutchinson, 1964), p. 211.
106 C. McGinn, *Mindsight* (London: Harvard University Press, 2004) p. 76f.
107 J. A. Stewart, *The Myths of Plato*, (London: Centaur Press, 1960), p. 346.
108 T. S. Eliot, *On Poetry and Poets* (London: Faber and Faber, 1957), p. 30.
109 Eliot, *On Poetry and Poets*, p. 30.
110 T. S. Eliot, 'East Coker', V, in T. S. Eliot, *Collected Poems (1909–1962)* (London: Faber and Faber, 1963) p. 203.

consciousness but co-extensive with it, and as Stewart says, 'inserted' into it.[111]

August von Kekulé disovered the structure of the benzene ring in 1865 in a state of reverie – the flames of his fire seemed to resemble snakes biting their tails. He subsequently exhorted his colleagues, 'Lernen Sie nur träumen, meine Herrschaften; lernen Sie nur träumen' (Simply learn dreaming, gentleman, learn dreaming).[112] The German is ambiguous. It could be construed as 'learn to dream'. Significantly it can also mean 'dream *while* you learn'.

The French phenomenologist Gaston Bachelard argues that we should not understand the operation of a poetic image in purely subjective or in 'timidly' *causal* terms, and uses the auditory metaphor of 'reverberation': 'The poet does not confer the past of his image upon me, and yet his image immediately takes root in me. The communicability of an unusual image is a fact of great ontological significance.'[113] In this sense poetry is a phenomenology of the soul rather than the mind, and this is because the poem awakens depths in the soul which are barely perceptible to the conscious mind. Bachelard uses the concept of an 'image' which 'has touched the depths before it stirs the surface'.[114] He employs the concept of 'reverie', which he distinguishes sharply from dream states.[115] In reverie the mind can relax, but 'the soul keeps watch, with no tension, calmed and active'.[116] Coleridge in his *Shakespeare Lectures* of 1811–12 describes the 'middle state of mind' as

> more strictly appropriate to the imagination than any other when it is hovering between two images: as soon as it . . . is fixed [on one of these] it becomes understanding and when it is wavering between them attaching itself to neither it is imagination . . . These were the grandest effects . . . where the imagination was called forth, not to produce a distinct form but a strong working of the mind still producing what it still repels and again calling forth what it again negatives and the result is what the Poet wishes to impress, to substitute a grand feeling of the unimaginable for a mere image.[117]

Freud quotes Schiller in his *Interpretation of Dreams* on the topic of poetic creativity and the 'constraint' or gate which intellect usually imposes upon the imagination:

> where there is a creative mind, Reason – so it seems to me – relaxes its watch upon the gates, and the ideas rush in pell-mell, and only then does it look them through and examine them in a mass. You

111 Stewart, *The Myths of Plato*, p. 28.
112 J. Herbert, *The German Tradition. Uniting the Opposites: Goethe, Jung and Rilke* (London: Temenos Academy, 2001), pp. 7–8.
113 G. Bachelard, *The Poetics of Space*, tr. M. Jolas (Boston: Beacon Press, 1994), p. vii.
114 Ibid., p. xxiii.
115 G. Bachelard, *The Poetics of Reverie: Childhood, Language and the Cosmos* (Boston: Beacon Press, 1969).
116 Bachelard, *Poetics of Space*, p. xxii.
117 Coleridge, *Lectures 1808–1819*, vol. I (Princeton: Bollingen, 1987), p. 311.

critics, or whatever else you may call yourselves, are ashamed or frightened of the momentary and transient extravagances which are to be found in all truly creative minds and whose longer or shorter duration distinguishes the thinking artist from the dreamer.[118]

One might say that real poetic power lies in its capacity to address what Cottingham calls the whole self rather than the controlling intellect or ratiocentric intellect. There is much to commend this view that psyche is more than consciousness. With Wordsworth's 'meditations, passionate from deep Recesses in man's heart', his poetry is 'thoughtfully fitted to the Orphean lyre'.[119] The image of the chariot evokes imaginatively the subrational and subconscious dimension of the soul. The charioteer represents rational control but he is working with pre-existing forces, the good and the bad horses. The story – and this is a justification of the employment of the myth – is that the myth engages the whole self and not just the controlling age. Furthermore, story or myth is transhistorical. In myth the soul encounters archetypal structures that recur and resonate throughout history. Indeed, myth endows history with intelligibility in so far as it is myth. Myth or story strikes the soul in its depths, even before the content is grasped by the discursive intellect.[120]

Stories and religion

Good story, like great music, is characterized by coherence and unity. Human life, too, strives towards an ideal of narrative and its attendant unity or coherence. This ideal is dependent upon, or coextensive with, the construction of a unified personality, which in turn is achieved partly by the integration of pain and suffering: a potential integration that sets us apart from other animals. Because of various factors – frailty, disease, death and the failure to inhabit our past – the ideal is never fully attainable. The story, or the eucatastrophic fairy tale, is a response to this condition, because it does not deny the existence of sorrow and failure, but proclaims a transcendent joy.

C. S. Lewis wrote a small critical gem on the nature of stories in which the religious dimension is pivotal.[121] In the preface to his *George MacDonald: An Anthology*, Lewis writes about myth what, in 'On Stories', he extends to all stories. He suggests that it is not the words but the structure of the narrative – its consistency – which is important:

The critical problem with which we are confronted is whether this art – the art of myth-making – is a species of literary art. The objection to so classifying it is that the Myth does not essentially exist in *words* at all. We all agree that the story of Balder is a great

118 Friedrich von Schiller, letter to Körner, 1 December 1788; quoted in S. Freud, *The Interpretation of Dreams*, p. 177.
119 Wordsworth, *The Prelude*, I, 230–4.
120 M. Cox and A. Theilgaard, *Mutative Metaphors in Psychotherapy: The Aeolian Mode* (London: Tavistock, 1997), p. xxiv.
121 Lewis, 'On Stories'.

myth, a thing of inexhaustible value. But of whose version – whose *words* – are we thinking when we say this? For my own part, the answer is that I am not thinking of any one's words. No poet as far as I know or can remember, has told this story supremely well. I am not thinking of any particular version of it. If the story is anywhere embodied in words, that is almost an accident. What really delights and nourishes me is a particular pattern of events, which would equally delight and nourish if it had reached me by some medium which involved no words at all – say by a mime or a film . . . Any means of communication whatever which succeeds in lodging those tricks in the imagination has, as we say, 'done the trick'.[122]

One might note in connection with Lewis's claim that the pattern of events does not require words that Goethe first encountered the Faust story in a puppet show.

'Lewis could see that good stories do not radically depend on surprise. Children want to hear them repeated word for word; adults reread with enjoyment, so it is familiarity that enchants, not novelty.'[123] It is not, Lewis argues, so much the surprise as the quality of surprisingness that counts. And why, if it is not for the thrill of the unexpected, do some stories persist and continue to delight?

'Lewis's answer was the classic humanist answer. Great stories echo the abiding aspirations of humankind: the search, the chase, the home-coming, in abiding figures like Cinderella, Don Juan and Faust. The classic fiction of Europe, whether epic, romance or novel, adds texture to such abiding myths; such works excel not by surprise but by a compelling consistency of atmosphere and mood.'[124] A story creates another world which is effective through inner coherence and unity, not surprise.

Something similar holds for the masterpieces of other artforms. A. E. Taylor writes:

There is, I understand, some doubt about the genuineness of the letter in which Mozart is supposed to speak of his ability to hear his own compositions 'all at once' by an interior audition, and of the incommunicable rapture of the experience. Yet I imagine it is not really doubtful that the great artist in every kind must really possess some such power of envisaging as a *totum simul*, however imperfectly, what he can only convey to us by means of a detail which he has to elaborate, and we to 'follow', in the form of long-drawn-out successiveness. Not to speak of the vision of the artist himself, which is, after all, the artist's secret, if we consider only our own imperfect appreciation and enjoyment of the artist's work when it is already there for us, it seems to me that as we learn to appreciate better, the work we appreciate and enjoy steadily sheds its successiveness.

122 George MacDonald: *An Anthology* (London: Geoffrey Bks, 1946), pp. 14–15.
123 See G. Watson, *Never Ones for Theory? England and the War of Ideas* (Cambridge: Lutterworth, 2000), p. 91.
124 Ibid., p. 92.

There was first a stage in which single stanzas of the poem, single scenes, or even speeches, of the drama, single phrases of the melody, were all that could fill our minds at one time; appreciation of the whole as a unity with structure had to be won with difficulty and the aid of conscious recollection and reflection. This is afterwards succeeded by a stage at which the impression is made by an interrelated whole, and our judgement of appreciation passed primarily on the whole as such, with a conscious immediacy.[125]

This unity encountered in story and music has a profound relationship to life itself. Charles Taylor argues that we need to endow our lives with sense and meaning, a set of goals and projects, and for this we require 'inescapable frameworks'[126] – a position kindred to MacIntyre's claim that we need to understand agency not as atomistic events but as located within a wider context – both in time and a given community. Hence MacIntyre says that 'narrative history . . . [is] the basic and essential genre for the characterisation of human actions'.[127] We look for significance in some events rather than others, links between aspects of our lives which may not be evident to an observer.

A life narrative is the attempt to view a life as meaningful. Even psychotherapy is story-based, so that the patient can escape from the grip of that particular story and develop another. John Cottingham has argued that much contemporary philosophical anthropology has signally failed to incorporate insights from psychotherapy in its reflection about rational decision-making processes, and he castigates much contemporary philosophy for persisting with an oddly desiccated model of deliberation. He writes eloquently:

in the key areas of human passion and emotion, when it comes to anger, jealousy, fear, ambition and sexual desire, linear rationality seems to fail us. What is amiss is not just that we imperfectly understand the past causes and future consequences of what we are 'choosing' to do and why. For if the structure of our deepest feelings and desires is conditioned by the influences and choices of the dormant past, to the extent that the significance of our actions will often be opaque to us, then the very notion of rational deliberation as a guide to action seems shaky. Unless and until the past is reclaimed, unless we can come to appreciate the significance of our past, and the role it plays in shaping our emotional lives, then the very idea of an ordered plan for the good life will have to be put on hold.[128]

However, actual lives are inescapably fragmentary and divided: 'just one damn thing after another' as Henry Ford notoriously said of history. Augustine famously observed of himself in the *Confessions*, 'Grant me

125 A. E. Taylor, *The Faith of a Moralist* (London: Macmillan, 1930), vol. 1, pp. 427–8.
126 C. Taylor, *Sources of the Self: The Making of Modern Identity* (Cambridge: Cambridge University Press, 1989), pp. 27, 47, 50.
127 A. MacIntyre, *After Virtue: A Study in Moral Theory*, 2nd edn (London: Duckworth, 1985), p. 194.
128 Cottingham, *Philosophy and the Good Life*, p. 135.

chastity and continence, but not yet'.[129] This was not cynicism or hypocrisy but the recognition of the Pauline divided self. Augustine realized that he consciously desired incompatible ends. Unity and coherence are ideals rather than attainments. Narrative means a series of events, minimally that there is a temporal and non-logical link between at least two events. But it usually means much more than this. A complete story has a beginning, a middle and an end: it has *unity*.

Narrative presupposes personal identity and yet personal identity is notoriously elusive. It has long been *de rigueur* in some literary circles to suggest that narrative *creates* identity. But this is a very strong and somewhat implausible claim. However, it is not entirely without merit. Plato in the *Republic* presents the soul as a sum of threefold and contradictory impulses. Unity must in some sense be constructed. Freedom is the capacity to pursue purpose and to subordinate or sublimate specific or random desires to an overarching purpose.[130] If pleasure is by definition fleeting and often momentary, like Burns' analogy in 'Tam o'Shanter',

> Or like the snow falls in the river
> A moment white – then melts for ever![131]

then it cannot sustain the well-being and fulfilment of an agent.

Human happiness must have more continuity and depth. It must be linked to the homogeneous functioning of different elements with an overarching personality. The stronger the personality, the easier its capacity to endure pain, suffering and misfortune. In the child or the immature adult (perhaps the adult suffering from a borderline personality disorder), momentary pleasure or pain dominates its consciousness and shapes decisions, whereas the powerfully unified personality integrates or assimilates particular pleasures or pains into a larger life plan and path. The agent who takes a merely prudential interest in his or her own affairs – health and fitness, savings, pensions – is a long way from being a properly moral agent but is acting as if life is a series of merely successive moments rather than a deeper unity. Prudence and morality (and supremely religion) may be thought of as a transformation of the self into a more permanent and abiding unity.

Of course, human frailty, disease and death means that the process of unification is an ideal and ultimately unattainable. Yet it marks a difference in kind and not merely in degree between human beings and the rest of the animal kingdom. Human beings are capable not just of pleasures but of happiness in the aforementioned sense. Adding to pleasures is not to add to happiness. The indulgence of impulse can, as in the case of the borderline syndrome, be linked to abject personal misery and insecurity and chronically low self-esteem. The happiness of a

---

129 Augustine, *Confessions* VIII.7.
130 See H. Frankfurt's classic article, 'Freedom of the Will and the Concept of a Person', repr. in G. Watson (ed.), *Free Will* (Oxford: Oxford University Press, 1982), pp. 81–95.
131 Robert Burns, 'Tam O'Shanter', ll. 61–2, *The Poems and Songs of Robert Burns*, ed. J. Kingsley, vol. 2 (Oxford: Clarendon Press, 1968).

reflective agent requires development of personality, and paradoxically for the sensualist, the suffering of pain and misfortune is a *sine qua non* of any developed personality, and hence happiness. The misery inflicted on cattle to produce cheap meat for supermarkets will not enhance the lives of the poor beasts in any way. Yet many of the most remarkable persons are not just strengthened but forged by suffering.

The drive for unity, albeit as an unrealizable ideal, generates a yearning for a state in which continuing unfulfilled striving finds some completion or goal. The homeward journey of Odysseus to Ithaca represented in late antiquity an image of the soul's longing for some *telos* in which it would find ultimate fulfilment.

The fairy tale in its most sublime form constitutes what Tolkien calls the 'eucatastrophe'. 'The eucatastrophic tale is the true form of the fairy tale and its highest function.'[132] The consolation of fairy stories, the joy of the happy ending – or more correctly, of the good catastrophe, the sudden joyous 'turn' – is not escapist. It does not deny the existence of the dyscatastrophe, of sorrow and failure. The possibility of these is necessary for joy and deliverance: 'it denies (in the face of much evidence, if you will) universal final defeat and in so far is *evangelium*, giving a fleeting glimpse of Joy, Joy beyond the walls of the world, poignant as grief.'[133] The word 'joy' has a clearly Romantic resonance:

Joy, Lady! is the spirit and the power,
Which wedding Nature to us gives in dow'r
A new Earth and new Heaven,
Undreamt of by the sensual and the proud –
Joy is the sweet voice, Joy the luminous cloud –
We in ourselves rejoice!
And thence flows all that charms or ear or sight,
All melodies the echoes of that voice,
All colours a suffusion from that light.[134]

C. S. Lewis gave a biographical exposition of such joy in *The Pilgrim's Regress* and *Surprised by Joy*. Joy is the happiness of a sense of unity with the Divine – it is rooted in the *desiderium naturale* of the soul, a longing for union with the Divine.[135]

William Temple wrote:

What we must completely get away from is the notion that the world as it now exists is a rational whole; we must think of its unity not by the analogy of a picture, of which all the parts exist at once, but by the analogy of a drama where, if it is good enough, the full meaning of the first scene only becomes apparent with the final curtain; and we are in the middle of this. Consequently the world as we see it is

---

132 Tolkien, *Tree and Leaf*, p. 60.
133 Ibid.
134 S. T. Coleridge, 'Dejection: An Ode', ll. 67–75, *Poems*, pp. 281–2.
135 See O. Barfield, 'Either: Or: Coleridge, Lewis, and Romantic Theology', in C. Hutter (ed.), *Imagination and the Spirit: Essays in Literature and the Christian Faith Presented to Clyde S. Kilby* (Grand Rapids, Mich.: Eerdmans, 1971), pp. 25–42.

strictly unintelligible. We can only have faith that it will become intelligible when the divine purpose, which is the explanation of it, is accomplished.[136]

Temple argues that the Logos should not be understood as 'a static principle of rational unity, but as an active force of moral judgment which calls upon us to be its fellow-workers and agents'.[137] Temple is placing emphasis upon the eschatological dimension of the divine Logos. Through language, and the enormously enhanced potential for experience and awareness which human consciousness affords, arises the conflict between inner images and outer reality and the desire to reconcile the two. This conscious estrangement is expressed in mythic terms as a Fall. Tolkien speaks memorably: 'a vivid sense of that separation is very ancient; but also a sense that it was a severance: a strange fate and guilt lies on us. Other creatures are like other realms with which Man has broken off relations, and sees now only from the outside at a distance, being at war with them, or on the terms of an uneasy armistice.'[138] This awareness of estrangement in Tolkien has a romantic, neo-Platonic provenance. The Romantics notoriously saw man's fall as division, isolation – and redemption as reconciliation.[139] Augustine in his *Exposition of the Psalms*, commenting on Psalm 101, writes:

God's years are not something different from God himself. God's years are God's eternity, and eternity is the very substance of God, in which there is no possibility of change. In him nothing is past, as though it no longer existed, and nothing is future, as though it has not yet come to be. There is nothing in God's eternity except 'is'.[140]

Augustine is using the language of Exodus 3.14: God revealed in the burning bush to Moses as 'I am who I am'. While we are 'in the body' we are on pilgrimage and away from the Lord – travellers and lodgers.[141] The goal of the pilgrimage is true being: 'Anyone who takes the road away from him who truly *is* necessarily goes toward non-being.'[142]

In his commentaries on the Psalms, Augustine links the language of being and eternity with the Exodus motif of exile, and the longing for the eternal sabbath which is the theme of the *Confessions* and expressed in its claim that our hearts 'find no peace until they rest in you'.[143] Rather as pagan Platonists used Ulysses returning to Ithaca as a model of the soul returning to its spiritual home, Augustine uses Eternity as the place of

---

136 F. A. Iremonger, *William Temple, Archbishop of Canterbury: His Life and Letters* (London: Oxford University Press, 1948), pp. 537–8.
137 Quoted ibid., p. 538.
138 Tolkien, *Tree and Leaf*, p. 58.
139 M. H. Abrams, *Natural Supernaturalism: Tradition and Revolution in Romantic Literature* (London: Oxford University Press, 1971), p. 272.
140 Augustine, *Expositions of the Psalms*, Exp. 2 of Ps. 101, § 10, tr. M. Boulding (New York: New City Press, 2000), vol. 5, p. 71.
141 Ibid., Exp. of Ps. 38, § 21; vol. 2., p. 192.
142 Ibid., Exp. of Ps. 38, § 225; vol. 2., p. 193.
143 Augustine, *Confessions*, tr. R. S. Pine-Coffin (Harmondsworth: Penguin, 1961), p. 21.

rest after the soul's sojourn in Egypt. His commentary on Psalm 38 dwells upon the soul's ascent to God: 'For myself, in my weakness I am so nearly non-existent that God has eluded my memory, God who said, I AM WHO I AM (Ex. 3.14).'[144] The sense of the imperfection of time presupposes an intimation of the perfection of eternity: 'I am making some progress, and already tending toward him; already I am beginning to attain true being'.[145]

But there is a rest for the soul in that spiritual Jerusalem, 'the bride of my Lord where there will be no death, no deficiency, where the day passes not but abides, the day that is preceded by no yesterday and hustled on by no tomorrow'.[146] The themes of the commentaries on the Psalms of the soul's frustrations in time and the longing for the eternity of God are pursued in books X to XIII of the *Confessions* as the conclusion to Augustine's story about his own conversion. The very first lines of the *Confessions* express the longing for rest in God and later in the first book he outlines the non-durational eternity of the divine being as the 'today' which contains years past and future and which is the source and measure of duration.[147] Narrative, whether autobiographical or not, involves a series of past, present and future. As Hamlet observes, man is a creature 'with such large discourse / Looking before and after'.[148] Although human beings experience time as fleeting 'nows', the unity of a narrative provides an intimation of the divine perspective of seeing whole.[149] It is this Augustinian longing for non-durational eternity that explains Lewis's conclusion in 'On Stories':

> We grasp at a state and find only a succession of events in which the state is never quite embodied. The grand idea of finding Atlantis which stirs us in the first chapter of the adventure story is apt to be frittered away in mere excitement when the journey has once begun. But so, in real life, the idea of adventure fades when the day-to-day details begin to happen. Nor is this merely because actual hardship and danger shoulder it aside. Other grand ideas – homecoming, reunion with a beloved – similarly elude our grasp. Suppose there is no disappointment; even so – well, you are here. But now, something must happen, and after that something else. All that happens may be delightful: but can any such series quite embody the sheer state of being which was what we wanted? If the author's plot is only a net, and usually an imperfect one, a net of time and event for catching what is not really a process at all, is life much more? . . . [Art] is an image of the truth. Art, indeed, may be expected to do what life cannot do: but so it has done. The bird has escaped us. But it was at least entangled in the net for several

144 Augustine *Exposition of the Psalms*, Exp. of Ps. 38, § 7; vol. 2, p. 176.
145 Ibid., Exp. of Ps. 38, § 13; vol. 2, p. 185.
146 Ibid., Exp. of Ps. 38, § 7; vol. 2, p. 178.
147 Augustine, *Confessions*, I, 6.
148 Shakespeare, *Hamlet*, IV.iv.36–7.
149 G. Lloyd, 'Augustine and the "Problem" of Time', in G. B. Mathews (ed.), *The Augustinian Tradition* (Berkeley, Calif.: University of California Press, 1999), pp. 40–59.

chapters. We saw it close and enjoyed the plumage. How may 'real lives' have nets that can do as much?

In life and art both, as it seems to me, we are always trying to catch in our net of successive moments something that is not successive.[150]

Lewis is arguing that the structure of a good story is satisfying because the reader can inhabit a world that bears some analogy to the completeness which the soul naturally longs for and yet finds frustrated by the fleeting and elusive nature of most other human joys and pleasures. The story seems to hold a mirror to eternity in its sequential representation of an ordered whole. Similarly, Coleridge sees the special prerogative of genius as the capacity to reduce 'multitude to unity, or succession to an instant'.[151] He once observed that

> The common end of all *narrative*, nay of *all*, Poems is to convert a *series* into a *Whole*: to make those events, which in real or imagined History move in a *strait* Line, assume to our Understandings a *circular* motion – the snake with it's Tail in it's Mouth.[152]

This is the snake that Kekulé saw. Coleridge continues:

> Hence the almost flattering and yet appropriate term – Poesy – i.e. poiesis = *making*. Doubtless to [God's] eye, which alone compre-hends all Past and all Future in one eternal Present, what to our short sight appears strait is but a part of the great Cycle – just as the calm sea to us *appears* level, though it be indeed part of a *Globe*. Now what the Globe is in geography, miniaturing in order to manifest the Truth, such is a poem to the Image of God, we were created into, and which still seeks that unity or revelation of the one in and by the many, which reminds it, that tho' in order to be an individual Being it must go forth from God, yet as the receding from him is to proceed towards nothingness and privation, it must still at every step turn back toward him in order to be at all.[153]

Let us return to J. A. Stewart. He links Plato's myth-making quite explicitly to literature. In particular he reflects upon the role of the poet's use of images and rhythm and melody as inducing a dream conscious-ness which exists fleetingly – as the dreamlike sense of the presence of eternity. The mood that the poet induces is that of our primordial pre-conceptual roots in the vegetative soul. However, the mind's return to normal consciousness is accompanied by an 'atmosphere of intense feeling' which pervades the waking consciousness: 'the poet performs his essential function as Poet only in so far as he rouses Transcendental Feeling in his patient, and that he does so by inducing in him a state of

---

150 Lewis, 'On Stories', pp. 44–5.
151 Coleridge, *Biographia Literaria*, vol. 2, p. 23.
152 Coleridge, *Collected Letters*, ed. E. L. Griggs, 6 vols (Oxford: Clarendon Press, 1956–71), vol. 4, p. 545.
153 Coleridge, *Collected Letters of Samuel Taylor Coleridge*, vol. 4, p. 545.

dream consciousness'.[154] The state so induced is one of transient or fitful episodes within the stream of waking consciousness:

The effect may be described as a feeling of having lately been in some divine region, where the true reasons of the things which happen in this world of ordinary experience are laid up; a Place in which one understood the significance of these things, although one cannot now explain what one then understood. In the *Phaedrus* Myth, where the Souls peep over the edge of the Cosmos for a moment into the Plain of Truth beyond, and then sink down into the region of the sensible, this feeling of "having just now understood the true significance of things" is pictorially rendered.[155]

For Stewart, the poet initiates a journey into the 'wonderland of dream consciousness' and we 'dream his dream':

The claim is that the kind of imaginative involvement in art bears a powerful kinship to dream states. We enter into the world of a play or novel rather in the way in which we are absorbed by our dreams, and dreams usually possess some kind of narrative structure, albeit often baffling. Some might argue that this analogy shows that the power of art is linked to th inclinations and instincts of the child. Just as the child is entranced by tales and stories, the dreamer has no rational guard or protection in the dream state: hence their often terrifying nature. One might conclude that the enjoyment of art is closely linked to the vestiges of childhood in the adult: a form of regression. Yet perhaps, following stewart, we could say that the deep analogy between the absorption in art and in dreaming is not a sign that enjoyment of art is linked infantile regression but, on the contrary, an encounter with great art confronts the soul with dimensions of reality of which the discursive intellect is often barely aware. Indeed, the coherence, consistency and unity of the story employed by the poet or the dramatist does not conflict with the state of immersion but is the very presupposition of absorption into the poem or tale.

We might contrast Lewis's Platonic account of stories with Martha Nussbaum's celebrated account of Odysseus's choice between a life with Calypso and returning to Penelope. Nussbaum interprets the former as a life with no risk – no vulnerability –

Our preference for Odysseus's life with Penelope over his life with Calypso actually stems, I think, from this more general uneasiness about the shapelessness of the life Calypso offers: pleasure and kindliness on and on, with no risks, no possibility of sacrifice, no grief, no children.[156]

---

154 Stewart, *Myths of Plato*, p. 344.
155 Ibid., p. 345.
156 M. Nussbaum, *Love's Knowledge: Essays on Philosophy and Literature* (Oxford: Oxford University Press, 1990), p. 366.

Her claim is that much of what makes a life worth living is internally linked to facts about our finitude and to our not desiring happiness if that means becoming other than human. She rejects 'as incoherent . . . the aspiration to leave behind altogether the constitutive conditions of our humanity . . . to seek for a life that is really the life of another sort of being'.[157] This even leads her to express a cautious preference for the Christian story of the incarnation ('if it can be made coherent') over against the invulnerable members of the Greek pantheon.[158] Much of her thought is rather Nietzschean in its polemic against the Platonic inheritance – the denigration of finitude and, indeed, the body – combined with the decadent pessimism of those *fin-de-siècle* novelists like Proust and James. She even insists that 'animals have forms of life apart from the pollution of religion; they show us what it could be to be alive without hope or fear or disgust or even love'.[159] But this is extremely fanciful. Human memory, culture and tradition mean that Nussbaum's suggestion is a hopeless illusion. Hope, fear, disgust and love create pain and anxiety unknown to brutes. Yet only a hedonist of the crudest stamp or an ancient Cynic could think that such pains can be readily erased without severe collateral loss to human well-being and happiness. Bergson and Heidegger have taught us how human consciousness is suffused by memories of the past (involuntary images and habits) and permeated by the anticipation of the future. Hence only the most adept and refined Buddhist can hope to live in the present, and certainly not the noble savage of Nussbaum's imagination.

Nussbaum's claim about life with Calypso is rather akin to Bernard Williams's use of the so-called 'Makropulos Case', a story by Karel Čapek developed into an opera by Janáček, concerning Elina Makropulos, who is 342, having been 42 for 300 years, and has lost any desire to live. Williams employs this story to show that there is some profit in death, that 'an endless life would be a meaningless one; and that we could have no reason for living eternally a human life'.[160] He argues that traditional views of the afterlife fail to appreciate adequately the unimaginable tedium of such an existence:

> In general we can ask, what is it about the imaged activities of an eternal life which would stave off the principal hazard to which EM succumbed, boredom? The Don Juan in Hell joke, that heaven's prospects are tedious and the devil has the best tunes, though a tired fancy in itself, at least serves to show up a real and (I suspect) a profound difficulty, of providing any model of an unending, supposedly satisfying, state or activity which would not rightly prove boring to anyone who remained conscious of himself and who had acquired a character, interests, tastes and impatiences in the course of living, already, a finite life. The point is not that for such a

157 Ibid., p. 379.
158 Ibid., p. 376.
159 Ibid., p. 304.
160 B. Williams, 'The Makropulos Case', in *Problems of the Self: Philosophical Papers 1956–1972* (Cambridge: Cambridge University Press, 1979), p. 89.

man boredom would be a tiresome consequence of the supposed states or activities, and that they would be objectionable just on the utilitarian or hedonistic ground that they had this disagreeable feature. If that were all there was to it, we could imagine the feature away, along no doubt with other disagreeable features of human life in its present imperfection. The point is rather that boredom, as sometimes in more ordinary circumstances, would not just be a tiresome effect, but a reaction almost perceptual in character to the poverty of one's relationship to the environment. Nothing less will do than something that makes boredom *unthinkable* . . . *The Platonic introjection*, seeing the satisfactions of studying what is timeless and impersonal as being themselves timeless and impersonal, may be a deep illusion, but it is certainly an illusion.[161]

One might raise the obvious objection that being an immortal among finite mortals is rather different from the traditional Christian idea of heaven. The Platonic tradition, as we have noted in Augustine, represents eternity as non-durational. Boethius's distinction between eternity as timelessness and everlasting time (sempiternity) is a classic instance of this. This has partly to do with the development in middle and later Platonism of the idea of the personality of the Deity and the placing of the Ideas or Forms into the mind of God not as an abstract ideal but as the concrete (as it were) unity of ultimate goodness. Divine consciousness and immutability require that God's thoughts are not a succession of discrete and ephemeral experiences of 'here and now' but a comprehensive and unified 'now' – the *interminabilis vitae tota simul et perfecta possessio*.[162]

This is an intimation of the God whose centre is everywhere and whose circumference is nowhere. The κόσμος νοητός, as Plotinus insists in his exposition of the *Phaedrus* myth,[163] is the vibrant one-in-many of the Divine Mind – a community of living translucent minds; a domain of fecund abundance. As we saw in Chapter 3, the monism of Plotinus is certainly not pantheistic, and nor is it monistic in the straightforward sense that the individual is dissolved into a transcendent unity. Rather, at the point of union with the Divine, the individual retains a unique perspective while aware of its identity with the all. Hence the individual is never more itself than in the moment of losing itself in God. Plotinus uses, quite deliberately, the imagery of 'boiling with life' to reinforce this vision imaginatively.[164]

Lewis uses the example of a drawing of a cathedral and the cathedral itself to illustrate the relation of the phenomenal to the noetic cosmos:

---

161 Ibid., p. 94–6.
162 Boethius, *De consolatione philosophiae*, V, pros. 6. On this, see J. Whittaker, *God, Time, Being: Two Studies in the Transcendental Tradition in Greek Philosophy* (Oslo: Oslo University Press, 1971), pp. 11–15.
163 Plato, *Phaedrus* 247c–248e.
164 Plotinus, *Enneads* VI.5.12.9. Meister Eckhart, in his commentary on Exodus, describes the 'seething and boiling' (*bullitio*) of the inner divine life as a dance of ideas. See W. Beierwaltes, *Platonismus und Idealismus* (Franfurt: Klostermann, 1972), pp. 55ff.

If flesh and blood cannot inherit the Kingdom, that is not because they are too solid, too gross, too distinct, too 'illustrious with being'. They are too flimsy, too transitory, too phantasmal.[165]

Here we have the case of a diffuse intimation of the presence of the spiritual, of an unfathomable divinity, as in a Caspar David Friedrich landscape. Friedrich's great rival, the Tyrolean artist Joseph Anton Koch, depicted Der Schmadribachfall in a seminal Romantic painting. Here the Alpine waterfall is a symbol of the infinite – the *coincidentia oppositorum*. Koch presents a visual paradox in his painting: the appearance of both vehement *motion* (of the water) and sublime *stability* – even fixity. This image fascinated Koch's contemporaries.[166] And the greatest poet of the age, Wordsworth, speaks of 'The stationary blast of waterfalls'.[167] Here is a concrete instance of Schelling's use of the word *Einbildungskraft* (imagination) to mean *in-Eins-bilden* (forming-into-one). The artist produces an artwork in which the finite object constitutes an image (*Bild*) of the infinite. This is the *in-eins-Bildung* or the *forming into a unity* of finite and infinite. The story, we have argued, can be an image of that infinity.

Art does not always lie. Paradoxically, the 'make-believe' of great art, as Aristotle insisted, is often a channel of insight into truth – art can convey truths through the 'mind's eye' and articulate the perplexing state of reflective self-consciousness and moral responsibility. But closely related to the mirroring function of art – the depiction of self-awareness – is art's unique capacity for expressing an experience of transcendence. 'Transcendence' is a very slippery word. The etymology of the word is from the Latin *transcendere*, to climb beyond, and here we are on the threshold of the Platonic cave. Martha Nussbaum speaks of a 'transcendence . . . of an *internal* and human sort',[168] but this, I think, is a rather Pickwickian account of transcendence. Let us take transcendence to mean the real existence of a spiritual realm of being upon which the physical cosmos – as known by the natural sciences – is dependent. A landscape of Caspar David Friedrich or certain Romantic symphonies are not clearly religious in a conventional institutional sense and yet are clearly not meant to be merely ornamental, merely decorative or simple entertainment for the eye or ear. Blake regarded poetry, painting and music as humanity's three ways of 'conversing with Paradise'.[169]

The historical importance of the aesthetic imagination, in both a positive and a negative sense, is quite clear. Many of the artefacts which we observe in museums had their original *Sitz im Leben* in temples or churches. But it would be naïve to think that art was traditionally at the service of religion. In some senses, it was a powerful and jealous rival – a

---

165 C. S. Lewis, 'Transposition', in *Weight of Glory and Other Addresses*, (New York: Macmillan, 1980), p. 68.
166 H. Frank, *Joseph Anton Koch: Der Schmadribachfall. Natur und Freiheit* (Frankfurt am Main: Fischer, 1995).
167 Wordsworth, *The Prelude*, VI, 626.
168 Nussbaum, *Love's Knowledge*, p. 379.
169 Quoted in K. Raine, *The Inner Journey of the Poet, and Other Papers* (London: Allen and Unwin, 1982), p. 33.

fact which can be observed in the recurrent attacks in great religions, occidental and oriental, upon images and idolatry.

Longings of imagination point to questions of salvation. Through the imagination we confront the question of alienation or being at home in the universe and how the wings of the soul cannot rise to its goal, its powers of imagination fail. As Dante writes, at the conclusion of the *Paradiso*:

> veder volea come si convenue
> l'imago al cerchio e come vi s'indova;
> ma non eran da ciò le proprie penne:
> se non che la mia mente fu percossa
> d a un fulgore in che sua voglia venne
> All'alta fantasia qui mancò possa;
> mia già volgeva il mio disio e 'l velle.
> sì come rota ch'igualmente è mossa,
> l'amor che move il sole e l'altre stelle.[170]

Perhaps it is not a matter of simple hostility between institutional religion and art, but that most religion needs art, and is therefore concerned about what kind of art is suitable. Precisely because religion needs art, it has reasons for being concerned about the truth or falsity, authenticity or inauthenticity, of artistic representation.[171] 'For now we see through a glass darkly; but then face to face.'[172]

---

170 'I wished to see how the image was fitted to the circle and how it has its place there; but my own wings were not sufficient for that, had not my mind been smitten by a flash wherein came its wish. Here power failed the high phantasy; but now my desire and will, like a wheel that spins with even motion, were revolved by the Love that moves the sun and the other stars': Dante, *Paradiso*, XXXIII, 137–45.
171 I owe this point to Dave Leal.
172 1 Corinthians 13.12.

7

Inspired Images, Angels and the Imaginal World

If I cried out, who would hear me among the angelic orders?[1]

After considering the apocalyptic dimension of metaphysics and the metaphysical mood of narrative, we now turn to the question of special revelation. In particular we concentrate upon the fusion of Athens and Jerusalem in the Christian tradition, the fusing of the Phaedran chariot with the heavenly vehicle of Ezekiel, by which the transcendent ideas become images beheld by the prophet. As Osborn observes, 'In Irenaeus, Athens and Jerusalem meet at Patmos. The visions of the prophets, which point to Christ, take the place of Plato's forms'.[2] In Christian Platonism, the prophet is not a predictor of marvels but whosoever can see into the mind of God. Philo took Moses in this sense; in Justin Martyr eschatology and ontology coalesce. The prophet sees the open heaven. The images of the biblical world – lamb, light, the servant, etc. – replace the Forms of Plato's dialectic; they are theophanic. This fusion of Platonism and scriptural revelation is not confined to Christianity: the twelfth-century Islamic philosopher Suhrawardi, among others, interpreted the Platonic ideas as angels. However, my interest is devoted in particular to a twentieth-century thinker, Austin Farrer. Though no avowed Platonist, he serves my purposes by producing a theory of revelation through inspired images. With the help of this theory, I can attempt to sketch my own theory of a Christian narrative which does not try to immunize itself from external critique in the fashion of various forms of Barthianism. Rather, the Christian narrative – though exhibiting deep affinities with other great scriptural traditions – depends less upon the verbal articulation of its revelation than it does upon its iconic structure. The Greek-Byzantine holy island of Patmos, the island of St John, serves as a fitting reference point for contemplating this revelation through inspired images, and I shall use Hölderlin's remarkable poem 'Patmos' as a point of departure. Yet Hölderlin was a lyric poet shaped by the Christian epic tradition of Milton through to Klopstock.

Milton's 'great argument' depicts the battle of the angels and Christ's victory over Satan in order to

1 'Wer, wenn ich schriee, hörte mich denn aus der Engel Ordnungen?': Rainier Maria Rilke, *Duineser Elegien*, 'Die Erster Elegie', ll. 1–2
2 Eric Osborn, *Irenaeus* (Cambridge: Cambridge University Press, 2001), p. xi.

211

I may assert th' eternal providence
And justify the ways of God to men.[3]

Had Christianity already begun, as it were, to concede significant territory to secular reason? Marx punned that Feuerbach's 'fiery brook' (his name means literally 'brook of fire') was a philosophical requirement in the modern age, and Milton's vision of supernatural warfare and Satan vanquished appears startlingly obsolete – perhaps, like Ovid, the last great articulation of a dying mythology. Yet this takes us into the heart of Christian reflection about the Scriptures and the breakdown of verbal inspiration in Protestant culture in the eighteenth and nineteenth centuries, and its wider ramifications throughout European culture in the twentieth. Milton is not a figure of random significance. His seminal role in modern European thought lies in his formative influence upon European Romanticism.[4] Wordsworth's *Prelude* and Goethe's *Faust* bear Milton's influence but both are demythologized narratives.[5] *Goethedienst* may have been a form of *Gottesdienst*, and Wordsworth became quite a conservative Anglican, but the genius of both poets is remote from Milton's passionate commitment to a Christological drama. Goethe's *Faust* is saved without either repentance or faith, quite in harmony with Goethe's neo-Spinozistic spirituality.

In Hölderlin's 'Patmos' the poet presents a defence of Christian belief against the more radical theology of the Enlightenment. Count Friedrich of Hessen-Homburg had initially asked the elderly Klopstock to do this, but he declined. It was this task Hölderlin took upon himself and he addresses the pious Count in his poem as a Christian poet. The Schwabian poet recounts an imaginary journey to the island of Patmos off the coast of Greek Asia Minor.

'Asia' (i.e. Asia Minor) draws the poet through its brilliance: the mountains (gold-decorated Paktol, and Taurus and Messogis), its 'göttlichgebauten Paläste', the snow on its mountains and its ivy, 'Zeug unsterblichen Lebens' (stuff of everlasting life). The evergreen ivy is a good image of immortality. But there is also the association of 'Zeuge' or witness. These are the poet's intimations of immortality. The poet can use his divine baton (*Stab*) to awaken redeemed humanity to its 'Unsterblicher Schicksal' (immortal destiny).

Yet in the midst of this blinding oriental Hellenic magnificence, the intense Greek light, the poet longs for the 'dunkeln Grotte' – the dark cave, presumably the cave where John was imprisoned by the Roman emperor Domitian, and where he received his revelation. Hölderlin envisages the elderly St John on the island of Patmos recalling his youth in Palestine with Christ as the beloved disciple:

---

3 John Milton, *Paradise Lost*, I, 25–6.
4 The Swiss critics Bodmer and Breitinger, as well as Herder and Klopstock, were instrumental in establishing Milton's fame on the Continent.
5 See J. Rohls, '"Goethedienst ist Gottesdienst": Theologische Anmerkungen zur Goethe-Verehrung', in J. Golz and J. Ulbricht, *Goethe in Gesellschaft: Zur geschichte einer literarischen Vereinigung vom Kaiserreich bis zum geteilten Deutschland* (Cologne: Böhlau, 2005), pp. 33–62.

once the beloved of the Divine,
The seer who in blessed youth
was inseparable
From the Son of the Most High.[6]

The great poets still have a strong sense of mankind's longing for redemption'. Painters and poets still invoke demons and angels – Wallace Stevens, Rilke and Klee, for example. Perhaps this is the phenomenon that M. H. Abrams called 'natural supernaturalism'[7] – the inherited supernatural structure reshaped and clipped to fit into non-supernatural premises. Another way of judging the same phenomenon is to observe that the poets articulate human experience and longing. Perhaps there are aspects of genuine human experience which cannot be expressed in scientific terms. The poets are not using allegories which they could translate if they wished into clinical objective terms, but symbols of irreducible phenomena.

Evil: from decadence to apocalypse

In Proust's *À la recherche du temps perdu* we have a vision of a paradise lost but retrieved in the memory of the artist. The artist becomes an aesthetic saint. Dislocated from a decaying society, he finds salvation in memory rescued through art: 'La vraie vie, la vie enfin découverte et éclaircie, la seule vie par conséquent réellement vécue, c'est la littérature.'[8] 'L'art pour l'art' is justified in terms of 'La tristesse du poète' and les 'Chagrins' du poète.[9] Creativity is the fruit of misery: 'Car le bonheur seul est salutaire pour le corps; mais c'est le chagrin qui développe les forces de l'esprit.'[10] Such art is 'le vrai Jugement dernier'.[11]

Thomas Mann's *Dr Faustus*, written in exile, could be interpreted as a critique of a Proustian aesthetics. He too draws upon the motif of artistic melancholy, in its paradigmatic emblem of genius in Dürer's *Melancolia*.[12]

Mann's novel produces a twentieth-century Faustus (his own contemporary) as a representative of the collapse of German intellectual culture between the Wilhelminian age and the wicked 'sans culottism' of the Nazi era,[13] and of the dark and sinister imaginative presence of supernatural forces. The novel is a particularly rich example of German literature of that time, as it was deeply influenced by Adorno and Tillich. Mann's Faustus is the composer and musician Adrian

---

6 'einst des gottgeliebten, / Des Sehers, der in seliger Jugend war / Gegangen mit / Dem Sohne des Höchsten, unzertrennlich': Friedrich Hölderlin, 'Patmos', in *Gedichte* (Stuttgart: Philipp Reclam, 2003).
7 M. H. Abrams, *Natural Supernaturalism: Tradition and Revolution in Romantic Literature* (New York: Norton, 1971).
8 M. Proust, *A la recherche du temps perdu*, (Paris: Laffont, 1987), III, p. 725.
9 Ibid., III, p. 138.
10 Ibid., III, p. 733.
11 Ibid., III, p. 713.
12 Mann, *Dr Faustus* (Frankfurt: Fischer, 2003), p. 317.
13 Ibid. p. 514.

Leverkühn. His story is told, in the form of a diary, by his friend, a gentle and humane schoolteacher (of Classics) aptly named Serenus Zeitblom. This serene humanist describes, though at distance and with suspicion, the sombre, irrationalistic intellectual milieu which shapes Leverkühn. Modelled on the life of Friedrich Nietzsche (also a composer), Leverkühn is an artist who sells his soul to the devil in order to attain creativity, seeking salvation in hell. Mann's Faust studies in Halle, famous for Pietism. Leverkühn produced a musical work, *Apocalipsis cum figuris*, inspired by Dürer's famous *Holzschnitt-Serie zur Apokalypse*. Dürer serves a number of functions – as the archetypal German artist and nationalist icon and as a good representative of Faustian ambitions. Yet the depiction of the Apocalypse is evidently symbolic of the demonic struggle which Mann wishes to articulate in his novel.

Satan meets Leverkühn while the musician is reading Kierkegaard's account of Mozart's *Don Giovanni* in *Either/Or*.[14] The devil lauds Kierkegaard's insight into the demonic nature of music.[15] Leverkühn's final composition is the atonal *Dr. Fausti Weheklag*. He invites friends to a performance in Munich in which the devil demands his due – and the syphilitic Leverkühn collapses.[16]

Mann depicts 'aestheticism as the forerunner of barbarism in one's own soul'.[17] 'Ästhetizismus als Wegbereiter der Barbarei in eigener Seele.' – 'Genius is a creative form of vitality, which deeply experiences, draws upon, and creates through sickness.'[18] Mann's Doctor Faustus reflects a move from 'decline to Apocalypse'.[19]

Why, one may ask, do the apocalyptic motif and the devil appear so powerfully in European literature three hundred years after Milton? Why does the devil still haunt the Western imagination?

The actuality of the apocalypse

Characters of the great Apocalypses,
the types and Symbols of Eternity.[20]

Mann's *Dr Faustus* draws upon Paul Tillich's experience of the conflict between liberal and conservative theology at the turn of the twentieth century. The former is the tradition of Ritschl, Harnack and Troeltsch; and Martin Kähler (1835–1912) represents the conservative tendency.

14 Ibid., p. 300.
15 Ibid., p. 325.
16 Ibid., pp. 648–63.
17 Ibid., p. 495.
18 'Genie ist eine in der Krankheit tief erfahrene, aus ihr schöpfende und durch sie schöpferische Form der Lebenskraft'. Ibid., p. 472.
19 E. Heftrich, *Vom Verfall zur Apokalypse: Über Thomas Mann* (Frankfurt: Klostermann, 1982).
20 Wordsworth, *The Prelude*, VI, 570–1.

Kähler is the model for Mann's Professor Kumpf. Zeitblom sees the failure of liberal theology as its failure to recognize evil and the demonic, and its confusion of religion with ethics and *Bildung*. Kähler/Kumpf is the product of a disillusionment with a German liberal theology which venerated the humanism and classicism of Goethe and Schiller (often known as *Kulturprotestantismus*) and a return to a more primordial Lutheranism.

Kähler was a theologian in the great Pietistic bulwark of Halle. He wrote a major work, *Der sogenannte historische Jesus und der geschichtliche, biblische Christus* (1892), in which he attacked the 'Jesus of history' of liberal Protestantism. He sees the Bible as the document of the early Church's preaching rather than an object of historical-biographical information concerning Jesus of Nazareth. For Kähler, Christ as presented in Scripture is the object of the theology of the New Testament rather than reconstructions of nineteenth-century rationalism and liberalism.[21] Here he is rejecting the distinction which goes back to David Friedrich Strauss and his work *Das Leben Jesu*, between the Jesus of history and the Christ of the Bible and Christian doctrine. It was quite in keeping with this anti-liberal stance that in Kähler's work *Zur Lehre von der Versöhnung* (1898) he sees the point of the Pauline and Lutheran doctrine of atonement as an objective event; thereby rejecting the subjective theory represented by Ritschl, with its roots via Schleiermacher, in which the death of Christ merely effects a subjective change in the believer. Kähler wanted to renew the objective theory as found in Anselm or Luther.

Gordon Graham makes the point that belief in spiritual powers needs to be distinguished from infantile superstition or magic. He notes that it has been ably demonstrated by Keith Thomas in *Religion and the Decline of Magic* that Christianity suppressed magic in the early modern period. Secondly, it is frequently assumed that spiritual powers (angels or demons) have been banished by science and that scientific naturalism provides a full and adequate explanation of human experience.[22] These two assumptions require scrutiny.

If a contemporary schizophrenic hears voices, we diagnose these as a malfunction. This is one instance of a tendency since the Enlightenment to explain such phenomena in terms of malfunction rather than external forces. But does the widening application of the concept of dysfunction extinguish the idea of possession? Our language still employs ideas of possession. Is this a quaint archaism like the German word for lumbago, *Hexenschuß* – the witch's shot? On the other hand, is the mass murderer an instance of dysfunction? Hitler wrote about his intentions in *Mein Kampf* and then proceeded to execute many of them. Hume observed:

21 See R. Morgan with J. Barton, *Biblical Interpretation* (Oxford: Oxford University Press, 1988), p. 109. It has been pointed out to me that Kähler seems to present a liberal view of the historical Jesus. Even though Kähler's claim about the lack of sources for the life of Jesus looks like anathema to modern Anglophone conservatives, he viewed himself, and was viewed by contempories, as a conservative figure.
22 Graham, *Evil and Christian Ethics*, (Cambridge: Cambridge University Press, 2001), pp. 71–2.

> Where a passion is neither founded on false suppositions, nor chuses
> means insufficient for the end, the understanding can neither justify
> nor condemn it. 'Tis not contrary to reason to prefer the destruction
> of the whole world to the scratching of my finger.[23]

Since Hume denies any external *telos*, like Plato's good, to which a
human being ought to strive, and because he thinks that practical reason
is and should be a slave to the passions, he can only account for the
abnormality but not the inherent wickedness of certain actions.

Feuerbach's claim, that the perfection which human beings attribute
habitually to God is their own projection, is preposterous, and not just
because it seems to presuppose a naïve optimism about human beings.
The naturalism professed by Feuerbach and Strauss (notwithstanding the
veneer of Hegelianism) cannot accommodate the widespread intuition of
evil. Without a prior awareness of goodness, how can we measure any
act as evil rather than abnormal?

The fact of genocide on such a large scale in the twentieth century is
philosophically puzzling for a naturalist. Animals do not commit
genocide, but this is not merely an empirical matter. Even the discovery
of fairly widespread violence among higher apes towards neighbouring
primates is distinct from genocide, as the latter requires greater
intelligence. The slaughter of the Armenians by the Turks at the
beginning of the twentieth century, and the more recent Hutu killings
of Tutsis in Rwanda, and the 'ethnic cleansing' of Bosnians by Milosevic,
were motivated by very human ideologies and carried out with rather
sophisticated technologies. My own view is that these horrors require a
theological explanation. This is not to be confused with the empirical role
of religion. The Serbs and the Hutus were Christian; Hitler, Stalin, Mao
and Pol Pot were militantly anti-religious. By 'theological explanation' I
mean simply that we need some robust account of evil as a supernatural
force which pervades empirical experience, and which Christians have
traditionally referred to as powers and principalities, and of why a
Christian prays, 'deliver us from evil'.

It may be countered that any such appeal to demonic powers is
incompatible with human freedom. Christ is presented in the New
Testament as forgiving sins and removing demons. Graham uses the
analogy of sexual seduction to respond to this challenge: 'Unlike the
rapist and kidnapper, seducers do not override the will of those they
seduce. Rather they work *through* it.'[24]

The propaganda of twentieth-century totalitarian states was a very
sophisticated machinery of seduction in a broader sense. One is
reminded of Milton's serpent ('pleasing was his shape, and lovely'[25]).
The puzzling issue is how intelligent and rational persons can desire
wicked goals. The banishment of the perpetrators of atrocities – multiple
or serial murders or genocide – to Bedlam is just as typical of

---

23 David Hume, *A Treatise of Human Nature*, II.iii.3 (Oxford: Clarendon, 1978), p. 416.
24 Graham, *Evil and Christian Ethics*, p. 144.
25 Milton, *Paradise Lost*, IX, 503–4.

rationalistic, technological societies as the banishment of fairy tales to the nursery. Hence the shock and irritation in discovering humane qualities in perpetrators of evil deeds. The idea that human agents can be, to use Graham's terminology, 'seduced' into wicked agency by an external force saves the appearances. The secular humanist account is much more hard-pressed to explain the evil actions of agents who are not themselves evil, or wicked agents who are not themselves diabolic.

Whiggish histories of thought delineate a move from a Homeric view of human agency being subject to external powers, divine and demonic, which overwhelm and overpower, to more rationalistic conceptions of self. But such sophisticates as Plato or Euripides still adhered to the idea of alien forces which can shape (and rough-hew) human ends. The sombre beauty of tragedy in Western culture from Sophocles to Shakespeare is linked to the acute sense of such pervading malevolent powers as structural evil, irreducible to the responsibilities or specific decisions of particular individuals. The Enlightenment quite correctly objected to the abuse of ideas of the demonic and angelic as superstitious or pseudo-rationalistic. Yet it thereby relinquished one of the central and irreplaceable ideas of the New Testament. Grace requires a concept of bondage to evil, mythologically expressed as Satan and the host of fallen angels, which is stronger than Aristotelian *akrasia*.

Yet by 'explanation' I do mean a quasi-scientific relation of *explanans* and *explanandum*. Evil has by definition a surd quality. It is precisely the unintelligible nature of evil as 'motiveless malignity' and as hatred of goodness that distinguishes it from deplorable selfishness, callousness or greed. Scarcity of resources, conflicts of interests, and limits of sympathy can account for much human malice and cruelty. But such empirical or psychological factors can barely *explain* the more egregious horrors of human behaviour. If I appeal to the use of the traditional language of powers and principalities, it is because this 'saves the appearances' in a manner which the psychological or sociological language fails to. Yet there are two great works of twentieth-century art which present a contrast to the narrative of cumulative disenchantment and the retreat of the artist into his own subjectivity: *Dr Faustus* and Mikhail Bulgakov's *The Master and Margarita*. The devil plays a dominant role in both novels, and these works were composed during the horrors of Stalin and Hitler.

Angelic and demonic combat

But now that we may lift up our eyes (as it were) from the footstool to the throne of God, and leaving these natural, consider a little the state of heavenly and divine creatures: touching Angels[26]

---

26 R. Hooker, *On the Laws of Ecclesiastical Polity*, in *The Works* (Oxford: Oxford University Press, 1841), vol. 1, p. 159.

The Greek word ἄγγελος means 'messenger'. In visions of the Old Testament prophets, angels surround the divine throne. The *locus classicus* is the theophany of Ezekiel's vision: a vehicle and a panoply of beings.[27]

In the Old and New Testament, angels represent both divine transcendence and immanence. They play parts in the economy of salvation: providence, redemption and judgement. Those Christians who openly challenged pagans, such as Origen in *Contra Celsum*, claimed that Christians had access to extra information about the fall of the angels. Augustine in various places, but notably in *The City of God*, argues that the fall of the angels was an important part of theodicy.[28] This argument, however, is open to the objection that this merely involves a regress, and that the fall of the angels still leaves unanswered for a monotheist the question of why and whence evil.

Tillich observes:

> If you want to interpret the concept of angels in a meaningful way today, interpret them as the Platonic essences, as the powers of being, not as special beings. If you interpet them in the latter way, it all becomes crude mythology. On the other hand, if you interpret them as emanations of the divine power of being in essences, in powers of being, the concept of angels becomes meaningful and perhaps important . . . The angels are the spiritual mirrors of the divine abyss . . . the essences in which the divine ground expresses itself first. [29]

Tillich is very plausible on this. Henry More insists that the book of Revelation is not crude 'Carnal Warfare' but a message of the renewal of the 'inner man'.[30] The psychological attraction of angelic entities or intermediaries is very clear. Whether one thinks of the *bodhisattva*s in Buddhism or Protestant martyrs, even the most austere religious systems have a tendency to cling to divine messengers. Logically, however, an *infinite* God can have no need of mediation. This is the common mistake of construing God's transcendence in quasi-spatial terms as remoteness. Eric Osborn describes the typical tendency of thinkers in late antiquity to stockpile redundant intermediaries as the 'bureaucratic fallacy'.[31]

Philosophers in the wake of Proclus are inclined to make the same error. As created, finite spiritual beings, angels are necessary spiritual intermediaries between God and man. But this is linked to an insistence, extreme even by Platonic standards, upon divine remoteness, and equally a tendency in Proclus to produce manifold principles of mediation – to the point of semi-polytheism. One of the main sources of Christian angelology, Pseudo-Dionysius, was closely allied to either

---

27 Ezekiel 1.4–28.
28 See J. Hick, *Evil and the God of Love* (Glasgow: Collins, 1979), pp. 66–70.
29 P. Tillich, *A History of Christian Thought* (London: SCM Press, 1968), pp. 94–5.
30 Henry More, *Apocalypsis Apocalypseos; or, The Revelation of St John the Divine Unveiled* (London: 1680), pp. 127, 52.
31 E. Osborn, *Irenaeus*, p. 69.

Proclus or some cognate form of late Neoplatonism which formed a very uneasy alliance with Christian theology. The brittle nature of this alliance was immediately recognized by Christian theologians, who were also required to give some philosophical account of the beings described as angels in Scripture because of their commitment to a pre-critical view of the texts. It is very difficult to avoid the conclusion that in speaking of angels one is either referring to human projections or divine attributes. If the former, angels do not really exist; if the latter, they are subsumed into God, and certainly are not the bodiless created spirits that mediate between God and man.

Gordon Graham agrees that there cannot be 'logical demonstration' of the existence of such spirits of the kind one finds in Aquinas, nor an empirical argument of the kind that one can find in Henry More.[32] Graham pleads for a supernatural account of evil, and argues that the New Testament language of powers and principalities and of a battle between 'elemental forces of good and evil' has residual power. [33] One might support his observation by invoking the famous image from the *Spiritual Exercises* of Ignatius of Loyola, in which he encourages meditation upon the two banners: that of Christ, the angels and the saints in opposition to the banner of Satan and the demonic powers.[34]

Graham correctly points to the exegetical problems which surround the old-style liberal humanist account of Jesus Christ as a teacher of ethical values. First, it is unclear that there is a distinctively Christian ethics. The precepts taught by Jesus are often presented as part of a tradition: even Christ himself does not appear to be claiming originality for the content of his ethics. Furthermore, within contemporary Christianity one finds Christians taking quite different sides over a number of ethical issues. Graham argues plausibly, and I think correctly, that it is the Christian motivation for morality that is unique, not its content, and the real task is that of 'connecting morality with Jesus as an agent of cosmic history rather than a teacher of precepts'.[35]

In the process of exploring the motivation of Christian morality, Graham turns to the New Testament account and quite rightly notes the fact that theology cannot be separated from history. Graham objects to setting up a priori dichotomies between, for example, natural and supernatural, literal and mythological, or indeed between the historical Jesus and the Christ of faith, and notes that some distinguished recent New Testament commentators such as N. T. Wright merge the categories. In so doing, such writers are following Martin Hengel, who has long argued that historical and dogmatic considerations are intricately interwoven and mutually reinforcing in New Testament scholarship. It could be added that some of the earliest material in the New Testament

---

32 See Henry More, *Antidote against Atheism* (London: 1655), ch. 3.
33 Graham, *Evil*, p. 159.
34 Ignatius of Loyola, *Personal Writings*, tr. J. A. Munitiz and P. Endean (London: Penguin, 1996), pp. 310–15.
35 Graham, *Evil*, p. 73.

employs a high Christology of Christ as a pre-existent divine being, such as the Philippians' hymn of St Paul, probably based on an existing hymn:

[Christ Jesus] was in the form of God,
[but] did not count equality with God a thing to be grasped,
but emptied himself,
taking the form of a slave,
being born in the likeness of man and in human form.
He humbled himself
And became obedient unto death,
even death on the cross.[36]

The Christian community at Philippi was founded in AD 49, and Paul's letter written approximately six or seven years later. Hence, as Hengel argues in his magisterial book *The Son of God*, the 'apotheosis of the crucified Christ' must have occurred within two decades of Christ's death.[37] If that is true, one could say that the effort expended in formulating the ultimate doctrine of Christ's relation to the Father as identity in substance, ὁμοούσιον, and not merely similarity ὁμοιούσιον, was the consequent explication of the New Testament message of God acting in Christ to save mankind.

Much emphasis has been laid in recent scholarship upon the role of the Second Temple in first-century Judaism until its destruction in AD 70. Margaret Barker has persuasively argued that the strong apocalyptic component in the milieu of Jesus had strong royal roots.[38] Hengel argues that the doctrine of atonement can be traced back to the words of Jesus himself.[39] Jesus understood himself as an agent of cosmic history and his claim to be Messiah, for which he was crucified, was part of a broader web of ideas tied to the Temple cult in Jerusalem.

The Temple cult of Jesus' day had a complex relationship to the Temple of David and Solomon, which was destroyed in 587 BC by the Babylonians. The Jewish diaspora began – the major place of exile being Babylon itself. 'In the exile and beyond it, Judaism was born.'[40] The religion of the pre-exilic Israelites was closely linked to a royal cult in Jerusalem, in which the inviolability of the city and the prophetic and priestly role of the monarch was established, as attested by the Psalms in particular. The cataclysm of 587 BC, attested by the great prophets Jeremiah and Ezekiel, destroyed the cult of the First Temple and the elite were deported. The return of the elite from Babylon occurred under the enlightened Persian king Cyrus, who ordered the rebuilding of the Temple in Jerusalem and allowed Jews to return to their native land. The Temple was rebuilt but the throne was not

---

36 Philippians 2.6–8.
37 M. Hengel, *The Son of God: The Origin of Christology and the History of Jewish-Hellenistic Religion* (Philadelphia: Fortress Press, 1976), p. 2. See also C. F. D. Moule, *The Origin of Christology*, (Cambridge: Cambridge University Press, 1977).
38 M. Barker, *The Older Testament: The Survival of Themes from the Ancient Royal Cult in Sectarian Judaism and Early Christianity* (London: SPCK, 1987) and *The Great High Priest: The Temple Roots of Christian Liturgy* (London: T.&T. Clark, 2003).
39 Hengel, *The Atonement*, pp. 65ff.
40 J. Bright, *A History of Israel* (London: SCM Press, 1967), p. 323.

re-established. Under the Persian Empire, a priestly theocracy was established, under which the royal elements of the old cult were either revised or removed. Yet as Barker has powerfully argued, the old hopes associated with the house of David did not die easily, and the religious traditions of Israel were so closely linked to the royal inheritance that post-exilic Judaism constituted a highly strained combination of restoration and radical reform.[41] Many of the motifs and structural elements of the cosmic narrative of Christianity are linked to this inherited conglomerate, but especially to the archaic-royal elements within the tradition, which fitted uneasily within the context of the post-exilic cult. It is striking that in the New Testament passion narrative, Christ's crucifixion is tied to the Temple and royal motifs. He is mocked as the King of the Jews who has come to replace the existing Temple.

Christ's prediction of the destruction of the Second Temple was not the wild jeremiad of a delirious eschatological prophet nor the tragic fate of an innocent victim of intrigue and jealousy, but the conscious enunciation and enactment of a cosmic atonement: God reconciling a world in bondage to demonic powers to himself and thus restoring creation.[42] Aulén famously described this as the 'classic idea' of atonement, Christus Victor:

> the old realistic message of the conflict of God with the dark, hostile forces of evil, and His victory over them by the Divine self-sacrifice; above all we shall hear again the note of triumph.[43]

Nygren set up the alternatives in Western theology as the objectivism of Anselm and the 'subjective' type of view, which he associates with Abelard. He criticizes the objectivism of Anselm as 'discontinuous' (its source is God but is an offering made by Christ to God in order to release us from the guilt of sin). The Christus Victor theory is 'continuous' in the sense that there are no forensic transactions between Father and Son.

Sacrifice

Then was the truth received into my heart,
That under heaviest sorrow earth can bring,
If from the affliction somewhere do not grow
Griefs bitterest of ourselves or of our Kind
Honour which could not else have been, a faith,
An elevation, and a sanctity,
If new strength be not given, nor old restored
The blame is ours, not Nature's.[44]

---

41 Barker, *The Older Testament*, pp. 184–200.
42 'God was in Christ, reconciling the world to himself': 2 Corinthins 5.19.
43 G. Aulén, *Christus Victor: An Historical Study of the Three Main Types of the Idea of Atonement* (London: SCM Press , 1980), p. 159.
44 Wordsworth, *The Prelude*, X, 422–9.

The strength of the classic idea of Christus Victor is that it starts from a phenomenology of sin and a fallen world: widespread poverty, genocide in Rwanda or the Sudan, serial killers. We need an imaginative apprehension of Christ's atoning action which avoids the alternatives of the forensic theory of penal substitution in Calvin and the exemplarist theory of old-style liberalism. The first has the advantage of upholding the cosmic significance of the cross and resurrection, even if expressed in obsolete feudal and juridicial ideas. The second claims that Christ's death is an example of divine love which inspires repentance and renewal. This is spiritually more satisfactory but seems to evacuate the objective events of Christ's passion of particular significance. Though the dramatic theory of Christus Victor avoids the subjectivism of the exemplarist theory, it seems less uplifting than Calvin's penal substitution and hardly more illuminating than exemplarism. The difficulty with Christus Victor is its crassly mythic nature. The sacrificial lamb is offered as a ransom to the demonic powers to pacify them. Are not the cultured despisers of religion thereby justified in seeing Christianity as the product of a credulous and barbarous era, ultimately crude and violent, however seductive its explicit paeans to humanity and love? Iris Murdoch is not unrepresentative in maintaining that the Christian ' "lie" about the conquest of death by Jesus' is 'deeply vulgar'.[45] Richard Dawkins is characteristically pungent:

> Jesus was tortured and executed to atone for sins. Not his own sins (which would be bad enough by the standards of enlightened penal thinking) but other people's sins. By some accounts he was atoning for the sin of Adam – a man who never existed and couldn't sin. By other accounts he was atoning for the sins of all humanity, even though most of us didn't yet exist and might decide not to sin when our time came. Isn't the New Testament doctrine of atonement a truly *nasty* idea, perhaps even nastier in its weird pretensions than the robust, Ayatollah-like cruelties of the Old Testament?[46]

The breezy Gibbonesque wit of Dawkins (who can refute a sneer?) begs the question. If sin means simply weakness of will, then the elaborate Christian machinery of atonement is both otiose and barbaric. Yet it is a crass failure of imagination to ignore the bondage of human beings to sinfulness – a universal and corporate structure of human experience 'who will deliver me from this body of death'[47] – to which Christian Scripture, Greek mythology, the greatest occidental poets and any of the daily newspapers attest.

Christians and Platonists alike have maintained that if God is perfect unity of essence and existence, the created realm is by definition 'fallen'.[48] Even Plotinus tends to personify the diminishing of initial divine

45 Quoted in P. Conradi, *Iris Murdoch: A Life* (London: HarperCollins, 2002), p. 354.
46 R. Dawkins, *Science and Faith* (London: Athenaeum, 2004), p. 9.
47 Romans 7. 24.
48 It has been put to me that many pre-modern Christians have upheld the literal truth of the unfallen state of initial creation. Yet equally many pre-modern Christians held to a biological view of sins as transmitted from Adam. I agree with the liberal tradition that these views are untenable.

perfection: he uses the semi- or quasi-Gnostic concept of τόλμα for the reckless self-assertion or foolhardiness at the root of the finite realm.[49] The Leibnizian law of the indiscernability of identicals means that if the created realm is to be genuinely different, it cannot share the perfection of its source.[50] Furthermore, the metaphysical idea of the self-sacrifice or contraction of the Divine is both pervasive and logically compelling: 'God makes the world make itself'.[51] If created beings make themselves, there is a contraction or diminution of the original divine plenitude, but also the surrender of absolute control. In the ushering of co-workers into the created order, God countenances and embraces rebellion.[52]

For Christians, the sacrifice of the second person of the Trinity, the eternal Logos made flesh, is a death in space and time. But as the death of the God-man it is the mirroring of that sacrifice which preceded the world, both logically and, as it were, temporally. Salvation should not be understood in the crude forensic terms of a propitiatory sacrifice made by man for God but rather vice versa: as part of an eternal and continual self-abnegation or contraction of the Divine. Christ reveals the character of God, and 'Christ liveth' in the believer in the sense that Christ the eternal Logos, as the hidden potential or divine spark in all human beings, becomes actualized in the Christian life.[53] Just as finite individuals can be 'possessed' by demonic forces without losing their rationality or human identity, they can also be 'possessed' by the 'Great Angel'[54] – the Logos who was God and was with God. The lives of the saints – the dedication of a Joan of Arc, a William Wilberforce or a Gandhi, say – is barely explicable psychologically without invoking a sense (deluded or not) of their being vehicles of a higher presence. Joan of Arc is perhaps the most mysterious and puzzling example. A seventeen-year-old girl, a shepherdess from Domrémy, Lorraine, liberating France from the English conquerors, has the air of fairy tale: but she was driven by her voices. And she is still a powerful symbol in France, rivalled perhaps only by Charlemagne and Napoleon. She embodied a spirit of resistance which inspired those around her – and created the fear which led to her trial and execution. The ethics of St Paul in Galatians 5, of 'living by the Spirit',[55] is an apocalyptic vision of human life in the grip of the transforming presence of Christ as opposed to demons. This is hardly the practice of prudence in the Aristotelian city-state, but the possession and renewal of the soul in Christ.

49 See A. H. Armstrong's characteristically lucid and judicious discussion in 'Plotinus', in A. H. Armstrong (ed.), *The Cambridge History of Later Greek and Early Medieval Philosophy* (Cambridge: Cambridge University Press, 1967), pp. 242ff.

50 J. Cottingham, *The Spiritual Dimension* (Cambridge: Cambridge University Press, 2004), pp. 27ff.

51 A. Farrer, *A Science of God?* (London: Geoffrey Bles, 1966), p. 90.

52 S. R. L. Clark, *The Mysteries of Religion: An Introduction to Philosophy through Religion* (Oxford: Blackwell, 1986), pp. 162–79.

53 My debt to Coleridge and F. D. Maurice is obvious. See especially F. D. Maurice, *The Doctrine of Sacrifice Deduced from the Scriptures* (London: Macmillan, 1854).

54 The phrase is from M. Barker, *The Great Angel: A Study of Israel's Second God* (London: SPCK, 1992).

55 Galatians 5.16ff.

L'homme moyen sensuel can be swept up by the inspired activities of individuals. Thanks to Wilberforce, no one defends the institution of slavery in the modern world, but it is easy to forget the radicalism of his innovation in his day. An essential element of the Christian-apocalyptic narrative is the overcoming and transformation of evil. Holiness is not purity in the sense of ritual *separation* from the cause of defilement or pollution. Christ is an object of derision – the lamb is the scapegoat, crucified alongside the corrupt and the wicked. And yet in the midst of evil, evil is overcome. Hence the justifiable dissatisfaction of Christian theologians throughout the centuries with merely *quantitative* justifications of the existence of evil, whether as a means to a higher end or mere shades of a broader and as yet invisible whole. The truly Christian vision of God's action in the world is not a static appreciation of goods relative to evils but the vision of the metamorphosis of evil through the conquest of Satan by Christ.[56] The image of the chariot makes it clear that it is God who saves mankind rather than the immanent powers of the soul, and that God is evident in history. Henry More discusses 'Ezekiel's Vision of the Four Cherubims or Chariot of God' in his *Divine Dialogues* (1679). The vision is interpreted Christologically – the vehicle is a symbol of 'the peremptory and irresistible progress of Divine Providence administered by [God's] Angelicall forces', depicting the 'Angelicall Orders in Heaven' and the Church driving towards the triumphant realization of it purpose, while the *'heavenly Humanity'* of Christ is enthroned inside the chariot.[57] The chariot represents both the battle and Christus Victor. Milton, that great Christian humanist and enthusiast for theology, gives a remarkable account of such a divine chariot in *Paradise Lost*:

> Forth rushed with whirl-wind sound
> The chariot of Paternal Deitie,
> Flashing thick flames, Wheele within Wheele undrawn,
> Itself instinct with Spirit, but convoy'd
> By four Cherubic shapes, Four faces each
> Had wondrous; as with Starrs thir bodies all
> And wings were set with Eyes, with Eyes the Wheele
> Of Beril, and careering Fires between;
> Over thir heads a chrystal Firmament,
> Whereupon a Saphir Throne, inlaid with pure
> Amber, and colours of the showrie Arch.
> Hee in Celestial panaplie all arm'd
> Of radiant Urim, work divinely wrought,
> Ascended, at his right hand Victorie
> Sate Eagle-winged, beside him hung his Bow
> And Quiver with thre-bolted Thunder stor'd,
> And from about him fierce Effusion rowl'd
> Of smoak and bickering flame, and sparkles dire.[58]

56 Graham, *Evil and Christian Ethics*, pp. 98ff., 165ff.
57 See Henry More, *Divine Dialogues*, comp. F. P. (London, 1668), pp. 284, 282, 296–7.
58 Milton, *Paradise Lost*, VI, 749–66.

This chariot, in one of the decisive moments in the poem, subdues the rebellious angels at the climax of the war in heaven. Some scholars have viewed the chariot as the 'principal image' of the epic.[59] The great cosmic chariot is triumphant and corresponds to, and guarantees, the inner victory of indwelling Logos within the human soul.[60]

Inspired images and *The Glass of Vision*

Austin Farrer argued in *The Glass of Vision* that poetic *imagination* is a key to the nature of scriptural *inspiration*. He maintained that scriptural revelation is effected through images rather than word, and that these images are inextricably linked to the history of Israel, Jesus and the Apostles. The images are the 'stuff of revelation' and they must be interpreted according to their own laws.[61] He held that the imagination of the Evangelists was the space of divine revelation:

> The lectures which follow are no more than a modest attempt to state what I do, in fact, think about the relation borne to one another by three things – the sense of metaphysical philosophy, the sense of scriptural revelation, and the sense of poetry . . . These three things rubbing against one another in my mind, seem to kindle one another, and so I am moved to ask how this happens.[62]

Farrer is a surprisingly elusive writer. Behind the limpid beauty and sheer vigour of his prose, we need to reconstruct the wider theological and philosophical context of his argument in relation to the question of faith and history. At one level Farrer seems to be presenting a theory about the authority of the Bible in an age when verbal inerrancy is untenable. More broadly, he seems to be claiming that God cannot be known directly but only through the mediation of images and parables: 'Faith discerns not the images, but what the images signify: and yet we cannot discern it except *through* the images.'[63] Since these images are taken from finite experience and refer to a transcendent object, we cannot check their accuracy. We cannot point away from the image to that which the image signifies. The images must be seen to possess an irreducible and definitive authority. Theology tests and determines the sense of the images, it does not create it. The images, of themselves, signify and

---

59 See Alastair Fowler's textual notes on these lines, in *The Poems of John Milton*, ed. J. Carey and A. Fowler (London: Longman, 1968), p. 763.

60 J. H. Adamson, 'The War in Heaven: The Merkabah', in W. B. Hunter, C. A. Patrides and J. H. Adamson, *Bright Essence: Studies in Milton's Theology* (Salt Lake City: University of Utah Press, 1973), pp. 103–14, and M. Lieb, 'Encoding the Occult: Milton and the Traditions of the Merkabah Speculation in the Renaissance', *Milton Studies*, 37 (1999), pp. 42–88.

61 A. Farrer, *The Glass of Vision* (London: Dacre Press, 1948), p. 51.

62 Ibid., p. ix. For an excellent account, see I. Dalferth, 'The Stuff of Revelation: Austin Farrer's Doctrine of Inspired Images', in A. Loades and M. McLain (eds), *Hermeneutics, the Bible and Literary Criticism* (London: Macmillan, 1996), pp. 71–95.

63 Ibid., p. 110.

reveal[64] – or as Farrer says in another passage, 'supernatural mysteries [speak] through living images'.[65] Farrer wishes to avoid the alternatives of the old theory of verbal inspiration and the more common modern theory that revelation is constituted by events witnessed and expressed in fallible documents: 'It does not seem as though the theory of revelation by divine events alone is any more satisfactory than the theory of dictated propositions.'[66]

Farrer claims that we have to understand the manner in which word and deed cohere together. Jesus used the language of the old royal cult and the Temple, and of the Suffering Servant, expressing these words and symbols in events like throwing out the money-lenders from the Temple, riding into Jerusalem, and the crucifixion and resurrection. But it was not just that Christ understood himself as a cosmic agent in a battle against evil: this was also how the Apostles understood Christ's life. For Farrer, revelation is constituted by the coincidence of Christ's understanding of his role and the inspired apostolic vision of his role and of the Spirit working in the Church: 'The choice, use and combination of images made by Christ and the Spirit must be simply a supernatural work.'[67]

This theory was attacked by H. D. Lewis in *Our Experience of God* and by Helen Gardner in *The Limits of Literary Criticism*. These attacks concentrated upon three major problems.

Lewis presents the first two:

1. In shifting the burden from words to images in presenting a theory of inspired images, Farrer has simply transferred the problem to a different domain: 'I do not know how far this is, at basis, a subtly disguised form of the appeal to the authority of the Bible as ultimate in itself.'[68] How can Farrer distinguish the normative biblical images from other images? Lewis thinks it is wiser to see divine action 'more directly in the very substance of living' than in images.[69]

2. Farrer's account of the process of inspiration itself is inadequate. How does prophecy relate to poetry? Farrer appeals to the 'supernaturalizing of events in the existing world' and claims that prophecy is both like and unlike poetry. Lewis holds that the division is unsustainable.[70]

Helen Gardner presents the third problem:

3. Farrer's apparent aversion to the historical and literal. Is Farrer simply another case of the theologian taking refuge in the mists of the figurative – to the annoyance of his more literal-minded colleagues, such as philosophers, historians and literary critics?

---

64 Ibid., p. 44.
65 Ibid., p. 56.
66 Ibid., p. 38.
67 Ibid., p. 109.
68 H. D. Lewis, *Our Experience of God* (London: Collins, 1959), p. 135.
69 Ibid., p. 138.
70 Ibid., pp. 209ff.

I cannot feel satisfied with a literary criticism which substitutes for the conception of the writer as 'a man speaking to men' the conception of the writer as an imagination weaving symbolic patterns to be teased out by the intellect, and in its concentration on the work by itself ends by finding significance in what the work suggests rather than in what it says, and directs our imaginations towards types and figures rather than towards their actualisation. As literary criticism I cannot regard the new symbolical or typological approach to the Gospels as satisfactory. It does not explain a prime historic fact; that for centuries Christian emotion directed towards the historic person of Jesus Christ, true God and true Man, has found in the Gospels the strength of its own conviction that 'Christ walked on this earth'.[71]

Gardner maintains that it is 'odd' to speak of St Mark's imagination being 'controlled' by the facts. If the faithful think they are facts, then it must be an instance of being 'filled by the wonder of those facts, and not merely respectful to them'.[72] Farrer, in his essay 'Inspiration: Poetical and Divine', claims to view his own theory as 'demolished'.[73] However, this essay is a reformulation of the position in *The Glass of Vision*. There is a sense in which Farrer's insouciance is justified. Neither Lewis nor Gardner hit their target.

Farrer is indebted to Romanticism, and has been criticized for allegedly being infected by it. The Romantic contagion amounts to both the view that imagination is more important than reason, and the view that art is a substitute for religion. I wish to claim that Farrer is a genuine inheritor of a certain Romantic legacy, indeed more so than he cares to admit, but it would be quite mistaken to assume that he is guilty of either of these charges. On the first point, we can reflect upon Henri Corbin's distinction between the 'imaginary' and the 'imaginal'. He coined this distinction to mark the difference between the secular either/ or of fact or fantasy and the older Platonic sense of the imaginal as a both-and state of perception of the noetic through the images of the physical cosmos.[74] Farrer is giving an account of how God *acts* through the imagination of the Gospel writers. There is a rebirth of images drawn from the Hebrew Temple and royal cult in the self-description of Jesus Christ and in the apostolic interpretation of Christ's life. To speak of inspired images is to invoke the activity of the incarnate eternal Logos and the Holy Spirit as bodying forth the same God in history. This is the context of Farrer's claim that the images interpreted the events of Christ's ministry, death and resurrection, and that the interplay of image and event constitutes revelation:

71 H. Gardner, *The Limits of Literary Criticism: Reflections on the Interpretation of Poetry and Scripture* (Oxford: Oxford University Press, 1956), p. 39.
72 Ibid., pp. 36–7.
73 A. Farrer, 'Inspiration: Poetical and Divine', in *Interpretation and Belief* (London: SPCK, 1976), pp. 39–53.
74 See H. Corbin, *Mundus Imaginalis: or, The Imaginary and the Imaginal*, tr. R. Horine (Ipswich: Golgonooza Press, 1976).

The events by themselves are not revelation for they do not by themselves reveal the divine work which is accomplished in them: the martyrdom of a virtuous Rabbi and his miraculous return are not of themselves the redemption of the world.[75]

Or as he says: 'the events without the images would be no revelation at all, and the images without the events would remain shadows on the clouds.'[76]

His concern is with supernatural action in the mind – specifically how God 'bestows an apprehension of divine mysteries, inaccessible to natural reason, reflection, intuition or wit'.[77] Yet he wishes to avoid any crass opposition of natural and supernatural. The act of supernatural faith appears to be only a 'fresh elevation of the faith' we place in other non-material objects; for example, the ethical, or sympathy with other human beings. The 'mysteries of faith' must cohere with 'one universe of sense' and with what we know of human beings, history, nature and being:[78]

Neither prophets nor apostles are inspired to devise simply new master images. That is an impossibility. It is only through images already implanted that revelation grows. But the images in growing, are transformed, they throw out fresh branches, they fertilize neighbouring and as yet purely natural imaginations.[79]

Poetry and the economy of revelation

The Epistles find their inspiration in the images, but they express them only in so far as serves the purpose of instruction or exhortation. But the Apocalypse writes of heaven and things to come, that is, of a realm which has no shape at all but that which the images give it.[80]

In the Apocalypse, St John sees the slain Lamb at the centre of the heavenly drama. This is clearly poetic imagery. Farrer insists that Scripture must be understood theologically: 'The images are supernaturally formed, and supernaturally made intelligible to faith'.[81] Farrer wishes to explain how these images can convey truth. The problem with the status of Scripture is that whereas in the age of verbal inspiration men nourished their soul on the Bible, now Higher Criticism has disclosed the

75 Farrer, *The Glass of Vision*, p. 43.
76 Ibid.
77 Ibid., p. 35.
78 Ibid., p. 33.
79 Ibid., p. 136.
80 A. Farrer, *A Rebirth of Images: The making of St John's Apocalypse* (London: Dacre Press, 1949), p. 17.
81 Farrer, *The Glass of Vision*, p. 110.

differing finite, fallible and even conflicting perspectives within the canon. How can God reveal himself in such an apparently flawed medium? Farrer observes that the liberal Enlightenment claims to have opened the spiritual casket, but there appears nothing inside. The Scylla and Charybdis of revelation as inerrant propositions or the response of human witnesses to divine events amounts to having no theory of inspiration at all, since in this case there is only a difference in degree between the Apostles and St Francis or John Wesley. It is clear that Farrer wants a theory of inspiration, but he does not want to be committed to the absurdity of the old theory – not because it is impossible or unscientific but because it is unworthy of God to be an extrinsic manipulator. The mechanical model of divine dictation does not cohere with a properly spiritual conception of deity – more precisely, the aim of the prophets and the Gospels to purify and to spiritualize our conception of God. Farrer examines the process in the inspired mind by which the images operate. He employs the analogy of poetry. Poetry rests on some fairly basic facts; language consists of many repetitive sounds which can be arranged in a musical mode, and we need to employ the imagination in understanding the work of another mind. These two, as it were, primitive facts of music and imaginative insight generate the 'joint possibility' of 'making the musical game the expression of the imaginative game'.[82] When the poet is producing poetry he is setting 'images in motion by rhythmical incantation, and then appreciating a certain way in which they "ought" to develop and express themselves. It is this "ought" which is the heart of the riddle'.[83]

Farrer wants to make a claim about literature. It is rather peculiar that Gardner should regard Farrer as an expression of an avant-garde in literature. Literature is not the expression of taste or ornament. Farrer's friend C. S. Lewis was fond of the anecdote of Coleridge concerning the waterfall described by tourists variously as sublime and pretty.[84] It is the first judgement which is correct. Here we can find an analogy to what Farrer describes as the poetic 'ought'. It is not just a fanciful way of construing aesthetic sensibility. There is a

> quality of human existence clamouring for expression and, as it were, pressing upon his mind and directing the manipulation of the poetical symbols. The poet's imagination is responsive to the possibilities of destiny in general as well as to the particular possibility of destiny realized in Hamlet: that is why he sees that he ought to make Hamlet speak as he does and not otherwise. Let us say, then, that the post-renaissance poet is responsive to qualities or patterns of human existence.[85]

This is the classic humanistic position. We still learn about reality from Shakespeare even after Marx, Nietzsche, Freud and Foucault. Our

---

82 Ibid., p. 115.
83 Ibid., p. 121.
84 C. S. Lewis, *The Abolition of Man* (London: HarperCollins, 1978), pp. 7ff.
85 Farrer, *The Glass of Vision*, p. 122.

common humanity comes to expression in the great poets, and this overrides any differences of race, gender or other contingent factors. Literature is a body of knowledge, not just entertainment. It is capable of being right or wrong. The post-Renaissance poet experienced in the *'ought* of his craft the pressure of life – what it is to be a man'.[86]

The fusing power of the poetic vision is in Farrer's mind when he draws analogies between poetical and prophetic inspiration. He states: 'this strange human passion for never saying what one means but always something else finds its most extreme and absolute development in the poets'.[87] What is the point of such bizarre convolution as 'The curfew tolls the knell of the parting day'? Why the use of metaphor? Is it mere drollery or relish of ingenuity? Sounding rather like John Ruskin, Farrer insists: 'The best figurative poetry speaks not to the frivolous intellect, but (if anything does) straight to the heart; and it does so better than plain prose. There seems then to be something which is better said with metaphor than without, which goes straighter to the mark by going crooked, and hits its aim exactly by flying at tangents. An odd fact, if true.'[88] Poetry, therefore, is not misrepresentation (as Bentham or Hume would insist), nor even ornament. It is *descriptive*. Farrer wants to attack two errors. One is that metaphor is the language of emotion. He makes the point that one can stir emotions often more effectively with literal language: 'A bull is charging you from behind' is more effective than talk of 'The playfellow of Europa'.[89] Farrer distinguishes between two senses given to the words 'subjective' and 'feeling'.[90] Poetry does express 'something subjective' and 'what is felt about things'. However, Farrer thinks it quite illegitimate to infer that poetry *only* tells us about the poet's emotions. He uses an analogy from the provincial (poorly lit) aquarium and the murky phenomena behind the glass with two observers: the philosopher (I think he means what we would usually call a 'scientist') and the poet. The first tries to distinguish the genuine fish from the distorting impact of the factors of light, glass, etc. The poet tries to describe the whole effect of the phenomenon of the fish in the tank in figurative language as a sea monster. The work of the poet is *descriptive*; but his domain of description is broader than that of the philosopher: 'the poet undoubtedly describes things just as he feels them, he does not describe what he feels *about* the things'.[91]

As we saw in Chapter 2, Coleridge proposes in the famous chapter 13 of his *Biographia Literaria*, 'On the Imagination', that the imagination is a *tertium aliquid* or 'an inter-penetration of the counteracting powers, partaking of both'– i.e. a middle point between subjective and objective.[92] Ultimately, Coleridge is trying to capture, I think, a similar insight about

86 Ibid., p. 125.
87 Farrer, *Reflective Faith* (London: SPCK, 1972), p. 24.
88 Ibid., p. 25.
89 Ibid., p. 26.
90 Ibid., p. 27.
91 Ibid., p. 29.
92 Coleridge, *Biographia Literaria*, vol. 1, p. 300. Coleridge is rather elliptical in this passage, but this is how I interpret him.

the nature of a poem as descriptive. Farrer distinguishes between the task of analysis and description. The scientist wishes to analyse the constituent elements of reality. The poet wishes to describe, 'to know *what it is like*'. If a lover wants to describe his beloved, no scientific analysis of her skin will do; 'You will have to compare her skin to flowers'.[93] Does the emotion blind or open the eyes of the lover? Farrer argues that it is reasonable to assume the latter. Perhaps the violence of passion can 'break down the dull custom of incomprehension, the blindness of the eyes and the hardness of heart';[94] 'It would be a strange fact if being passionately interested in something were always a bar to appreciating it truly.'[95] This is a point which Burke and the Romantics (including Newman) made against the quasi-objectivity of 'sophisters, economists and calculators': knowledge is much more likely to be obtained if the mind is really committed to and passionate about truth.[96] But this must mean a greater role for the emotions and imagination in the formation of belief than classical empiricism can concede. Farrer writes,

> In poetic vision, then, and in amatory passion we are convinced that the object of our contemplation has a vividness of being, a distinctness of incommunicable individuality which scientific analysis would in vain hope to express – we are driven into metaphor. Science considers things in so far as they are the same; poetry, in so far as each is irreducibly itself. But what can we say about that which is truly unique?[97]

'What is it like?' means 'What other thing does it resemble?' This is a question of analogies:

> All the unique creatures God has made resemble one another, at greater or less distance; for all reflect in diverse manner and degree their one creator, and imitate his existence, as far as their lowliness allows, by being each themselves. But if they have a family resemblance, they have an unlikeness too.[98]

Furthermore, Farrer insists 'it is only by comparison and contrast with other things that we become aware of their individualities, and find out, as the saying is, what they are like'.[99]

Basil Mitchell has a telling argument against any exhaustive and exclusive dichotomy between the literal and the metaphorical. Drawing on Berkeley's distinction between metaphorical and proper analogy, he argues that it is perfectly reasonable to apply concepts such as knowledge, faithfulness or love as attributes of the Deity. This can be done in a manner which vastly exceeds our experience of these

---

93 Farrer, *Reflective Faith*, p. 30.
94 Ibid., p. 31.
95 Ibid., p. 30.
96 Edmund Burke, *Reflections on the French Revolution* (London: Dent, 1955), p. 73.
97 Farrer, *Reflective Faith*, p. 31.
98 Ibid., p. 32.
99 Ibid. Cf. Shakespeare: 'Love looks not with the eyes but with the mind; / And therefore is winged Cupid painted blind': *A Midsummer Night's Dream*, I.i.234–5.

properties, while avoiding relegating these terms to mere metaphor. Stretched these concepts may be, but they express *literal* truths about God. Through a 'controlled exercise of imagination' by the use of proper analogy, we can develop a 'framework of theistic theory'.[100] Within such a context Farrer's claim that 'divine truth is supernaturally communicated to men in an act of inspired thinking which falls into the shape of certain images' does not itself have to be regarded as a metaphor that we are at a loss to interpret; for the language of 'speaking' or 'communicating' in this context is an instance of 'proper' rather than 'metaphorical' analogy. There is good metaphysical precedent for this in one of the greatest poets. When Dante speaks of love moving the sun and the other stars, it would make a nonsense of his *Commedia* if it were just a metaphor.

I. A. Richards and the Cambridge school envisaged the criticism of literature as breaking down inherited values and sentimentalism. It is also the period of much positivistic attack on metaphysics. When Farrer distinguishes between mysteries, puzzles and problems, he is engaged in a defence of metaphysics as a genuine field of knowledge, even though conceding that the old idea of metaphysics as a deductive science is quite untenable. He writes:

> Free existential description is really prior to metaphysical system, it is the soil out of which it grows: and it is for the health of systematic metaphysics that there should always be minds in revolt against what they esteem its sterile dogmatism[101]

But he does not think that metaphysics can be dispensed with. He thinks we have to distinguish the central problems of metaphysics – free will, the relation of the subject to the body, etc. – as unlike scientific questions because natural science deals with specific problems relating to the specific questions and instruments of the enquiry. The results are real but 'highly abstract or selective'.[102] On the other hand, philosophical puzzles depend upon the prior philosophical assumptions of any particular position. The relation of the active and the receptive intellect is a 'puzzle' for Aristotelians but not for behaviourists or Berkelians. God is a genuine mystery like free will or the nature of the self because God is not open to scientific procedure, but nor is that mystery simply to be disposed of as a 'factitious puzzle'.[103] Farrer sees the work of metaphysics as the sober criticism of images which we can naturally employ to describe reality:

> The so-called problems of metaphysics are difficulties of description: that does not make them either unimportant, or easy to manage. On the contrary, they may be quite agonizing; nor are any questions of greater importance to a mind which desires to understand the

100 B. Mitchell, 'The Place of Symbols in Christanity', in *How to Play Theological Ping-Pong, and Other Essays on Faith and Reason* (London: Hodder and Stoughton, 1990), p. 193.
101 Farrer, *The Glass of Vision*, p. 73.
102 Ibid., p. 65.
103 Ibid., p. 81.

nature of its real world. There is no finality about the descriptions offered by metaphysics for the mysteries of existence, but there is an advance in apprehension of the mysteries by the refining of the descriptions.[104]

We can see that this account of both the real nature of metaphysical problems and their conceptual elusiveness is relevant to his robustly realist views about literature. The great post-Renaissance poets are not criticizing our images of reality like the metaphysician, but they too are 'constrained' by the exterior pressure of reality, and while expressing their imaginative visions are able to refine and enrich our beliefs and aspirations.

There are two remarks I would like to make here. The first is that it is odd that Farrer's clear admiration for Aristotle should be allied to a certain scepticism towards the conceptual. The knowledge which literature and metaphysics can deliver is not to be confused with definitive articulation. This knowledge is, in a sense, experiential. It also means that I remain puzzled by H. D. Lewis's criticism that God works through 'the very substance of living' rather than 'given images'.[105] Lewis asserts firmly that 'images must . . . be anchored in experience and never allowed to take wing very far on their own'.[106] I think it is clear from Farrer's excursion into the nature of metaphysical reasoning that he is concerned to do justice to the experiential component in metaphysics, which eludes exhaustive definition. He uses the Platonic language of participation:

> Yet in our degree we all participate in supernatural act, for we do not receive revealed truth as simply a tale told about God in the third person by others; we apprehend it as assured to us by God himself, or to put it otherwise, the description of divine mysteries ceases to be experienced by us as mere description: in the lines laid down by the description, the mysteries shine with their own light and presence; or rather, with the light and presence of God.[107]

This is very close to the passage where he describes the liberating effect of Spinoza, which helped him to think of the Divine not as an alien 'other', but rather as the 'underlying cause of my thinking', so that there might be a perception of the 'divine cause shining through the created effect'.[108]

Poetry, Farrer observes, is a technique of divination. It is *in* the poetic process that the prophet receives his message:

> Whatever signs or omens set the incantation of shapely words moving in the prophet's mind, it went on moving and forming itself with a felt inevitability, like that of a rhapsodical poetry which

---

104 Ibid., pp. 63–4.
105 Lewis, *Our Experience of God*, p. 138.
106 Ibid., p. 139.
107 Farrer, *The Glass of Vision*, pp. 31–2.
108 Ibid., p. 8.

allows for no second thoughts: it formed itself under a pressure or control which the prophet experienced as no self-chosen direction of his own thinking, but as the constraint of a divine will.[109]

Here we can see a clear instance of Farrer's theory of double agency. The emphasis is upon the organic and vital nature of the process. The great images are 'alive and moving',[110] 'vital images';[111] and these 'images are the stuff of revelation'.[112]

However,

If we surrender metaphysical enquiry, we shall vainly invoke supernatural revelation to make up for our metaphysical loss of nerve. For if our cravenheartedness surrenders the ground of metaphysics, it will have surrendered the bridgehead which the supernatural liberator might land upon. Get a man to see the mysterious depth and seriousness of the act by which he and his neighbour exist, and he will have his eyes turned upon the bush in which the supernatural fire appears, and presently he will be prostrating himself with Moses, before him who thus names himself 'I am that I am'.[113]

The move here to Exodus 3.14 is very important. It was this passage, partly as a result of a strange translation of the Hebrew, that became read as God's own identifying himself with ultimate being. Here we come back to the 'Barthian captivity' of a theology that refuses to mediate between revealed and natural truth. The organic model of revelation through the medium of the imagination is linked, however paradoxical this may seem, to Farrer's passionate defence of metaphysics. Although God is 'absolutely unique', we expect, he claims, religious mysteries

to bear some analogy with natural realities because they are revealed in the stuff of our human experience. So it seems that God's encounter with us must be a sort of encounter analogous to our encounters with men; and that the parables or symbols through which God teaches us to imagine his action must be some sort of symbols parallel, perhaps, to the symbols of valid poetry'.[114]

The point is really about divine agency rather than religious language. Farrer is not trying to translate talk of divine action into the merely figurative expression of a sense of deity, but to give an account of the status of talk about divine action.

Farrer is comparing the post-Renaissance poet with Jeremiah. Jeremiah is a poet who 'sets images moving by musical incantation' and allows them to arrange and express themselves as they 'ought'. But what is the 'ought' that constrains Jeremiah? The 'ought' which constrains

109 Ibid., pp. 128–9.
110 Ibid., p. 146
111 Ibid., p. 126.
112 Ibid., p. 51.
113 Ibid., p. 78.
114 Farrer, *Interpretation and Belief*, p. 45.

Shakespeare is not a metaphor. Farrer thinks there are certain facts about human nature which great poetry is responsive to. Similarly Jeremiah is constrained by the impact of the will of God upon his mind. He is 'not responding to the quality of human life, he is responding to the demands of eternal will on Israel as they make themselves heard in the determinate situation where he stands'.[115]

The difference between these two controlling pressures is egregious.[116] The scope of prophecy is much narrower than poetry because of the 'elastic possibilities of human nature', and the determinate nature of the divine will. The poet is a maker, the prophet is a mouthpiece.[117] But there is control in both cases. In the case of prophecy, imagination mediates between the intelligible and the sensible. Islamic philosophers speak of imagination as an isthmus or meeting point of the noetic and empirical. Henri Corbin remarks upon the significance of mirror imagery. The substance of the mirror is distinct from the mirror image. He writes: 'Active imagination is the mirror par excellence, the epiphanic places for images of the archetypal world'.[118] It is no accident that Farrer's title is *The Glass of Vision*. The prophet's imagination is the meeting place of the noetic and the sensible. It is expressed in both the language and symbols of first-century Palestine and the vision of a transcendent reality. The belief in the unchanging *reality* of a world beyond space and time, which can only be pictured inadequately through likenesses, is the prerequisite of such a distinction between the prophetic and the poetic. Heaven and hell are not geographical locations and yet apocalypse – the revelation of divine mysteries – requires and cannot avoid symbolic expression. As Coleridge observes: 'An IDEA, in the *highest* sense of that word, cannot be conveyed but by a *symbol*.'[119] Henry More argued that John composed his revelation while his mind was 'vacant from this earthly body, and external senses, and wholly seised by this Divine and Angelical Power, which caused in it the following Visions, and Prophetical Impressions, but as lively and clear as any objects to the outward or corporeal senses'.[120]

The privileging of the prophet as the seer of divine mysteries and as possessing poetic gifts is a Romantic contribution which goes back to Robert Lowth's *De sacra poesi Hebraeorum* (1753), which influenced both Herder and the great Göttingen scholar Johann David Michaelis.[121] Lowth was Professor of Poetry at Oxford, and subsequently Bishop of Oxford and then London. He noted that the prophets of ancient Israel were employing poetic techniques in order to express prophecy, against Augustan wits who sneered at the stylistic infelicity of Scripture compared with Graeco-Roman literature. Lowth extols the simplicity

115 Farrer, *The Glass of Vision*, pp. 126–7.
116 Ibid., p. 126.
117 Ibid., p. 129.
118 Corbin, *Mundus Imaginalis*, p. 9.
119 Coleridge, *Biographia Literaria*, vol. 1, p. 156.
120 More, *Apocalypsis Apocalypseos*, p. 5.
121 See S. Prickett, *Words and the Word: Language, Poetics and Biblical Interpretation* (Cambridge: Cambridge University Press, 1989).

and sublimity of the *poetry* of the Hebrew prophets. Hebrew poetry is characterized by its parallelism – the 'Correspondence of one verse, or line, with another'.[122] The word 'Nabi' meant in Hebrew both 'prophet' and 'poet'. As Lowth observes:

> From all these testimonies it is sufficiently evident, that the prophetic office had a most strict connection with the poetic art. They had one common name, one common origin, one common author, the Holy Spirit. Those in particular were called to the exercise of the prophetic office, who were previously conversant with the sacred poetry. It was equally a part of their duty to compose verses for the service of the Church, and to declare the oracles of God.[123]

Lowth also emphasized the importance of an exegetical imagination – of seeing things through the eyes of the Hebrews: 'We must endeavour as much as possible to read Hebrew as the Hebrews would have read it.'[124] This stress upon *eorum oculis* was seminal for the future development of German higher criticism. Thirdly, Lowth argued that the Semitic context is important. The poetry of the Hebrews is essentially oriental. This latter stress upon the oriental inspired both Herder and Goethe, culminating in the latter's masterpiece *West-östlicher Divan* and Herder's work *Vom Geist der Hebraischen Poesie* (1782). Lowth, however, unintentionally opened up the path to the appreciation of forms of literature and life which did not conform to French neo-classicism.[125]

Narrative and images

Farrer produces an answer to two questions: the issue of inspiration after the demolition of verbal inerrancy and the issue of the relation of historical to eternal divine truth, otherwise known as Lessing's ditch. The first target is clear, but the second is much less so. Farrer is trying to answer Lessing on both fronts: scriptural inspiration and divine action. In other words, there is both the vertical and horizontal perspective: how the particular prophet or the apostle can be thought of as a 'mouthpiece' of the divine and how the historical process of revelation can be conceived of as a genuine divine economy without recourse to crude anthropomorphisms or the notion of revelation as an inexplicable rupture.

Farrer gives us an interesting piece of theological biography:

> I had myself . . . been reared in a personalism which might satisfy the most ardent of Dr Buber's disciples. I thought of myself as set over against deity as one man faces another across a table, except

---

122 Robert Lowth, *Lectures on the Sacred Poetry of the Hebrews*, tr. G. Gregory (London: J. Johnson, 1787), vol. 2, p. 12.
123 Ibid., vol. 2, p. 18.
124 Ibid., vol. 2, p. 114.
125 See John Barton's remarks in Morgan, *Biblical Interpretation*, pp. 207ff.

that God was invisible and indefinitely great. And I hoped that he would signify his presence to me by way of colloquy; but neither out of the scripture I read nor in the prayers I tried to make did any mental voice address me. I believe at that time anything would have satisfied me, but nothing came: no 'other' stood beside me, no shadow of presence fell upon me. I owe my liberation from this *impasse*, as far as I can remember, to reading Spinoza's Ethics. Those phrases which now strike me as so flat and sinister, so ultimately atheistic, *Deus sive Natura* (God, or call it Nature), *Deus, quatenus consideratur ut constituens essentiam humanae mentis* (God, in so far as he is regarded as constituting the being of the human mind) – these phrases were to me light and liberation, not because I was or desired to be a pantheist, but because I could not find the wished-for colloquy with God.

Undoubtedly I misunderstood Spinoza, in somewhat the same fashion as . . . St. Augustine misunderstood Plotinus, turning him to Christian uses. Here, anyhow is what I took from Spinozism. I would no longer attempt, with the psalmist, 'to set God before my face'. I would see him as the underlying cause of my thinking, especially of those thoughts in which I tried to think of him. I would dare to hope that sometimes my thought would become diaphanous, so that there should be some perception of the divine cause shining through the created effect, as a deep pool, settling into a clear tranquillity, permits us to see the spring in the bottom of it from which its waters rise. I would dare to hope that through a second cause the First Cause might be felt, when the second cause in question was itself a spirit, made in the image of the divine Spirit, and perpetually welling up out of his creative act.[126]

This passage gives us an important insight into Farrer. Written in 1948, its context is an attack on the personalism in the philosophy and theology of Martin Buber and Karl Barth: 'When Germans set their eyeballs and pronounce the terrific words "He speaks to thee" (Er redet dich [sic] an) . . . they are not speaking to my condition.'[127] Farrer is placing himself within the Platonic-Aristotelian tradition of which St Thomas is a good example, a tradition allied to the God of the philosophers as well as the God of Abraham, Isaac and Jacob. This also explains why Farrer is at pains to insist upon the hierarchy of the mind: mankind is defined by the 'luminous apex of the mind', not the 'shadowy base'.[128] *Pace* David Brown in his excellent article on Farrer, 'God and Symbolic Action',[129] I do not think we can say that Farrer is hostile to the creative role of the unconscious or subconscious realm. Farrer is making a point about his anthropology: man made in the image of God is primarily a rational

126 Farrer, *The Glass of Vision*, pp. 7–8.
127 Ibid., p. 8.
128 Ibid., p. 22.
129 D. Brown, 'God and Symbolic Action', in *Divine Action: Studies Inspired by the Philosophical Theology of Austin Farrer*, ed. B. Hebblethwaite and E. Henderson (Edinburgh: T. & T. Clark, 1990), pp. 103–22.

creature. This is the basic conviction lying behind the idea of 'a double personal agency in our one activity':[130] God can act within and through finite human agents. Again, I think the target is the anthropological pessimism of Freud, or again Barth. My point is that Farrer is clearly standing in the tradition of natural theology and he wants a theory of inspiration as part of an account of divine action which coheres with his philosophical tenets. Farrer's emphasis upon 'images' is not arbitrary: it allows him to keep his philosophical theology and his biblical theology in harmony. The images allow Farrer, like Irenaeus, to pursue the idea of a continuous typology. Incarnation corresponds with creation and is its fulfilment – a God who acts but is not arbitary, and whose action is not intervention from without in a mechanical sense, but paradigmatically within the created realm in an organic or plastic sense. Redemption and creation form a continuum, and Farrer's stress is upon the unique nature of God's relationship to the world. Finite agents are mutually exclusive but there is no excluding the infinite. This is clearly not pantheism or a pan-metaphoric account of divine action.

Typology

Whereas many twentieth-century theologians have been concerned that divine action might be incompatible with complete scientific explanation, ancient theologians tended to be more worried about such action being incompatible with divine dignity: to attribute action to the supreme being is blasphemy. The problem is not that God cannot act, but that he should not act. This is, of course, tied to a rather lower estimate of history. It was easy for Aristotle to think poetry more philosophical than history.

We might say that St Augustine is quite frank about his debts to the pagans. In a sense the *Confessions* is about how the books of the Platonists brought him to the threshold of the Church. Those books conceived of the cosmos as the *theophany* of an invisible Deity: the theology of these Hellenists of late antiquity rejected as too remote the God of book XI of Aristotle's *Metaphysics*; they rejected as too immanent the God of the Stoics. It was this *via media* of a God both transcendent and immanent which lured Augustine from the Manichees. But for Plotinus or Porphyry, the restriction of revelation to Jesus Christ and the Church was a scandalous claim. The ancient pagans rejected divine action in the Christian sense because it seemed to them unworthy of deity. Any change in God can only mean a change for either better or worse, and neither one nor the other can be attributed to the Godhead as perfection. Plotinus is very keen to dispel the anthropomorphism which might be attributed to the *Timaeus* myth. The world-soul directs the cosmos internally not externally, like nature not a doctor.

It is interesting to see how a theologian like Irenaeus denies resolutely the claim that God does not intervene, and how close his position is, say,

---

130 Farrer, *The Glass of Vision*, p. 33.

to Plotinus. Irenaeus rejects the idea that God is only in the world when intervening. God is omnipresent and Irenaeus claims that a gulf between God and finite being would reduce God to a finite being. He is also surprisingly reticent to speak of any contingency in the Divine. In his polemic against the Gnostic writers who stressed the radical break between creation and redemption, Irenaeus stresses the continuity between them.[131] The one God has progressively revealed himself since creation through Adam, the pagans, the prophets and the Gospels, and Christ's pre-existence is an index of the essential immutability of divine revelation. Divine revelation is not contingent and arbitrary. That which is novel in revelation is congruous with what is already known about God. The divine economy provides a gradual education of the human race because man requires free growth into knowledge, but of course God is quite above any change. God does not need man, because of the mutual adoration of the Trinity; yet 'the glory of God is a living man and the life of man is the vision of God'.[132] The typology which Irenaeus employs serves to illuminate God's progressive revelation, which constitutes the expression of unchanging divine love for the world. One of the keys to the Irenaean emphasis upon the continuity between the God of the philosophers and the Christian revelation is his use of the prophets and his fusion of the ontological and the eschatological. The providence which informs history is more than the sum of merely historical events. Philo intepreted Moses as seeing the ideas of God and in Justin and Clement one has the idea that the prophets were able to perceive the divine economies. The prophets have glimpsed the glory of God in different phases. Hence Jesus was not just predicted by the prophets – his revelation was preceded by a framework of images which both provide the context of, and are transformed by, the teaching and life of Christ.

Just like Clement, Augustine and Irenaeus, Farrer insists that 'men have always been apprehending the shadow of God in Nature, but in many partial aspects and under much confusion of mind'. This is evident in his discussion of archetypes and creative intentions. Man begins with a 'fertile but superstitious idolatry of archetypes.'[133] Such archetypes can be viewed, in a philosophical spirit, as God's creative intentions, and hence all of creation as a theophany. Such is the move from archetypes to universality. But Farrer asserts that there is another road – this is the path of the incarnation itself.

Even though the archetypes look heathenish, they 'hold the promise of revelation'.[134] The old archetypes were at hand and already half transformed. The great images were undergoing a change in a super-natural direction through the prophets themselves, though the prophets were not conscious of the process:

---

131 See Osborn, *Irenaeus*, p. 89, where he speaks of the 'horizontal' Platonism of Irenaeus.
132 See Ibid., p. 13.
133 Farrer, *The Glass of Vision*, p. 104.
134 Ibid., p. 105.

The prophets do not know that the images are changing their natures . . . they are so purifying and exalting the image that nothing merely natural will ever be able to embody it. In this sense the great images themselves are undergoing change in the prophets: and the act of soul by which this happens in them is a supernatural act, it is the process of the incarnation of God preparing its own way and casting its shadow before.[135]

Christ took up these images, and the images were further transformed. It was not a slight change of basic images revealed in the prophets and something greater in the Apostles: the prophets spiritualize the imagery of the cult, and in the Apostle we find a rebirth of these images and the opening of the heavens in the Son of Man.[136] But the continuity remains. We have a clear thread from the natural to the supernatural: redemption is the fulfilment of creation. 'The choice, use and combination of images made by Christ and the Spirit must be simply a supernatural work: otherwise Christianity is an illusion.'[137] But we must remember that the 'supernatural acts . . . are continuous with natural functions, of which they are, so to speak, the upward prolongations. The boundary between the two need be neither objectively evident nor subjectively felt'.[138]

With aphoristic concision, Farrer says that the religion of the Israelites was in 'suspense' between idolatry and incarnation. But modern theology is caught between a pure rational theology on the one hand and a superstitious reverence for the supposed Jesus on the other: idolatry and theistic rationalism. What does he mean by this?

Let me try and translate the languid allusiveness of Farrer into the nuts and bolts of those Enlightenment and Romantic debates about faith and history which lie behind modern theology – Kierkegaard and Ritschl on the one hand, Lessing and Kant on the other: the pure Jesus of history as the paradoxical appearance of God in time, or the symbolic representation of eternal verities with no essential link to the life of any particular rabbi.

Farrer agrees with modern Teutonic theologians that the primary revelation in the New Testament is Jesus Christ, but, as we have noted, he insists that this means *both* the words and the deeds of Christ. The New Testament is not the sum of the fact of Christ and the apostolic commentary upon this fact. Rather, the Evangelists and St Paul were pursuing the imagery employed by Christ himself of the Kingdom of God, the Son of Man, Israel, or the sacrificial supper and covenant. Farrer employs the example of St Paul's experience of his own discipleship as continual death and resurrection as an example of a creative extension of images rooted in Christ's own teaching. I think we can sense Farrer's attempt to bestride the ugly ditch of Lessing whereby accidental historical truths can never prove rational truths. Rather than accept the alternative of either the contingent facticity in the history of Jesus of

135 Ibid., p. 135.
136 Ibid., p. 136.
137 Ibid., p. 109.
138 Ibid.

Nazareth or universal symbols and images, Farrer insists upon blending the two. Word and deed coalesce in Christ crucified and risen in a genuinely historical revelation. Whereas Barth or Bultmann separate revelation from history, Farrer argues for history as the revelatory locus.

It is within the broader or horizontal context of divine action *through* history that we have to understand Farrer's proposal concerning inspiration. The triumph of revelation is not its surprise but its coherence. Providence must be bodied forth; it must be made *visible à la fantaisie* if it is to be made *sensible au cœur*.[139]

Ingolf Dalferth objects that Farrer unnecessarily privileges the apostolic interpretation of the images,[140] but privileging a particular epoch has some justification. One could draw analogies with sculpture, painting, drama or music. Sculpture in ancient Greece, painting in Renaissance Italy, drama in late Renaissance England, and the Romantic symphony in Germany exhausted certain possibilities. The providential blending of Hellenism, with its distinctive individualism and universalism, and the prophetic religion of the Hebrews in the Roman Empire under the rule of Tiberius, produced the most spiritual of religions in Christianity, even if that only meant the sublime and intense vision of Christ in Palestine. A Christian has a further reason to think that the heavens opened in the life of Christ: the divine economy in history.

In his justly celebrated *The Eclipse of Biblical Narrative*, Hans Frei describes a shift from a world in which the biblical narrative defines reality to a world in which Scripture was tested by the secular standard. This historical analysis of a shift from the Enlightenment is linked to a Barthian emphasis upon the autonomy of Christian revelation. Frei relates his Barthian agenda, somewhat bizarrely one might imagine, to an emphasis on practice in Gilbert Ryle's behaviouristic philosophy of mind. The world of the believer, for Frei, is constituted by the overt and public practices of Christian community.[141] The narrative and practice (behaviour) of the Christian is reinforced by other proponents of the Yale school such as George Lindbeck.

Farrer is free of the exclusivism which mars the Barthian tradition of theology, especially the narrative theology of the Yale school. Yet Farrer is more robustly theological than admirable thinkers like Ricœur, whose emphasis is upon the *parables* of Christ as a way of awakening new imaginative possibilities for human life, but who gives little scope to the centrality of Christ's action as opposed to what he taught. As Dalferth writes in relation to Farrer's theology: 'Jesus not only taught in parables but also became himself a parable: the self enacted parable of God's saving love.'[142] Farrer shares the Christocentrism of Frei without the Barthian isolationism; he can match Ricœur's sense of the centrality of

---

139 Ibid.
140 Dalferth, 'The Stuff of Revelation', p. 88.
141 H. W. Frei, *The Eclipse of Biblical Narrative: A Study in Eighteenth and Nineteenth Century Hermeneutics* (New Haven, Conn.: Yale University Press, 1974), p. 116.
142 Dalferth, 'The Stuff of Revelation', p. 82.

the poetic in any adequate understanding of Scripture, without losing sight of the protagonist of the Christian drama.

The cultic drama

The central Christian sacrament of the eucharist is the celebration of a redemption achieved: the triumphal presence of God in the midst of suffering – the vision of God in a fallen world. It is the celebration of the divine triumph and the ultimate redemptive import of human suffering. The crucifixion in John's Gospel is quite explicit on this point. Christ's suffering on the cross is an act of victory culminating with the words 'It is finished' (John 19.30). Thus Hölderlin can sing of the divine triumph and the mystery of the redemptive significance of human suffering. He insists that John is the seer who saw the divine countenance, especially at the Last Supper:

> The face of God exactly,
> There, at the mystery of the Vine, they
> sat together at the hour of the Banquet.[143]

The syncretistic elements of Hölderlin's vision are pronounced. John's memory of his physical vision of Christ culminates with the recall of the Last Supper. 'Zu der Stunde des Gastmahls' is associated with the wine deity Dionysus (Hölderlin associates Christ with Hercules and Dionysus in *Der Einzige*). Dionysus as the dismembered deity can represent or be an allegory of Christ's own death – 'the infinite dispersal of the living God':

> But it is dreadful how hither and thither
> The Living God is scattered infinitely.[144]

Gastmahl means 'banquet' and in German carries specific associations of Plato's *Symposium*. (Hölderlin described his muse Susette Gontard as Diotima, the visionary teacher of Socrates in Plato's dialogue, the figure who explained to Socrates the nature of love.) Hölderlin recounts in his poem how John the Divine sees in the figure of Christ the victory of the power of the spirit over the spirit of power:

> And in the great soul, gently sensing death
> The Lord and the ultimate love spoke, since in words
> he could never speak enough
> of goodness in that time, and in order to rouse them, because
> he saw the tumult of the world.
> Since all is good. Thereupon he died. Much
> could be said.

---

143 'Das Angesicht des Gottes genau, / Da, beim Geheimnisse des Weinstocks, sie / Zusammensaßen, zu der Stunde des Gastmahls': Friedrich Hölderlin, 'Patmos', ll. 80–2, in *Gedichte*, ed. G. Kurz (Stuttgart: Philipp Reclam, 2003), p. 90.

144 'Doch furchtbar ist, wie da und dort / Unendlich hin zerstreut das Lebende Gott': ibid., ll. 121–2. p. 91.

And, as triumphant he gazed, the most joyous of the friends saw
him at the very end.[145]

The disciples saw Christ's triumphant vision of joy in extremity. It is
characteristic of John's Gospel that the cross is presented as victory, and
the trained theologian Hölderlin sees here the vision of the divine
presence and communion with humanity apprehended through the
symbolic imagination.

The eucharist can easily be misunderstood. Early Christians were
accused of cannibalism. Again, it is important to avoid both the
mythological and the over-conceptual rationalization. A sense of pollution and guilt can be given a Marxist or Freudian interpretation, but I
would plead for an understanding of this sense as having a more
profound cause in those demonic structures which pervade human life.
Doubtless the imagery of sacrifice has its roots in ritual practices that can
be traced back to archaic man, and which found drastic literal expression
in the religious cults of savage civilizations like those of the Aztecs. To
compare the *cibus spiritualis* of the Christian eucharist with the atrocities
of Aztec cannibalism and ritual sacrifice is indefensible. It would be as
absurd as the etymological fallacy of thinking that in my use of the word
'truth' I am still, in part, inhabiting the world of my Saxon ancestors
through the word's direct ancestor, *treowth*. This, *pace* Heidegger, is
absurd. But Farrer has given us a very good theological account of how
such images can become part of a providential narrative.

We commented in the previous chapter on Huizinga and Gadamer in
relation to the question of make-believe. Huizinga explores the idea of
play as an ineluctable part of culture; Gadamer explores how play should
not be construed in narrowly subjective terms. Gadamer notes that play
differs from any merely aesthestic experience because it involves
participation in the experience of 'being played'. The play provides the
boundaries, rules and objectives: a domain in which the player is
absorbed. Peter Berger in his eloquent little book *A Rumour of Angels*
refers to the element of suspension of the 'serious' world and the fact that
in playing 'one steps out of one time into another'.[146]

The eucharist shares with other religious rituals the symbolic arrest of
profane time.[147] The ritual of the eucharist fulfils a desire for order, the
reassurance of an overarching providential framework. But it also allows
Christians to take part in the drama of the Last Supper. Aristotle saw
catharsis as a means of purging certain emotions through seeing the tragic
drama. In ritual, Christians are engaging in the story recounted by the
priest at the altar to rediscover their real identity as children of God – as
parts of the divinely instituted covenant. It is not a relic of primordial

---

145 'Und in der großen Seele, ruhigahnend den Tod / Aussprach der Herr und die letzte
   Liebe, denn nie genug / Hatt er von Güte zu sagen / Der Worte, damals, und zu
   erheiten, da / Er's sahe, das Zürnen der Welt. / Denn alles is gut. Drauf wäre starb er.
   Vieles ware / Zu sagen davon. Und es sah ihn, wie er siegend blickte / Den
   Freudigsten die Freunde noch zuletzt': ibid., ll 83–90; p. 90.
146 P. L. Berger, *A Rumour of Angels* (Harmondsworth: Penguin, 1969), p. 76.
147 M. Eliade, *Images and Symbols: Studies in Religious Symbolism*, pp. 71–9.

cannibalism or a vestige of crude attempts to placate and manipulate jealous and dangerous gods, but participation in the divine life. In this way we can avoid the extremes of viewing the eucharist as either mechanical re-enactment or merely the remembrance of the past.

The eucharist is an instance of how the imagination helps serve to overcome the debilitating forces of individualism and pessimism. It is the encounter with the divine life, a presence which transcends comprehension but which is intimated by – and apprehended through – symbols and the symbolic imagination. The prayers of penitence acknowledge the fact of sins of fallen humanity, of our selfish interests and obsessions, of our collusion and complicity with the cruel demons of the world. In taking the bread and the wine, Christians are recalled to their true identity as part of a wider body as children of God.

Conclusion

In this chapter I have tried to steer a middle path between those liberal theologies which fail to take the apocalyptic dimension of Christianity seriously (and in particular the drama of Christ's victory over the principalities and powers), and that opposed neo-orthodox tradition that sees any appeal to reason as succumbing to the 'secular'. In my account of the imagination as a form of mediation between the intelligible and the sensible – the isthmus or meeting point of the noetic and empirical – and my discussion of Hölderlin and Gadamer, we have endeavoured to bring the puzzling apocalyptic-Temple imagery within a broadly philosophical context, in particular those images of sacrifice and atonement that were a scandal to the Enlightenment.

8

Social Imaginary

The One remains, the many change and pass;
Heaven's light forever shines, Earth's shadows fly;
Life, like a dome of many-coloured glass,
Stains the white radiance of Eternity[1]

The religious imagination suffuses human society. The greatest monuments of Graeco-Roman antiquity are their temples. The same applies to medieval Europe and the Gothic cathedral. Some of the greatest monuments of English poetry are meditations upon Christian holy places such as 'Tintern Abbey' and 'Little Gidding'.

The German word for imagination, *Einbildungskraft*, includes the word for education, *Bildung*. *Bildung* in Gadamer's sense is education into the particular prejudices of one's own *Wirkungsgeschichte*, an awareness of that which has indelibly shaped our self-understanding. This is why Gadamer can famously state that 'history does not belong to us, but we belong to it'.[2] Outer facts – accidents of kith and kin, national history and tradition – have already formed our attitudes before we can reflect upon the validity of our own inner states. In this sense *Bildung* is a 'Begreifen, was uns ergreift', a 'grasping of that which grips us'.[3] That 'being grasped' involves imagination: the 'social imaginary'.

For philosophers, it is perhaps natural to link politics and society with the imagination. Plato in the *Republic* uses his myth of the cave to support his ideal state; Hobbes uses the image of Leviathan. Yet we should not forget that even the image of the original social contract is powerful as a pervasive work of the imagination. The great twentieth-century American political philosopher John Rawls enquired: 'How is it possible that there may exist over time a stable and just society of free and equal citizens profoundly divided by reasonable though incompatible religious, philosophical and moral doctrines?'[4] The theoretical basis for his model of such a society is the image of the 'social contract'.

---

1 P. B. Shelley, 'Adonais: An Elegy on the Death of John Keats', ll. 460–4, *Shelley's Poetical Works*, vol. III, ed. H. Buxton Forman, (London: Reeves and Turner, 1882), p. 28.
2 H.-G. Gadamer, *Gesammelte Werke* (Tübingen: Mohr, 1985–9), vol. 1, p. 281.
3 Ibid., vol. 2, p. 108.
4 J. Rawls, *Political Liberalism* (New York: Columbia University Press, 1993), p. xx.

Modern social imaginaries

Charles Taylor has developed a rich and subtle account of the genealogy of the 'social contract' in his *Modern Social Imaginaries*. The term 'imaginary' has for many French *Marxisant* commentators pejorative connotations of some alienating ideology. But it does not have this negative meaning for Taylor. He defines the social imaginary broadly as 'the way people imagine their social existance'.[5]

Symbolic values and the force of the imagination loom large in conflicts between and within societies. Peoples forget the dead and wounded of their conflicts surprisingly quickly, but the loss or destruction of shrines or monuments or symbolic territory remains active in the popular imagination for centuries. It is obvious why we care about other human lives: why should we care about cultural artefacts? Sometimes the acts involved are merely ritual. The storming of the Bastille was not a very significant practical liberation, since there were very few prisoners or weapons within it, but it was a foundational symbolic action of popular sovereignty over against monarchic-aristocratic despotism. The crowning of the King of Prussia as the German emperor in the Hall of Mirrors in Versailles was a symbolic revenge for the humiliation that Louis XIV imposed on seventeenth-century Germany. But we know that it was the prelude to one of the cruellest of all European wars.

That which originally developed as an idea becomes embedded in the collective imagination and it has 'become so self evident to us that we have trouble seeing it as one possible conception among others'.[6] This is the idea of society as a contract that defends the rights of each member and provides for the reciprocal benefit of all. Taylor is explicitly drawing on Habermas's seminal work on the development of a 'public sphere' in France in the eighteenth century. What is public opinion? It is a rather puzzling, if not paradoxical, notion: a community of opinion formed by people who do not and cannot meet each other. The social imaginary is '*imagined* because members of even the smallest nation will never know most of their fellow-members, meet them, or even hear of them, yet in the minds of each lives the image of their communion'.[7]

Taylor's book is an exploration of the unprecedented and unparalleled synthesis of institutions, techniques and forms of life generated during the modern period through the scientific revolution, the industrial revolution and urbanization, and of how contemporary Western consciousness has been suffused by the modern principle that the purpose of society is to attain mutual benefits for its members and to protect their rights. His book is a description of how ideas of popular sovereignty, equality and rights emerged from the initial contract theories of Grotius and Locke and came to be dominant. He also describes how these theories changed from having a largely *hermeneutical* status, i.e. interpreting the social contract as

5 C. Taylor, *Modern Social Imaginaries* (London: Duke University Press, 2004,), p. 23.
6 Ibid., p. 2.
7 B. Anderson, *Imagined Communities: Reflections on the Origin and Spread of Nationalism* (London: Verso, 1983), p. 15.

the principle of justification for an existing political order, to a prescriptive principle, inspiring ever-increasing reforms. Furthermore, the society in which both Grotius and Locke lived – both in England and the Low Countries – was still deeply hierarchical. Modern societies have come to reflect much more accurately in their collective imagination the individualism inherent in the theories of Grotius and Locke.

Nor can we ignore the religious context of many of these ideas. Congregationalism, with its central principle of the autonomy of the worshipping congregation based upon its own covenant, and not admitting any external authority – whether synods or individual persons – provides a clear religious precedent in the Anglo-Saxon context. Both the English Civil War, especially Cromwell himself, and the congregationalism of New England, in particular Connecticut, provided a powerful paradigm for secular theories of government justified by consent.[8]

Taylor starts from a narrative of the purging of the enchanted universe of pre-modern Europe. But he sees the roots of the process in the so-called 'post-axial' age, the foundational eras in China, Greece, India and Israel of a number of the major world religions. It was characteristic of the post-axial religions, on Taylor's account, that they challenged inherited views of human flourishing which were more deeply embedded in the community.[9] Archaic religion embedded the agent in the clan or tribe and cosmos. Post-axial religions all challenged the individual's relation to both society and the cosmos.

This post-axial challenge developed through the early modern period into a model of a society constituted by the free will of rational agents. It was devised in the seventeenth century and is a product of the wars of religion which shook early modern Europe. In Grotius, consent provided a justification and legitimization of political authority, but consent theories soon came to subvert those monarchical-aristocratic feudal structures that seemed embedded in the theory of a divinely ordained order. Locke's formulation of the theory coincided with, and provided a justification for, the Glorious Revolution of 1688. Locke's *Two Treatises of Government* were a defence of constitutional government and individual freedom. The first treatise was an attack on the divine right of kings and the theory of a divinely sponsored social hierarchy as expressed in Robert Filmer's *Patriarcha* (1680). In the second treatise, Locke argues that naturally men are free and equal. Nature is, however, often in fact infringed. The social contract is an artifice by means of which human beings can exercise these natural rights. It is the basis of the government of a society, laws, and adjudication of conflicts of interest. Filmer's theory, as its title suggests, was that authority is essentially paternal. Locke replies: 'the Governments of the World, that were begun in Peace, had their beginning laid on that foundation, and were made by the Consent of the People'.[10] Furthermore, the 'beginning of Politic Society

---

8 Taylor, *Modern Social Imaginaries*, p. 109.
9 Ibid., pp. 57ff.
10 John Locke, *Two Treatises of Government*, ed. P. Laslett (Cambridge: Cambridge University Press, 1967), II, §104; p. 354.

depends upon the consent of the Individuals, to joyn into and make one Society'.[11] Here we have the *locus classicus* of the view that consent and contract are the essence of political life.

John Rawls wished to develop the notion of a political structure which facilitates tolerance and regards pluralism as a 'permanent feature of the public culture of democracy'. Furthermore, 'reasonable pluralism is the long-run outcome of the work of human reason under enduring free institutions'.[12] This idea of the reasonable is very important in Rawls's pluralism. In recognizing others' comprehensive views as reasonable, citizens also recognize that in the absence of a public basis for establishing the truth of their beliefs, to insist on their comprehensive view must be seen by others as insisting on their own beliefs.[13]

This idea of being 'reasonable' is related inextricably to co-operation. Agreement rather than justification is the real issue in politics – procedure rather than substance.[14] Indeed, the paradigm for modern formulation of the idea is in Rawls's modern classic *A Theory of Justice*. In this model the state is conceived as redistributing goods and status so that inequalities can be justified as benefiting the most vulnerable. The strategy employed to defend this model is essentially imaginative. Rawls requires us to contemplate what he calls the 'original position'. In this 'original position' we find ourselves behind a 'veil of ignorance' which involves knowledge about human nature but ignorance concerning one's own status, talents or wealth. The model of the 'original position' encourages the choice for equality.[15] Given that human nature requires incentives to endure the asperities of training and so on, however, certain incentives to encourage special skills are in the ultimate interest of all. The impartial reasoner does not have knowledge of his own advantages or disadvantages (akin to the ideal observer of utilitarianism). What I wish to emphasize here is the imaginative nature of the model. A number of commentators have observed that the contractual model cannot justify the impartial liberalism which Rawls wishes to propound. In fact the model presupposes the view that impartiality is at the core of morality. But it helps, as Will Kymlicka argues, to present a compelling image of commitment to impartiality.[16] The veil of ignorance presents how we may think of thinking of others and the effect of particular principles upon all members of society.

We have to employ the imagination to appreciate the roots of our culture. Yet also we need something deeper than merely arbitrary and conventional attachments to form a state. This leads to the difficult

---

11 Ibid., II, §106; p. 356.
12 See John Rawls, *A Theory of Justice* (Oxford: Oxford University Press, 1973), pp. 17–22, 129.
13 Rawls, *Political Liberalism*, p. 247.
14 R. Trigg, *Rationality and Religion: Does Faith Need Reason?* (Oxford: Blackwell, 1998), pp. 11ff.
15 See Rawls, *A Theory of Justice*, pp. 136–50.
16 W. Kymlicka, *Liberalism: Community and Culture* (Oxford: Clarendon Press, 1991), pp. 194ff.; see also M. La Caze, *The Analytic Imaginary* (Ithaca, NY: Cornell University Press, 2002), pp. 112ff.

question of the status of religion in a modern democratic society. Many secular philosophers, such as Richard Rorty, see religion as incompatible with public debate. Others, like Alasdair MacIntyre or Charles Taylor, see many of the ethical problems in modern democratic societies as the result of the decline of religion. I wish to reflect upon the contemporary significance of Coleridge's reception of Rousseau. Here I wish to draw a parallel with Taylor's qualified and critical support of Rousseau and Coleridge, in opposition to MacIntyre's continuation of a more strictly Burkean critique of the modern project. Indeed, MacIntyre might be characterized as a modern Edmund Burke, especially in his savage critique of the 'Enlightenment project' of basing morality upon abstract rationality and his view that emotivism is the dominant ethical theory of contemporary philosophy. For him, Rousseau embodies the flaws of modern ethics. MacIntyre's project to revive Aristotelian virtues might be seen as a response to the cult of spontaneity and sincerity as well as abstract universalism. Given Rousseau's debt to the tradition of Hobbes and his vast impact upon the modern mind, MacIntyre could be seen as attacking precisely this legacy of modernity, which has dislocated moral agency from any deeper objectivity or order.[17]

There is much force to MacIntyre's Burkean critique. The free market is a radical dissolvent of inherited loyalties, traditions and principles. Ancient and historic communities, like colleges, universities or churches, can exercise a potent role in the communication of values which resonate through generations, a role which neither government nor individuals can emulate: in England, for example, those innumerable schools and colleges founded in the Renaissance or Romantic eras.

Charles Taylor, though prima facie having much in common with MacIntyre – an emphasis upon community, a critique of negative freedom and of positivism – nevertheless expresses a view of Rousseau which is much closer to Coleridge. This is quite clear in his magisterial *Sources of the Self*. Rousseau marks the development and transformation of certain themes of selfhood, freedom and rationality that were implicit in the Hellenic-Christian synthesis originating largely from Augustine. For Taylor, Rousseau is a paradigm of the continuity between Augustine and the modern sense of subjectivity. Rousseau's *Confessions* is a deliberate reference to Augustine's autobiography. His novel *Julie* is a paradigm of the affirmation of ordinary life and exalted sentiments. In this sense as in many others, Taylor sees Rousseau as reinforcing and developing a view of subjectivity which goes back to Augustine, for whom God is 'interior intimo meo et superior summo meo'[18] and Plotinus, for whom 'we are each of us the intelligible world'.[19] Taylor places Rousseau within an Augustinian tradition because Rousseau denies the perfectionistic and mechanistic tenets of the Encyclopaedists

17 See É. Perreau-Saussine, 'Une spiritualité libérale? Charles Taylor et Alasdair MacIntyre en conversation', *Revue française de science politique*, 55.2, (2005), pp. 299–315.
18 Augustine, *Confessions* III.6.11.
19 Plotinus, *Enneads* III.4.3.22.

and replaces it with a secularized version of the Augustinian requirement of a 'transformation of the will'.[20]

MacIntyre is profoundly pessimistic about the resources available to
modern society to achieve any ethical coherence, and blames this upon
the ultimately ruinous 'Enlightenment project' of universal reason as the
basis of ethics and, intertwined with this utopian hubris, the distinctively
modern cult of a deracinated authenticity detached from community and
tradition. Modern society is frequently 'nothing but a collection of
strangers'.[21] The ethical malaise of contemporary culture is due to the
forlorn attempt to retain a moral vocabulary without the resources to
sustain it. Lacking these traditional structures, contemporary moral
discourse becomes a random fantasy within ultimately nihilistic param-
eters, proximate convention and whim in a landscape devoid of ultimate
meaning.

Yet I wish to argue that MacIntyre's pessimism is excessive. Taylor is
far less gloomy and rejects MacIntyre's claim that modern subjectivity
amounts to no more than desiccated emotivism and/or nihilism. He
affirms the expressivist/Romantic ideal. His remarks on John Stuart Mill
are revealing:

> Mill suffered deeply in his own life from the conflict between the
> demands of the most austere disengaged reason and the need for a
> richer sense of meaning, which he ultimately found through the
> Romantic poets. He had somehow to integrate Bentham and
> Coleridge, and he put together a synthesis, which one sees in such
> works as *Utilitarianism* and the *Essay on Liberty*, which combines a
> disengaged, scientistic utilitarianism with an expressivist conception
> of human growth and fulfilment, and which owes a lot to German
> Romanticism, through Coleridge and Humboldt.[22]

I wish to suggest that, for reasons illustrated by Taylor, Coleridge is
closer to Rousseau than his polemic suggests. Coleridge thinks that
Burke fails to provide a positive account of the 'rightful constitution of
government'. Coleridge tries to find a *via media* between idealistic
abstraction, and prudence and tradition. He is at one with Rousseau in
emphasizing reason in politics, but differs in his account of reason.

Coleridge distinguished 'culture' and 'civilization', a distinction which
has inspired critics of utilitarianism such as Carlyle, Matthew Arnold,
T. S. Eliot and Raymond Williams.[23] In his model of the 'clerisy', a body of
scholars and teachers, we have a fine example of how Coleridge thought
that a reasoned and non-instrumentalist view of rationality can transform

---

20 Taylor, *Sources of the Self: The Making of the Modern Identity* (Cambridge: Cambridge
   University Press, 1989), p. 356.
21 A. MacIntyre, *After Virtue: A Study in Moral Theory*, 2nd edn (London: Duckworth, 1985)
   p. 233.
22 Taylor, *Sources of the Self*, p. 458.
23 The distinction is derived from Rousseau via German philosophy. It was Rousseau, in
   his prize essay 'First Discourse', who argued that science and the arts had not merely
   failed to improve mankind but had corrupted it.

a nation or civilization.[24] But in fact the general optimism of *Bildung* and culture has a certain (and perhaps surprisingly) Platonic origin.

Culture, religion and detachment: Rousseau and Coleridge

During the French Revolution, Rousseau's *Social Contract* exerted massive influence, not least upon the repellent Robespierre himself. But Rousseau is a very important figure in the European social imaginary because of his expression of what later becomes known as alienation. For Rousseau, human society is inherently divided and the redress of society's ills is achieved through the reconstitution of unity, in which the individual will is fused with the general will. Rousseau thereby became the fountainhead of the German idealist/Romantic attempt to transform human agency from being merely *an sich* to being *für sich* and *an und für sich* – a state of non-alienated self-legislation.[25] The exalted pathos of sincerity and authenticity, much mocked by Hume, Burke and Voltaire, has irrevocably shaped contemporary political sensibility. Here we ought to note the brilliant rhetoric of Rousseau, employed to describe the misery inflicted upon mankind by social injustice and oppression, and not least upon the individual psyche. But he touches upon that dimension of human happiness and flourishing neglected by the technocrats and advocates of enlightened self-interest. A deeply modern figure, Rousseau is the most strident critic of the malaise and failings of the modern order. His ideals are lofty and yet he shares much of the hostility to transcendent ideals and supernatural order expressed by the radical Enlightenment. In the twenty-first century, many inhabit an imaginary shaped by Rousseau without having read a word of the man.

On the other hand, Coleridge scarcely refers to Rousseau, and ever since the 1817 review of his *Biographia Literaria* by Hazlitt and Jeffrey he has been seen as a follower of Burke: as a Tory critic of the quintessentially modern or secular views of the state represented by Rousseau. It is certainly the case that Burke's link between the national character, the Church of England and the historical British constitution was pursued by Coleridge. As a young man, Coleridge wrote:

> I do not particularly admire Rosseau [sic]. Bishop Taylor, Old Baxter, David Hartley and the Bishop of Cloyne are *my men*.[26]

Later on in his writing career, he observes:

> Of the heirs of fame few are more respected by me, though for very different qualities, than Erasmus and Luther: scarcely any one has a larger share of my aversion than Voltaire; and even of the better-

24 See A. P. R. Gregory, *Coleridge and the Conservative Imagination* (Macon, Ga: Mercer University Press, 2003), pp. 178–9.
25 Taylor, *Modern Social Imaginaries*, p. 81. See also C. Taylor, *Hegel* (Cambridge: Cambridge University Press, 1975), pp. 111–12.
26 S. T. Coleridge, *Collected Letters* ed. E. L. Griggs (Oxford: Oxford University Press , 1956–71), vol. 1, p. 146.

hearted Rousseau I was never more than a very lukewarm admirer.[27]

The comparison between the two is damning of Rousseau:

> the heroic LUTHER, a Giant awaking in his strength! and the crazy ROUSSEAU, the Dreamer of lovesick Tales, and the Spinner of speculative Cobwebs; shy of light as the Mole, but as quick-eared too for every whisper of the public opinion; the Teacher of stoic *Pride* in his principles, yet the victim of morbid *Vanity* in his feelings and conduct![28]

This comparison is based upon the resolutely anti-deterministic and anti-materialistic theory that philosophical ideas are real forces in history and influence the great political events of mankind. Coleridge claims that we can predict the politics of an age given knowledge of the philosophical ideas which were common in the preceding period. For Coleridge, Rousseau's doctrine of the general will prepared the way for the satanic tyranny of Napoleon, just as Luther's prophetic genius had liberated much of Europe from stupor and superstition.

Despite the picture of Rousseau as a harbinger of horrors, when we examine Coleridge's critique of Rousseau – and it is largely critique in the Burkean mould – he evinces much common ground with Rousseau. I wish to propose that Coleridge's mature political theory can be viewed as a *synthesis* of Burke and Rousseau, but not because Coleridge accepted Rousseau's view of the natural goodness of man corrupted by society and his link between evil and civic structures. Like Kant, Coleridge thinks that human agency has a propensity to evil which is grounded in the will – this is radical, innate evil. However, Coleridge also insists that even though we are not naturally good, equally we are not driven by mere instinct or whim. Free agency involves the use of maxims or principles, and these can be good or bad. But our freedom and rationality are inextricably linked and must be given a central place in any proper account of the body politic. I shall argue that this Rousseauian legacy can be seen in Coleridge's concept of the clerisy. I am not convinced that there is much direct influence, but I am suggesting that there is an overlap of concerns and ideas. This should not be surprising: Rousseau read Plato and decisively influenced Kant. The use of the word 'conscience' in Coleridge overlaps with that of all three thinkers.

Burke on Rousseau

> It is now sixteen or seventeen years since I saw the queen of France, then the dauphiness, at Versailles; and surely never lighted on this orb, which she hardly seemed to touch, a more delightful vision . . .

27 S. T. Coleridge, *The Friend*, ed. B. Rooke (Princeton, NJ: Princeton University Press, 1969), vol. 1, pp. 130–1.
28 Ibid., p. 132.

little did I dream that I should have lived to see such disasters fallen upon her in a nation of gallant men, in a nation of men of honour, and of cavaliers. I thought ten thousand swords must have leaped from their scabbards to avenge even a look that threatened her with insult. But the age of chivalry is gone. That of sophisters, economists, and calculators, has succeeded; and the glory of Europe is extinguished for ever.[29]

Burke contrasts his dazzling portrayal of Marie Antoinette with the 'barbarous philosophy' of Rousseau and his like:

We are not converts of Rousseau; we are not the disciples of Voltaire; Helvetius has made no progress amongst us. Atheists are not our preachers; madmen are not our lawgivers . . . We have real hearts of flesh and blood.[30]

Coleridge was a young man in Cambridge when he read Burke's *Reflections on the Revolution in France* in 1790. Charles LeGrice speaks of Coleridge discussing Burke in the anti-Pitt environment of undergraduate Cambridge. The conflicts between Burke and the French-inspired Radicals were a formative feature of Coleridge's young mind.

Burke views Rousseau as vain, subjectivistic and full of morbid sentimentalism (the correlate of the desiccated rationalism of Voltaire). In Rousseau natural affection is perverted: his own abandoning of his children reveals the sham nature of Rousseauian sentimentalism and benevolence. However, Coleridge moves beyond Burke's *ad personam* polemics. Burke's rhetoric is ultimately, according to Coleridge, *ad hoc*:

If his opponents are Theorists, *then* every thing is to be founded on PRUDENCE, on mere calculations of EXPEDIENCY: and every man is represented as acting according to the state of his own immediate self interest. Are his opponents calculators? *Then* calculation itself is represented as a sort of crime. God has given us FEELINGS, and we are to obey them! and the most absurd prejudices become venerable, to which these FEELINGS have given consecration.[31]

Coleridge perceives a lack of overarching theory in Burke's account of social institutions and structures, and consequently posits Burke veering between incompatible principles: prudence and sensibility. Coleridge employs the Kantian distinction between persons and things: 'Man must be *free*; or to what purpose was he made a Spirit of Reason, and not a Machine of Instinct?'[32] He wishes to negotiate the realm between 'the magic circle of pure Reason' and 'the sphere of the understanding and prudence'.[33] Coleridge neverthless criticizes Rousseau on partially Burkean grounds, quoting with approval Burke's remark that 'It is fittest that sovereign authority should be exercised where it is most likely

29 Edmund Burke, *Reflections on the French Revolution* (London: Dent, 1955), p. 73.
30 Ibid., p. 83.
31 Coleridge, *The Friend*, vol. 1, p. 188.
32 Ibid., p. 191.
33 Ibid., p. 193.

to be attended with the most effectual correctives.'[34] Once this happens, we are moving into the realm of probabilities:

in this distinction, established by Rousseau himself, between the *Volonté de Tous* and the *Volonté generale*, (i.e between the collective will, and a casual over-balance of wills) the falsehood or nothingness of the whole system becomes manifest. For hence it follows, as an inevitable consequence, that all which is said in the *contrat social* of that sovereign will, to which the right of universal legislation appertains, applies to no one Human Being, to no Society or assemblage of Human Beings, and least of all to the mixed multitude that makes up the PEOPLE: but entirely and exclusively to REASON itself, which, it is true, dwells in every man *potentially*, but actually and in perfect purity is found in no man and in no body of men.[35]

Rousseau's theory

Coleridge's critique has two principal elements: Rousseau's system is too abstract and it confuses the actual and the ideal. Hence it fails to recognize the impossible utopianism of one system applying to diverse cultures:

Neither an individual, nor yet the whole multitude which consti-tutes the state, can possess the right of compelling him to do any thing, of which it cannot be demonstrated that his own Reason must join in prescribing it. If therefore society is to be under a *rightful* constitution of government, and one can impose on rational beings a true and moral obligation to obey it, it must be framed on such principles that every individual follows his own Reason while he obeys the laws of the constitution, and performs the will of the state while he follows the dictates of his own Reason. This is expressly asserted by Rousseau who states the problem of a perfect constitu-tion of government in the following words: *Trouver une forme d'Association – par laquelle chacun s'unissant à tous, n'obeisse pourtant qu'à lui-même, et reste aussi libre qu'auparavant.* i.e. To find a form of society according to which each one uniting with the whole shall yet obey himself only and remain as free as before.[36]

This became the pretext for 'the satanic Government of Horror under the Jacobins, and of Terror under the Corsican'.[37] Coleridge is sometimes thought to be complicit 'in the injustices of a regressive monarchical regime after turning his back on the revolutionary hopes of his youth'.[38] Coleridge's monarchism was, at least in part, the result of his observation of Napoleon's tyranny and cruelty. This seemed to Coleridge, as to many

34 Ibid., p. 193., quoting Burke, *Works*, vol. 1 (London, 1792), pp. 647–8.
35 Ibid., pp. 193–4.
36 Ibid., p. 192.
37 Ibid., p. 194.
38 J. Stout, *Democracy and Tradition* (Princeton, NJ: Princeton University Press, 2004), p. 107.

other observers, the result of unchecked power. Constitutional monarchy seemed preferable – not because of the divine right of kings, but precisely because of the constitutional limits on the monarch. Coleridge's interest in monarchy, and indeed aristocracy in general, is part of a vision of society as constituted by a dynamic equilibrium, in which the forces of tradition and those of innovation are in a state of uneasy but creative balance. Coleridge diagnoses a failure to recognize the necessary limits of human society in Rousseau's political idealism, and notes that

> Rousseau indeed asserts, that there is an inalienable sovereignty inherent in every human being possessed of Reason: and from this the framers of the Constitution of 1791 deduce, that the people itself is its own sole rightful legislator, and at most dare only recede so far from its right as to delegate to chosen deputies the power of representing and declaring the general will.[39]

To counter this claim, Coleridge uses the example of children – they are excluded on the basis of immaturity. Yet are not ignorance and superstition 'equal impediments to the rightful exercise of the Reason, as childhood and early youth'? He uses the example of women. They are excluded because of their dependence upon a husband – however, what about poor or sick men, and 'to all in short whose maintenance, be it scanty or be it ample, depends on the will of others'? These are all questions of degrees and yet 'Reason is not susceptible of degree'.[40] Any appeal to 'reason' must consider what is meant by the term:

> That Reason should be our guide and governor is an undeniable Truth, and all our notion of right and wrong is built thereon . . . From Reason alone can we derive the principles which our understandings are to apply, the Ideal to which by means of our Understandings we should endeavour to approximate. This however gives no proof that Reason alone ought to govern and direct human beings, either as Individuals or States. It ought not to do this because it cannot.[41]

This is the key distinction. Divine Reason is contrasted with the finite Understanding. We can intuit the Divine Reason or the realm of Forms – the invisible ideas of visible phenomena in mathematics or the moral sciences – but we need to employ our discursive epistemic faculty to engage with, and form inductive generalizations concerning, the physical cosmos. Reason is the apex of mind – our link with the Divine – and Understanding the necessary and ubiquitous tool which we share with other intelligent animals:

> the moral laws of the intellectual world, as far as they are deducible from pure Intellect, are never perfectly applicable to our mixed and sensitive nature, because man is something besides Reason; because

39 Coleridge, *The Friend*, vol. 1, p. 195.
40 Ibid., p. 196.
41 Ibid., p. 199.

his Reason never acts by itself, but must clothe itself in the substance of individual Understanding and specific Inclination, in order to become a reality and an object of consciousness and experience.[42]

Reason is the intelligible world of Forms, the divine intellect, whereas Understanding is the tool by which finite beings negotiate a transitory world of spatially located objects. Therefore, though Coleridge is as anxious as Rousseau to ground ultimately his political thought in reason, he insists that it must be mediated through the finite human understanding, and hence mediated through

> *expedience* founded on *experience* and particular circumstances, which will vary in every different nation, and in the same nation at different times, as the maxim of all Legislation and the ground of all Legislative Power . . . universal principles, as far as they are principles and universal, necessarily suppose uniform and perfect subjects, which are to be found in the *Ideas* of pure Geometry and (I trust) in the *Realities* of Heaven, but never, never, in creatures of flesh and blood.[43]

An argument Coleridge offers against Rousseau is based on the institution of property:

> The chief object for which men first formed themselves into a State was not the protection of their lives but of their property . . . Now it is impossible to deduce the Right of Property from pure Reason[44]

For Locke, the social contract provided a legitimation of property; in Rousseau, as for Marx later, property distribution demands revolutionary revision. John Stuart Mill thought that Coleridge's 'greatest service' in political thought was in his 'reviving the idea of a *trust* inherent in landed property'[45] and his denial of any absolute rights thereto.

Can the contractual model sustain the natural human aspiration for deeper significance in the social-political domain? One of the obvious problems with such a contractual model, in which all the relevant agents are rational, and at least relatively autonomous (behind the veil of ignorance), is the position of dependants and children. The increasing separation of sexuality, parenting and children in Western consumer-orientated society raises very serious moral problems.[46] As Stephen Clark observes:

> The origin of moral and political bonds lies with . . . immediate natural relationships, and care for children is not marginal but central. That is why contemporary discussion of the 'rights' of future

---

42 Ibid., p. 201.
43 Ibid., p. 202.
44 Ibid., pp. 199–200.
45 J. S. Mill, 'Coleridge', in *Utilitarianism and Other Essays* (Harmondsworth: Penguin, 1987), p. 219.
46 See J. Rist, *Real Ethics: Rethinking the Foundations of Morality* (Cambridge: Cambridge University Press, 2002), p. 184.

generations must strike traditionalists as scholastic. The issue is not about their rights, but about our duties.[47]

Herein lies the major difficulty for all contract models – excessive abstraction and/or circularity. We imagine a contract being made by pre-social beings. But contractual agreement presupposes an already existing web of ties and bonds – a society, in fact. A common morality is necessary as the cement of society and relations with others; 'my station and its duties', as F. H. Bradley liked to argue, is constitutive of the human self, not an additional component. The pre-social rational agent is a desiccated abstraction, far too narrow a foundation for either self or society. In fact, the nearest thing we can imagine to non-social human beings is a group on the very edge, rather like Turnbull's 'Mountain People'.[48]

An interesting instance of the weakness of contractual theories is Karl Popper's view of the 'open society', a famous critique of utopianism in the form of totalitarian ideologies. The opposite of the open society is, naturally, the closed society, which may be tribal, feudal or totalitarian, where all submit to the direction of the party. In the open society, there is no overarching vision and no centrally planned society, which Popper sees exemplified in Plato and Marx. But it is subject to continual and universal criticism, and by implication continual modification of institutions, in view of their suitability for solving specific problems. At the heart of Popper's political thought is negative utilitarianism. The minimal constraint on the open society for Popper is the avoidance of harm. Politics is constituted by general consent in regard to the reduction of manifest evils. It is essentially a pluralist vision: what is ruled out of court is the employment of an overarching vision of what should be. The basis of the open society is the idea that reasoned and reasonable debate can solve problems and forge social harmony. But it is not clear that this negative utilitarianism is really coherent. Is not the idea of a 'manifest ill' parasitic upon some idea of the good? If we take those ethical issues which really do impinge on public policy, agreement upon a manifest ill may not help at all. We may all agree that prolonged human suffering is a manifest ill, but does that justify euthanasia?[49] After all, one of the closed societies which was the direct target of Popper's strictures, Nazi Germany, enthusiastically supported euthanasia.

On such issues, governments have to make decisions, but it is not clear that there will be real agreement. The solutions will be largely pragmatic. And of course there is no a priori reason why, even if consensus is reached, the truth will ensue. Virtually everyone in ancient and medieval Christendom accepted slavery but that did not make it right. Consider an issue where there is broad consensus. We are all convinced that child pornography is wicked – no amount of intellectual exploration, I think,

---

47 S. R. L. Clark, *Civil Peace and Social Order* (Oxford: Clarendon Press, 1989), p. 58.
48 C. Turnbull, *The Mountain People* (London: Johathan Cape, 1973).
49 I owe this point to Anthony O'Hea, see 'The Open Society Revisited', in *Karl Popper: Critical Appraisals*, ed. P. Cotton and G. Macdonald, (London: Routledge, 2004), pp. 189–202.

would incline us to say 'the child pornographer may be right'. And it seems that something deeper than questions of social utility is at stake. A society which abuses its young and tolerates this abuse is not just irrational but sick. Burke speaks of 'that tribunal of conscience which exists independently of edicts and decrees'.[50] Such bonds of morality are prior to any contract.[51] And as we know from Nazi Germany or the Soviet Union, neither democracy nor a liberal constitution guarantees freedom from tyranny. Thus the rationalism of a thinker like Popper leads into conflict with deeply held moral intuitions.

Anthony O'Hear convincingly analyses Popper as offering a crude and false alternative: between irrational societies on that one hand, and rational societies who have rejected tradition on the other. The 'open' society is itself part of a flourishing tradition and such a society will be undermined if those values and beliefs about the virtues of consent and debate are eroded and rejected from within. It is clear that Burke is also casting doubt on the notion that our convictions can be subject to perpetual critique. Even in a pluralistic society within which opposing traditions exist, the individual needs to identify with a tradition in order to avoid superficiality. The identification requires imaginative and emotional engagement. The democrat has to care about certain practices and traditions and to empathize with them. The extreme liberal's attempt to refrain from imparting any kind of bias which is not strictly rational is self-subverting. In T. S. Eliot's words:

A people without history
Is not redeemed from time.[52]

Coleridge's loathing of abstraction was pronounced. Writing in support of the Factory Bill of 1818, Coleridge observed: 'Generalities are apt to deceive us. Individualize the sufferings which it is the object of this Bill to remedy, follow up the detail in some one case with a human sympathy, and the deception vanishes.'[53]

Indeed, if democratic conviction is subjected to the canons of purely instrumental abstract rationality, its basis appears very fragile. Democratic praxis should not be misunderstood as a means to a perfect end as *poesis*, but as a rational commitment to a complex set of practices and values which have grown up within a certain historical context and suffuse our social imaginary. One might observe that belief in a Whiggish march of progress from the American and French Revolutions to modern parliamentary democracy is deeply questionable. The beginning of the twentieth century was dominated in Europe by anti-democratic movements:

50 Quoted in A. O'Hear, *After Progress: Finding the Old Way Forward* (London: Bloomsbury, 1999), p. 42.
51 Ibid., pp. 38ff.
52 T. S. Eliot, 'Little Gidding', V, in *Collected Poems 1909–1962* (London: Faber and Faber, 1974), p. 222.
53 Quoted in R. J. White, *The Political Thought of Samuel Taylor Coleridge* (London: Jonathan Cape, 1938), p. 220. Coleridge was scathing in his criticism of Pitt as a man who employed 'Abstractions defined by abstractions! Generalities defined by generalities': ibid., p. 72.

Russia, Germany, Italy, Romania and Spain were all anti-democratic and the German Weimar Republic was under siege until it collapsed. Even in France, democracy was challenged by the far right and the far left. Parliamentary democracy was an exception and it is rather remarkable that the military collapse of fascism and the subsequent economic collapse of socialism produced a Europe in which parliamentary democracy has come to dominate. Yet this, in a sense, is a very welcome but hardly predictable outcome.

Bildung

. . . the communication
Of the dead is tongued with fire beyond the language of the
living. Here, the intersection of the timeless moment
Is England and nowhere.
Never and always.[54]

Historically one can see Burke drawing upon an essentially Thomist-Aristotelian view of prudence, while Coleridge has more Platonic sympathies. For Coleridge, intelligent will, that is man's spiritual nature, is the capacity of action determined by reference to ultimate goals. The problem with Rousseau is that he has employed 'truths, but most important and sublime Truths; and that their falsehood and their danger consist altogether in their misapplication.'[55] On Rousseau's account, 'All voluntary actions say they, having for their objects, good or evil, are *moral* actions.'[56] Here Coleridge is at one with Rousseau: 'Car l'impulsion de l'appétit est esclavage, et l'obéissance à une loi qu'on s'est préscrite est liberté.'[57]

Coleridge is, I suggest, subtler than either Rousseau or Edmund Burke in avoiding the extremes of contractualism and traditionalism. *On the Constitution of the Church and State* (1830) is a work on the nature and history of the English constitution which is a response to the contractualism of the French and Scottish Enlightenment.[58] Coleridge saw the state as based upon a dynamic and irresolvable tension between permanence (the landed aristocracy) and progression (manufacturing and professions). The constitution is formed by the 'law of balance' between these principles, and change in the constitution is best understood, Coleridge thinks, as an organic process rather than the mechanical substitution of one system of government for another. Yet he importantly included a third principle which he calls the 'National Church', a group of

54 Eliot, 'Little Gidding', I, in *Collected Poems*, p. 215.
55 Coleridge, *The Friend*, vol. 1, p. 185.
56 Ibid., p. 184.
57 Jean-Jacques Rousseau, *Du contrat social* (Paris: Flammarion, 1992), p. 44.
58 S. T. Coleridge, *On the Constitution of the Church and State* (Princeton NJ: Princeton University Press, 1976).

teachers called the 'clerisy' distributed throughout the land. Mill claims that Coleridge 'vindicated against Bentham and Adam Smith and the whole eighteenth century, the principle of an endowed class, for the cultivation of learning, and for diffusing its results among the community'.[59] This should not be confused with the Christian Church, but represents a common trust of the nation which serves the cultural and spiritual growth of the population.[60] The National Church, constituted by the clerisy, serves to cultivate 'the harmonious development of those qualities and faculties that characterize our *humanity*'.[61] Human minds are not inert instruments which respond passively to stimuli from without; the discipline and cultivation of the mind is the educating of souls. Culture, as opposed to mere civilization, is the formation of self-conscious, reflective rational beings capable of contemplating eternal truths through the symbols of religion.[62] On the other hand, unity is not to be confused with mere uniformity. Society is not merely the sum of individuals but also a spiritual community in which eternal values constitute an essential component. Coleridge would concur with Taylor that a merely secular society 'involves stifling the response in us to some of the deepest and most powerful aspirations that human beings have conceived'.[63] Coleridge says of the healthy body politic:

> Thus the dignity of Human Nature will be secured, and at the same time a lesson of humility taught to each individual, when we are made to see that the universal necessary Laws, and pure IDEAS of Reason, were given us, not for the purpose of flattering our Pride and enabling us to become national legislators; but that by an energy of continued self conquest, we might establish a free and yet absolute government in our own spirits.[64]

Coleridge's theory of culture is directed against a doctrine of *pleonexia*.[65] Coleridge sees Adam Smith as formulating a theory that appeals to the worst aspect of the imagination. In *The Theory of Moral Sentiments* Adam Smith writes:

> What are the advantages which we propose by that great purpose of human life which we call bettering our condition? To be observed, to be attended to, to be taken notice of with sympathy, complacency, and approbation, are all the advantages which we can propose to derive from it. It is the vanity, not the ease or the pleasure, which interests us.[66]

---

59 See Mill, 'Coleridge', p. 212.
60 Ibid., p. 208.
61 Ibid.
62 Ibid., pp. 42–3
63 Taylor, *Sources of the Self*, p. 520.
64 Coleridge, *The Friend*, vol. 1, p. 185.
65 See Plato, *Republic* 359c.
66 Quoted in P. Manent, *The City of Man* (Princeton, NJ: Princeton University Press, 1998), p. 88.

The theory that vanity is the source of 'bettering our condition' fits in well with contemporary theories of morality, like that of his friend David Hume:

> Our imagination . . . expands itself to every thing around us. We are then charmed with the beauty of that accommodation which reigns in the palaces and the economy of the great; and admire how everything is adapted to promote their ease, to prevent their wants, to gratify their wishes, and to amuse and entertain their most frivolous desires. If we consider the real satisfaction which all these things are capable of affording, by itself and separated from the beauty of that arrangement which is fitted to promote it, it will always appear in the highest degree contemptible and trifling . . . The pleasures of wealth and greatness, when considered in this complex view, strike the imagination as something grand, and beautiful, and noble, of which the attainment is well worth all the toil and anxiety which we are apt to bestow upon it.[67]

In Smith's theory the imagination feeds upon human vanity. Smith notes the gap between the actual benefits of goods and their significance for human vanity. But he notes that 'it is well that nature imposes upon us in this manner. It is this deception which arouses and keeps in continual motions the industry of mankind.'[68] This industry can found agriculture and civilization and 'improve all the sciences and arts, which ennoble and embellish human life'.[69] Yet one might challenge the notion that the advance of the economy is an unqualified good. Coleridge saw this notion as part of a general malaise – the 'OVERBALANCE OF THE COMMERCIAL SPIRIT'.[70]

And one can see that materialistic values may generate wealth but also produce much human misery. Depression, anxiety and personality disorders are clearly widespread in Western Europe and North America, and the imaginative identification of self with competitive symbols of prestige and status, clearly evinced in the advertising industry – where evidently fantasy is manipulated to stimulate greed – fuels much of the dissatisfaction and disappointment experienced.

Coleridge's plea is for a group of teachers whose major task is not merely to instruct with facts or information but to educate and cultivate the rational spirit in the young. This education provides contemplative detachment from immediate concerns and needs, and the capacity for contemplation of – and assent to – those immaterial values and principles that distinguish man from beast:

> cvilization is itself but a mixed good, if not far more a corrupting influence . . . where [it] is not grounded in *cultivation*, in the

---

67 Quoted ibid., 90.
68 Quoted ibid., 90.
69 Quoted ibid., 90.
70 Coleridge, *Lay Sermons*, p. 169.

harmonious development of those qualities and faculties that characterize our *humanity*. We must be men in order to be citizens.[71]

Coleridge agrees with Rousseau that 'whatever law or system of law compels any other service, disennobles our nature, leagues itself with the animal against the godlike, kills in us the very principle of joyous well doing, and fights against humanity'.[72]

The theory of the clerisy is ostensibly anti-Rousseauian – the view expressed in *Émile* is that clergy should play no role in education – but Coleridge's theory incorporates elements which are close to Rousseau. Coleridge's own view of the ideal constitution of the Church and the state is a scathing critique (Mill says the 'severest satire'[73]) of the Church's de facto arrangements.

In the *Table Talk* of September 1830, Coleridge refers to the bitter error of the Church 'clinging to the court and state instead of cultivating the people'. He argues that the state regards people as groups rather than as individuals, such as with regard to birth and property. The (ideal) Church operates from the reverse perspective – treating people as individual persons without gradation of rank: 'A Church is therefore in Idea the only pure Democracy'.[74]

It is often precisely those who claim to be free of the dead weight of history and tradition who are most vulnerable to the unchallenged dogmas, presumptions and unreflective prejudices of the *Zeitgeist*. Gadamer has argued vigorously that those who labour under the illusion that they are free from prejudices will be unconsciously dominated by them. It is no paradox that T. S. Eliot produced the most striking protocol of the mood of the interwar years of the twentieth century – and he was the man who insisted on the need for individual creativity to flourish on the basis of tradition, and who consciously sought to reappropriate Homer and Dante.[75] As Newman observed, 'In a higher world it is otherwise; but here below to live is to change, and to be perfect is to have changed often.'[76]

Charles Taylor describes very eloquently the shift in the Western imaginary from a social 'hierarchical complementarity' reflecting cosmic order to an instrumental contract for the sake of reciprocal benefits of equal members, in which security and economic welfare constitute the prime ends. Taylor's account comes together with his limpid analysis of the three pivotal aspects of the economy, the public sphere and popular sovereignty. The book is a subtle critique of those neo-liberals who fail to appreciate the genealogy of Western 'modernity'. In the spirit of

---

71 Coleridge, *On the Constitution of Church and State*, pp. 42–3.
72 Coleridge, *The Friend*, vol. 1, p. 191.
73 Mill, 'Coleridge', p. 211.
74 S. T. Coleridge, *Table Talk*, vol. 1 (Princeton NJ: Princeton University Press, 1990), p. 189.
75 See T. S. Eliot, 'Tradition and the Individual Talent', in *Selected Essays*, 3rd edn (London: Faber and Faber, 1953), pp. 13–22.
76 J. H. Newman, *Essay on the Development of Christian Doctrine* (Harmondsworth: Penguin, 1974), p. 100.

Gadamer, Taylor's work is a challenge to those who are unaware of their own prejudices as such.

European culture, with its cosmopolitanism and universalism, is perceived by many (especially Muslims) as a particularly insidious form of Western imperialism. Rémi Brague, however, in his book *Eccentric Culture: A Theory of Western Civilisation*, has emphasized the fact that European culture has an external source. Seeing Rome, and more directly Charlemagne, as the key to European identity, he argues that European culture owes its vigour to its *derivative* qualities – Roman culture drew from both Athens and Jerusalem. Rather than seeing Europe's identity as its own original creation and as self-defined, Brague identifies its capacity to learn as its most striking feature. The Californian campus may try to change the curriculum to reflect the politics of minority groups in order to counteract occidental hegemony. But Brague argues that this is based upon a mistake:

> The question should never be one of knowing if an author belongs to our tradition or not, and yet less if he has the same sex or the same 'race' as we do. The only legitimate question seeks to know whether an author is worth the trouble of being read for himself.
>
> This is, besides, just what the Europeans have done in the past. They have not studied the Greek and Latin classics because they were the sources of Europe, and therefore because they were fundamentally themselves, so that in studying them they came to know themselves better, and were able to affirm their own particularity. To the contrary, they studied them, as they studied besides Muslim or Jewish thinkers, because they found their works true, beautiful, interesting etc. One could thus extract something like a cultural law according to which the appropriation of a source is fruitful only if it is disinterested. In stark terms: only what is free pays.[77]

Brague is surely making a very important point when he highlights the significance of the plurality of sources at the foundation of the inheritance of European culture. Thus Brague can note that within Christendom there was no uncritical sense of a single sacred language linking the community to the supernatural order. Latin did not have the status of Classical Arabic, Sanskrit, Pali, or Classical Chinese, and could not, because of its dependence upon the source languages of revelation. This has enormous implications for the Latin European imaginary if the philosophers still speak Greek and the angels Hebrew!

Brague's account of the 'disinterested' is a fine explanation of the importance of an inherited tradition and culture. Multiculturalism is an ingrained feature of the organic and inherited tradition of the European mind. Brague is surely correct that respect for non-European culture will not be enhanced by ignoring or denigrating Europe's intellectual and

---

77 R. Brague, *Eccentric Culture: A Theory of Western Civilization* (South Bend, Ind. St Augustine's Press, 2002), p. 143.

cultural inheritance. Let me draw an analogy from child psychology. It is the child with a good family context who is most capable of leaving that home and forming good relationships with others. The capacity for imaginative empathy with other cultures must presuppose a strong imaginative engagement with the home culture. We cannot appreciate the meaning of certain aspects of another heritage or form of life without first having a real engagement with our own.

On images

The attack on fanaticism had its roots in the critique of enthusiasm by the Cambridge Platonists during the Civil War. Both Burke and Coleridge saw themselves as inheritors of this tradition. It was Coleridge's conviction that England's spiritual decline began with the Glorious Revolution. Locke and Grotius became the dominant figures for the eighteenth century, and for the prosaic compromise and worldliness of the Hanoverian Church. Coleridge was fascinated by the *aesthetische Wende* (aesthetic turn) of the English seventeenth century. Charles Taylor, with justification, concentrates on the American and French Revolutions, and he does not particularly dwell upon the English Civil War. This was a period in which there was a vehement struggle within the Church of England concerning images and iconoclasm. The Elizabethan Settlement led to a stripping of the churches. Under Archbishop Laud there was a revival of the conscious use of images within the Church – the 'beauty of holiness'. This was a source of bitter controversy. The main targets were the Oxford colleges and cathedrals, and Cambridge followed their lead. Priests who objected to the innovations were punished severely. This battle between the iconophiles and the iconoclasts within the Church of England was one of the factors which led to the Civil War and culminated in the execution of Laud. It was a development which affected music and architecture as well as producing vitriolic debates about stone altars and communion tables, or the use of railings.

One of the figures integral to the development of a theological aesthetic was the Christian Platonist and Arminian Thomas Jackson (1579–1640). Jackson pleaded for the value of art. He argued that Christians should look to the Divine through the medium of the visible – not away from it. Jackson would have approved of Ruskin's adage: 'To see clearly is poetry, prophecy and religion.' In a discussion of emblems and art, Jackson claims that 'we cannot contemplate incorporeal substances without imagination of some corporeal form'.[78] In a passage redolent of Michelangelo, he observes that the sculptor 'only makes that visible and apparent to the eye which was formerly hidden or inveiled in the stone'.[79]

---

78 Thomas Jackson, *Treatise of the Divine Essence and Attributes* (London, 1628), p. 40.
79 Ibid., p. 239.

One of the most glorious products of seventeenth-century Oxford was Thomas Traherne. His is a theology of the world's beauty, linked to a profound sense of the immanence of the Divine in the created realm.

Your Enjoyment of the World is never right, till you so esteem it, that everything in it, is more your treasure then a King's exchequer full of Gold and Silver. Can you take too much joy in your Father's works? He is Himself in every Thing.
. . . You never Enjoy the world aright till the Sea itself floweth in your veins, till you are clothed with the heavens and crowned with the Stars.[80]

The age of Shakespeare and Donne through to Jeremy Taylor, Henry More and George Herbert was the age not just of the greatest flowering of the arts in England but the development of a theological aesthetic.

The roots of Cambridge Platonism can be traced back through Thomas Jackson. Furthermore, Jackson can be identified as one channel through which Platonism was mediated to literary circles: he was linked to George Herbert through their close mutual friend Nicholas Ferrar of Little Gidding, and through his patrons the Danvers and the Earl of Pembroke. He was also read by Thomas Traherne. Henry Vaughan was a student in Oxford in Jackson's time. The religious poetry of such writers as Milton, Vaughan, Traherne and Marvell is in many ways the poetic counterpoint of the Cambridge Platonists' philosophical theology.[81]

Lying behind this theory of the 'image' is the conviction that the mind should be purged of false attachments determined by particular longings and loyalities and selfish desire (*pleonexia*) to the exclusion of universal truths, the eternal and immutable noetic cosmos. But it can learn a detachment which contemplates particular beauties as a guide to, and symbol of, a far greater world than the transitory domain revealed by the senses.

'Image' in Shakespearean English did not mean figure of speech but a painting or sculpture, as in this passage from *King Lear*:

KENT: Is this the promised end
EDGAR: Or Image of that horror?
ALBION: Fall, and cease![82]

The image here possesses a strongly religious sense, close to that of 'icon'. The word 'end' can mean limit (Land's End), conclusion, line or the end of life. However, the word also has a further, important meaning: end as ultimate goal or purpose. The physical world is doomed. If we take the second law of thermodynamics seriously as the principle that the universe is in a state of inexorably increasing entropy, the best we can

---

80 Thomas Traherne, *Centuries of Meditations*, I, 25, 29 (London: Dobell, 1927), p. 19.
81 See A. Baldwin and S. Hutton, *Platonism and the English Imagination* (Cambridge: Cambridge University Press, 1994), p. 74. Cf. P. White, *Predestination, Policy and Polemic* (Cambridge: Cambridge University Press, 1992), pp. 256–71.
82 William Shakespeare, *King Lear*, V.iii.37–9.

hope for in a fallen world is to try to ameliorate and improve matters, while perfection is unattainable.

Aristotle distinguishes between two characteristic kinds of human activity, *praxis* and *poiesis*: between an instrumental making, and action or conduct.[83] Building a house and thinking might represent instances of the two kinds of activity. In the first case there is a beginning and an end to the process, and an obvious goal. The object is well or badly constructed. In the second case, the question of the goal is more elusive. Certainly there is not a *product* as such. Much worthwhile human activity is *praxis* in the broadly Aristotelian sense. There is no clear result to be attained or a clearly defined goal. Health or education are good instances of areas where specific targets can be deeply misleading. If one is learning a sport or musical instrument, it is not clear what defines success. Certainly there are no clear guidelines for both beginner and expert as to what constitutes, say, learning a language. Achievement must depend upon contingent factors surrounding the particular activity. Furthermore, in many areas there are no procedural rules. The right action must depend upon the imagination and judicious prudence of the agent. A striking aspect of the political developments after 1789 is in terms of the failure of utopian political schemes. Robert Spaemann has argued that modern radicalism from Rousseau to Marx fundamentally misconstrued human *praxis* as *poiesis*.[84] Instead of understanding politics as the practice of striving for the good within the limits of human nature and society with its inherited traditions and forms of culture, Marx presented an eschatological immanentism in which reform could achieve a stable end and goal – that of the classless society. Such an eschatological utopianism was evinced in the horrors of Bolshevism and the Nazi sense of 'history'. Taylor refers to the 'troubling legacy' which he sees in the 'link between democratic revolution and scapegoating violence' as 'one of the most disquieting features of modernity'.[85]

Taylor views Rousseau as a key figure in the development of a revolutionary ideology which justified the radical purges of twentieth-century regimes in the name of the people through his theory of the fusion of the individual and common wills. This, Taylor insists, is 'Manichaean, highly "ideological", even quasi-religious in tone'.[86] Those who did not conform to the 'general will' were a justified target of 'scapegoating violence'.

The narrow and instrumental rationalism of many contractual theorists fails to appreciate the proper role of imagination and emotion. A rational individual develops his or her rationality within a cultural

83 Aristotle, *Nicomachean Ethics* 1139b1.
84 R. Spaemann, 'Aufhalter und Letztes Gefecht', in K. Stierle and R. Warning (eds), *Das Ende Figuren einer Dankform* (Munich: Fink, 1996), pp. 564–77. Thanks to Barbara von Wulffen. The peculiarity of the modern idea of progress was to consider progress as the object of the *poiesis*, of making; yet simultaneously to think of this making as indefinite', R. Rorty, *Philosophy and the Mirror of Nature* (Oxford: Blackwell, 1980), p. 574.
85 Taylor, *Modern Social Imaginaries*, p. 138.
86 Ibid, p. 125.

tradition. Belief in democracy, for example, is the application of what Burke calls 'prejudice with reason involved':

> because prejudice, with its reason, has a motive to give action to that reason, and an affectation which will give it permanence. Prejudice is of ready application in the emergency; it previously engages the mind in a steady course of wisdom and virtue, and does not leave the man hesitating in the moment of decision, sceptical, puzzled and unresolved. Prejudice renders a man's virtue his habit; and not a series of unconnected acts. Through just prejudice his duty becomes part of his nature.[87]

Burke can place such a high estimate upon 'prejudice' because he is operating with an essentially providential view of history. This can provide a defence against fanaticism and utopianism because of the mysterious yet providential workings of the Divine in human history; but it can also provide a bulwark against the pernicious and corrosive effect of pessimism and individualism. I suggest that our imaginary still requires that our fragile sense of justice and honour, even our most maimed and abortive efforts to improve a world which is in a state of entropy, are grounded in a transcendent hope and the intimation of the *imago Dei* in the human soul, the Romantic 'mood' or *Stimmung* which we explored in Chapter 3. Coleridge, picking up on Burke's idea of the state as a partnership between 'the living, the dead, and the unborn', presented its institutions as inadequate, transient embodiments of an eternal and perfect idea. The City of Man, if it is to be more than a collection of strangers, reflects, if only imperfectly, the City of God.

All human beings require community and a sense of belonging, and the communities they belong to are necessarily imperfect. A country like England, with its rich, continuous, evolving tradition, possesses providential boons in its universities and cathedrals. These institutions may be hard to justify in strictly rational terms, but they form organic realities. The inherited wealth of the ancient universities is a bulwark against the draconian measures of governments with short-term electoral interests and mandates.

The Church of England's established position and the non-congregational parish system seem equally a precarious anomaly, yet only if one forgets Burke's and Coleridge's strictures about contingency and human frailty. Erasing tradition will obliterate innovation rather than stimulate it. The parish system points to the dimension of religion which extends beyond the bonds of the existing congregation of Christians. The Church, like the monarchy, represents dimensions of the partnership between dead and future generations, though, unlike the monarchy, it points beyond space and time to the communion of saints in the heavenly Jerusalem. The glories of the Book of Common Prayer and the King James Bible, the magnificent choral tradition of the cathedral and college choirs, are parts of the wider fabric of the imaginary. For example, as Anderson notes, 'The United Kingdom of Great Britain and Ireland' does

---

87 E. Burke, *Reflections on the French Revolution*, p. 84.

not name a nation reflecting the legacy of the old dynastic order.[88] And yet English imaginary – the sense of being English – is a very deep conviction, whether in Bede, Shakespeare or Wordsworth. The fact that Westminster Abbey includes poets and social reformers, whereas the cathedral of St Denis near Paris holds only monarchs, reveals a significant difference between national histories. To understand our roots is to employ the past so that we are not absorbed by mere history:

> History may be servitude,
> History may be freedom. See, now they vanish,
> The faces and places, with the self which, as it could, loved them,
> To become renewed, transfigured, in another pattern.[89]

When we accept the spiritual temper of our ancestors and can share their aspirations, we can have communion with the past:

> All touched by a common genius,
> United in the strife which divided them.[90]

It is a common tenet of much contemporary ethical thought that we have neglected the plurality of forms of human flourishing. Particularly after the collapse of the 'Enlightenment Project' we can safely reject the idea of an overarching paradigm of human life. John Dewey insisted that the idea of the *summum bonum* was a genuine obstacle to ethics because it implied the rejection of the fluidity of human nature and human potential. However, the *transcendent* horizon of the theist should be no more susceptible to intolerance than its secular counterpart. Civil government should be subordinate to ultimate values which can only be realized imperfectly. The infinite good which is God can only be imitated in a variety of imperfect ways. This conviction is a bulwark against the excesses of utopianism.[91] Yet it helps one avoid a debilitating relativism, whether this be based on the satisfaction of individual desires or group interests, and the cynical resignation to the corrosive power of materialism or envy. As Brian Hebblethwaite observes: 'The pure white of the divine light will for ever be refracted in the many colours of created being and goodness.'[92]

Imagination and *Bildung*

In *Philosophy and the Mirror of Nature* Richard Rorty famously takes the espousal of Gadamer's concept of *Bildung* as an 'effort to get rid of the classic picture of man-as-essentially-knower-of-essences',[93] and as akin to

---

88 B. R. O'G. Anderson, *Imagined Communities* (London: Verso, 1983), p. 12.

89 T. S. Eliot, 'Little Gidding', III; *Collected Poems*, p. 219.

90 Ibid., p. 220.

91 See Chris Insole's excellent book *The Politics of Human Frailty: A Defence of Theological Liberalism* (London: SCM Press, 2004), pp. 33ff..

92 B. Hebblethwaite, 'Varieties of Goodness', in *Ethics and Religion in a Pluralistic Age: Collected Essays* (Edinburgh: T&T Clark, 1997), p. 60.

93 Rorty, *Philosophy and the Mirror of Nature*, p. 364.

his own proposal that 'edifying philosophy' (Rorty's term for *Bildung*) 'aims at continuing a conversation rather than at discovering truth'.[94] Yet it was empiricists such as Locke and Hume who saw the mind as a passive 'mirror' of nature, reflecting independent items and events. *Bildung* does contain the active element of production – *shaping* – which could fit with Rorty's anti-realistic account. But it also has connotations of *imitation* – or the relation between icon and archetype.

Gadamer explicitly rejects the deep pessimism of Heidegger's apocalyptic-Gnostic conviction of the *Seinsvergessenheit* (forgetting of being) of occidental culture. He rejects the iconoclastic, anti-humanist component in Heidegger's thought that was part of the reception of *Lebensphilosophie*, Nietzsche, Kierkegaard and Dostoevsky, dialectical theology and expressionism – the febrile and portentous milieu of Thomas Mann's *Dr Faustus*.

The concept of *Bildung* has been revived in the twentieth century through Gadamer. His interest in this very un-Heideggerian concept is an instance of Gadamer's humanism – 'urbanising the Heideggerian province', to use the celebrated expression of Habermas.[95] In his attack upon a narrowly Cartesian obsession with method and the limits of a narrowly technocratic and instrumental rationality, Gadamer draws upon Herder and the Romantic tradition. There is no equivalent of the concept of *Bildung* in other Germanic languages, or in Romance languages. Through the mystical associations of *bilden*, *Bildung* became associated with German reaction against Western Europe and Descartes in particular. The *aesthetische Wende* (aesthetic turn) in the mid-eighteenth century was a reaction to the paradigm of mechanistic scientific models. It culminated in Hegel, where self-consciousness and the history of Spirit is at the centre of thought.[96] This idea of *Bildung* drew upon the philological humanism of the eighteenth century – Weimar Classicism, especially reflection on poetry – and idealism. Hence for Schiller, *Bildung* is expression or externalization. Schiller's *Aesthetische Briefe* drew Hegel, Hölderlin and Schelling away from Kant's moralism.[97] But the Romantics reinvested the *Bildung* concept of Weimar with the religious resonances of its pre-history via Pietism and medieval mysticism. Gadamer is perfectly aware of this dimension of the *Bildung* concept. Far from being, as Rorty portentiously proposes in *Philosophy and the Mirror of Nature*, an alternative to the mirror-image paradigm,[98] the concept of *Bildung* is dependent upon it. The word *Bildung* has its roots in Eckhart's highly spiritualized and Neoplatonic interpetation of 2 Corinthians 3.18, *in eandem imaginem transformamur*. The translation of *transformare* (as referring to the work of the indwelling Divine Spirit or Platonic Intellect) was into *Überformen* or *Überbilden*. *Forma* and *imago* were fused to convey the transformation of the soul into the image of its divine

94 Ibid., p. 373.
95 J. Grondin, *Hans-Georg Gadamer: Eine Biographie* (Tübingen: Mohr Siebeck, 2000) p. 5.
96 E. Lichtenstein, *Zur Entwicklung des Bildungsbegriffs von Meister Eckhart bis Hegel* (Heidelberg: Quelle und Meyer, 1966), p. 22.
97 Lichtenstein, *Zur Entwicklung des Bildungsbegriffs*, p. 30.
98 Rorty, *Philosphy and the Mirror of Nature*, pp. 12ff., 392ff.

source in Christ. Hence for Eckhart, *Bildung* ultimately means deification. Jung liked to quote Eckhart's remark that God must be born in the soul again and again. Jung envisages the drama of the self as acted out in an inhospitable world devoid of meaning. But the self that Eckhart thinks should be reflected is the cosmic Christ, begotten not made, eternal Son of the Father, God from God. This Lamb who seems so harsh – demanding that we die to the old self – presents a message of deep hope, of being transformed into his image. *Überbilden* is not just 'images above all' but a transformation into the image of the God who transcends all images. The biblical starting point is St Paul, but the link between image and apophaticism is just as Neoplatonic as it is biblical.

We should consider the fact that, compared with the other Abrahamic religions, Christianity is not without qualification a religion of the law. Judaism centres around the Torah, Islam the revelation delivered to Muhammad; but there is no need to postulate an essential link between the essence of the Godhead and the deliverances of the divine will. Christianity is an incarnational religion. Christ is image (2 Corinthians 4.4; Colossians 1.15) and the Christian is restored to the image of God (Colossians 3.9; 1 Corinthians 11.7). The Christian is explicitly described as an image of Christ (Romans 8.29; 1 Corinthians 15.49; 2 Corinthians 3.18). Christianity has the doctrine of the Word made flesh – a Word which is consubstantial with the Father. It is a strict implication of the doctrine of the Trinity that the essence of God is revealed in his Son – he is a light and mirror of the Father. Accordingly it is a central tenet of Christian theology that this presence should be seen in the sons of God of the new creation of which Paul speaks in Romans. Hence Christians, like Platonists, have good reasons to try to see the invisible in the visible and to have faith in the religious imagination. Coleridge coins a word in English for the imagination: esemplastic:

"Esemplastic. The word is not in Johnson, nor have I met with it elsewhere." Neither have I! I have constructed it myself from the Greek words εἰς ἕν πλάττειν i.e. to shape into one[99]

Bild carries the dynamic sense of form (i.e. formation or plastic). Cudworth's pupil Shaftesbury forges the link between plastic nature and forms as active spiritual principles. In this manner the personality and genius of man is revealed. The formative principle of the soul is the inward form – moral aesthetic unity. The goal of *Bildung* is that self-formation which is not an external copy but comes from within, through aesthetic education. But aesthetic education or *Bildung* retained, through its evident etymology and Christological provenance (Herder, Lessing, Hegel, Schelling and Scheiermacher were all learned theologians) a resolutely theological resonance. As Charles Taylor notes,

Most of the great Romantic poets saw themselves as articulating something greater than themselves: the world, nature being the word of God. They were not concerned primarily with an expression of their own feelings.[100]

T. S. Eliot was deeply influenced by Coleridge's vision. The proximity to Coleridge can be seen clearly in 'Little Gidding' and Eliot's deeply Platonic distinction between detachment and indifference. The source of detachment is the contemplation of eternal verities, which is the vision of God. Detachment should not, however, be confused with inertia generated by indifference to the world:

There are three conditions which often look alike
Yet differ completely, flourish in the same hedgerow:
Attachment to self and to things and to persons, detachment
From self and from things and from persons; and, growing between
    them between indifference
Which resembles the others as death resembles life,
Being between the live and the dead nettle. This is the use of
    memory:
For liberation – not less of love but expanding
Of love beyond desire, and so liberation
From the future as well as the past.[101]

In 'The Dry Salvages', Eliot draws upon the story in the *Bhagavadgita* where Arjuna in his war chariot is exhorted by his charioteer Krishna to action on the battlefield, but an action which is detached. The story of the great battle has a clearly symbolic dimension: the struggles of the soul. In Shakespeare's last masterpiece, *The Tempest*, Prospero accuses himself of neglecting his worldly duties:

those being all my study,
The government I cast upon my brother,
And to my state grew stranger, being transported
And rapt in secret studies.[102]

The philosopher-magus must return to the cave and, indeed, Prospero restores order. Eliot wrote the poem in wartime, when indifference was evidently intolerable. The context is that of the extraordinarily remote Little Gidding, and Eliot has driven to Little Gidding 'from the place you would be likely to come from', i.e. from Cambridge. This chapel is the site of detachment from the world, the place of a religious community set up in the seventeenth century by Nicholas Ferrar and destroyed by the Puritans. The detachment practised here is not apathy or indifference.

---

100 Taylor, *Sources of the Self*, p. 427.
101 T. S. Eliot, 'Little Gidding', III; *Collected Poems*, p. 219.
102 William Shakespeare, *The Tempest*, I.ii. 74–7.

Contemplation and the Temple

Faire is the heav'n, where happy soules have place,
In full enjoyment of felicitie,
Whence they doe still behold, the glorious face
Of the Divine, eternall Majestie . . .

Yet farre more faire be those bright *Cherubins*,
Which all with golden wings are overdight,
And those eternal burning *Seraphins*,
Which from their faces dart out fiery light:
Yet fairer than they both, and much more bright
Be th'Angels and Archangels, which attend
On God's owne person, without rest or end.

These thus in faire each other farre excelling,
As to the Highest they approach more neare,
Yet is their Highest farre beyond all telling,
Fairer than all the rest which there appeare,
Though all their beauties joynd together were;
How then can mortall tongue hope to expresse,
The image of such endless perfectnesse?[103]

The classical philosophical tradition holds that contemplation is the highest good. What if contemplation can motivate? The mechanical model of motivation is classically expressed by Hobbes, Hume and Smith as self-motivated desire or calculation. For Hume, reason is 'perfectly inert, and can never either prevent or produce any action or affection'.[104] Hence his vivid paradox: 'Reason is, and ought only to be the slave of the passions.'[105] But the rational egoism model has its limitations: precisely those which Rousseau identified in his critique of the *philosophes*. One does not in fact calculate the maximum utility in matters of friendship or family, simple pleasures or aversions, or humdrum duties. Self-help literature exists because many human beings feel alienated from their immediate context, unable to fulfil their potential. Our 'being in the world' has a strong non-reflective component. But we can be 'inspired' to action. Religion is inspiring in the sense of being a motivating force. Wordsworth speaks movingly of the vision of Tintern Abbey as inspiring

103 Edmund Spenser, 'A Hymn of Heavenly Beauty', *Daphnaïan and other poems*, ed. W. L. Penwick, (London: The Scholartis Press, 1929), pp. 147–8.
104 David Hume, *A Treatise of Human Nature*, III.i.1, ed L. A. Selby-Bigge and P. H. Nidditch, II.iii.3; 2nd edn (Oxford: Clarendon Press, 1978), p. 458.
105 Ibid., p. 415.

an 'aspect more sublime', the serene mood that lightens the 'heavy and the weary weight' of the world:

> in this moment there is life and food
> For future years.[106]

Contemplation is often pilloried as unintelligible and empty. Yet it is clearly a source of inspiration. Etymologically it is linked to pre-scientific animistic beliefs. But enthusiasm can be taken literally too – *Deus in nobis*. Is this not the transcendental mood of Wordsworth's 'Tintern Abbey', where the great poet says,

> we are laid asleep
> In body, and become a living soul:
> While with an eye made quiet by the power
> Of harmony, and the deep power of joy,
> We see into the life of things.[107]

Is this not the divine madness of which Plato speaks in the *Phaedrus* and *Ion*?[108] The mythic images of the chariot and the Temple express symbolically the need for a broader and higher purpose, an eternal and immutable morality which transcends finite existence and can unleash the potential energy of the soul: 'The wing'd Chariots of Plato's school'[109] As Henry More, philosophical poet among the Cambridge Platonists, speaks of 'The wing'd Chariots of Plato's School', while his great contemporary Traherne declares:

> Thoughts are the wings on which the soul doth fly,
> The messengers which soar above the sky,
> Elijah's fiery chariot, that conveys
> The soul, even here, to those eternal joys.
> Thoughts are the privileged posts that soar
> Unto His throne, and there appear before
> Ourselves approach. These may at any time
> Above the clouds, above the stars may climb.
> The soul is present by a thought; and sees
> The new Jerusalem, the palaces,
> The thrones and feasts, the regions of the sky,
> The joys and treasures of the Deity.[110]

Contemplation is often identified with 'quietism'. However, many of the great advances in the astronomy of early modern science were the result of a Platonic contemplative ideal, in which mathematics was of central importance. And in more modern science, one can take the

---

106 William Wordsworth, 'Lines Composed a Few Miles above Tintern Abbey', ll. 37, 39, 64–5.
107 Ibid., ll. 45–9.
108 Plato, *Phaedrus* 244–5., *Ion* 534.
109 Henry More, *Philosophical Poems* (Lewisberg, Pa: Bucknell University Press, 1998), p. 486.
110 T. Traherne, 'Thoughts V', II, 4–12, *Selected Poems and Prose*, pp. 70–1.

example of great technical innovations that have relied upon purely contemplative-theoretical discoveries which in turn could then be exploited with enormous practical consequences. Electromagnetism and the telephone might be an example of this: the theoretical knowledge of electromagnetism *preceded* any perceived need to communicate across vast distances. The telegraph and telephone were developed as products of the practical employment of the fruits of theoretical enquiry.[111] The detached contemplation of truth does not imply indifference regarding the fruits of discovery; however, it does presuppose that the goal of science is truth, not utility. The Platonists proper are not averse to action per se, but see action as derived from contemplation. The theorems of Euclid and Pythagoras have, in fact, changed the world, though they were hardly practical discoveries. Plotinus likes to express this idea by saying that 'Action is a weakening of contemplation'.[112] The 'expanding of love beyond desire' means the *detached* enjoyment of earthly beauty and goods – precisely in opposition to the *attachment* to possession and manipulation, the greed which Plato and Aristotle viewed as causing war and strife. That is why we are told in Plato's *Symposium* by Diotima that the person who has a vision of the Good will no longer be distracted and perturbed by desire for possession.[113] A pertinent illustration of contemplative control outside the bounds of strict science can be found in Coleridge's fine depiction of Shakespeare's genius – one who 'first studied patiently, meditated deeply, understood minutely, till knowledge become habitual and intuitive wedded itself to his habitual feelings, and at length gave birth to that stupendous power, by which he stands alone . . . '[114]

And perhaps, one might suggest, inner vision is more important for the intelligent and sensitive transformation of the world than any merely mechanical modification of the external environment. One might think of the enormous *practical* effect of contemplative individuals like Moses, Socrates, Muhammad or Hegel, to say nothing of William Wilberforce or Gandhi, upon world affairs. Mahatma Gandhi is a striking instance. His asceticism and political engagement were closely linked to his adherence to the great Indian monistic Vedantic metaphysics of Sankara (eighth century AD). The frequently serendipitous relationship between discovered fact and the formation of hypothesis can be observed in figures such as Newton and Einstein. Both were men of great imagination and neither lacked a contemplative sensibility. The story of Newton's apple or Einstein brooding over the town clock in Berne may be apocryphal stories, but they illustrate the complex relationship between control of the world and contemplation of its nature. A. E. Taylor states most eloquently:

111 A. E. Taylor, *Does God Exist?* (London: Collins, 1966), p. 78.
112 Plotinus, *Enneads* III.viii.4.
113 Plato, *Symposium*, 211d.
114 Coleridge, *Biographia Literaria*, vol. 2, p. 27.

It would be a false psychology that should treat 'contemplation' as passive, in the sense of being inert. To contemplate aright we must, indeed, be wholly *receptive* towards suggestions from without; we must lay the whole self open to the object contemplated, lose the self in it. But to be thus receptive takes all the energy with which a man is endowed. Contemplation and laziness will not keep house together; and we should merely misunderstand the great master of the mystic way if we supposed their traditional language about passive contemplation to mean that our highest felicity is a state comparable with the lazy enjoyment of a hot bath. Rightly understood, the life of fruition of the vision is not the supersession, but the fulfilment, of the life of dutiful practice of the modest virtues of the family, the city and the nation. What is superseded is only the conflict with adverse elements in the self and its environment, and that is only superseded because it has been brought, by God's grace to a victorious issue.[115]

It is perhaps natural that we should still identify contemplation with its etymological link with 'templum' and its Greek cognate τέμενος. The Temple is a separate area which can serve as a locus for contact between the human and the Divine. In chapter 4 of the Revelation of St John, the seer seems to reflect, and reflect upon, Ezekiel's chariot vision. In this chapter John sees an opening to the heavens and, again like Ezekiel, the seer of Patmos sees a man upon a throne beneath a glassy firmament amid light and a rainbow, and surrounded by strange beasts.[116] The opening of the heavens within the Temple was often seen in the Jewish and Christian tradition as the fulfilment of the contemplation activity that Plato and Aristotle saw as the fulfilment of the Delphic oracle: know thyself![117] In Patmos the legacy of Athens is fused into the new Temple of the heavenly Jerusalem.

Through the exploration of the imagination we can still fulfil the Delphic imperative: the great poets are guides and mirrors of our nature. In this, Shakespeare plays a role for modern occidentals akin to that of Homer in the ancient world. But the greatest poets point beyond self-knowledge of matters all too human to the transcendent poetry of revelation and salvation in which the eternal archetypes and divine forms are bodied forth into human existence and history. The temple is the sacred place of contemplation: an image of the heavenly archetype, and a place of detachment from the world, not indifference to it. From this perspective the world may be viewed through universal poetical forms, what Vico most memorably called 'universali fantastici'. Such forms are both transhistorical and yet appear in concrete historical manifestations or epiphanies. The forms become historical and history is redeemed through the Logos.

115 Taylor, *The Faith of a Moralist*, p. 433.
116 Christman, *What Did Ezekiel See?*, pp. 10ff.
117 H. Corbin, *Temple and Contemplation* (London: KPI, 1986), pp. 290ff.

The religious social imaginary has often, not least in the British Isles, stiffened the habits of the tribe; or worse: reinforced compliance, complacency and servility. However, the living forms of the social imaginary, bodied forth through the Logos, made visible in the pilgrimage from Exodus to Resurrection, can be a vehicle of the highest mode of imagination: the transforming vision that poets, priests and seers trace to the love of God.

Epilogue

Faith is a supply of Reason in things intelligible, as the Imagination is of *light in things Visible.* The *Imagination,* with her *witty,* and *laborious* Pensil, *draws,* and *represents* the *Shapes, Proportions,* and *Distances* of *Persons* and *Places;* taking them onely by the help of some *imperfect Description,* and tis fain to stay here, till it be better satisfied with the *very sight* of the things *themselves.* Thus *Faith* takes things upon an heavenly *representation* and *description,* upon a *Word* upon a *Promise,* it sees an heavenly Cannan in the Map before an *Intellectual Eye* can behold it in a way of *clear* and *open Vision,* for men are not here capable of a *present Heaven,* and happiness of a *compleat,* and vision beautifical ...[1]

This argument or narrative has been the attempt to expound a Platonic intimation expressed in the Romantic 'visionary gleam':

Human life is perceived through the imagination as a drama of the soul and the physical cosmos a temple of the Divine. For Hölderlin, the poet can employ a divine baton (*Stab*) to awaken redeemed humanity to its immortal destiny, the 'Unsterblicher Schicksal'. The prophets and the Scriptures are not merely poetic but paradigmatically so. I have tried to support this tenet through the defence of the apocalyptic dimension of Christianity and the mythical/eschatological aspect of the Platonic tradition. I have offered a defence of the Romantic view of religion as grounded in the intimation of the eternal, and the closely associated view of the centrality of the symbolic as a form of mediation between the finite and the infinite. Evidently, my first target has been those who disparage the ancient doctrine, notably expressed in Plato's *Phaedrus,* that human creativity is a gift of the Divine. I have argued that the imagination is inalienably linked to this irreducible creativity. My second target has been certain anthropological and sociological theories which challenge the Romantic notion of religion as a defining characteristic of humanity – and indeed a *sui generis* phenomenon – reducing religion to a form of social cement, or a by-product of evolutionary mechanisms.

If the imagination is a central component of human ethics and aesthetics, and can serve as a tracking mechanism for truth, then we have

---

1 Nathaneal Culverwel, *An elegant and learned Discourse of the Light of Nature with several other Treaties* (London, 1661), p. 145.

277

a prima facie reason for accepting the parallel legitimacy of imagination in the case of religion. Indeed, my major concern in this work has been to show how ethics, aesthetics and religion – the good, the beautiful and the true – form a complex unity.

Considerations inspired by Donald MacKinnon concerning truth, ethical normativity and beauty led to reflections about stories and narrative inspired by C. S. Lewis and J. R. R. Tolkien. After considering the problem of story, I addressed the idea of the *Christian* story as neither crudely literalistic nor merely figurative, and in particular drew upon Austin Farrer's theory of revelation through inspired images. Finally – and perhaps most controversially – drawing upon Burke and Coleridge, I considered the Christian imaginative framework as a neglected component of the social imaginary and the body politic.

The dazzling syncretistic, oriental-Hellenic magnificence evoked by Hölderlin's 'Patmos' – with its paradoxical coincidence of intense Greek light and the 'dunkeln Grotte' – the dark cave of St John the seer – is a suitable locus to reflect upon how images can point to an unseen reality as icons of an eternal and immutable world: not as sterile abstractions but as living forms of the imagination which furnish a chariot for the soul to ascend to God.

Bibliography

Abrams, Meyer Howard, *Natural Supernaturalism: Tradition and Revolution in Romantic Literature* (London: Oxford University Press, 1971).

Allen, Michael J. B., *Marsilio Ficino and the Phaedran Charioteer* (Berkeley: University of California Press, 1981).

——*The Platonism of Marsilio Ficino: A Study of his 'Phaedrus' Commentary, its Sources and Genesis* (Berkeley, Calif.: University of California Press, 1984).

Alston, William P., *Perceiving God: The Epistemology of Religious Experience* (Ithaca, NY: Cornell University Press, 1995).

Anderson, Benedict R., *Imagined Communities: Reflections on the Origin and Spread of Nationalism* (London: Verso, 1983).

Anscombe, Gertrude Elizabeth Margaret, *The Collected Philosophical Papers of G. E. M. Anscombe*, 3 vols (Oxford: Blackwell, 1981).

Aristotle, *The Ethics of Aristotle: The Nicomachean Ethics*, tr. J. A. K. Thomson, rev. Hugh Tredennick (Harmondsworth: Penguin, 1976).

——*Metaphysics*, tr. Hugh Tredennick (Cambridge, Mass.: Harvard University Press, 1977).

Armstrong, A. H. (ed.), *The Cambridge History of Later Greek and Early Medieval Philosophy* (Cambridge: Cambridge University Press, 1967).

Auerbach, Eric, *Mimesis: The Representation of Reality in Western Literature*, tr. Willard R. Trask (Princeton, NJ: Princeton University Press, 1971).

Augustine, *The City of God*, tr. Henry Bettenson (Harmondsworth: Penguin, 1984).

——*Confessions*, tr. R. S. Pine-Coffin (Harmondsworth: Penguin, 1961).

——*De Trinitate*, tr. E. Hill (New York: New City Press, 1991).

——*Expositions of the Psalms 33–50*, ed. John E. Rotelle, tr. Maria Boulding (New York: New City Press, 2000).

Aulen, Gustav, *Christus Victor: An Historical Study of the Three Main Types of the Idea of the Atonement*, tr. A. G. Herbert (London: SCM Press, 1980).

Bachelard, Gaston, *The Poetics of Reverie: Childhood, Language, and the Cosmos*, tr. Daniel Russell (Boston: Beacon Press, 1969).

——*The Poetics of Space*, tr. Maria Jolas (Boston: Beacon Press, 1994).

Baldwin, Anna P., and Sarah Hutton (eds), *Platonism and the English Imagination* (Cambridge: Cambridge University Press, 1994).

Balint, Enid, *Before I Was I: Psychoanalysis and the Imagination*, ed. J. Mitchell and M. Parsons (London: Free Association Books, 1993).

Barfield, Owen, 'Either: Or: Coleridge, Lewis, and Romantic Theology', in *Imagination and the Spirit: Essays in Literature and the Christian Faith Presented to Clyde S. Kilby*, ed. Charles A. Huttar (Grand Rapids, Mich.: Eerdmans, 1971), pp. 25–42.

——'Matter, Imagination and Spirit', *Journal of the American Academy of Religion* 42 (1974), pp. 621–9.

Barker, Margaret, *The Great Angel: A Study of Israel's Second God* (London: SPCK, 1992).

——*The Great High Priest: The Temple Roots of Christian Liturgy* (London: T&T Clark, 2003).

——*The Older Testament: The Survival of Themes from the Ancient Royal Cult in Sectarian Judaism and Early Christianity* (London: SPCK Press, 1987).

Barrett, William, *The Illusion of Technique: A Search for the Meaning of Life in a Technological Age* (Garden City, NY: Anchor Press, 1978).

Bate, Jonathan, *The Genius of Shakespeare* (London: Picador, 1997).

——'Shakespeare and Original Genius', in *Genius: The History of an Idea*, ed. Penelope Murray (Oxford: Basil Blackwell, 1989), pp. 76–97.

Beach, Edward Allen, *The Potencies of God(s): Schelling's Philosophy of Mythology* (Albany, NY: State University of New York Press, 1994).

Beierwaltes, Werner, 'Logos im Mythos: Marginalien zu Platon', in *Weite des Herzens, Weite des Lebens: Beiträge zum christsein in moderner Gesellschaft. Festschrift für Abt Odilo Lechner*, ed. M. Langer and A. Bilgri (Regensburg: Friedrich Pustet, 1989), pp. 273–285.

——*Platonismus und Idealismus* (Frankfurt am Main: V. Klostermann, 1972).

Benjamin, Walter, *Ursprung des deutschen Trauerspiels*, ed. Rolf Tiedemann (Frankfurt am Main: Suhrkamp Verlag, 1963).

Benz, Ernst, 'Theogony and Transformation in Schelling', in *Man and Transformation: Papers from the Eranos Yearbooks*, ed. Joseph Campbell, tr. Ralph Manheim (Princeton, NJ: Princeton University Press, 1964), pp. 203–49.

Berger, Peter L., *A Rumour of Angels: Modern Society and the Rediscovery of the Supernatural* (Harmondsworth: Penguin, 1969).

Bergson, Henri, *Creative Evolution*, tr. Arthur Mitchell (London: Macmillan, 1954).

Berkeley, George, *Philosophical Works*, ed. M. Ayers (London: Dent, 1993).

Bernard, Hildegaard, *Hermeias von Alexandrian: Kommentar zu Platons 'Phaidros'* (Tübingen: Mohr Siebeck, 1997).

Bettelheim, Bruno, *The Uses of Enchantment: The Meaning and Importance of Fairy Tales* (Harmondsworth: Penguin, 1978).

Blackmore, Susan J., *The Meme Machine* (Oxford: Oxford University Press, 1999).

Blumenberg, Hans, *Höhlenausgänge*, 2nd edn (Frankfurt am Main: Suhrkamp, 1988).

Blunt, Anthony, *Artistic Theory in Italy: 1450–1600* (Oxford: Clarendon Press, 1978).

Boyer, Pascal, *Religion Explained: The Evolutionary Origins of Religious Thought* (New York: Basic Books, 2001).

Bradley, F. H., *Appearance and Reality: A Metaphysical Essay* (Oxford: Clarendon Press, 1930).

Brague, Rémi, *Eccentric Culture: A Theory of Western Civilisation*, tr. Samuel Lester (South Bend, Ind.: St Augustine's Press, 2002).

Braithwaite, R. B., 'An Empiricist's View of the Nature of Religious Belief', in *The Philosophy of Religion*, ed. Basil Mitchell (London: Oxford University Press, 1971), pp. 72–91.

Brandeis, Irma, *The Ladder of Vision: A Study of Dante's Comedy* (London: Chatto and Windus, 1960).

Brann, Eva T. H., *The World of the Imagination: Sum and Substance* (Lanham, Md: Rowman and Littlefield, 1991).

Bréhier, Émile, *La Philosophie de Plotin* (Paris: J. Vrin, 1961).

Bright, John, *A History of Israel* (London: SCM Press, 1967).

Brisson, Luc, *How Philosophers Saved Myths: Allegorical Interpretation and Classical Mythology*, tr. Catherine Tihanyi (Chicago: University of Chicago Press, 2004).

——*Plato the Myth Maker*, tr. Gerard Naddaf (Chicago: University of Chicago Press, 1998).

Brown, Robert F., *Schelling's Treatise on "The Deities of Samothrace": A Translation and an Interpretation* (Missoula, Mont.: Scholars Press, 1977).

Burke, Edmund, *A Philosophical Enquiry into the Origin of our Ideas of the Sublime and Beautiful*, ed. Adam Phillips (Oxford: Oxford University Press, 1990).

——*Reflections on the French Revolution* (London: Dent, 1955).

Burke, Sean, *Authorship: From Plato to the Postmodern* (Edinburgh: Edinburgh University Press, 1995).

Burns, Robert, *The Poems and Songs of Robert Burns*, ed. J. Kinsley, 3 vols (Oxford: Clarendon Press, 1968).

Burwick, Frederick, *Illusion and the Drama: Critical Theory of the Enlightenment and Romantic Era* (University Park, Pa: Pennsylvania State University Press, 1991).

——*Mimesis and its Romantic Reflections* (University Park, Pa: Pennsylvania State University Press, 2001).

Butler, Joseph, *Fifteen Sermons Preached at the Rolls Chapel*, ed. John Henry Bernard (London: Macmillan, 1913).

Caird, John, *An Introduction to the Philosophy of Religion* (Glasgow: J. MacLehose, 1894).

Cassirer, Ernst, *The Philosophy of Symbolic Forms*, ed. John Michael Krois and Donald Phillip Verene, tr. John Michael Krois, 4 vols (New Haven, Conn.: Yale University Press, 1996).

Castoriadis, Cornelius, *The Imaginary Institution of Society*, tr. Kathleen Blamey (Cambridge: Polity Press, 1987).

Christman, Angela Russell, *Ezekiel's Vision of the Chariot in Early Christian Exegesis* (Ann Arbor, Mich.: University of Michigan Press, 1995).

Clark, Stephen R. L., *Civil Peace and Sacred Order* (Oxford: Clarendon Press, 1989).

——*God's World and the Great Awakening* (Oxford: Clarendon Press, 1991).

——*The Mysteries of Religion: An Introduction to Philosophy through Religion* (Oxford: Basil Blackwell, 1986).

Clement of Alexandria, *Le Protreptique*, tr. C. Mondesert (Paris: Cerf, 1976).

Coleridge, Samuel Taylor, *Aids to Reflection*, ed. John Beer (London: Routledge, 1993).

——*Biographia Literaria*, ed. John T. Shawcross, 2 vols (Oxford: Oxford University Press, 1907).

——*Biographia Literaria: or, Biographical Sketches of my Literary Life and Opinions*, ed. H. N. Coleridge, completed Sara Coleridge, 2nd edn, 2 vols (London: n.p., 1847).

——*Biographia Literaria: or, Biographical Sketches of my Literary Life and Opinions*, ed. James Engell and Walter Jackson Bate, 2 vols (London: Routledge and Kegan Paul, 1983).

——*Collected Letters of Samuel Taylor Coleridge*, ed. Earl Leslie Griggs, 6 vols (Oxford: Clarendon Press, 1959).

——*The Collected Works of Samuel Taylor Coleridge*, ed. Kathleen Coburn and Bart Winer, 16 vols (London: Routledge and Kegan Paul, 1969–2001).

——*Miscellanies Aesthetic and Literary*, ed. T. Ashe (London: Bell, 1885).

——*The Notebooks of Samuel Taylor Coleridge*, ed. Kathleen Coburn, 8 vols (London: Routledge and Kegan Paul, 1957–90).

——*The Philosophical Lectures*, ed. Kathleen Coburn (London: Pilot Press, 1949).

——*Poems*, ed. J. Beer (London: Dent, 1986).

——*The Political Thought of Samuel Taylor Coleridge*, ed. Reginald James White (London: Jonathan Cape, 1938).

Collingwood, R. G., *The Principles of Art* (Oxford: Clarendon Press, 1938).

Conradi, Peter J., *Iris Murdoch: A Life* (London: HarperCollins, 2001).

Cook, Nicholas, *Music, Imagination and Culture* (Oxford: Clarendon Press, 1990).

Corbin, Henry, *Alone with the Alone: Creative Imagination in the Sufism of Ibn Arabi* (Princeton, NJ: Princeton University Press, 1997).

——*Avicenne et le récit visionnaire: Étude sur le cycle des récits avicenniens* (Verdier: Lagrasse, 1979).

——*Temple and Contemplation*, tr. Philip Sherrard and Liadain Sherrard (London: KPI in association with Islamic Publications, 1986).

Coriando, Paola-Ludovica, *Affektenlehre und Phänomenologie der Stimmungen: Wege einer Ontologie und Ethik des Emotionalen* (Frankfurt am Main: Vittorio Klostermann, 2002).

Cottingham, John, *Philosophy and the Good Life: Reason and the Passions in Greek, Cartesian, and Psychoanalytic Ethics* (Cambridge: Cambridge University Press, 1998).

——*The Spiritual Dimension: Religion, Philosophy, and Human Value* (Cambridge: Cambridge University Press, 2005).

Coulson, John, *Religion and Imagination: "In Aid of a Grammar of Assent"* (Oxford: Clarendon Press, 1981).

Cox, Murray, and Alice Theilgaard, *Mutative Metaphors in Psychotherapy: The Aeolian Mode* (London: Tavistock, 1987).

Cudworth, Ralph, *A Sermon Preached before the Honourable House of Commons, March 31, 1647* (repr. New York: Facsimile Text Society, 1930).

——*A Treatise Concerning Eternal and Immutable Morality*, ed. Sarah Hutton (Cambridge: Cambridge University Press, 1996).

——*The True Intellectual System of the Universe. The First Part, wherein All the Reason and Philosophy of Atheism is Confuted and its Impossibility Demonstrated: With a Treatise Concerning Eternal and Immutable Morality*, ed. John Harrison, 3 vols (London: Thomas Tegg, 1845).

Currie, Gregory, and Ian Ravenscroft, *Recreative Minds: Imagination in Philosophy and Psychology* (Oxford: Oxford University Press, 2002).

Dalferth, Ingolf U., 'The Stuff of Revelation: Austin Farrer's Doctrine of Inspired Images', in *Hermeneutics, the Bible and Literary Criticism*, ed. Ann Loades and Michael McLain (Basingstoke: Macmillan, 1992), pp. 71–95.

Damasio, Antonio R., 'Some Notes on Imagination and Creativity', in *The Origins of Creativity*, ed. Karl H. Pfenninger and Valerie R. Shubik (Oxford: Oxford University Press, 2001), pp. 59–68.

Dante Alighieri, *The Divine Comedy of Dante Alighieri*, tr. John D. Sinclair, 3 vols (London: John Lane, 1939–46).

Dawkins, Richard, *The Blind Watchmaker* (London: Penguin, 2000).

——*Science and Faith* (London: Athenaeum, 2004).

de Man, Paul, 'The Rhetoric of Temporality', in *Blindness and Insight: Essays in the Rhetoric of Contemporary Criticism*, 2nd edn (London: Methuen, 1983), pp. 187–228.

Dennett, Daniel C., *Darwin's Dangerous Idea: Evolution and the Meanings of Life* (London: Allen Lane, 1995).

Descartes, René, *The Philosophical Writings of Descartes*, tr. John Cottingham, Robert Stoothoff, Dugald Murdoch, and Anthony Kenny, 3 vols (Cambridge: Cambridge University Press, 1985–91).

Dickinson, Emily, *The Complete Poems of Emily Dickinson*, ed. Thomas H. Johnson (London: Faber and Faber, 1975).

Dillon, John, 'Plotinus and the Transcendental Imagination', in *Religious Imagination*, ed. James P. Mackey (Edinburgh: Edinburgh University Press, 1986), pp. 55–64.

Dreyfus, Hubert L., *Being-in-the-World: A Commentary on Heidegger's 'Being and Time', Division I* (London: MIT Press, 1991).

Dronke, Peter, *Imagination in the late Pagan and Early Christian World: The First Nine Centuries AD* (Florence: Sismel, 2003).

Eckhart, Meister, *Die Lateinischen Werke*, ed. J. Koch (Stuttgart: Kohlhammer, 1936).

Eliade, Mircea, *Images and Symbols: Studies in Religious Symbolism*, tr. Philip Mairet (Princeton, NJ: Princeton University Press, 1991).

——*Myths, Dreams and Mysteries: The Encounter between Contemporary Faiths and Archaic Realities*, tr. Philip Mairet (London: Harvill, 1960).

Eliot, T. S., *Collected Poems 1909–1962* (London: Faber and Faber, 1974).

——*On Poetry and Poets* (London: Faber and Faber, 1957).

——'Tradition and the Individual Talent', in *Selected Essays*, 3rd edn (London: Faber and Faber, 1953), pp. 13–22.

Emmel, H., 'Gemüt', in *Historisches Wörterbuch der Philosophie*, ed. Joachim Ritter, 13 vols (Basle: Schwabe, 1971–2007), vol. 3, pp. 258–64.

Engell, James, *The Creative Imagination: Enlightenment to Romanticism* (London: Harvard University Press, 1981).

Farmer, H. H., *God and Men* (London: Nisbet, 1948).

Farrer, Austin M., *Faith and Speculation: An Essay in Philosophical Theology* (Edinburgh: T. & T. Clark, 1988).

——*The Glass of Vision* (Westminster: Dacre Press, 1948).

——'Inspiration: Poetical and Divine', in *Interpretation and Belief*, ed. Charles C. Conti (London: SPCK, 1976), pp. 39–53.

——*A Rebirth of Images: The Making of St John's Apocalypse* (Westminster: Dacre Press, 1949).

——*Reflective Faith: Essays in Philosophical Theology*, ed. Charles C. Conti (London: SPCK, 1972).

——*A Science of God?* (London: Geoffrey Bles, 1966).

Festugière, André Jean, *Contemplation et vie contemplative selon Platon* (Paris: J. Vrin, 1936).

——*Personal Religion among the Greeks* (Berkeley, Calif.: University of California Press, 1954).

Ficino, Marsilio, *Platonic Theology*, tr. M. J. B. Allen (Cambridge, Mass.: Harvard University Press, 2001).

Finke, Ronald A., Thomas B. Ward, and Steven M. Smith, *Creative Cognition: Theory, Research, and Applications* (Cambridge, Mass.: MIT Press, 1996).

Fish, Stanley E., 'How To Do Things with Austin and Searle', in *Is There a Text in This Class? The Authority of Interpretive Communities* (Cambridge. Mass.: Harvard University Press, 1980), pp. 197–245.

Flamant, Jacques, *Macrobe et le néo-platonisme latin, à la fin du IVe siècle* (Leiden: E. J. Brill, 1977).

Flanagan, Owen J., *Dreaming Souls: Sleep, Dreams, and the Evolution of the Conscious Mind* (Oxford: Oxford University Press, 2000).

Foucault, Michel, *Les Mots et Les Choses* (Paris: Gallimard, 1966), p. 398.

Foley, Robert, *Humans Before Humanity: An Evolutionary Perspective* (Oxford: Blackwell, 1995).

Frank, Hilmar, *Der Joseph Anton Koch, Der Schmadribachfall: Natur und Freiheit* (Frankfurt: Fischer Taschenbuch Verlag, 1995).

Frankfurt, Harry G., 'Freedom of the Will and the Concept of a Person', in *Free Will*, ed. Gary Watson (Oxford: Oxford University Press, 1982), pp. 81–95.

Frye, Northrop, *The Great Code: The Bible and Literature* (Toronto: Academic Press Canada, 1982).

Gadamer, Hans-Georg, *Wahrheit und Methode*, 4th edn (Tübingen: J. C. B. Mohr Siebeck, 1975).

Garber, Marjorie B., *Dream in Shakespeare: From Metaphor to Metamorphosis* (New Haven, Conn.: Yale University Press, 1974).

Gardner, Helen L., *The Limits of Literary Criticism: Reflections on the Interpretation of Poetry and Scripture* (Oxford: Oxford University Press, 1956).

Gibbon, Edward, *The Decline and Fall of the Roman Empire*, introd. Hugh Trevor-Roper, 6 vols (London: David Campbell, 1993–4).

Glanvill, Joseph, *Saducismus triumphatus, or, Full and Plain Evidence Concerning Witches and Apparitions in Two Parts: The First Treating of their Possibility, the Second of their Real Existence. With a Letter of Dr. Henry More on the Same Subject and an Authentick but Wonderful Story of Certain Swedish Witches Done into English by Anth. Horneck* (London: n.p., 1681).

Goldammer, Kurt, *Paracelsus in der deutschen Romantik. Eine Untersuchung zur Geschichte der Paracelsus-Rezeption und zu geistesgeschichtlichen Hintergründen der Romantik: Mit einem Anhang über die Entstehung und Entwicklung der Elementargeister-Vorstellungen seit dem Mittelalter* (Vienna: Gesellschaften Österreichs, 1980).

Gould, Stephen Jay, *Wonderful Life: The Burgess Shale and the Nature of History* (London: Vintage, 2000).

Graham, Gordon, *Evil and Christian Ethics* (Cambridge: Cambridge University Press, 2001).

Green, Garrett, *Theology, Hermeneutics, and Imagination: The Crisis of Interpretation at the End of Modernity* (Cambridge: Cambridge University Press, 2000).

Green, T. H., *Prolegomena to Ethics* (Oxford: Clarendon Press, 1899).

Gregory, Alan P. R., *Coleridge and the Conservative Imagination* (Macon, Ga: Mercer University Press, 2003).

Gregory, Richard L., and Oliver Louis Zangwill (eds), *The Oxford Companion to the Mind* (Oxford: Oxford University Press, 1987).

Griswold, Charles L., Jr, *Self-Knowledge in Plato's 'Phaedrus'* (New Haven, Conn.: Yale University Press, 1986).

Grondin, Jean, *Hans-Georg Gadamer: Eine Biographie* (Tübingen: Mohr Siebeck, 2000).

Grumett, David, *Teilhard de Chardin: Theology, Humanity and Cosmos* (Leuven: Peeters, 2005).

Gulyga, A., *Schelling Leben und Werk* (Stuttgart: Deutsche Verlags Anstalt, 1989).

Hadot, Pierre, *Exercices spirituels et philosophie antique* (Paris: Albin Michel, 2002).

——*Porphyre et Victorinus*, 2 vols (Paris: Études Augustiniennes, 1968).

Hannay, Alastair, *Kierkegaard* (London: Routledge and Kegan Paul, 1982).

——*Mental Images: A Defence* (London: George Allen and Unwin, 1971).

Harris, Paul L., *The Work of the Imagination* (Oxford: Blackwell, 2000).

Hebblethwaite, Brian, 'Butler on Conscience and Virtue', in *Joseph Butler's Moral and Religious Thought: Tercentenary Essays*, ed. Christopher Cunliffe (Oxford: Clarendon Press, 1992), pp. 197–207.

——*Ethics and Religion in a Pluralistic Age: Collected Essays* (Edinburgh: T&T Clark, 1997).

——*Philosophical Theology and Christian Doctrine* (Oxford: Blackwell, 2005).

Hedley, Douglas, *Coleridge, Philosophy and Religion: Aids to Reflection and the Mirror of the Spirit* (Cambridge: Cambridge University Press, 2000).

——'Coleridge's Intellectual Intuition, the Vision of God, and the Walled Garden of "Kubla Khan"', *Journal of the History of Ideas* 59 (1998), pp. 116–34.

——'Ecstasy, Imagination and Divine Agency: Reflections upon S. T. Coleridge and the Platonic Tradition', in *Pensées de l'"un" dans l'histoire de la philosophie: Études en hommage au Professeur Werner Beierwaltes*, ed. Jean-Marc Narbonne and Alfons Reckermann (Paris: J.Vrin; Sainte-Foy, Que.: Presses de l'Université Laval, 2004), pp. 443–58.

——'The "Future" of Religion', in *Truth, Religious Dialogue and Dynamic Orthodoxy: Reflections on the Work of Brian Hebblethwaite*, ed. Julius Lipner (London: SCM Press, 2005), pp. 96–111.

——'Philosophia Trinitatis', in *Coleridge's Assertion of Religion: Essays on the Opus Maximum*, ed. Jeffrey W. Barbeau (Leuven: Peeters, 2006), pp. 213–31.

——'The Platonick Trinity: Philology and Divinity in Cudworth's Philosophy of Religion', in *Philologie und Erkenntnis: Beiträge zu Begriff und Problem frühneuzeitlicher "Philologie"*, ed. Ralph Häfner (Tübingen: Max Niemeyer Verlag, 2001), pp. 247–63.

——'Theology and the Revolt Against the Enlightenment', in *Christianity: World Christianities c.1815–c.1914*, ed. Sheridan Gilley and Brian Stanley (Cambridge: Cambridge University Press), pp. 30–52.

Hedley, Douglas and Hutton, Sarah, ed. *Platonism and the Origins of Modernity* (Dordrecht: Springer, 2007).

Heftrich, Eckhard, *Vom Verfall zur Apokalypse* (Frankfurt am Main: Vittorio Klostermann, 1982).

Heidegger, Martin, *Being and Time*, tr. John Macquarrie and Edward Robinson (Oxford: Blackwell, 1962).

——*Erläuterungen zu Hölderlins Dichtung* (Frankfurt am Main: Klostermann, 1971).

——*Platons Lehre von der Wahrheit* (Bern: Branke, 1947).

——*Poetry, Language, Thought*, tr. Albert Hofstadter (New York: Harper and Row, 1972).

——*Schellings Abhandlung über das Wesen der menschlichen Freiheit*, ed. H. Feick (Tübingen: Max Niemeyer, 1971).

——*Sein und Zeit*, 17th edn (Tübingen: Max Niemeyer, 1993).

——*Der Ursprung des Kunstwerkes* (Stuttgart: Reclam, 1967).

Hegel, Georg Wilhelm Friedrich, *Vorlesung über Äesthetik* (Frankfurt am Main: Suhrkamp, 1986).

——*Vorträge und Aufsätze* (Pfullingen: Günter Neske Verlag, 1954).

Herbert, Jack, *The German Tradition. Uniting the Opposites: Goethe, Jung and Rilke* (London: Temenos Academy, 2001).

Hick, John, *Evil and the God of Love* (Glasgow: Collins, 1979).

Hillman, James, 'Plotinus, Ficino and Vico as Precursors of Archetypal Psychology', in *Loose Ends: Primary Papers in Archetypal Psychology* (Dallas: Spring Publications, 1978), pp. 146–69.

——*Re-Visioning Psychology* (New York: Harper and Row, 1975).

Hobbes, Thomas, *Leviathan* (Oxford: Clarendon Press, 1958).

Holmes, Richard, *Coleridge: Early Visions* (London: Hodder and Stoughton, 1989).

Hooker, Richard, *The Works*, ed. John Keble, 2 vols (Oxford: n.p., 1841).

Hopkins, Jasper, *Nicholas of Cusa on Learned Ignorance: A Translation and an Appraisal of 'De docta ignorantia'* (Minneapolis: A. J. Banning Press, 1981).

Horrocks, Don, *Laws of the Spiritual Order: Innovation and Reconstruction in the Soteriology of Thomas Erskine of Linlathen* (Carlisle: Paternoster Press, 2004).

Howald, Ernst, *Kampf um Creuzers Symbolik* (Tübingen: J. C. B. Mohr, 1926).

Huizinga, Johan, *Homo ludens: A Study of the Play-Element in Culture* (London: Routledge, 1998).

Hume, David, *Dialogues Concerning Natural Religion*, ed. J. C. A. Gaskin (Oxford: Clarendon Press, 1993).

——*A Treatise of Human Nature*, ed. L. A. Selby-Bigge and P. H. Nidditch, 2nd edn (Oxford: Clarendon Press, 1978).

Hüttig, Albrecht, *Macrobius im Mittelalter: Ein Beitrag zur Rezeptionsgeschichte der Commentarii in Somnium Scipionis* (Frankfurt am Main: Peter Lang, 1990).

Ignatius of Loyola, *Personal Writings: Reminiscences, Spiritual Diary, Select Letters*, tr. Joseph A. Munitiz and Philip Endean (Harmondsworth: Penguin, 1996).

Insole, Christopher J., *The Politics of Human Frailty: A Theological Defence of Political Liberalism* (London: SCM Press, 2004).

Iremonger, F. A., *William Temple, Archbishop of Canterbury: His Life and Letters* (London: Oxford University Press, 1948).

Jackson, Thomas, *A Treatise of the Divine Essence and Attributes* (London: Clarke, 1628).

James, William, *Varieties of Religious Experience: A Study in Human Nature* (Harmondsworth: Penguin, 1985).

——*The Will to Believe, and Other Essays in Popular Philosophy* (New York: Dover Publications, 1956).

Jay, Martin, *Downcast Eyes: The Denigration of Vision in Twentieth Century French Thought* (Berkeley, Calif.: University of California Press, 1993).

Jeffreys, Harold, *Scientific Inference* (Cambridge: Cambridge University Press, 1931).

Jowett, Benjamin, *Dialogues of Plato: Introduction to the Republic*, 4th edn (Oxford: Clarendon Press, 1953).

——*Select Passages from the Introductions to Plato*, ed. Lewis Campbell (London: John Murray, 1902).

Kant, Immanuel, *Grundlegung einer Metaphysik der Sitten* (Berlin: Walter de Gruyter, 1968).

——*The Moral Law: or, Kant's Groundwork of the Metaphysics of Morals*, tr. H. J. Paton (London: Hutchinson, 1981).

Keats, John, *The Letters of Keats, 1814–1821*, ed. Hyder Edward Rollins (Cambridge, Mass.: Harvard University Press, 1958).

Kierkegaard, Søren, *Philosophical Fragments: Johannes Climacus*, ed. and tr.

Howard V. Hong and Edna H. Hong (Princeton, NJ: Princeton University Press, 1985).

Kirschner, Suzanne R., *The Religious and Romantic Origins of Psychoanalysis: Individuation and Integration in Post-Freudian Theory* (Cambridge: Cambridge University Press, 1996).

Koestler, Arthur, *The Act of Creation* (London: Hutchinson, 1964).

Kolakowski, Leszek, *Modernity on Endless Trial* (Chicago: University of Chicago Press, 1990).

Kristeller, Paul Oskar, *The Philosophy of Marsilio Ficino* (New York: Columbia University Press, 1943).

Kruger, Steven F., *Dreaming in the Middle Ages* (Cambridge: Cambridge University Press, 1992).

Kymlicka, Will, *Liberalism: Community and Culture* (Oxford: Clarendon Press, 1991).

La Caze, Marguerite, *The Analytic Imaginary* (Ithaca, NY: Cornell University Press, 2002).

Lang, Wolfram, *Das Traumbuch des Synesius von Cyrene: Uebersetzung und Analyse der philosophischen Grundlagen* (Tübingen: J. C. B. Mohr, 1926).

Lear, Jonathan, *Open Minded: Working Out the Logic of the Soul* (Cambridge, Mass.: Harvard University Press, 1998).

Leclercq, Stéphan, *Plotin et l'expression de l'image: Les Paradoxes du réel* (Mons: Sils Maria, 2005).

Lewis, C. S., *The Abolition of Man* (London: HarperCollins, 1978).

——'The Anthropological Approach', in *English and Medieval Studies Presented to J. R. R. Tolkien on the Occasion of his Seventieth Birthday*, ed. Norman Davis and Charles Leslie Wrenn (London: Allen and Unwin, 1962), pp. 219–230

——*The Discarded Image: An Introduction to Medieval and Renaissance Literature* (Cambridge: Cambridge University Press, 1964).

——*God in the Dock: Essays on Theology*, ed. Walter Hooper (London: Fount, 1979).

——*Of this and Other Worlds*, ed. W. Hooper (London: Collins, 1982).

——*Weight of Glory and Other Addresses*, ed. with an introduction by W. Hooper (New York: Macmillan, 1980).

Lewis, H. D., *Our Experience of God* (London: Allen and Unwin, 1959).

Lichtenstein, Ernst, *Zur Entwicklung des Bildungsbegriffs von Meister Eckhart bis Hegel* (Heidelberg: Quelle und Meyer, 1966).

Lloyd, Genevieve, 'Augustine and the "Problem" of Time', in *The Augustinian Tradition*, ed. Gareth B. Matthews (Berkeley, Calif.: University of California Press, 1999), pp. 40–59.

Locke, John, *An Essay Concerning Human Understanding*, ed. Peter H. Nidditch (Oxford: Oxford University Press, 1975).

——*Two Treatises of Government*, ed. Peter Laslett, 2nd edn (Cambridge: Cambridge University Press, 1970).

Lovejoy, A. O., *The Great Chain of Being: A Study of the History of an Idea* (Cambridge, Mass.: Harvard University Press, 1961).

Löwith, Karl, *Meaning in History: The Theological Implications of the Philosophy of History* (Chicago: Chicago University Press, 1970).

Lowth, Robert, *Lectures on the Sacred Poetry of the Hebrews*, tr. G. Gregory, 2 vols (London: J. Johnson, 1787; repr. London: Routledge/ Thoemmes Press, 1995).

Macaulay, Thomas Babington, *Critical and Historical Essays Contributed to the Edinburgh Review* (London: Longmans, Green, Reader and Dyer, 1878).

MacIntyre, Alasdair, *After Virtue: A Study in Moral Theory*, 2nd edn (London: Duckworth, 1985).

MacKinnon, Donald, *The Problem of Metaphysics* (London: Cambridge University Press, 1974).

Macrobius, Ambrosius Aurelius Theodosius, *Commentary on the Dream of Scipio*, tr. William Harris Stahl (New York: Columbia University Press, 1952).

Malcolm, Norman, *Dreaming* (London: Routledge and Kegan Paul, 1977).

Manent, Pierre, *The City of Man*, tr. Marc A. LePain (Princeton, NJ: Princeton University Press, 1998).

Mann, Thomas, *Doktor Faustus* (Frankfurt am Main: S. Fischer, 2003).

Marignac, Aloys de, *Imagination et dialectique: Essai sur l'expression du spirituel par l'image dans les dialogues de Platon* (Paris: Les Belles Lettres, 1951).

Maurice, F. D., *The Doctrine of Sacrifice Deduced from the Scriptures: A Series of Sermons* (Cambridge: Macmillan, 1854).

McDowell, John, *Mind and World* (Cambridge, Mass.: Harvard University Press, 1994).

McGann, Jerome J., *The Romantic Ideology: A Critical Investigation* (Chicago: University of Chicago Press, 1983).

McGinn, Colin, *Mindsight: Image, Dream, Meaning* (Cambridge, Mass.: Harvard University Press, 2004).

Mill, John Stuart, and Jeremy Bentham, *Utilitarianism and Other Essays*, ed. Alan Ryan (Harmondsworth: Penguin, 1987).

Miller, Patricia Cox, *Dreams in Late Antiquity: Studies in the Imagination of a Culture* (Princeton, NJ: Princeton University Press, 1994).

Milton, John, *The Poems of John Milton*, ed. John Carey and Alastair Fowler (London: Longman, 1968).

Mitchell, Basil, *How to Play Theological Ping-Pong and Other Essays on Faith and Reason*, ed. William J. Abraham and Robert W. Prevost (London: Hodder and Stoughton, 1990).

Mithen, Steven J, 'A Creative Explosion? Theory of Mind, Language, and the Disembodied Mind of the Upper Paleolithic', in Steven Mithen (ed.), *Creativity in Human Evolution and Prehistory* (London: Routledge, 1998), pp. 165–191.

Moore, Thomas, *The Planets Within: The Astrological Psychology of Marsilio Ficino* (Hudson, NY: Lindisfarne Press, 1990).

More, Henry, *An Antidote Against Atheism: or, An Appeal to the Naturall Faculties of the Minde of Man, Whether There Be Not a God* (London: n.p., 1655).

——*Apocalypsis Apocalypseos: or, The Revelation of St. John the Divine Unveiled. Containing a Brief but Perspicuous and Continued Exposition from Chapter to Chapter, and from Verse to Verse, of the Whole Book of the Apocalypse* (London: n.p., 1680).

——*Enthusiasmus Triumphatus: A Brief Discourse of the Nature, Causes, Kinds, and Cure of Enthusiasm* (London: n.p., 1662; repr. Los Angeles: Augustan Reprint Society, University of California Press, 1966).

——*Philosophical Poems* (Lewisburg, Pa: Bucknell University Press, 1998).

——*A Platonick Song of the Soul*, ed. Alexander Jacob (Lewisburg, Pa: Bucknell University Press, 1998).

Morgan, Robert, and John Barton, *Biblical Interpretation* (Oxford: Oxford University Press, 1988).

Morris, Simon Conway, *Life's Solution: Inevitable Humans in a Lonely Universe* (Cambridge: Cambridge University Press, 2003).

Moseley, C. W. R. D., *J. R. R. Tolkien* (Horndon, Devon: Northcote House Publishers, 1997).

Mulhall, Stephen, 'Can There Be an Epistemology of Moods?', in *'Verstehen' and Humane Understanding*, ed. Anthony O'Hear (Cambridge: Cambridge University Press, 1996), pp. 191–210.

Murdoch, Iris, *Existentialists and Mystics: Writings on Philosophy and Literature*, ed. Peter Conradi (London: Chatto and Windus, 1997).

——*Metaphysics as a Guide to Morals* (London: Chatto and Windus, 1992).

Nagel, Thomas, *Mortal Questions* (Cambridge: Cambridge University Press, 1979).

Narbonne, Jean-Marc, *Lévinas et l'héritage grec* (Paris: J. Vrin, 2004).

Nettle, Daniel, *Strong Imagination: Madness, Creativity and Human Nature* (Oxford: Oxford University Press, 2001).

Newman, John Henry, *An Essay in Aid of a Grammar of Assent* (Notre Dame, Ind.: University of Notre Dame Press, 1979).

——*An Essay on the Development of Christian Doctrine*, ed. James Munro Cameron (Harmondsworth: Penguin, 1974).

Nietzsche, Friedrich, *Twilight of the Idols; and, The Anti-Christ*, tr. R. J. Hollingdale (Harmondsworth: Penguin, 1981).

Novalis, *Philosophical Writings*, tr. and ed. Margaret Mahony Stoljar (Albany, NY: State University of New York Press, 1997).

Nussbaum, Martha C., *The Fragility of Goodness: Luck and Ethics in Greek Tragedy and Philosophy* (Cambridge: Cambridge University Press, 1986).

——*Love's Knowledge: Essays on Philosophy and Literature* (Oxford: Oxford University Press, 1990).

O'Flaherty, Wendy Doniger, *Dreams, Illusions and Other Realities* (Chicago: University of Chicago Press, 1984).

O'Hear, Anthony, *After Progress: Finding the Old Way Forward* (London: Bloomsbury, 1999).

——'The Open Society Revisited', in *Karl Popper: Critical Appraisals*, ed. P. Cotton and G. MacDonald (London: Routledge, 2004), pp. 189–202.

Origen, *Contra Celsum*, tr. Henry Chadwick (Cambridge: Cambridge University Press, 1980).

——*Homélie sur les Nombres*, ed. A. Mehat (Paris: Cerf, 1951).

Osborn, Eric, *Irenaeus of Lyons* (Cambridge: Cambridge University Press, 2001).

Penner, Hans, 'You Don't Read a Myth for Information', in *Radical Interpretation in Religion*, ed. Nancy K. Frankenberry (Cambridge: Cambridge University Press, 2002), pp. 153–70.

Perreau-Saussine, Émile, 'Une spiritualité libérale? Charles Taylor et Alasdair MacIntyre en conversation', *Revue Française de Science Politique* 55 (2005), pp. 299–315.

Perry, Seamus, *S. T. Coleridge: Interviews and Recollections* (Basingstoke: Palgrave Macmillan, 2000).

Philo of Alexandria, *Philo*, tr. F. H. Colson and G. H. Whitaker, 12 vols (London: Heinemann; Cambridge, Mass.: Harvard University Press, 1929–62).

Pickstock, Catherine, *After Writing: On the Liturgical Consummation of Philosophy* (Oxford: Blackwell, 1998).

Pietikäinen, Petteri, *C. G. Jung and the Psychology of Symbolic Forms* (Helsinki: Academia Scientiarum Fennica, 1999).

Plato, *Opera*, ed. John Burnet, 5 vols (Oxford: Clarendon Press, 1986).

——*Phaedrus*, tr. Reginald Hackforth (Cambridge: Cambridge University Press, 1952).

——*Phaedrus*, tr. Walter Hamilton (Harmondsworth: Penguin, 1973).

——*The Republic*, tr. Desmond Lee (Harmondsworth: Penguin, 1987).

——*Theaetetus*, tr. Robin A. H. Waterfield (Harmondsworth: Penguin, 1987).

Plotinus, *Opera*, ed. P. Henry and H.-R. Schwyzer (Oxford: Clarendon Press, 1964).

——*Plotinus*, tr. A. H. Armstrong, 7 vols (Cambridge, Mass.: Harvard University Press, 1984–8).

Prickett, Stephen, *Words and the Word: Language, Poetics, and Biblical Interpretation* (Cambridge: Cambridge University Press, 1986).

Proclus, *Trois études sur la providence*, tr. and ed. Daniel Isaac, 3 vols (Paris: Les Belles Lettres, 1977–82).

Proust, Marcel, *A la recherche du temps perdu* (Paris: Laffont, 1987).

Pseudo-Dionysius, *The Complete Works*, tr. Colm Luibheid and Paul Rorem (New York: Paulist Press, 1987).

Raine, Kathleen, *Inner Journey of the Poet, and Other Papers* (London: Allen and Unwin, 1982).

Raven, Charles E., *Natural Religion and Christian Theology*, 2 vols (Cambridge: Cambridge University Press, 1953).

Rawls, John, *Political Liberalism* (New York: Columbia University Press, 1993).

Revonsuo, Antti, 'The Reinterpretation of Dreams: An Evolutionary Hypothesis of the Function of Dreaming', in *Sleep and Dreaming: Scientific Advances and Reconsiderations*, ed. E. F. Pace-Schott, M. Solms, and M. Blagrove (New York: Cambridge University Press, 2003), pp. 85–109.

Rickman, Hans Peter, *Wilhelm Dilthey: Pioneer of the Human Studies* (London: Elek, 1979).

Ricœur, Paul, *The Conflict of Interpretations: Essays in Hermeneutics*, ed. Don Ihde (Evanston, Ill.: Northwestern University Press, 1974).

Rinon, Y., 'The Rhetoric of Jacques Derrida. II: *Phaedrus*', *Review of Metaphysics* 46 (1993), pp. 537–58.

Rist, John M., *Real Ethics: Reconsidering the Foundations of Morality* (Cambridge: Cambridge University Press, 2002).

Roberts, Julian, *Walter Benjamin* (London: Macmillan, 1982).

Rohls, Jan, 'Goethedienst ist Gottesdienst: Theologische Anmerkungen zur Goethe Verehrung', in *Goethe in Gesellschaft: Zur Geschichte einer literarischen Vereinigung vom Kaiserreich bis zum geteilten Deutschland*, ed. J. Golz and J. Ulbricht (Cologne: Böhlau, 2005), pp. 33–62.

Rorty, Richard, 'The Contingency of Language', *London Review of Books*, 17 April 1986, pp. 3–6.

——*Philosophy and the Mirror of Nature* (Oxford: Blackwell, 1980).

Rousseau, Jean-Jacques, *Du contrat social* (Paris: Flammarion, 1992).

Runco, Mark A., and Steven R. Pritzker (eds), *Encyclopedia of Creativity*, 2 vols (San Diego: Academic Press, 1999).

Ruskin, John, *The Works of John Ruskin*, ed. E. T. Cook and Alexander Wedderburn, 39 vols (London: George Allen, 1903–12).

Russell, Bertrand, *Philosophical Essays* (New York: Longmans and Green, 1910).

Ryle, Gilbert, *The Concept of Mind* (London: Penguin, 1949).

Sallustius, *Sallustius Concerning the Gods and the Universe* [*De diis et mundo*], tr. and ed. Arthur Darby Nock (Cambridge: Cambridge University Press, 1926).

Sartre, Jean-Paul, *L'Imaginaire: Psychologie-phénoménologique de l'imagination* (Paris: Gallimard, 1940).

Schelling, Friedrich Wilhelm Joseph von, *Ausgewählte Schriften*, 6 vols (Frankfurt: Suhrkamp, 1995).

——*Ueber die Gottheiten von Samothrace: Vorlegesen in der öffentlichen Sitzung der Baier'schen Akademie der Wissenschaften am Namenstage des Königes den 12 Oct.1815. Beylage zu den Weltaltern* (Stuttgart and Tübingen: n.p., 1815).

Schiller, Friedrich, 'Das Ideal und das Leben', in *Sämtliche Werke*, ed. Eduard von der Hellen (Stuttgart and Berlin: J. G. Cotta, 1904–5), vol. 1, pp. 191–6.

——*On the Aesthetic Education of Man: In a Series of Letters*, tr. and ed. Elizabeth M. Wilkinson and L. A. Willoughby (Oxford: Clarendon Press, 1985).

Schilling, Hans, *Bildung als Gottesbildlichkeit: Eine motivegeschichtliche Studie zum Bildungsbegriff* (Freiburg im Breisgau: Lambertus-Verlag, 1961).

Schmidt-Biggemann, Wilhelm, *Philosophia perennis: Historische Umrisse abendländischer Spritualität in Antike, Mittelalter und früher Neuzeit* (Frankfurt am Main: Suhrkamp, 1998).

Scholem, Gershom, *Walter Benjamin: The Story of a Friendship* (London: Faber and Faber, 1982).

Scruton, Roger, *Gentle Regrets: Thoughts from a Life* (New York: Continuum, 2005).

——*An Intelligent Person's Guide to Modern Culture* (London: Duckworth, 1998).

——*A Short History of Modern Philosophy: From Descartes to Wittgenstein*, 2nd edn (London: Routledge, 1995).

Searle, John R., *Minds, Brains and Science: The 1984 Reith Lectures* (Harmondsworth: Penguin, 1984).

Shaftesbury, Anthony Ashley Cooper, Earl of, *Characteristicks of Men, Manners, Opinions, Times*, 4th edn, 3 vols (London: John Darby, 1727).

Shelley, Percy Bysshe, *Shelley's Literary and Philosophical Criticism*, ed. John T. Shawcross (London: Henry Frowde, 1909).

Sidney, Sir Philip, *A Defence of Poetry*, ed. J. A. van Dorsten (London: Oxford University Press, 1966).

Smith, John, *Select Discourses* (Cambridge: n.p., 1660).

Spaemann, Robert, 'Aufhalter und Letzes Gefecht', in *Das Ende: Figuren einer Dankform*, ed. K. Stierle and R. Warning (Munich: Fink, 1996), pp. 564–77.

Spenser, Edmund, *Daphnäida and Other Poems*, ed. R. L. Penwick (London: The Scholartis Press, 1929).

Sperber, Dan, *Explaining Culture: A Naturalistic Approach* (Oxford: Blackwell, 1996).

Stevens, Wallace, *Collected Poetry and Prose* (New York: Library of America, 1997).

Stewart, John Alexander, 'Cambridge Platonists', in *Encyclopaedia of Religion and Ethics*, ed. James Hastings (Edinburgh: T. and T. Clark, 1910), vol. III, pp. 167–73.

——*The Myths of Plato*, ed. Gertrude R. Levy (London: Centaur Press, 1960).

——'Platonism in English Poetry', in *English Literature and the Classics*, ed. George Gordon Stuart (Oxford: Clarendon Press, 1912), pp. 25–48.

Stout, Jeffrey, *Democracy and Tradition* (Princeton, NJ: Princeton University Press, 2004).

Taylor, A. E., *Does God Exist?* (London: Collins, 1966).

——*The Faith of a Moralist*, 2 vols (London: Macmillan, 1930).

Taylor, Charles, *Hegel* (Cambridge: Cambridge University Press, 1975).

——*Modern Social Imaginaries* (London: Duke University Press, 2004).

——'Self-Interpreting Animals', in *Human Agency and Language* (Cambridge: Cambridge University Press, 1985), pp. 45–76.

——*Sources of the Self: The Making of the Modern Identity* (Cambridge: Cambridge University Press, 1992).

Temple, William, *Christus Veritas: An Essay* (London: Macmillan, 1930).

Tillich, Paul, *A History of Christian Thought*, ed. Carl E. Braaten, 2nd edn (London: SCM Press, 1968).

Tolkien, J. R. R., *The Letters of J. R. R. Tolkien*, ed. Humphrey Carpenter (London: George Allen and Unwin, 1981).

——*The Lord of the Rings* (London: HarperCollins, 1968).

——*The Monsters and the Critics, and Other Essays*, ed. Christopher Tolkien (London: Allen and Unwin, 1983).

——*Tree and Leaf* (London: George Allen and Unwin, 1975).

Traherne, Thomas, *Centuries of Meditations*, ed. Bertram Dobell (London: Dobell, 1927).

——*The Poetical Works of Thomas Traherne*, ed. Gladys I. Wade (London: Dobell, 1932).

——*Selected Poems and Prose*, ed. Alan Bradford (Harmondsworth: Penguin, 1991).

Trevelyan, G. M., *England Under the Stuarts* (London: Methuen, 1904).

Trigg, Roger, *Rationality and Religion: Does Faith Need Reason?* (Oxford: Blackwell, 1998).

Trowitzcsch, Michael, *Zeit zur Ewigkeit: Beiträge zum Zeitverständnis in der "Glaubenslehre" Schleiermachers* (Munich: Christian Kaiser, 1976).

Tugendhat, Ernst, *Self-Consciousness and Self-Determination*, tr. Paul Stern (Cambridge, Mass.: MIT Press, 1986).

Turnbull, Colin M., *The Mountain People* (London: Jonathan Cape, 1973).

Turner, Denys, *The Darkness of God: Negativity in Christian Mysticism* (Cambridge: Cambridge University Press, 1995).

——*Faith, Reason and the Existence of God* (Cambridge: Cambridge University Press, 2004).

Walton, Kendall L., *Mimesis as Make Believe: On the Foundations of the Representational Arts* (Cambridge, Mass.: Harvard University Press, 1990).

Wasserstrom, Steven M., *Religion After Religion: Gershom Scholem, Mircea Eliade, and Henry Corbin at Eranos* (Princeton, NJ: Princeton University Press, 1999).

Watson, George, *The Certainty of Literature: Essays in Polemic* (Hemel Hempstead: Harvester Wheatsheaf, 1989).

——'Contributions to a Dictionary of Critical Terms: Imagination and Fancy', *Essays in Criticism* 3 (1953), pp. 202–14.

——*Never Ones for Theory? England and the War of Ideas* (Cambridge: Lutterworth Press, 2000).

Watson, Gerard, 'Imagination and Religion in Classical Thought', in *Religious Imagination*, ed. James P. Mackey (Edinburgh: Edinburgh University Press, 1986), pp. 29–54.

——*Phantasia in Classical Thought* (Galway: Galway University Press, 1988).

Weber, Max, 'Wissenschaft als Beruf', in *Max Weber: Gesamtausgabe*, ed. W. J. Mommsen and W. Schluchter with B. Morgenbrod (Munich: Mohr Siebeck, 1992), pp. 99–101.

Westcott, B. F., 'The Myths of Plato', in *Essays in the History of the Religious Thought of the West* (London: Macmillan, 1891), pp. 1–50.

White, Patrick, *Riders in the Chariot* (London: Eyre and Spottiswoode, 1956).

White, Victor, *God and the Unconscious* (London: Harvill, 1952).

Whitehead, Alfred North, *Adventures of Ideas* (Cambridge: Cambridge University Press, 1933).

Whittaker, John, *God Time Being: Two Studies in the Transcendental Tradition in Greek Philosophy* (Oslo: Universitetsforlaget, 1971).

Whyte, Lancelot Law, *The Unconscious Before Freud* (London: Friedmann, 1978).

Williams, Bernard, *Descartes: The Project of Pure Enquiry* (Hassocks, West Sussex: Harvester Press, 1978).
——*Ethics and the Limits of Philosophy* (London: Fontana, 1985).
——*Problems of the Self: Philosophical Papers 1956–1972* (Cambridge: Cambridge University Press, 1973).
Winnicott, Donald Woods, *Playing and Reality* (Harmondsworth: Penguin, 1980).
Wolin, Richard, *Walter Benjamin: An Aesthetic of Redemption* (New York: Columbia University Press, 1982).
Wordsworth, William, *Poetical Works*, ed. Thomas Hutchinson, rev. Ernest de Selincourt (London: Oxford University Press, 1936).
——*Prelude*, ed. Ernest de Selincourt and Stephen Gill (Oxford: Clarendon Press, 1970).
——*The Prelude: or, Growth of a Poet's Mind (Text of 1805)*, ed. Ernest de Selincourt and Stephen Gill, 2nd edn (Oxford: Oxford University Press, 1996).
——*William Wordsworth: The Poems* (London: Yale University Press, 1981).
Wykstra, Stephen J., 'The Humean Obstacle to Evidential Arguments from Suffering: On Avoiding the Evils of "Appearance"', in *The Problem of Evil*, ed. Marilyn McCord Adams and Robert M. Adams (Oxford: Oxford University Press, 1990), pp. 138–60.
Wynn, Mark, *Emotional Experience and Religious Understanding: Integrating Perception, Conception and Feeling* (Cambridge: Cambridge University Press, 2005).
Young-Eisendrath, Polly, and Terence Dawson (eds), *The Cambridge Companion to Jung* (Cambridge: Cambridge University Press, 1997).
Zeki, Semir, *Inner Vision: An Exploration of Art and the Brain* (Oxford: Oxford University Press, 1999).

Index of subjects

Index of Names